17484541

WITHDRAWN
NDSU

INDUSTRIALIZATION, FAMILY LIFE, AND CLASS RELATIONS

INDUSTRIALIZATION, FAMILY LIFE, AND CLASS RELATIONS

SAINT CHAMOND,

1815–1914

Elinor Accampo

The University of California Press
Berkeley · Los Angeles · London

University of California Press
Berkeley and Los Angeles, California

University of California Press, Ltd.
London, England

© 1989 by
The Regents of the University of California

Library of Congress Cataloging-in-Publication Data

Accampo, Elinor Ann
    Industrialization, family life, and class relations: Saint
Chamond, 1815–1914 / Elinor Accampo.
        p.   cm.
    Bibliography: p.
    Includes index.
    ISBN 0–520–06095–4 (alk. paper)
    1. Family—France—Saint-Chamond—History.   2. Labor and laboring
classes—France—Saint-Chamond—History.   3. Work and family—
France—Saint-Chamond—History.   I. Title.
HQ623.A15 1989
306.8′5′0944581—dc19   88–459
                                                                      CIP

Printed in the United States of America
1 2 3 4 5 6 7 8 9

To Bob

Contents

Illustrations

Tables

APPENDIXES (*pages 221–233*)

Preface

In the eighteenth and nineteenth centuries, three simultaneous events touched the core of European family life: while the demographic revolution transformed family structure, industrialization changed gender roles and Enlightenment philosophies inspired new ideals of equality, personal freedom, and individualism. The convergence of these three revolutions caused the family to become more nuclear, private, and child-centered as it also shrank in size. Male and female spheres came to be more sharply defined. Emotional functions replaced economic ones.

The study of family history provides a unique opportunity to understand the conjuncture of these major events that shaped modern Europe. The family, after all, is the starting point of any society and rarely remains untouched by social change, whether as a cause or as an effect. But its history poses an overwhelming challenge as well. The private nature of family life has kept it hidden from history, particularly among people who left few or no records of their past. The changes described above most closely fit the European middle classes—the victors of all three revolutions—who left the most ample documentation of their everyday lives. That the lower classes experienced these massive social changes very differently is indisputable. Their fertility and mortality remained high and they continued to have large families; the shift from home-based production to mechanized factory production in most cases left a large portion of the working class disinherited. Benefits of democratic ideals came to them very late, and only after bitter struggles to add to the political meaning of freedom a social one: the basic right to exist.

Whatever their response or fate, the industrial proletariat endured a precarious existence and created new strains on the societies in which it lived. Records of conflict with employers and police and of militant protest that often translated into political movements provide some of the best evidence of these workers' histories. And yet those records represent only a fraction of all workers and only one facet of their past. The family is a key to understanding the effects that economic, political, and demographic change had on the "inarticulate" as well as on those who protested their condition. The story of how the urban proletariat experienced the upheavals of its age must include a detailed examination of the family.

A basic notion among many historians is that the lower classes followed the lead of those above them, that, for the most part, their families eventually adopted the same structural patterns and basic functions the middle class had evolved. Yet family life among urban workers remains relatively unexplored. This study argues that industrialization weakened the working-class family. Though its impacts may have been temporary and transitional, industrialization set the family on a path of change quite distinct from that of the middle class and helped to create deeper class differences.

A starting point for understanding family life among workers is its demographic structure. A fundamental premise here is that fertility, nuptiality, and mortality provide measures of well-being. All workers left records of their individual vital histories: birth, marriage, death. Much of the analysis in this book is based on the reconstruction of these vital events. Records of these events offer a means to study life among workers who otherwise left little or no documentation about themselves. Because work and family were so interconnected, this study also treats the family as a point of departure for understanding broader aspects of the working-class world such as work organization and class relations.

While this book is a social history, it is my hope that it will also engage readers in other disciplines. Chapters 2 and 4, in particular, rely on demographic methods of analysis and are addressed to demographers as well as historians. It has not been my intention, however, to treat the methodology and problems of measurement for their intrinsic interest. Instead my purpose has been to utilize this methodology in order to gain more insight into working-class life. Indeed, I initially approached demographic measurements rather naively and only learned the hard way that a scholar trained in a single discipline cannot simply appropriate the methods of another. Collecting data, coding, computerizing, and running programs on it and, most important, analyzing it with any sort of critical judgment required several more years than I had originally anticipated. In addition to being indebted to mentors and colleagues in the historical profession, numerous people with demographic and computer expertise make the list of those to whom I owe gratitude a long one.

I would first like to acknowledge and thank the sources of funding that supported this project: a University of California Travel Grant, a French Government Fellowship, and a Haynes Foundation Fellowship funded research trips to France. The University of Southern California Faculty Innovation and Development Grant provided generous support for computer use and research assistance. A Mabelle McCleod Lewis Fellowship and a German Marshall Fund Fellowship at various points released me from teaching responsibilities so that I could devote full time to writing, and the latter also supported a final research trip.

In the conception of and inspiration for this project, as well as in the discipline to carry it out, I owe a great debt to faculty members at the University of California, Berkeley. Gerald Cavanaugh first sparked and nurtured my interests in French history. Hans Rosenberg, more than any other single individual, introduced me to concepts of social history and imbued me with a sense of self-discipline. Susanna Barrows, Fryar Calhoun, Natalie Z. Davis, Jan de Vries, and Neil Smelser gave me invaluable guidance in conceiving and developing this topic, as well as in researching and writing.

When I began research in France, Michelle Perrot offered suggestions for possible directions my work might take. Throughout my stay, the Centre d'Histoire Economique et Sociale at the University of Lyon II offered gracious hospitality. I particularly thank Maurice Garden for including me in his seminars and making computer services available, Alain Bideau and Robert Estier for guidance in family reconstitution and demographic analysis, Jean Lorcin for advice on local archives, and all the participants of the center's Saturday seminars for their intellectual stimulation. I am especially grateful to Claire Auzias for her ideas, support, and friendship.

Achieving my research goals would have been far more difficult without the friendship of Hélène Mouriquand and her three children, Laurent, Pascal, and Béatrice Amieux, who frequently provided me with lodging and familiarized me with the Lyonnais region. They not only helped me overcome practical difficulties of Alpine proportions but made me a part of their family. Laurent and Pascal helped reproduce many of the illustrations in this book. Similarly, the weeks I spent in Saint Chamond and Saint Etienne would have been lonely indeed without the friendship of Jean-Claude and Marie Bonnet and their family, who shared many meals and much knowledge about the Stéphanois people. Not only did Michelle Zancarini and her husband, Jean-Claude, provide lodging, but Michelle shared her library and archival material and offered many research suggestions.

I would also like to express my appreciation to the staffs of the various archives and libraries where I conducted this research: the Archives Nationales, the Bibliothèque Nationale, and the Musée Social in Paris, the Archives Départementales of the Rhône, the Hôtel de Ville of Saint Chamond, the Greffe du Tribunal de Grande Instance in the Palais de Justice in Saint Etienne, the Chambre de Commerce in Saint Etienne. Most particularly, I owe thanks to Mlle Viallard and the staff at the Archives Départementales of the Loire in Saint Etienne, where I spent the major portion of my time.

The coding and computing of the family reconstitution data would not have been possible without guidance and help from Gene Hammel, Ruth Deuel, and Madeline Anderson. Naintara Gorwaney and Larry Logue helped integrate new data and gave indispensable demographic expertise. Larry Logue spent many hours helping me refine the computer analysis.

Many friends and colleagues have commented on various parts of my research, most often as responses to papers presented at meetings of the Social Science History Association and other conferences: George Alter, Rachel Fuchs, Michael Haines, Michael Hanagan, James Lehning, David Levine, Leslie Page Moch, Mary Lynn Stewart (who read the entire manuscript), and Louise Tilly have all in some way given me critical insights. I am particularly grateful to Don Reid, whom I met when I started this project and who has read various parts and entire versions throughout its development. Friendship and critical advice from Kristen Neuschel helped me through some of the most difficult stages of writing. I also appreciate the advice and encouragement given by Lois Banner, Rudy Koshar, and Lloyd Moote.

To several people I owe an especially large debt. Lynn Dumenil and Steven Ross each gave this manuscript detailed and critical readings in its later stages, and while the shortcomings that remain are of course my own, its final form owes much to their respective insights and suggestions. David Weir contributed to this book by opening a fundamentally resistant mind to the broader possibilities and analytical demands of quantification. He spent several patient hours teaching me some of the intricacies of demographic analysis and suggesting ways in which I could refine my statistics and their interpretations. John Merriman became a mentor and friend at the inception of this project, has offered advice and support through every stage, and has read every version of the manuscript. Few people would debark from the train passing through Saint Chamond, as he did, to see the city about which he had read so many chapters. His archival and cultural (including gastronomic) knowledge of France has enriched my own education beyond measure and has become an inherent part of this book.

Yves Lequin, who also became a mentor and friend when I began this project, helped me in countless tangible and intangible ways; to him I owe the most. It was he who suggested that I study Saint Chamond and use the method of family reconstitution. He provided unstinting support and guidance by introducing me to archives and to other scholars, by making facilities available at the University of Lyon II, and by supplying a coding system for birthplaces and occupations in marriage records. He too gave each metamorphosis of the manuscript a careful reading.

To my husband, Robert Hern, I am also indebted. In addition to his patience, his humor, his insights about working-class family life, and the boundless moral support he gave me while I was writing this study, during the final stage of research he sacrificed a vacation to help track down names in census reports and vital records. As he gave the entire manuscript a mercilessly critical reading, he will appreciate that my gratitude can find no appropriate words. To him I dedicate this book.

Map 1. Department of the Loire

Introduction

A traveler taking autoroute A–47 southwest from Lyon will first pass by the industrial city of Givors and then descend into the Gier valley. The traffic passes speedily by a cluster of somber little industrial towns that darken an otherwise verdant and pleasant valley: Rive-de-Gier, La Grande Croix, L'Horme. After L'Horme, one comes upon Saint Chamond, the least forgettable of these towns, for there the road goes through, instead of by, the city. A signal, which seems always to be red, halts traffic. The tall smokestacks, darkened old factories, and old houses that retain traces of black smoke impress themselves upon the traveler's consciousness. The green light permits the traveler to continue on to Saint Etienne, a larger version of these industrial towns, but dotted with recently cleaned public buildings and renovated town squares that burst with fountains.

Few tourists would feel inspired to explore Saint Chamond. But a narrow street that goes off to the right leads the venturesome up a steep hill into a neighborhood whose origins date back to the year 640. This hill certainly lacks the charm of Lyon's *vieille ville* or Croix Rousse. Its past, however, contains a comparable richness. Originally the home of Archbishop Ennemond who came from Lyon, this hill hosted numerous seigneurial lords and religious orders.[1] But apart from street names—rue du Château, rue des Capucins—and the ruins of the chapel of Saint John the Baptist, little of that past remains. Instead one finds the small, unsightly church of Saint Ennemond (see figure 1) and an architecture that speaks to an industrial rather than a religious past.

From at least the sixteenth century, this hill teemed with iron forgers, ribbon weavers, silk workers, and, later, miners, stonecutters, and carpenters. At its base, clustered along the Gier River (currently paved over), millers worked their silk on water-run spindles. The neighborhood of Saint Ennemond today appears much as it did in the middle of the nineteenth century. As one

1

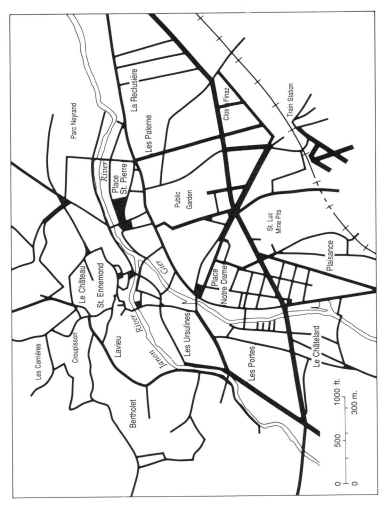

Les Carrières

Croupisson

Le Château

St. Ennemond

Bertholet

Lavieu

River

Janon

Gier

River

Parc Neyrand

River

Place
St. Pierre

La Reclusière

Les Palerne

Public
Garden

Clos Finaz

Train Station

St. Luc
Mine Pits

Plaisance

Les Ursulines

Place
Notre Dame

Les Portes

Le Châtelard

0   500   1000 ft.

0   300 m.

Map 2. Saint Chamond, 1890

military officer described it in 1843, "the houses are of simple construction, built with cut stone." The streets are "generally dirty and poorly paved in round stone."[2] Now blotted with timeworn layers of asphalt, the cobblestone streets twist among old apartments that once housed enormous ribbon looms and shops for iron forges (see figure 2).

The houses designed for tools of production as much as for people testify to a past that knew little distinction between work life and home life. They remind us that one of the most common elements in preindustrial work was its heavy reliance on families rather than factories as work units. From the top of the hill in Saint Ennemond, one can look down upon the lower city, on the other side of the autoroute, where in the nineteenth century industries built their own shrines—braid factories, steel plants, and the immense churches of Notre Dame and Saint Pierre, renovated with bourgeois funds in the 1870s. Today, urban, working-class apartments—tall, gray HLMs (Habitations à Loyer Modéré) built since World War II—dominate the landscape.

Saint Chamond's architecture alone hints at the multiple layers of its history. The differences between the hill and the lower city represent the transformation in workers' lives that came with industrialization. Indeed, the drama that unfolded within these structures during the nineteenth century repeated itself countless times throughout industrializing Europe: productive labor left the home and became concentrated in factories.

When production took place within the home, work and family fused in a number of ways. Labor shared time and space with eating, sleeping, lovemaking, childbearing and childrearing, and socializing with friends and kin. Family and household concerns frequently and spontaneously broke up the sixteen-hour workday. Equally important, the bond between work and family had cultural significance. Men, women, and children often labored as a team. Parents passed skills on to their children, trained and disciplined them, and initiated them into the secrets and associations of their trades. Marriages formed around work relationships and in turn reinforced those relationships. Even when the family members labored at unrelated tasks, the common effort to sustain a family income bound them together.[3]

In removing work from the home and centralizing it near sources of power, mechanization transformed the interrelationship between family and labor. Merchants no longer put out work to cottagers; instead, the latter had to leave their homes to earn a daily wage. Frequently they had to abandon their homes in the countryside and migrate to the towns and cities where production became concentrated. Not only did such migration often break up families, but factory labor itself changed the relationship between parents and children. Mechanization made some skills obsolete and created other new skills. Training no longer took place in the home and, for the most part, sons no longer learned from their fathers. Factory work also transformed the economic role of women. Because leaving the home to work conflicted with child care, mothers could no longer easily contribute to the family income.

The object of this book is to examine precisely what this dramatic change in the relationship between work and family meant for the lives of nineteenth-century workers. Specifically, it uses family formation and family structure as windows onto the world of workers and as points of departure for understanding workers' material experiences with industrialization and changes in the organization of work. How workers adapted to industrial change in turn cannot be understood apart from their relations with employers and the local elite, whose behavior—benevolent, utilitarian, or a combination of both—created the context in which workers' consciousness developed. Thus a secondary focus of this study is an analysis of class relations in the light of changes in family structure. Industrial change pressed workers into new modes of survival. It also forced the elite to develop new strategies to preserve and discipline the working class and to try to mold workers in their own image.

The city of Saint Chamond and its surrounding region offer rich opportunities to examine the relationship between family structure and economic and technological transformations, as well as implications family change had for class relations. The city is located in the Stéphanois basin, an area which corresponds roughly with the arrondissement of Saint Etienne in the department of the Loire. Referred to frequently as "the cradle of the industrial revolution in France," this basin has long attracted scholarly attention.[4] Its mountains and valleys provided industry with abundant primary resources—particularly in water power and coal deposits—and set the stage for industrialization along classical lines. The region attracted industry not just because of its resources but also because agriculture alone could no longer support the growing population.[5]

Cottage industry, and especially the employment it provided for women and children, thus contributed significantly to the sustenance of the rural population. An extensive network of domestic workshops produced nails, bolts, files, luxury arms, glass, ceramics, silk ribbon, and thread. By 1790, these industries supported a population of 118,981 in the Stéphanois region. Beginning about 1820, the importation of English metal-working processes, combined with the introduction of steam power, radically transformed this region's economy, demography, and social relations. By 1866, the Loire ranked as one of the most densely populated departments in France.[6] Most of this population crowded into the principal Stéphanois cities of Saint Etienne, Firminy, Le Chambon-Feugerolles, Saint Chamond, and Rive-de-Gier. Stéphanois industrialization also forged a militant working class and an entrepreneurial bourgeoisie committed to republicanism. This workshop of France has become a laboratory for historians interested in studying the economic, social, and political impacts of industrialization.

Saint Chamond's development pivoted on the commercial manufacturing of iron and silk. During the seventeenth and eighteenth centuries, ribbon merchants and forge masters expanded the domestic industries of ribbon weaving and nail making throughout Saint Chamond and deep into the adjacent countryside. In the second quarter of the nineteenth century, heavy metallurgical production and mechanical braid-making became established. By the 1850s, for a number of reasons that varied from industry to industry, ribbon and nail merchants either left Saint Chamond entirely or invested their capital in the new factory-based industries. The simultaneous mechanization of silk and iron production industrialized Saint Chamond more completely and dramatically than its neighbors. This development in turn transformed the town's labor force, environment, and architecture. Industrialization largely eliminated domestic production, polluted the environment, and drew thousands of migrants from the surrounding countryside. Over the course of the nineteenth century, the town's population grew from 4,000 to 14,000 inhabitants.

Saint Chamond's transition from artisan-based production to full-scale factory production and the pattern of migration and urban growth there make it an ideal setting for the study of family change among workers. Its combination of metallurgy and textiles makes possible a comparison among different types of artisans and industrial workers; previous social, economic, and political histories of the region, moreover, offer an implicit comparative perspective with other towns and cities.

This book argues that among both artisans and industrial workers a strong relationship existed between the organization of labor and gender roles, the number of children born to workers, and the number of their children who died early in life. Among artisans, family structure depended upon gender-specific demands of labor and varied by occupation. Occupational differences became less important with industrialization. By removing work from the home, mechanization forced workers to restructure their family lives. They had smaller families for both voluntary and involuntary reasons. Most couples clearly attempted to limit the number of their children more than they had in the past, but many had smaller families also as a result of poor health and infant and child deaths.

As workers lost control over their work lives, curtailing family size became more important as a means of exercising self-determination. But many working-class families did not succeed in surviving independently and had to rely on material assistance. In this regard, industrialization meant new forms of dependence on the employer class. Removal of work from the home not only made material independence more difficult but undermined workers' power in other ways. Factory work deprived them of the ability to develop skills and authority within their own families. Apprenticeship either disappeared entirely or came under factory control. Factory work attracted to the city migrants who also suffered a loss of independence from employers because they lacked strong familial bonds and social ties.

This study of industrialization and the working-class family fits into a broad body of literature that spans a century and a half, and its conclusions will clash with those of many studies that have preceded it. Little dispute is engendered by the statement that the removal of work from the home had significance for workers' lives; what that significance was, however, escapes consensus. Throughout the nineteenth century, many observers sharply criticized factory labor. As early as the 1830s, sociomedical economists such as

Louis René Villermé brought attention to the miserable, insalubrious conditions in factories.[7] Later in the century, when working conditions had improved somewhat, political economists still had reason for concern. The concentration of workers into industrial urban slums made them more visible. Crime and poverty made it apparent that workers' home lives had become a source of moral degeneracy. Consternation over working-class morality grew more intense with every social upheaval in which they participated: the revolution of 1830, pervasive working-class unrest shortly thereafter, the revolution of 1848, the increased incidence of strikes in the 1860s, and most important, the Paris commune of 1871. This last event presented the specter of socialism in its most pronounced form yet.

In response to the apparent moral decay in French society, by the 1870s Frédéric Le Play had begun to formulate a sociology of the working-class family. With a methodology based on observation and induction, he concluded that partible inheritance, legislated during the Revolution of 1789, had proletarianized rural workers and devastated their families. It destroyed the traditional stem family, in which the father perpetuated his authority by transferring family property to only one heir, who would provide a pension for his parents and cash or dowries for his siblings. Equal inheritance weakened paternal authority and destroyed the family as a moral and economic unit. Large-scale industrialization accelerated this destruction, particularly for the working classes, for it further destabilized family life.[8]

Le Play inspired many followers who adopted his methodology as well as his conclusions. Among them was the abbé Cetty, who in 1883 published *La famille ouvrière en Alsace*. Based on interviews with workers in the industrial centers of Alsace, this study attempted to uncover the roots of working-class misery. Although Cetty's perceptions are often skewed by his own moralistic predisposition, his thorough investigation leaves rich material for historians of the working class. Following Le Play's reasoning, Cetty believed that lack of patrimony and the removal of work from the home destroyed the power and authority of fathers over their sons. In former times, the worker's children "grew up under his eyes, were raised by his side, and when they came of age, he made them a part of his work, took them by the hand, and guided their first efforts." But with the introduction of factory labor, young boys associated talent, art, and progress only with the machine and not with their fathers' experience.[9] Factory organization encouraged insubordination toward the father, for the son did not work under his direction. Working for the same employer placed father and son in a position of equality and sometimes even put the latter in a superior position.[10]

Cetty also attributed the "almost irredeemable decadence" of the family to the unhappy fate that industrialization had imposed on women. He pointed to the central question of the family wage: women had almost no choice but to enter the factory. Prostitution offered the only other alternative. Their departure from the home to the factory attacked domestic life at its very source. And removal of productive labor itself disorganized the family and reduced the home to a mere shelter for eating and sleeping: "[The family] is no longer a hearth around which a new generation grows and develops with the same faith, the same soul, the same character." Parents and children returned from the factories too exhausted for conversation or education. The family lost its role as a source of moral authority and knowledge.[11]

The decline in parental, particularly paternal, authority created a vicious cycle in each generation that weakened the structure of the family. It led to early marriages and numerous children, which in turn resulted in high rates of infant mortality and death from childbirth. Women worked in factories until they delivered babies and then immediately resumed work. Between 1861 and 1870, Mulhouse averaged 33 infant deaths per 100 legitimate births. Worse than early marriages was the habit of *concubinage* (cohabitation) when workers could not afford to marry. Cetty found the practice reproachable in and of itself, and he showed it also helped produce higher rates of infant mortality: 45 of every 100 illegitimate babies died before they were a year old.[12]

The decline of paternal authority, the necessity for women to work outside the home, the destruction of family traditions, and premature marriages made the family unable to meet its own needs. The death of either parent, which frequently came early, would throw the family into a state of dependence. Other relatives no longer cared for family members as they had in the past. Institutions thus developed to meet those needs. Orphanages, kindergartens (*salles d'asile*), and hospices had become establishments of "first necessity"; in Mulhouse, the *salles d'asile* "render such great services, that have so entered the customs of the inhabitants, that it would be hard to imagine this city without them."[13] Although Cetty praised charitable activities in the industrial centers of Alsace, he did not look to charity as a solution to the problems of the working-class family. Instead, the family had to be strengthened from within. He cited efforts among some industrialists to reinforce morals both in and outside the workplace.[14]

Cetty and Le Play condemned industrialization because it ruined the family and thus undermined the moral basis of society. Noteworthy about their position is that they did not blame the worker for moral degeneration. Instead, the family had become the "first victim of industrialism," whose situation required the invention of a new word, *pauperism*.[15]

Not all contemporary observers shared the views of the Le Play school. The well-known inquiries of Louis Reybaud and Armand Audiganne, for example, did not consider the removal of work and of women from the home as destructive to the family. The fact that women had always performed productive labor made their entry into the workshops and factories seem logical. Indeed, many investigators believed factory work to be beneficial to women because machine-tending suited their strength. They did not, moreover, view factory work as a source of family decay. Employers and observers alike frequently indicated that unmarried women supplied most of the labor force; they left the factory either after marrying or after the birth of their first child. Unlike Cetty, Reybaud and Audiganne believed the miserable slums they witnessed in their travels resulted, not from industrial capitalism leading systematically to pauperism, but from individual moral failings.[16]

The most recent generation of scholarship echoes these latter observers insofar as it has treated the working class as maker of its own history rather than as passive victim of the industrial process. E. P. Thompson pioneered new avenues of research by bringing to light the existence of a positive, rich working-class culture that enjoyed independence.[17] Labor movement activity grew out of that culture. As social history came to focus on working-class life rather than on labor movements and strike activities alone, the working-class family emerged as an important source of culture.

Recent research tends to support the view that industrialization did not severely disrupt family life among workers, and certainly that it did not destroy it in the ways Cetty and others suggested.

Examples abound. Nearly thirty years ago, Neil Smelser noted that mechanization in the English cotton industry did not break up the family; parents employed their own children in factories and thus replicated some of the teamwork they had depended upon in their homes. Michael Anderson later demonstrated that, if anything, migration and industrialization strengthened relations among family and kin. Migrants from the countryside did not travel alone to the city. They came with, or after, family, friends, and neighbors. Hardship forced them to rely on one another even more than before. During critical life situations—unemployment, sickness, the death of a key wage-earner in the family, widowhood—workers relied on one another and used bureaucratic forms of assistance only as a last resort. In his more recent study of the Lyonnais region, Yves Lequin also stressed continuity in the industrial process: industry moved to the countryside long before workers moved to urban industry. When they did migrate to the city, many came from only a day's journey away, and they maintained contact with the countryside. Moreover, they came from regions that already had the same industries as those in the city. In other words, occupational and thus cultural continuity mediated the move from country to city.[18]

Lequin's conclusions complement another direction of research that further turns attention away from industrialization per se as the most important watershed in the history of the working class. Wage labor in the context of cottage industry proletarianized workers and transformed their family lives long before mechanization did. Artisans became proletarianized because they lost control over the purchase of raw materials, tools of production, and the marketing of finished products. This process, recently labeled *proto-industrialization*, prepared workers for urban factories and was a phase not only preceding industrialization but necessary to it.[19]

The focus on proto-industrialization has brought to the surface the darker side of domestic industry. In addition to proletarianizing workers, it also reshaped the working-class family by encouraging workers to have large numbers of children so that they could contribute wages to the family income.[20] It could and did lead to the exploitation of men, women, and children. In the light of recent research, the Le Play school's nostalgia for domestic industry looks extremely romantic. Not only did the working-class family survive factory labor intact, but the mode of production preceding it offered a far from ideal situation for the traditional family as they conceived it.

In their path-breaking study of industrialization and women's work, Joan Scott and Louise Tilly also downplay the severity of change that mechanization brought to the family. They conclude that the family provided "a certain continuity in the midst of economic change" in the contexts of domestic and of factory production. Even though industrialization removed work from the home, the spheres of family and work did not separate completely; the family "continued to influence the productive activities of its members."[21] Most important, they called attention to the crucial relationship between production and reproduction. In the transition from the family economy to the family wage economy and family consumer economy, workers adjusted their fertility strategies. According to this scholarship, the family turned out to be remarkably flexible in the face of industrial change.

The studies of these researchers and others investigating the family economy have demonstrated that although most production ultimately did leave the home, the process occurred gradually. New types of domestic industry replaced those that became mechanized. The introduction of electricity began another era of home industry, much as did the personal computer in recent years. Married women and mothers, by continuing to work in the home, carried on the same kind of productive activities they always had. Home industry permitted them to continue to juggle productive and reproductive responsibilities.[22]

Implicitly and explicitly, this scholarship suggests that the family served not only as a source of continuity but, indeed, a source of strength, if not defense. Echoing Michael Anderson's findings, Jane Humphries has offered the hypothesis that family hardship promoted a "primitive communism" among workers that, in turn, helped promote class consciousness. In the effort to avoid the "degradation of the workhouse," only kinship ties could "provide an adequate guarantee of assistance in crisis situations." Not only were kin ties strengthened, but the struggle to provide for nonlaboring members of the family created a consciousness of social obligation that extended to nonkin. This sense of obligation in turn established a basis for class consciousness and class struggle. The family's ability to survive independently of state institutions provided a foundation for class resistance to economic exploitation.[23]

The existence of a powerful labor movement by the end of the nineteenth century demonstrates that industrialization did not destroy the moral fabric of the working class. Workers could not have organized if factory labor had reduced their family lives to total disarray. Complete demoralization would have resulted in apathy. On the contrary, a positive culture gave workers the class consciousness, inspiration, and courage to resist exploitation and demand more rights in the workplace. William Reddy, for example, has recently documented that protest often derived from the effort to protect not just the family income but a way of life organized around it.[24]

The recent empirical research seems to overturn the assessments of working-class life that are based on eyewitness accounts of the Le Play school. This study of workers in Saint Chamond, however, argues that while the modern research corrects the Le Play school it goes too far in downplaying the extent and profundity of change that occurred in family life. It has also left unexplored the implications those changes had for class relations. The argument presented here turns to an analysis of demographic patterns as a key to understanding economic change and working-class family life. A close examination of marriages, births, and deaths among proto-industrial and industrial workers reveals that an enormous change in the family did occur with industrialization: through deliberate control over births as well as through high mortality, family size declined; the working-class family also became weakened as a basis for class culture as it lost a certain measure of autonomy.

Nineteenth-century observers and modern historians have noted that industrialization caused a lowering of the age at marriage, reduced life expectancy, and increased infant and maternal mortality. But at the same time, in part because of earlier marriages, it also caused a larger than average family size among workers. While workers supposedly continued to have large families, contraceptive practices spread regionally and conquered all of geographical France. Thus in the face of this overall decline, the newest of social classes, that of urban industrial workers, apparently remained a bastion of high fertility. While considered "laggers" in the general demographic transition of Western society, they eventually joined the middle class in having smaller families once infant mortality decreased and their standard of living rose.[25]

Analyses of family structure among industrial workers have been based mostly on aggregate data from vital events or from census reports, neither of which can provide a completely accurate picture of fertility or trends in fertility. Aggregate data, for example, cannot control for such factors as duration of marriage; census reports supply information for households rather than for families and do so only at five-year intervals. A more accurate method for documenting fertility change in a local context is through family reconstitution—the actual reconstruction of individual families through linkage of birth, death, and marriage records over two or more generations for the entire population of a single locality. Most family reconstitution studies have concentrated on preindustrial populations, in part because they seek to establish the roots of the fertility transition, which began prior to industrialization. Moreover, in practical terms, the task of family reconstitution is an overwhelming one even for small village populations. Few family reconstitutions have been conducted in an urban context, and none has been done, to my knowledge, for a nineteenth-century industrial city.[26] Yet without this technique, gaining a detailed picture of fertility and mortality among urban workers and thus better insights into the material conditions of their family lives remains beyond the historian's grasp. Through a method of cohort analysis, I have overcome most of the obstacles inherent in reconstituting families in an urban population.[27]

Using family reconstitution, Part 1 of this book explores the relationship between work and family in two contexts: among proto-industrial artisans in the first half of the nineteenth century, and among factory workers in the second. Although workers did continue to have relatively larger families, family size declined considerably with industrialization. More important than the decline itself are the conditions under which it took place: workers had fewer children not because they began to follow the path of their middle-class counterparts, but because the industrial work organization pressed them into doing so. The decline in fertility neither stemmed from an improved standard of living, as is often argued, nor did it necessarily lead to a higher standard of living. Instead, fertility and mortality signified distress among certain elements of the industrial population.

Part 1 also explores the meaning that change in work organization had for the family by reexamining and questioning the continuity between rural and factory industries, as well as occupational continuity between generations. Registers of births, deaths, and marriages used for family reconstitution contain detailed information about occupation, birthplace, and residence. The linkage of these records in the individual family histories over two or three generations in Saint Chamond thus makes possible a close examination of migration and occupational change. Despite the proletarianization prior to mechanization, and the continuity it provided for urban industry, migration and new modes of production indeed produced a generational break with the past. Occupational inheritance did decline, and where it persisted it created fewer and less meaningful bonds among family members. Migration also broke up families even when it strengthened ties among those members who stayed together.

This study of occupational change and family structure also touches on the question of whether patriarchal authority within the family deteriorated, leaving family life more permeable to employers' paternalistic incursions. Removal of work from the home meant a decline in occupational inheritance as well as a loss of family cohesion. This process portends a loss of social power as well as of authority over the work process itself. When skills and their perpetuation remained in the domain of the family rather than of the capitalist, workers had leverage over who attained skills. The decline in occupational inheritance and the fact that its very nature changed clearly transformed the relationship between parents and children, because parents lost much of their ability to shape a child's future, and children had to leave the family to obtain skills. The family lost custody over technological knowledge. This process also changed the relationship between employers and workers, for the former began to control apprenticeships.[28]

A third area of investigation in this book is class relations, to which Part 2 is devoted. This subject has certainly received more than its share of attention from historians. And yet scholars have focused mostly on workers who exerted power. They have not often enough questioned why the majority of workers did not organize and why those who did failed in their efforts to construct a society according to their own vision. This study examines class relations in a society where workers did not exercise very much power and seeks to explain why this was the case despite their efforts to organize. One area of investigation is the practice of paternalism, a topic that has received increased attention in recent years. Paternalism has generally been examined in the context of workers who rejected it, which has led to the conclusion that it did not succeed in its goal of pacifying the working class. Many workers did indeed shun material assistance. Others, however, had no choice but to rely on it. Whether or not it achieved its goal, material assistance did play a role in class relations that has, as of yet, remained relatively unexplored.

The use of *paternalism* to describe various forms of charity in the late nineteenth century has confused the issue because the word connotes an anachronistic, Old Regime view of the world and thus one whose policies were doomed to failure in the nineteenth century. The analysis of charity in Saint Chamond is based primarily on the archives of the city's hospice—a source rarely used in studies of the working class—as well as on employer practices within and outside the workplace. These sources show that industrialists in Saint Chamond tailored their paternalistic activities to conditions of urban industrialization. They adopted new ways of administering material assistance such as employer-controlled insurance and child-care centers. These institutions not only addressed the new pressures that came with industrial society but also attempted to moralize workers. Rather than restoring power and authority to the working-class family, these paternalistic practices assumed some family functions and further deprived workers of independence. What happened in Saint Chamond at least partially supports recent theories regarding industrial discipline derived from Michel Foucault and Jacques Donzelot and applied by Michelle Perrot.[29] The inability to survive independently made many working-class families permeable to intervention from local caretaking institutions. The family became a medium for class relations and an arena for elite influence.

Part 2 also examines local politics and the labor movement in this context. Here previous work done on the Stéphanois region provides a comparative perspective. Yves Lequin, Sanford Elwitt, Michael Hanagan, and David Gordon have analyzed working-class and middle-class left-wing political activity in this region during the nineteenth century.[30] In both its bourgeois and its working-class political consciousness, Saint Chamond proved exceptional

for this region and provides interesting points of contrast. Its bourgeoisie remained devoutly Catholic and politically conservative, if
not monarchist, through the end of the nineteenth century, while
the working class was relatively tranquil. This book argues that
rapid industrialization, the need to rely on material aid, and the
Catholic, monarchist, and paternalist stance of employers weakened workers' propensity to develop a strong political movement;
moreover, because local priests were friends of the poor, workers
could not fully sympathize with the anticlericalism of the left wing.
At the same time, workers did retain a cultural independence and
many of them resisted elite domination even though it did not become effectively translated into political opposition. Their resistance is all the more remarkable given the cultural barriers to the
formation of worker associations and the pervasiveness of employer efforts at political hegemony.

Every city or region is unique. The hope of a local study is to
speak, not to that uniqueness, but to common human experience.
In Saint Chamond, the years between 1860 and 1880 mark a period
of discontinuity in working-class culture and family formation
strategies. These workers' experience does not fit easily with the
thrust of recent scholarship. But perceptions of continuity and discontinuity do not necessarily contradict one another. Instead, they
represent coexisting realities. Neither proto-industrialization nor
industrialization assumed homogeneous forms in their respective
developments. Nowhere did industrial capitalism develop linearly.
Thus the impacts of industrialization on the working-class family
varied as well. In Saint Chamond, mortality and fertility rates suggest that industrialization caused distress for the working-class
family. Rarely are demographic patterns unique to a single locality,
and Saint Chamond was not alone in its high rates of death and
low rates of birth. Nor was it unique in its strong paternalism. In
the structural weakening of the family and its vulnerability to assistance from the elite, the experience of the Saint-Chamonais
should provide insight into workers' lives in other industrial
centers.

PART 1

WORK AND FAMILY STRUCTURE

1

Labor and Family among
Artisan Workers, 1815–1840

In 1807, Jean-François Richard-Chambovet, a prominent ribbon merchant in Saint Chamond, traveled to Paris, a journey few Saint-Chamonais of the nineteenth century ever made. He certainly had the leisure to travel during this year, for revolution and war had nearly decimated his business. While wandering about Paris trying to distract himself from commercial troubles, Richard-Chambovet came upon a shop of antiques and used goods. There a curiosity caught his eye: a loom with thirteen spindles. How strange this mechanism appeared to him, for it was completely unlike the ribbon looms with which he had great familiarity. The shop had three of these looms; Richard-Chambovet purchased them all, for the hefty sum of 390 francs apiece, and brought them back to Saint Chamond.[1]

Little did this ribbon merchant know that his simple purchase would eventually reshape the economy of his native town and, indeed, change the direction of its history. These looms braided threads rather than weaving them. Their arrival coincided with the introduction of steam power. Much less delicate than ribbon looms, braid mechanisms adapted well to steam. By 1820, Richard-Chambovet had a factory with 298 braid looms. A decade later, steam powered 4,000 spindles in Saint Chamond, and by 1860 this number had multiplied by no less than one hundred. Mechanically produced braids did not replace the shinier and more delicate woven ribbons. Indeed, the Restoration brought a return to fancier tastes, and the ribbon industry experienced a golden age between 1815 and 1825. But by the 1840s factory-produced braids replaced ribbons as the primary textile industry of Saint Chamond.[2]

The Saint Chamond economy simultaneously expanded in the metallurgical sector. The extensive coal deposits of the Stéphanois region attracted entrepreneurs who introduced blast furnaces and

rolling mills in the 1820s and 1830s. They built English forges in
Saint Chamond and the surrounding communes of Terrenoire,
Lorette, Izieux, Saint-Julien-en-Jarrez, and Saint-Paul-en-Jarrez. By
1831, large-scale industry in two sectors vital to the French economy,
textiles and metal, had been installed in Saint Chamond. Meanwhile, the two traditional craft industries that had established
Saint Chamond as a commercial town, nail making and ribbon
weaving, had all but disappeared by 1850.[3]

During the first half of the nineteenth century the basis of the
Saint Chamond economy thus became transformed from domestic
production to large-scale factory production. Capital and labor
were transferred from craft to mechanized industries. In this complex process, the choices, activities, and capital of Saint Chamond's
merchants and entrepreneurs played a decisive role. The transfer
of labor, however, required a distinctly human shift and thus entailed the decisions, choices, and will of workers in Saint Chamond
as well. Industrialists certainly felt pleased with this town's technological transformation; but how did workers experience it?

In some other parts of France where industrial capitalism similarly transformed industries and local economies, artisans resisted
change and retarded its effects by maintaining control over their
own labor. Although the Le Chapelier Law of 1791 was intended
to abolish guilds and other worker associations, many persisted.
Craft guilds, confraternities, *compagnonnages*, and other quasi-
religious associations helped artisans extend their work identity to
a sense of fellowship with other members of their trade. Associations enabled them to maintain some control over their work by
regulating entry into the craft through apprenticeships and by
regulating standards of production.[4]

In other cases, however, economic development alone undermined the power of worker associations to preserve their way of
life. In Saint Chamond, for example, merchants controlled raw materials, imposed standards of work, and monopolized the sale of
finished products. *Confréries* persisted throughout the nineteenth
century, but they came to be dominated by employers and confined
themselves primarily to religious functions.[5] As associations weakened, the family assumed more significance as a repository for culture centered around work, and particularly as a main source for
apprenticeships. Consciously or not, it developed into the primary

theater in which tactics for preserving a way of life became formulated; equally, it became the arena in which workers relinquished their way of life. How they responded to economic change in large part depended on the degree to which the family operated as a production unit and on the extent of their success in passing skills on to new generations.

While during the course of the nineteenth century industrialization reshaped family life, what happened within the family also largely determined the fate of domestic industries. In Saint Chamond, the majority of men and women devoted themselves to some stage in the production of nails, ribbons, and the processing of silk. Most work took place in the home, and in both silk processing and iron working, parents passed skills on to their children. Each craft, however, responded to economic change in Saint Chamond very differently. Despite a decline in the ribbon industry, weavers clung to their trade and persisted in passing it on to their children. Nail makers and their sons more readily abandoned their craft.

One reason for the divergent patterns in these responses stems from the nature of the work itself. In the end products as well as in the labor that created them, these two crafts could not have differed more. Ribbon weavers turned organic material into beautiful luxury items that had little utilitarian purpose beyond the satisfaction of consumer vanity. Their value was subject to the whims of constantly changing fashion. At the same time, their production required lengthy apprenticeship, highly developed skills, dexterity, patience, and, for the best ribbons, a true artistic talent. Nail makers turned inorganic material into an exclusively utilitarian object with little aesthetic value. Only seasoned nail makers appreciated aesthetic qualities in details of difference among the thousand or so varieties. Their indispensability insured more consistent employment. The creation of nails, however, required more practice than training, more brute force than talent.

Ribbon weavers indeed felt more pride in their work, which partly explains their greater attachment to it. But this attachment did not stem from the nature of the work alone. The relationship between family and work among both nail makers and ribbon weavers provides insight into cultural approaches that informed their behavior. A key difference between the two crafts helps to explain their divergent responses to economic change: though both industries took place in the home, ribbon weaving depended upon the family as a unit, while nail making relied primarily on adult male labor. To survive in the face of technological change and loss of control over various stages of production, ribbon weavers drew more heavily on the productive capacities of their wives and children. Nail makers, on the other hand, turned outward from the family and tended to seek opportunities that were less domestically oriented.

From the preparation of raw materials to the marketing of the final product, ribbon production had a complex organization, of which weaving constituted but one stage. It was this stage, however, that involved the family most completely as a work unit. A master weaver usually owned three to six looms on which he, his family, and his journeymen worked. His wife and children provided invaluable assistance in auxiliary tasks such as winding bobbins. Wives also supplemented the family income by spinning or warping silk for merchants.[6] As heads of a family enterprise, weavers exercised considerable independence.

Yet because weaving was only one stage in ribbon production and, indeed, dependent upon the other stages, weavers could not enjoy complete autonomy. All phases of ribbon production were seasonal, contingent on the silk harvest between May and July as well as on orders from fashion houses in London, Paris, and New York. Silk preparation lasted from three to six months, and looms operated for about eight months of the year. It was in silk preparation and marketing that merchants had gained considerable control by the end of the eighteenth century. Called *maîtres faiseur fabricant*—they put others to work, or they "put work out"—they had come to direct the bulk of the Saint Chamond labor force that worked in silk. The *fabricant* experimented with patterns, textures, and colors and decided which ones he would have produced for firms in Paris, London, and New York. He then had raw silk prepared and dyed according to the specifications of the pattern and hired a weaver to produce it. The leading ribbon *fabricants* of Saint Chamond—especially the Dugas brothers, Dugas-Vialis and Co., Bancel, Gillier and Sons, and David-Dubouchet—were the wealthiest and most important in France.[7]

After purchasing the silk cocoons, the *fabricant* hired young girls to unravel their single threads and wind them onto skeins. This work lasted approximately three months after the cocoon harvest and was the most distasteful in the silk preparation process. The worker first had to find the end of the single strand that composed the cocoon. She took about six cocoons at once and plunged them in extremely hot water to loosen the gum. She next unraveled all six cocoons while twisting the strands together and then placed them on a skein.[8]

Workers could perform this task in their own homes, but increasingly *fabricants* employed them in workshops. By the 1830s skeining workshops were equipped with motorized spools and furnaces for centralized heating of water basins. This job especially relied upon migrant labor—young girls who usually returned to their rural villages after the season. As such, skeiners "belonged to the poorest class" and suffered the most miserable conditions. The stench of cocoons permeated the workshop and penetrated their clothing. The constant submersion of their hands into nearly boiling water caused chronic pain. Soaking them in red wine and cold water during breaks and after work provided meager relief. Skeiners earned 60 to 90 centimes for their sixteen-hour workday. *Fabricants* usually lodged them, but under conditions Villermé described as miserable. They slept two together in beds of straw and ate meals consisting of "weak bouillon, legumes, potatoes, potherbs, a few milk products and sometimes a little codfish."[9]

After having the silk skeined, the *fabricant* then sent it to a miller. Silk millers exercised a profession in their own right, but they too came under the direction of *fabricants*—they worked as jobbers, fulfilling precise orders. Millers "threw" silk for merchants in Lyon and Saint Etienne as well as for those in Saint Chamond. They too relied on a female labor force, most of whom worked under their supervision in a workshop. Workers placed the skeined strands of silk on a mill consisting of rotating vertical spindles and bobbins. The mill twisted each thread in one of two directions to form the warp and weft, respectively. The tightness of the twist depended on the kind of thread required for the weave of a particular design.[10]

Water powered the spindles that twisted the silk, so the millers clustered along the Gier River, where they employed and lodged in workshops at least eight to ten workers, and sometimes as many as thirty or forty, who each supervised up to sixteen spindles. The women who worked for silk millers suffered conditions not much better than those of the skeiners. They too labored a sixteen-hour day for 90 centimes. Their employment lasted about six months.[11]

Once the miller completed the job he sent the silk back to the *fabricant*, who in turn sent it out to a dyer. After scouring, cleaning, and dyeing the silk, the dyer returned it, still on skeins, to the *fabricant*. There the warp thread underwent one further stage of twisting on wooden spindles. Finally, warpers (*ourdisseuses*) performed the delicate task of placing all the strands in a parallel fashion and stretching them with equal tension. Spinners and warpers worked either in their own homes, on the premises of the *fabricant*, or in the workshops of headmistresses. These processes too became increasingly centralized in the first decades of the nineteenth century. Because their work required skill, practice, and patience, warpers fared somewhat better than skeiners, mill workers, and spinners. They earned 1f40 per day, and some of the older, more experienced women were permitted to work in their own homes. Their work also lasted only six months.[12]

After warping, the *fabricant* finally sold both the warp and the weft to the weaver. The weaver wove the silk into ribbons which he sold back to the *fabricant*, who then again employed a female labor force to perform the finishing, including folding and packaging the ribbons for marketing.

With the exception of the weaving and dyeing, this industry from start to finish relied upon an extensive, protean female labor force drawn from both town and country. The women could perform almost all these preparatory processes in their homes, provided they could obtain the proper materials and equipment. But in the first half of the nineteenth century, *fabricants* and silk millers increasingly organized these workers into workshops. A number of factors made centralization more practical. Most important, *fabricants* could better supervise the workers as well as the silk itself. In addition, silk could not tolerate changes in temperature or humidity, and keeping the raw materials under the *fabricant*'s supervision assured proper treatment. The concentration of workers in shops also helped prevent the theft of silk and its waste products.[13]

The government inquiry of 1848 reported, not surprisingly, very poor conditions among the mill workers, skeiners, and spinners who labored in workshops. Respondents complained of overly strict supervision, stomach ailments, and leg varices induced by having to stand for long periods of time or by pumping the spinning-wheel pedal. Because silk could not tolerate atmospheric variations, these women suffered winter cold, summer heat, and high levels of humidity and breathed foul air because windows and doors had to be kept closed. Silk particles caused serious chest irritation. Long hours and workshop discipline surely made conditions there worse than those in workers' own homes.[14]

The history of family and occupational life in Saint Chamond can be retrieved from marriage records, especially when used in conjunction with birth and death records for the purpose of reconstituting families. Records from couples who married between 1816 and 1825 and proceeded to have families in Saint Chamond through the first half of the century provide insight into the relationship between work and family life and into family responses to the technological change that took place during these years. Of the 539 women who married in Saint Chamond between 1816 and 1825, nearly 50 percent declared their occupation as silk workers of some kind (Table 1). Of those, 20 percent wove silk and the remainder declared jobs as silk worker, warper, skeiner, or spinner. Forty-one percent had fathers who wove ribbons.[15] It is impossible to know how many of these women worked in their own homes and how many in workshops; no doubt those who came from ribbon-weaving families assisted their parents when they were needed and worked outside the home during various periods as well.

Whether these women wove ribbons in their own homes or skeined silk in the workshops of *fabricants*, or both, they could bring valuable knowledge and experience into a marriage with a ribbon weaver. The assistance of a weaver's wife and children played a particularly important role in his productivity. Once the *fabricant* sold the prepared weft and warp to the weaver, the family had to operate as a tightly coordinated unit. *Fabricants* habitually gave weavers last-minute rush orders and ruthlessly demanded that deadlines be met. The weaver first had to "mount" the loom according to the pattern and type of ribbon specified in the order. This process took anywhere from one day to more than a week, depending on whether plain or patterned ribbons had been ordered. The task was accordingly painstaking.[16]

Table 1.   Occupations of Men and Women Married 1816–1825

	Men		Women	
	No.	*%*	*No.*	*%*
Agriculture	9	1.7	1	0.1
Mining	5	1.7	0	0
Small metallurgy	102	18.9	0	0
Large metallurgy	27	5.0	0	0
Textiles (primarily silk)	133	24.7	256	47.5
Construction	59	11.0	0	0
Clothing	36	6.7	53	9.8
Misc. crafts	38	7.1	20	3.7
Land transport	9	1.7	0	0
Shopkeeping and food	83	15.6	12	2.2
Misc. services	37	6.9	29	5.4
None	0	0	168	31.2
Total	539	100.0	539	100.0

Note: The data here and, unless otherwise indicated, in all subsequent tables come from ADL, sous-série 3E 208, 1815–1865, and from the *état civil* in the Palais de Justice de Saint Etienne, Greffe du Tribunal de Grande Instance, 1865–1914.

In addition to weaving, wives assisted their husbands in a number of other indispensable ways. As the weaver set up the loom, his wife worked over a *canetière*, a mechanism that passed the weft thread from the bobbin onto *canettes*, smaller bobbins that fit into the interior of the loom shuttle. Once her husband finished a ribbon, she picked floss and impurities from it (*émouchetage*). Throughout the ribbon production process, she also ran important errands. She often obtained the thread and other materials from the *fabricant* and did the negotiating with him over prices of materials and labor. Here she could draw on her own experience, either from having grown up in a ribbon-weaving family or from having previously worked under a *fabricant*. Nearly 60 percent of the ribbon weavers who married between 1816 and 1825 chose brides who had already worked with silk; nearly 40 percent married the daughters of ribbon weavers. The importance of a wife's skills in this trade is even reflected in the literacy rates: 40.2 percent of ribbon weavers' wives were able to sign their marriage records, a rate more than twice as high as that of nail makers' wives. Ribbon weavers themselves were more literate than other types of workers, because of the accounts they had to keep; it helped if their wives also had such skills.[17] Indeed, marriage served as the point of departure for a family enterprise, for ribbon production depended heavily on the participation of all family members.

If marriage served to consolidate skills, family formation perpetuated them. Of all the ribbon weavers in the older generation present at the weddings celebrated between 1816 and 1825, 83 percent had passed their skills onto a new generation. More than two-thirds of them had daughters who declared occupations in the silk industry. Of ribbon-weaving grooms whose fathers declared professions, 65 percent also wove ribbons.[18] Although the information about fathers' occupations remains incomplete, it does indicate a strong degree of occupational inheritance. As these figures suggest, apprenticeship almost always took place within the family. It began at about age fifteen or sixteen and lasted two to five years. Each of the specialties—plain ribbons, patterned or velvet ribbons, and, later, elastic—required a separate apprenticeship. Though training usually prepared the young weaver to be a journeyman before he reached age twenty, according to one observer it often took three generations to produce an able ribbon-weaver. The ability to weave the fanciest ribbons depended not just on skills learned from one's father but on inborn artistic talent. Occupational inheritance served as the wellspring for each generation of weavers. It also helped shape the industry. In his 1929 thesis on the silk ribbon production Henri Guitton attributed loom innovations to "modest workers who watched looms working under the hands of their fathers, and who, remaining the rest of their lives in their presence . . . felt the perfection that technology demanded as a function of the needs and possibilities of the moment."[19]

If occupational inheritance helped weavers become inventors and entrepreneurs, innovations in this industry in turn, ironically, made it more difficult for weavers to become masters and to pass skills on to their sons. Although some workers exploited new opportunities and attained a higher status, innovations during the first three decades of the nineteenth century had some negative consequences for the average weaver: looms became less affordable, their greater complexity made the traditional apprenticeship insufficient, and the weaver lost further control over the production process to an increasing number of middlemen. While ribbon production remained a family enterprise, survival became more difficult and fewer sons carried on the trade.

The first major technological change that ultimately began to proletarianize the weaver came with the Zurich or high warp loom, which brothers Jean-Baptiste and Jacques Dugas first introduced to Saint Chamond in 1765. This loom made possible the simultaneous production of thirty-two ribbons. A single bar in the front that the weaver raised and pushed moved its numerous shuttles. This new loom held such importance for the industry that Louis XVI ennobled the Dugas brothers and the government granted premiums of 70 francs annually for eight years to anyone who would obtain one. By 1777, Saint Chamond's *fabricants* supplied silk to 2,400 Zurich looms in and around the town.[20]

Their size and complexity made Zurich looms much more expensive than the low warp or tambour looms. Moreover, the simpler looms continued to operate because the shuttles of the Zurich could not produce the same variety in size and patterns. Jacquard originally designed his mechanism for the looms in Lyon that wove single pieces of fabric. Its adaptation to the Zurich took several years, but it ultimately improved the versatility. Weavers in the Stéphanois began using the Jacquard with a single shuttle for simple designs in 1824. The same loom with several shuttles for large designs and brocades became standard throughout the region within the next eight years (see figure 3).[21]

As a result of the Jacquard, the situation of ribbon weavers became worse in some respects than that of silk weavers in Lyon. By the 1850s, looms in Lyon cost 250 or 300 francs. But in Saint Chamond and Saint Etienne, because of the adaptations made in order to produce numerous ribbons simultaneously, the Zurich and Jacquard looms cost 1,000 francs. Those made of walnut or mahogany sold for 2,000 to 3,000 francs. Such enormous capital outlay began as early as the French Revolution to restrict the number of loom owners, especially since government premiums had ceased by this time.[22]

In addition to raising the price of looms, the Jacquard mechanism made them much more complex. Its main innovative characteristic was that it reproduced patterns automatically. Two specialized workers, a sketcher (*dessinateur*) and reader (*liseur*) performed the preliminary work to set up the mechanism. Their task bore similarity to that of a modern computer programmer. The sketcher drew the design on graph paper with conventional symbols to indicate how the weft thread would produce the pattern. Using a mechanical language, the reader punched into cardboard the intended movement of the warp threads during the passage of the loom shuttle. He then placed this program on a cylinder in the loom, and the pattern reproduced itself automatically as the weaver moved the shuttle. This job required more skill than that of the sketcher and at least three years of apprenticeship—as much training as most weavers required.[23]

The Jacquard mechanism thus removed from weavers one of the stages in ribbon production: implementation of the designs. As one observer put it, with the Jacquard "the ribbon weaver has no need to know how to read the cardboard designs in order to reproduce them. He is no longer anything but a simple agent who executes an operation."[24] Instead, the sketcher and reader took over this task in the fabrication of patterned ribbons. They too were hired by the *fabricant*. The reader in particular became a key intermediary between the *fabricant* and the weaver, for he installed the punched cardboard for the latter. This mechanism also made the job of mounting looms far more painstaking, because the weaver had to avoid damaging the punched cardboard and the cylinder. *Fabricants* imposed stiff financial penalties if any damage did occur.[25]

Though weavers continued to work in small family workshops, these technical advances divided the labor by gender and by geography. Women mostly wove on the low warp and tambour looms, which produced plain ribbons. Looms fit for patterned ribbons became increasingly difficult for them to operate because decorative and metallic thread made the shuttles weigh at least 130 pounds. In addition to becoming male-dominated, the production of patterned ribbons became urban-centered. Their delicacy required closer supervision both in their production and in regulation of the patterns themselves—in the hilly and mountainous countryside within a radius of five or six kilometers from Saint Chamond, weavers tended to plagiarize designs. Thus advances in loom mechanisms during the first thirty years of the nineteenth century were concentrated in towns and cities; weaving in some of the rural areas outside Saint Chamond became exclusively a female occupation, while in the city itself it became predominantly male.[26]

From about 1830, when the Jacquard loom became standard in Saint Chamond, the multiplication of processes carried out by others complicated the weaver's task and denied him access to some of the specializations. Once he had received an order, for example, he had to make as many as twenty errands to the *fabricant*'s shop to obtain the necessary silk and loom pieces. Often he would be promised silk in the morning and then waste an entire day standing at the shop's door waiting for it. Sometimes it took ten to fifteen days to collect all the necessary prepared pieces just to begin weaving. As respondents to the government inquiry of 1848 put it, the time a weaver spent running errands and waiting cut into his work, "his only property."[27]

The ribbon weaver was held fully responsible for the quality of the finished ribbon. If the dyer, sketcher, reader, or warper had made mistakes, the weaver had to correct them or see that they were corrected, which stole more time from his weaving. His wife's contribution toward these time-consuming chores, particularly the running of errands, became ever more important as the *fabrique* grew more complex.

The increased need to supervise the production of patterned ribbons led to the introduction of a third middle person between the weaver and *fabricant*: the *commis de barre*, who took over functions the weaver had once performed himself. *Barre* referred to the bar on the front of the loom that moved the numerous shuttles. The *commis* found "bars"—weavers—to carry out the orders for the *fabricants*. In addition to scouting for weavers, the *commis* negotiated prices, surveyed the work, and regulated disputes on behalf of the *fabricant*. Most often the *commis* had been a ribbon weaver himself and continued to oversee a workshop. He might own three or four looms worked by his family and journeymen. His own experience as a weaver had taught him the commercial side of the industry. He had learned to negotiate shrewdly with *fabricants* and *commis* and had acquired a business sense about the prices of raw materials and the market for finished products.[28]

The increased reliance on *commis* caused considerable vexation. They received 5 percent of the price the *fabricant* paid the weaver for ribbons, further cutting into the weaver's wages. More complaints had to do with the humiliation to which *commis* subjected weavers. It was the *commis* who often demanded the order be filled within an unreasonably short period of time so that he could then extract more from the weaver's pay as a fine. Under pressure from the *fabricant*, the *commis* also went out of his way to detect imperfections in the ribbon. He frequently cheated the weaver by finding fault with the ribbon's color, texture, or pattern and holding him responsible for mistakes the sketcher, reader, dyer, or warper had made. Most often the weaver would not risk going before the Conseil des Prud'hommes to complain, for fear that the *fabricant* or *commis* would stop giving him orders. Although weavers worked successively for several *fabricants*, they could not afford to alienate any of them for fear that they would not be chosen to work during the commercial slowdowns that came so frequently in the ribbon industry.[29]

The higher prices of looms, the increased subdivision of work into specialties, and the greater reliance on *commis* began to influence the ribbon industry most profoundly after the Jacquard loom became a mainstay in the Stéphanois region during the 1820s and early 1830s. Responses to the government inquiry of 1848 reflect their impact. Most complaints referred to the cheating *commis*. Saint-Chamonais described the relationship between weavers and *commis* as "feudalistic": weavers received "protection" if they were family members of the *commis* or if they had provided certain "services" to the *commis* or *fabricant*, particularly sexual favors from their wives or daughters.[30]

Weavers also expressed deep concern about their loss of control over specializations and their decreasing ability to equip their children with the skills necessary to operate the more complex looms. They deplored the traditional methods of apprenticeship for their arbitrariness. In other words, inheriting skills from a family did not adequately equip a young weaver for the new technology. A father's knowledge and experience no longer sufficed. They called for a professional school that would provide theoretical as well as practical instruction in all types of looms, in punching cards for the Jacquard (*mise en carte*), in designing patterns, and in loom mechanics.[31]

Respondents to the government inquiry also complained bitterly about the occupational hazards of ribbon weaving, some of which had always plagued weavers, others of which intensified with technological change. Silk work rendered homes extremely insalubrious. Workers lived in tall, narrow apartments, built to accommodate looms rather than people. Just as in silk workshops, doors and windows had to be kept closed to maintain an even temperature and level of humidity and to shut out the pervasive dirt and ash from the increasing number of forges in the town. Inside, silk dust thickened the air and depleted it of oxygen. Journeymen and children slept on *soupentes*, platforms suspended from the walls near the ceiling. Though this arrangement well suited the operation of looms, it placed those who slept on *soupentes* in even greater jeopardy. Warm air rose and brought with it more of the deadly silk particles. Weavers contracted a number of degenerative illnesses from these conditions. Most common was the disease whose symptoms modern medicine now recognizes as those of tuberculosis.[32]

Operating Zurich and Jacquard looms entailed new physical hardships for the weaver. To the government inquiry, Saint Chamond's ribbon weavers reported that for the production of the fanciest ribbons, they had to manipulate up to 650 pounds of silk when lifting and pushing the wooden bar in front of these looms. At the same time they had to move it evenly and continuously without becoming winded. "A large number of workers do not have enough strength for this," the report stated, "and when they do, they can only do it for three or four years." To move the bar even with threads that weighed much less, workers had to lean on it with their stomachs and do this constantly over a period of several days at a time. Mounting the looms and tying broken threads also compressed the stomach. Such constant pressure caused internal membranes to thicken and become cancerous.[33]

Weavers risked other hazards as well, such as varices in their limbs and scrotum, especially when they began work at too young an age. Production of the fancier ribbons ruined the eyesight. The delicate silk threads often broke, and the weaver had to reattach the broken ones to those of matching color, grouped together in a large bundle. The government inquiry noted that "To this rude labor the worker is in some way attached like a beast of burden, which ruins temperaments and decimates a good number of individuals in the flower of their age. Usually by 48 or 50, a man can no longer work in this state, whether by weakness of temperament or by failing eyesight that prevents him from functioning properly."[34]

Ribbon weavers in Saint Chamond faced a further dilemma which those in the rest of the Stéphanois basin suffered only much later: the local decline of the industry itself. Fierce rivalry between Saint Chamond and Saint Etienne began in the second half of the eighteenth century and intensified after the Revolution, to Saint Chamond's disadvantage. One of the most frequently cited reasons for the lead Saint Etienne took in this competition is that the ribbon industry in Saint Chamond continued to respect guild regulations while Saint Etienne's did not, and wages and prices in Saint Etienne responded more effectively to the market. As the capital of ribbon weaving long before Saint Etienne started producing ribbons, traditions in the small town had become more firmly imbedded. By 1813, the Consultative Chamber of Arts and Manufactures in Saint Chamond requested that the prefect enforce regulations in the Saint Etienne ribbon industry. They bitterly referred to their Stéphanois counterparts as "oppressors" who engaged in a "war of ribbons" that threatened "1,200 fathers of families." The competition developed beyond wages and prices, for manufacturers in Saint Etienne made a practice of stealing some of the designs made in Saint Chamond.[35] Other factors further weakened the Saint Chamond ribbon industry. One local historian thought the building of the railway between Lyon and Saint Etienne in 1827 enabled buyers to ignore the small town. Another suggested that they purposely avoided Saint Chamond because its hotels did not offer enough luxury and because Saint Etienne had a more centrally located and convenient train station.[36]

By 1840, ribbon production in Saint Chamond had declined to one-tenth the size of the trade in Saint Etienne. A military officer sent to report on the region in 1843 noted that the "population of Saint Chamond had been diminishing appreciably for a dozen years because of the almost complete ruin of its ribbon trade." It lost a fifth of its population, which fell from 10,000 inhabitants to 8,000. Many ribbon manufacturers simply liquidated their businesses; some changed over to new industries, particularly the mechanical production of braids and cords. By 1848, only eight ribbon-manufacturing firms, fewer than half of what had existed in the 1830s, remained in Saint Chamond.[37]

The ribbon weavers who married between 1816 and 1825 began their conjugal lives at a time of relative prosperity and promise but bore and raised many of their children when the Jacquard loom and industrial capitalism began to have their most intensive effects. The greater obstacles to buying looms and mastering necessary skills, the loss of control over production, and the shrinking of the industry itself challenged not only the traditional organization of work but the very basis of family life among weavers and silk workers.

What strategies did they adopt to meet these challenges? Surprisingly few took the apparently logical step of leaving the town or changing professions. Only 8 percent of the ribbon weavers who married failed to start having families in Saint Chamond, and at least 43 per cent of them showed evidence of their presence in 1850 or later. Among those who started families in Saint Chamond, only eight of them, or 17.5 percent, met the new challenges of the industry by assuming seventeen other occupations: baker, schoolteacher, publican, grocer, café keeper, gardener, nail maker, mattress maker, carter, charcoal merchant, mason, iron worker, day laborer, dyer, wood mechanic, braid maker, and braid tagger. The last four occupations derived from their experience in the ribbon industry. *Menuisier, menuisier-mécanicien,* and *mécanicien sur bois* referred to the job of loom mechanic, an occupation that grew more specialized and important as looms became more complex. Although ribbon looms began to decrease in Saint Chamond, the number of braid looms multiplied rapidly. Since weavers had to become masters of their looms, specializing as a loom mechanic even for the braid industry exhibited a continuity in their occupational history.[38]

Among the few who did change occupations, about half alternated their jobs with ribbon weaving. Michel Bonnard, for example, declared his occupation as ribbon weaver at the time of his marriage in 1819. Ten years later he worked as a tavernkeeper, then as a schoolteacher. Through 1838 he alternately declared these two occupations. In 1839 he worked as a grocer and once again declared himself a ribbon weaver in 1841. His occupation appeared upon the registration of his death in 1844 as "former teacher and tavernkeeper." A ribbon weaver at the time of his marriage in 1820, Claude Marie Labeaune declared himself to be a joiner (*menuisier*) two years later and in 1828 again referred to himself as a ribbon weaver. From 1833 to 1869 he alternately listed his occupation as joiner, as mechanic, and, finally, as *ex-menuisier-sur-bois*.[39]

Given the increased hardships in the profession of ribbon weaving, that more did not abandon it is remarkable, especially since the expansion in the braid and metallurgical industries provided new employment opportunities. Assuming that they were highly motivated to remain in their craft, what made it possible for weavers to do so? Apart from the increased cost of looms and loss of control over several stages of production, the specific changes ribbon weavers faced in their industry entailed an increase in the time spent mounting looms and in the number of troublesome errands and negotiations. These latter chores were activities that the wife could perform in addition to the auxiliary tasks she had always done for her husband. Thus ribbon weavers increased the efficiency of their production by relying more on their wives. Their family structure suggests that such was the case. In comparison with the rest of the Saint-Chamonais, ribbon-weaving couples had fewer children, spaced them more deliberately, and tended to send more of them to wet nurses. Mothers thus limited their reproductive obligations so that they could devote more attention to productive responsibilities.[40]

A continued high rate of occupational inheritance in the second generation, remarkable in itself, further indicates that ribbon production persisted by virtue of that fact that it remained family-intensive. Offspring of the generation who married between 1816 and 1825 grew to adulthood in the 1830s, 1840s, and 1850s. Only 20 percent of all male children, regardless of father's occupation, married in Saint Chamond. Despite the hardships of their local trade, a surprisingly higher proportion of ribbon weavers' sons (23 percent) married in town.[41] Of 38 sons who married, more than half declared their occupations as ribbon weaver. Others declared closely related activities: reader, braid tagger, dyer. Even joiners and mechanics performed work related to passementerie, because they worked on wooden looms. Workers and employees in rubber manufacturing performed tasks related to the weaving of elastic—an extension of ribbon weaving. If these related jobs are included as an indirect form of inheritance, 75 percent of these sons in some manner carried on skills to which their fathers had exposed them. Conspicuously absent is any entry into metal working, small or large; this absence is noteworthy because heavy metallurgy, like loom construction and elastic production, had begun to expand by this point. One exception stands out. Jean Marie Chavanne wed a second time in 1865, at which point he stated his occupation as "ex–ribbon weaver, turner at the Petin forges." His first wife had died in Bourg Argental, which suggests that he had married and settled in that town as a ribbon weaver. After his wife's death, he returned to Saint Chamond where metal work, at this point, offered the only opportunity for employment.[42]

Daughters born to the cohort of couples who married between 1816 and 1825, regardless of father's occupation, wed in Saint Chamond at a rate of 21.4 percent, slightly higher than that of sons. But only 19 percent of the ribbon weavers' daughters married there, a percentage lower than that of their brothers. Many of the daughters who did marry in their native town, like their brothers and fathers, adhered to the craft traditions originating with the family. Forty-three percent of them married ribbon weavers or workers with associated skills. Many of the others married men in petit-bourgeois or even middle-class occupations, suggesting a measure of upward mobility.[43]

If the power of family resources and work traditions made it possible for ribbon weavers to continue practicing their craft in Saint Chamond, one must still ask what motivated them to become masters in the face of so many obstacles and to withstand numerous hardships after attaining that status. What, indeed, made so many ribbon weavers and their sons stay in Saint Chamond, "attached to this rude labor like beasts of burden"? Ribbon weavers lived in a paradoxical world. They could command among the highest of wages, yet because they produced luxury items the work available to them fluctuated with the whims of fashion. A sudden downturn in commerce could wipe out the money they had saved to buy looms and homes. In the middle of the century, weavers received about 13 centimes per meter of patterned ribbon or 8 centimes for plain ribbon. They could produce about sixty meters of plain ribbon and only about thirty-six meters of patterned ribbon in one day. For both, wages per day of work thus ranged from about 4f70 to 4f80. Since ribbon weavers worked only eight months out of the year, this wage averaged about 3f60 a day overall unless they took on other jobs in the off season.[44]

However, particularly skillful and efficient ribbon weavers could weave more and acquire more work. Herein lay the source of their pride: the ambition to do well at their craft, if not to perfect it. They lived in the constant hope that their superior talents would bring them work even during hard times. Inheritance of tools as well as skills could also place them in an advantageous position, as could extensive assistance from their wives and children.

Ribbon weavers' pride in their work and the commitment to stay with it derived from the looms, the training, and the traditions they had inherited from their fathers, grandfathers, and great-grandfathers. Young weavers in Saint Chamond after 1830 would not have tried to establish themselves as masters if their own fathers had not already encouraged their talents, instilling a respect for the work they performed and an appreciation of its beauty. They spoke of their products with a language of love: "rich and sumptuous brocades, the most iridescent satins, taffetas of delicate tones."[45] They took pride in making twills and satins for epaulets, gold braid for hats, velvet ribbons with fine gold for church ornaments; they were proud that their products found use in haute couture.

Silk working and its products posed a curious and problematic juxtaposition to the other major industry of Saint Chamond, metal working. Travelers through the Stéphanois region continually expressed shock to find "workshops of silk ribbons and laces . . . where so many forges fed by coal continually pour black and dirty smoke into the atmosphere." Silk working in Saint Chamond and Saint Etienne had to locate itself as far as possible from "smoky places where metal is cast."[46] Even the small domestic forges posed difficulties over the centuries during which these two industries cohabited, and the introduction of large forges in the nineteenth century brought new dimensions to their conflict. As one "Monsieur Capnophobe" protested to a newspaper in 1854, *fabricants* did not want to give orders to ribbon weavers living in any proximity to the forges, when a "gaping mouth will at every instant vomit smoke and soot on their dwellings, and [ruin] the delicate colors of rose, white, lilac, that require so much care and precaution to conserve their beautiful and pleasant brightness which delights the elegant Parisians."[47]

Bitter controversies between the two industries led to somewhat unfair characterizations about the life-styles and personalities of those who worked with metal and silk. Early in the nineteenth century, Duplessy declared the silk worker as "more gentle, more disciplined than the iron worker. He shows more thought, invention, and intelligence. Maker of delicate fabrics, he carries this work to a high degree of perfection, while the works of ironmongery . . . remain imperfect and unfinished; the men who occupy themselves with this work earn little and hardly dream of perfecting it, a type of carelessness which seems to reflect these words of Holy Writ: 'He who works iron, sits near the anvil and gazes upon the fire that he works up; the fumes from the fire parch his flesh and nevertheless he delights in the intense heat of the oven.'"[48] Others noted that iron workers behaved in a "coarse and noisy manner," while ribbon weavers had expensive habits and a "pronounced taste for all that shines."[49] Iron workers crowded into "low and humid places on clayish soil," where they "breathed" iron; ribbon weavers worked in clean and well-lit apartments and touched only silk, "whose emanations are not harmful."[50]

As late as 1871, in his travels through Saint Chamond and the Stéphanois valley Louis Reybaud associated silk working with the family and metal working exclusively with men: "Family life is often identified with [the work of the] weaver; women and children become involved with it and find in the works of detail a use for their time and the opportunity for a little profit. But the iron industry is more harsh and less accessible. It hardly ever admits anyone but men built for services which demand . . . strong arms."[51]

These characterizations contain no small amount of caricature. Duplessy's description almost suggests that iron workers felt attracted to hell. Some ribbon weavers' apartments may have been well lit, but none were clean. And the "emanations" from silk certainly harmed their occupants. These observers no doubt nostalgically romanticized silk working for its juxtaposition to the more palpably industrial craft. Distortions aside, nail makers did have a relationship with their work that was different from that of ribbon weavers in at least two ways: their work did not organize itself as much around family life, and they manifested a much weaker attachment to their craft. The particular nature of their work-family relationship also shaped their response to the industrialization of Saint Chamond in a manner distinct from that of ribbon weavers.

Insofar as nail making was a putting-out industry, it bore some resemblance to ribbon weaving in its organization. Nail merchants— *fabricants*—received orders for nails from retailers in the bourgs and villages of the Massif Central and from Lyon. They bought iron from the Bourgogne or Dauphiné and had it split into bars or fine rods in splitting mills. These splitting mills, equipped with a tilt-hammer and usually operated by water, employed five to ten workers each. In 1818, eleven such mills operated in the arrondissement of Saint Etienne. Two prominent Saint-Chamonais families, Neyrand and Thiollière, were among the owners of these mills and as *fabricants* also sold the split iron to nail makers.[52]

Like ribbon *fabricants* in Saint Chamond, nail *fabricants* employed workers in the countryside as well as in the town. Geographical dispersion did not, however, produce a division of labor as it did in the ribbon industry. Instead, the amount of time devoted to forging distinguished country from city. Overpopulation in the countryside pressed peasant cultivators into supplementing their income with nail forging during winter and in the evenings. But in Saint Chamond itself, most nail makers devoted full time to their task.[53] Nail making employed the second largest proportion—19 percent—of the men who married between 1816 and 1825 (see Table 1).

Typically, the nail maker bought about twenty-five kilos of iron, which he then carried to his workplace, a home and workshop combined. Often a forge occupied the first floor of his home, and the family cooked and slept upstairs. Over the forge, the worker first heated the nail blank and hammered it out to a thin strip. He sharpened the four edges of the stem, shortened it to its required length by breaking it off, and then hammered the head onto it.[54]

The energy required to forge nails depended on their type. They were manufactured in hundreds of different forms for uses ranging from shoes, horseshoes, and bellows to ships, roofs, and floors. Those more difficult to shape brought better wages. Some workers did develop their own specializations, but the types of nails workers produced depended largely on what merchants ordered. In Saint Chamond, most forgers made nails for shipbuilding. The work required little skill, but it did demand enormous strength and a good deal of patience and attention. Once the forger had heated the iron he had to work it continuously or it would cool and turn brittle. The hammer weighed nearly five pounds, making it difficult to strike the metal smoothly and evenly. Though nail-making tools did not compare in their complexity or technology with Jacquard looms, they required constant conditioning: the worker had to tighten the nail anvil about every two weeks but avoid adjusting it to the point that it would dent and twist the nail stem.

Like their counterparts in ribbon production, nail *fabricants* held forgers responsible for all imperfections. They added to nail makers' frustrations by providing poor-quality split iron that required great delicacy in handling. At the same time, they paid less for damaged nails and expected orders to be filled with precision. Nail making paid poorly. Estimates of wages between 1815 and 1855 ranged from 1 to 2 francs per day, depending on the amount of time workers devoted to the forge. Nail makers in Saint Chamond earned slightly more since they spent full time at it, but they earned only half to two-thirds the wages of ribbon weavers and suffered a lower standard of living. Their conditions also depended on the extent to which they could control their own work. Like ribbon weaving, nail making required capital investment. Nail makers had to buy hammers, files, anvils, and bellows, as well as fish oil to grease the bellows and seven to eight kilos of coal for each day's work. They also had to have enough capital to purchase the iron.[55]

As in ribbon weaving, workers' status ranged from that of the *chef d'atelier* who employed his own family and other workers to the day laborer who only made nails at someone else's forge when he could find no other work. Even for those who acquired the proper tools, the investment necessary for buying the iron generally exceeded their means. Most nail makers had to make their purchases from day to day or buy on credit, which cost them an additional 10 percent of their wages.[56]

Although the work depleted strength and the workday sometimes lasted from 5 A.M. to 10 P.M., forgers did not labor under the pressures endured by ribbon weavers. Testimony from former nail makers suggests that most of those who practiced the trade resigned themselves to permanent low wages. Unlike ribbon weaving, this craft offered no room for improvement either in the nails or in the tools that produced them. Indeed, Duplessy and others condemned nail makers for their unwillingness to "perfect" their work. What attracted nail makers to their craft was the relative freedom it provided. They could work when and for how long they pleased. And although they put in long, exhausting days, especially when they relied on forging full time as they did in Saint Chamond, the forge became a fulcrum of sociability. Men would drink wine and gossip as they made nails and then together celebrate at taverns after having delivered the nails. This sociability in turn produced marriages built around nail making. Forty-five percent of the nail makers' daughters who married between 1816 and 1825 married nail makers, a proportion higher than that of the ribbon weavers' daughters who married into their father's profession.[57]

The social life built around nail making thus provided a basis for family formation. Moreover, forging took place in the home and often grouped the entire family around it. Adolescents and children placed rods in the fire, operated the bellows, and recharged the coal furnace. Wives, just like those of ribbon weavers, often ran errands such as delivering nails and negotiating with merchants.[58]

The work of nail makers, however, did not build upon marriage and family life in the same manner that it did among ribbon weavers. Only very rarely did women do any forging and hammering themselves. In fact, in Saint Chamond the bulk of their contribution to the family income came from silk production. Wives and daughters worked seasonally in the silk-milling, skeining, spinning, and warping workshops. Well over half of the nail-making fathers between 1816 and 1825 had daughters who worked in the textile industry. Sixty-five percent of the nail makers who married between 1816 and 1825 wedded silk workers, and many of these women continued working with silk after their weddings. Local testimony even confirms that women spun silk on the second stories of houses in which forging took place on the first, despite problems of dust and ash dirtying the silk.[59] Although wives contributed to the family income through silk work in the home or in workshops and although they helped to perform the tasks involved in nail making, they did not assist their husbands with the same intensity as did ribbon weavers' wives. Marriage did not combine skills in the same manner it did among silk workers and ribbon weavers.[60]

The family nonetheless remained the single most important vehicle through which skills passed from one generation to another. No formal apprenticeship existed in nail making; it was the older who taught the young, and most usually fathers taught sons. Nail making was not difficult to learn, but it required strength, endurance, and many hours of practice in hammering steadily and regularly. Boys usually took up the hammer only in late adolescence after having spent years watching their fathers closely. Among fathers present at the marriages between 1816 and 1825, 71 percent of those who declared their occupation as nail maker passed their skills on to their sons. Fifty-six percent of the nail makers who married had inherited skills from their fathers. These rates fall below those of ribbon weavers but clearly highlight the predominance of occupational inheritance in this industry.[61]

The generation of nail makers who married between 1816 and 1825 and started families in Saint Chamond did not face the same structural transformations in their craft as did ribbon weavers. The organization of their work remained constant and they had no need to acquire new skills. Lower wages made living conditions more miserable for nail makers, but they did not suffer the same pressures ribbon weavers faced from commercial fluctuations due to changes in fashion, increasingly expensive looms, more specialized technology, and a larger number of middlemen who put a tighter squeeze on their wages.

In a structural sense, therefore, the craft of nail making remained more stable than that of ribbon weaving. In the latter craft, technological change and local commercial decline forced many weavers to take their skills to Saint Etienne, Lyon, or Paris. Less skilled, and less attached to their skills, nail makers had a greater tendency to remain in Saint Chamond but changed jobs more frequently. Ninety-three percent of those who married remained in Saint Chamond to begin families. At least 61 percent, in contrast to the ribbon weavers' 43 percent, showed evidence of their presence in Saint Chamond in 1850 or later.[62] The willingness to change occupations made this geographical stability possible. Unlike ribbon weavers, who remained doggedly attached to their craft despite its decline, nail makers responded to the expanding and diversifying economy of Saint Chamond by changing their jobs more frequently. Of the eighty who left ample evidence of their occupational histories in the *état civil* (through births, deaths, and marriages of their children or through their own deaths in the town), 54 percent—a proportion more than three times as great as that of ribbon weavers—changed occupations. This pattern bears a remarkable similarity to that in another community of artisans, Salem, Massachusetts. Artisans who engaged in crafts requiring lesser skills had a lower tendency to pass those skills on to their children and also had less impetus to leave the community.[63]

Like the ribbon weavers who did change occupations, many Saint-Chamonais nail makers continued to alternate their original craft with other work, especially as day laborers in a wide assortment of jobs. Of the seventy-four who changed jobs, only fourteen moved into other types of metal work. Excluding those who declared themselves to be day laborers, forty-two nail makers registered thirty different occupations unrelated to metal. Rather than entering the new metal and braid industries, nail makers revealed an attachment to jobs in traditional economic sectors. Examples from reconstituted families illustrate the variety of their paths. Over a forty-two-year period, Claude Journoud listed his occupation as nail maker, stonecutter, charcoal burner, and then, finally, scraper at the steel plant. He alternated among these occupations and mentioned nail making until 1843. Other nail makers clearly moved upward in abandoning their craft. Jean Marie Preynat became a master mason and tavernkeeper. Less than ten years after his marriage, Etienne Preynat became a dyer. Jacques Monnier became a municipal employee and then a police inspector. Between his marriage in 1816 and his death in 1869, Michel Virieux listed his profession as tavernkeeper (1830), café keeper (1843), and ex–nail merchant (1861). Significantly, in their choice of jobs these individuals tended to stay in trades and occupations untouched by technological change. The expanding heavy metallurgical and braid industries accounted for only 21 percent of the jobs they listed.[64]

Sons as well as fathers exhibited geographical stability. Of those born to couples married between 1816 and 1825, 27.8 percent married in Saint Chamond, 5 percent more than the sons of ribbon weavers. Fewer of these sons, however—only 20 percent—inherited their father's craft.

According to nail makers' testimonies, low wages, the coercive nature of their relationship with merchants, and the tediousness of the work itself ultimately tempted younger nail makers or sons of nail makers into factory work. Nail production as a handicraft began to decline, not when nails came to be produced mechanically, at the end of the century, but when heavy metallurgy started to develop in the Stéphanois region after 1815. Regular and salaried work, according to these testimonies, apparently held more appeal for many of the younger workers than did nail making. They preferred the rigidity of impersonal factory labor to the repetition and strain of hammering. The factory alternative seemed to make the young less patient with artisanal nail making and all the difficulties it entailed. *Fabricants* shared these perceptions. As early as 1825, they complained that "the workers are becoming more and more rare, the large industrial establishments which are forming in the arrondissement [of Saint Etienne] are employing the best among them and few new nail makers are being trained." [65]

Contrary to this testimony, however, not many sons of nail makers actually entered modern metallurgy. Occupations recorded for those who married, died, or served as witnesses to the registration of births, deaths, and marriages indicate a remarkable tenacity in traditional jobs. Large-scale metallurgy did lure more nail makers' sons away from their fathers' craft than ribbon weavers and their sons, but the former entered new plants at the same low rate as did their fathers: only 21 percent took work in heavy metallurgy. The vast majority in both generations assumed any of a large array of jobs in the traditional sectors. [66]

Though nail makers and their sons did not flock to the new industries, neither did they manifest the same kind of attachment to their craft as ribbon weavers. Nail making also ceased to bring couples together in the second generation. Fewer daughters of nail makers (24.4 percent) remained in Saint Chamond to marry than did their brothers. The number of those who married nail makers dropped from 45 percent in their mothers' generation to 34 percent. The distribution of occupations among the men they married repeated that of their husbands and fathers: only 23 percent entered the new metal industries, and the remainder practiced a variety of occupations in the traditional sectors.[67]

Nail makers and their sons willingly abandoned their craft but, contrary to contemporary perceptions, not as a direct result of large-scale metal production. The labor force for the new industries came not from native Saint-Chamonais but from migrants to the city. The resulting population growth after 1840 helped to expand traditional sectors of the economy such as building, carting, stone-cutting, tavern- and cafe-keeping. It was for these occupations that workers deserted the domestic forge.

The logic behind decisions or the circumstances surrounding them are not always immediately discernible to the historian. Surely economic need and economic opportunity narrowed the workers' realm of choices and often dictated those choices. But work-associated traditions also affected them. Family life composed a major part of these traditions because work frequently took place in or around the home and families often worked as a unit. Family structure served as a natural basis for work organization. For most families in any trade, domestic production took precedence over work outside the home. When wives and children were needed for domestic production, they were available. Demand for labor was often seasonal, and family members left the home only when their labor could not be used there.

No industry illustrates the importance of family-related work traditions better than ribbon production. Weaving relied on the family as a work unit, on the cooperation of men, women, and children, and especially on the teamwork between wife and husband. Work traditions contributed to family formation, and family formation in turn reinforced work traditions. Passing the craft from generation to generation, the family provided a physical as well as psychological space in which men, women, and children labored. A man's sense of identity as a ribbon weaver developed more intensely if he had learned the craft from his father and grandfather beginning in his early childhood. As an adult, his identification with ribbon weaving grew stronger if his wife had come from the same environment and if she participated in creating the same product through silk throwing, spinning, warping, or weaving.

The artisan had a further stake in his skills if he expected them to provide a source of livelihood for his children as well. Skills constituted a form of family property unlike money or land. Rather than being divided through inheritance, skills became more consolidated, and because they had a nonmaterial base, they fostered strong familial bonds and solidarity.[68] Family life consisted of parents not simply reproducing and raising children but reproducing and cultivating skills and traditions as well.

The importance of work traditions rooted in family life varied considerably by craft. Apart from the raw materials and end products which so distinguished the iron and silk industries, a key difference set them apart: nail production did not involve as much family cooperation as silk work. Though production took place in a domestic context and required the assistance of family members, women and children devoted themselves primarily to tasks unrelated to the nail maker's work. Social relationships formed around the forge, but marriage and family formation did not reinforce work organization.

Varying degrees of family involvement influenced workers' attachment to their craft and in turn informed their responses to economic change. Within Saint Chamond's very mixed environment, ribbon weavers and nail makers responded in distinctly different patterns. In greater numbers than did their nail-making counterparts, weavers and their children left Saint Chamond so that they could continue to exercise their skills. But the majority remained, and did so in the face of numerous obstacles. When conditions grew worse for ribbon weavers in Saint Chamond, family-related work traditions informed their manner of coping with crisis. Drawing further on labor resources of the family provided not only a more logical but an easier alternative to leaving the town or changing occupations.

Nail makers and their children more frequently remained in Saint Chamond, but they readily deserted their craft, whose perpetuation, like that of ribbon weaving, depended on the transmission of skills through the family. By leaving nail production, they contributed to its decline. About one out of five entered the new metallurgical plants and in so doing at least continued a tradition of working with metal. But the majority assumed different skilled or unskilled jobs in the traditional sector, some of which moved them upward in social and economic status. Nail makers and their offspring thus met economic challenges in Saint Chamond not only in leaving their trade more readily but in pursuing opportunities outside the realm of family-oriented production. It is noteworthy that both older and younger generations in silk and metal mostly shunned the new metallurgical industries that offered steadier employment.

The economic history of Saint Chamond illustrates concretely a process central to European industrialization: the transfer of raw materials, capital, and labor power from domestic craft to large-scale mechanized production. It also affords the opportunity to compare this process in two very different industries, textiles and metal. One salient point that emerges from the occupational histories of metal and textile workers is the flexibility and variability in survival strategies. The skilled or unskilled occupation with which an individual entered adulthood did not in any strict manner define or determine his or her future. The mixed nature of the Saint Chamond economy—iron and silk, domestic and factory industries—permitted and in many instances forced workers to change or to alternate occupations frequently, sometimes to practice crafts of contrasting or even opposite natures, such as nail making and ribbon weaving.

The strength or weakness in work-related family traditions at least in part explains why workers in these industries took divergent paths in their response to the economic transformation of Saint Chamond. The differences in their work organization and their work-family relationships suggest, furthermore, that pre-industrial and proto-industrial artisans had a wide variety of experiences with family and work even as they became proletarianized. In Saint Chamond, as in most of France, industrialization did not assume revolutionary forms. Instead, it consisted of numerous families taking relatively small steps to adjust to new economic situations. In some cases, against all odds, families remained attached to the old craft industries. They did not make decisions based on the logic of economic gain but, rather, on the logic of work organized around family life and structure. In other cases, workers willingly left old industries for the new ones, perceiving opportunities for employment or for a better life. Whatever their response to Saint Chamond's changing economy, the relationship between work and family and the traditions that this relationship cultivated informed their choices. So too, as the next chapter will show, did it shape the very structures of their families: the number of children they had, when they had them, and the chances their children had for survival into adulthood.

2

Family Formation, 1816–1840

The development of industries in Saint Chamond during the first half of the nineteenth century involved a complex interaction between work and family. The participation of wife and children in the father's work, the transference of skills from father to son, and marriages between men and women who shared a common work background demonstrate how tightly work and family were interwoven. Ribbon weavers in particular manifested this interdependence, especially as they faced dramatic changes in the nature of their craft. Nail makers generally lived in miserable circumstances, and in their greater degree of proletarianization they more frequently changed occupation than did those who worked with silk. They too, however, labored in a domestic setting where family activities and work regularly intermixed.

The situation of silk and iron workers in Saint Chamond can in many respects be considered "proto-industrial." This newly coined and somewhat controversial term refers, in its strictest sense, to the process by which merchants came to dominate and control much of the production process and, most important, to expand it into the countryside. The more capital they accumulated, the more raw materials they could put out to the countryside, where peasants needed to supplement food cultivation with industrial production in order to survive. In so doing, merchants bypassed guild restrictions and paid cottage workers less than urban artisans, thus multiplying their profits.[1]

A looser application of this term applies to urban artisans who did not supplement their wages with cultivation.[2] Capital accumulation empowered merchants to win control over urban crafts by subdividing stages of production, especially those dealing with the preparation of raw materials and the marketing of finished goods. Proto-industrialization in towns and rural areas thus transformed the workers' relationship to the means of production long before factory work did. This process, furthermore, made the family an agent of economic development. In both the rural context and that of the small town, output expanded through the multiplication of production units—families—rather than through mechanized tools of production. The family's role in this expansion also had a profound impact on its structure. Wage labor encouraged workers to marry relatively early, because husband and wife could combine their wage-earning capacities. The fact that children could begin contributing to the family income at a very young age permitted couples to have large families and may even have made numerous children necessary for long-term economic survival.[3]

At first sight, economic and demographic development in the region around Saint Chamond attests to the association between work and large families. In a period when birth rates in France had begun to decline, the department of the Loire continued to manifest high fertility. Until 1831, crude birthrates there remained among the highest in France.[4] Widespread devotion to Catholicism in the region partly accounts for high fertility. But according to at least one historian, proto-industrial development provided the crucial mechanism for growth: "multiple sources of revenue and the fact that children became profitable at an early age encouraged marriage and large families both in the town and in the countryside. . . . The silk and metallurgical industries not only sustained a large population, but also encouraged people to breed overlarge families in a desperate attempt to survive on the minimal earnings of several children."[5]

Recent scholarship has demonstrated that proto-industrialization helped promote what might be termed a demographic counterrevolution, by encouraging large families.[6] While couples in late-eighteenth-century peasant, middle, and upper classes began to have smaller families, workers married younger and had numerous children. Lack of property or patrimony meant that they did not have to delay marriage for an inheritance. Wage labor encouraged earlier marriage because the wages of a wife and children could increase chances for survival or for a higher standard of living. With no contraception, marriage to young brides meant large families. This was precisely the situation against which Thomas Malthus railed in 1798. Many workers indeed became caught in the Malthusian dilemma. Families with numerous children could survive during periods of full employment, but crisis years, which came so frequently in the first half of the nineteenth century—1816–1817, 1826–1827, 1840–1841, 1846–1847—could turn children into an insupportable burden.

Most of the empirical investigations supporting the hypothesis that proto-industrialization promoted high fertility among workers have been conducted in a rural context. Some contemporary observers and historians have suggested that wage labor in urban, industrial settings also promoted high fertility among workers. In 1841, for example, Louis Blanc pointed to the "incontrovertible" fact that "population grows far faster in the poor class than in the rich class," noting that in Paris, births were "1/32nd of the population in well-to-do districts, and 1/26th in others."[7]

Modern methods for analyzing fertility and family size have certainly grown more sophisticated than those of the 1830s and 1840s. Recent work has suggested that city dwellers, including workers, began to exercise fertility control before the end of the eighteenth century. If urban workers did indeed limit or at least try to limit the number of children they had, it would certainly lend irony to the observations and value judgments derived from the crude statistics upon which Louis Blanc and others relied. It would demonstrate that workers appeared to have many children only because numerous families were crowded together in slums. It would also suggest that workers indeed tried to exert some control over their lives and that their poverty resulted from factors other than their own improvidence. A more precise picture of working-class family structure, whatever form that structure took, will also provide a fuller context for understanding industrialization and the lives of workers.

Between 1816 and 1850 the population of Saint Chamond ranged in size from 6,000 to 9,000 inhabitants, technically making the town "urban," according to administrative definitions. But while Saint Chamond attracted migrants from the countryside and grew in size, urbanization hardly fostered the conditions normally associated with environments in cities such as Saint Etienne, Lyon, Paris, or Rouen. An analysis of Saint Chamond's demographic profile will test whether urbanization can be associated with family limitation. Of greater concern here, however, is determining the influence that work itself exercised on family structure. An analysis of the re-

Table 2.   Mean and Median Age at First Marriage,
by Occupation, 1816–1825

Husband's occupation	Husbands			Wives		
	No.[a]	Mean age	Median age	No.[a]	Mean age	Median age
Agriculture	2	32.1	32.1	2	23.6	23.6
Mining	3	23.8	22.1	4	26.0	23.0
Small metallurgy	66	25.1	24.1	72	24.7	23.1
Large metallurgy	16	27.1	24.3	18	24.7	24.9
Textiles (silkwork)	93	25.9	24.5	103	24.1	23.5
Construction	42	25.6	24.6	46	23.1	22.0
Clothing	28	26.7	24.1	30	24.8	23.3
Furniture	2	26.1	26.1	3	23.2	22.6
Leather	1	21.3	21.3	1	20.0	20.0
Misc. industry	9	34.2	29.2	12	26.0	26.0
Misc. crafts	8	24.2	23.3	8	21.0	21.0
Land transport	6	40.0	39.2	5	26.7	29.0
Food and shopkeeping	44	26.6	24.9	48	23.4	22.8
Misc. services	17	33.3	30.2	18	26.3	25.7
Total	337	26.7	25.0	370	24.2	23.1

[a]The numbers of husbands and wives differ because only first marriages are included here.

spective family structures among nail makers and ribbon weavers will expose ways work and economic conditions mediated family formation.

To examine family structure among the population of Saint Chamond during the nineteenth century, I have employed the technique of family reconstitution. The procedure consists of linking birth, death, and marriage records in order to reconstruct the vital histories of individual families. Dates of the vital events of each family member provide data for the measurement of fertility and mortality.[8] The reconstitution of families in Saint Chamond begins with marriages that took place between 1816 and 1825. During this ten-year period an average of about one hundred marriages took place each year. Table 2 breaks down the marriages by age and by occupation.

The bride's age had the greatest importance for family size, since it determined the number of childbearing years. In Saint Chamond women married for the first time at an average age of 24.2, nearly two years earlier than women of rural parishes in other parts of France during roughly the same period. They married four years younger than had their counterparts in Lyon during the previous century. Ages did not vary much by husband's occupation, except in those categories, such as mining, with numbers too small to have statistical significance. Men married more than a year younger than the national average of 28.[9] These comparatively young married workers apparently lacked the "moral restraint" Malthus urged of their generation.

Beyond its demographic meaning, age at first marriage can be an important index of social, cultural, and economic norms that regulate family life in any community. A drop in marriage age suggests the presence of new incentives to marry young. Historians have argued that it also hints at a greater freedom from community or family controls, and particularly from any economic restrictions patrimony may have imposed.[10] The early marriages of nail makers and ribbon weavers contrast only slightly with those of retail and wholesale merchants but do suggest that wage labor may have influenced the timing of their weddings. Early marriages also signify a reversal in the relationship between family and work: masterships among artisans had at one time been a requirement for marriage, but with the spread of wage labor, the economic partnership of marriage became necessary to attain masterships.[11]

Because family and household organization remained inextricably bound to work, the decision to marry did not occur independently of parents and siblings. Throughout the nineteenth century, even with wage labor adult children continued to view themselves as part of a family economy.[12] When they married often depended on their particular economic role in the family, their birth order, and their gender. Many young people married only after one or both of their parents had died; parental death not only released patrimony, it released young people from the need for parental consent. In Saint Chamond between 1816 and 1825, the fathers of more than 50 percent of the grooms and the mothers of 39 percent had died by the time the sons married. A smaller proportion of brides' parents—the fathers of 44 percent and the mothers of 36 percent—were deceased.[13]

What happened between couples prior to their weddings provides further clues to the timing and meaning of their marriages. The social and economic changes that led to earlier marriage some- times resulted in more frequent premarital sexual activity and thus in higher illegitimacy. Just as industrial capitalism weakened patri- archal community norms regulating marriage, so did it release workers from some traditional norms regulating courtship. Illegiti- macy rates increased dramatically after 1750.[14] In France prior to 1750, for every 100 births there were 3 illegitimate births. This rate rose to 4.7 between 1780 and 1820.[15] These rates reflect regional averages that include rural areas; rates in cities were much higher. In Saint Chamond, the number of illegitimate births per 100 births reached a relatively high average of 5.8 between 1824 and 1830, but it was less than half the rate in nearby Lyon. The illegitimacy rate in Saint Chamond approximated those of rural areas, whose pop- ulations remained more traditional.[16]

Sexual relations during courtship among proletarian couples had long been common in France, as in much of Western Europe. But as a part of courtship, such behavior anticipated marriage and indeed often precipitated the wedding. Data available from various parts of France indicate that 13.2 percent of all firstborn children between 1780 and 1820 had been conceived prior to marriage. The average in Saint Chamond fell near that level. Birth records subse- quent to marriages that took place between 1816 and 1825 indicate that 12.6 percent of the brides came to the altar with child, a rate similar to that of other towns with 5,000 to 10,000 inhabitants.[17] Thus, in Saint Chamond, while proto-industrialization did permit earlier marriage it did not foster an especially high level of sexual activity outside wedlock. No doubt the strong Catholicism in this city, combined with its small size, helped reinforce cultural norms that economic change would otherwise have threatened. More than 50 percent of the men and women who married between 1816 and 1825 had been born in Saint Chamond and did not experience the sense of anonymity or uprootedness often associated with high levels of illegitimacy in urban areas.[18]

The relative restraint or precaution Saint-Chamonais couples practiced prior to their weddings carried over to their married lives. Though on the average they had large families, many did exhibit signs of pursuing a deliberate family formation strategy

Table 3.   Age-Specific Marital Fertility Rates
of Women Married 1816–1825

	Saint Chamond[a]				France	
Age group	Years at risk	Children born	Rate/ 1,000	Index of marital fertility (20–24 = 100)	Rate/ 1,000[b]	Rate/ 1,000[c]
20–24	514	214	435	100	458	412
25–29	854	326	398	91	383	360
30–34	957	293	319	73	329	295
35–39	932	181	205	47	245	219
40–44	889	89	105	25	120	102
45–49	790	6	8	2	—	10
Total marital fertility rate			7.4		—	6.9

Note: For index of fertility control m (.337803), see Appendix B, Table B-8. Mean square error = .00213.

[a] Marriages with prenuptial conceptions were backdated and rates were corrected for under-registration of births. See Appendix A.

[b] Rates based on weighted means from reconstituted families in sixty parishes from 1780 to 1820 in Michael W. Flinn, *The European Demographic System, 1500–1820* (Baltimore: Johns Hopkins University Press, 1981), pp. 106–7.

[c] Rates here are for the years 1790–1819. Rates based on INED data from forty villages analyzed by David Weir. "Fertility Transition in Rural France, 1740–1829," Ph.D. diss., Stanford University, 1982.

within marriage. Family reconstitution provides data for the calculation of several rates that indicate not only the overall level of fertility but the pacing and possible planning of childbearing.

The age-specific marital fertility rate (Table 3) is based on the number of children married women bore according to the number of years they remained married in each of the five-year age groups.[19] The index of marital fertility measures the sharpness with which fertility declined through the woman's childbearing years. In populations exercising no control, demographers expect the level of fertility to remain constant throughout most of the childbearing period. The "total marital fertility rate" is the sum of age-specific rates multiplied by five, the number of years in each of the age groups. This rate estimates the number of children each woman would have if her marriage lasted through her childbearing years and thus gives a figure larger than the actual average family size. As a measure, however, the total marital fertility rate is much more accurate than actual average family size, because it takes into account the duration of marriage.

Two other sets of family reconstitution data from France are presented in the far right-hand columns of this table. They are not strictly comparable to the data from Saint Chamond, because they have not been modified to account for prenuptial conceptions, they apply to an earlier generation, and they come from rural France. These factors would lead us to expect somewhat lower rates in Saint Chamond. The comparative fertility decline becomes most apparent after age thirty-five.

The population of Saint Chamond clearly followed the trend throughout France as a whole. During the eighteenth century, total marital fertility in France declined from about 9 to around 7 births per family. Age-specific and total marital fertility rates demonstrate that the population of Saint Chamond, despite its largely proletarian composition, joined with the bulk of France in practicing some sort of family limitation. Finally, a standardized measure of fertility control, *m*, clearly establishes that this population systematically limited family size.[20] Any value of *m* greater than 0 indicates deviation from natural fertility; the closer it approaches 1, the more closely it approaches fertility schedules from the 1960s. The measure of *m* in Table 3, .337803, demonstrates clearly that Saint-Chamonais couples had consciously begun to limit family size.[21]

Breaking down these families by age at marriage demonstrates a further degree of family limitation. Contrary to Malthusian fears that earlier marriages among the lower classes would result in larger families, some demographers have found that the younger women were when they married, the sooner they stopped having children.[22] This tendency apparently increased through the eighteenth century. The majority of women in Saint Chamond married under age twenty-five. Table 4 provides marital fertility rates for women married under twenty-five for the entire cohort, as well as for those whose husbands belonged to the most largely represented occupational categories. Levels of fertility declined sharply among women in the entire cohort as they grew older, and particularly after age twenty-nine.

A lower rate of childbearing later in a marriage, particularly among women who married young, could result from temporary

Table 4.   Age-Specific Marital Fertility, by Husband's Occupation, of Women Married under Age Twenty-five, 1816–1825

Age group	Years at risk	Children born	Rate/1,000	Index of marital fertility (20–24=100)
Entire cohort				
20–24	513	214	438	100
25–29	693	263	395	90
30–34	635	172	283	65
35–39	568	95	177	40
40–44	520	40	81	19
45–49	452	2	4	1
Total marital fertility rate			6.9	
Nail makers				
20–24	113	45	419	100
25–29	162	61	393	94
30–34	152	43	294	70
35–39	130	26	213	51
40–44	114	15	139	33
45–49	100	1	10	2
Total marital fertility rate			7.3	
Ribbon weavers				
20–24	116	48	434	100
25–29	180	71	413	95
30–34	170	45	277	64
35–39	160	26	172	40
40–44	151	9	62	14
45–49	137	0	0	0
Total marital fertility rate			6.8	
Commerce				
20–24	79	34	452	100
25–29	93	37	414	92
30–34	89	26	305	68
35–39	73	9	130	29
40–44	56	1	19	4
45–49	45	0	0	0
Total marital fertility rate			6.6	

Note: Marriages backdated to include prenuptial conceptions and rates corrected for under-registration of births. See Appendix A.

sterility, a decline in fecundity, or less frequent intercourse. But the fact remains that these women, regardless of age at marriage, were having fewer children than their predecessors in the same age group.[23] In the absence of any reason to believe that health declined or conjugal relations changed, the increase in this trend during the early nineteenth century suggests that the lower fertility later in marriage resulted from a conscious effort to limit family size.

Of particular interest here are occupational differences. Not surprisingly, shopkeepers' and wholesale merchants' wives exhibit a more abrupt drop in their fertility than any of the other groups.[24] But the ribbon weavers stand out for the few children they had after their wives reached age thirty-four. They joined merchant families in their relatively high fertility early in marriage, followed by a sudden end to childbearing. This pattern resulted in a total marital fertility rate lower than both that of nail makers and that of the cohort average.

David Levine discovered this same pattern among workers in Shepshed during the second quarter of the nineteenth century. He suggests that it signifies a conscious desire to pass quickly over the "dependency hump" in which couples had several children in rapid succession and then stopped or, more accurately, tried to stop. For workers, this pattern formed part of a family formation strategy in which the period of child dependency on parents would pass quickly and children would soon be able to contribute their labor to the family wage-earning effort.[25]

Second-to-last and last intervals between births, along with the mother's mean age at the last child's birth, constitute two further standard measures for detecting efforts to limit family size and for analyzing family formation strategies. When these later intervals are substantially longer than others, it indicates a deliberate effort to avoid pregnancy. Table 5 provides these measures and compares them with data from other parts of France. In contrast to birth intervals from families in eighteenth-century France, as well as from those contemporary to this cohort, parents in Saint Chamond separated the births of their last two children by a relatively long period. Ribbon weavers particularly distinguished themselves in this regard, as they did in the young age at which their wives stopped having children.

Available data indicate that French women between 1780 and

Table 5.   Intervals between Births, and Mother's Age at Last Child's Birth, for Women Married 1816–1825 (Intervals in months)

Parity	Marriage to 1st birth	1st to 2d birth	2d to 3d birth	2d to last birth	Last birth	Mother's age at last birth
France[a]						
Pre–1750	16.1	22.9	26.2	30.3	35.4	40.4
1740–1790	14.3	22.5	24.5	29.8	37.6	39.3
1780–1820	14.6	26.1	27.1	30.7	42.4	36.7
Saint Chamond, 1815–1840						
Entire cohort	15.2	24.9	28.3	32.5	43.6	37.0
Nail makers	17.3	24.0	28.0	35.6	43.7	38.6
Ribbon weavers	19.9	23.4	28.9	36.2	45.7	36.6

[a] Weighted mean averages from Michael W. Flinn, *The European Demographic System, 1500–1820* (Baltimore: Johns Hopkins University Press, 1981), pp. 113–15. Data from Saint Chamond are based on women married at all ages whose marriages lasted past their fiftieth birthday.

1820 may have shortened their childbearing by as much as 5.8 years. Prior to 1750, women spent about 15.8 years bearing children; data from reconstitution studies show that women in the later period spent an average of only ten years bearing children. But such data vary considerably by region. David Weir found that by the first decade of the nineteenth century, women who married between ages 20 and 24 stopped having children after age 36.8, and the childbearing period lasted 14.8 years.[26] Women in Saint Chamond who married at all ages demonstrated clear signs of fertility control in a mean age of 37 at the births of their last children and an average childbearing period of 12 years. Yet ribbon weavers' and nail makers' wives diverged in interesting ways: the former stopped bearing children after an average of only 11 years, while the latter spent 14.4 years giving birth, a period closer to that of the rural women Weir analyzed.[27]

Intermediate intervals between births present more interpretive difficulty, and an attempt to analyze their significance touches on the uncertain territory of demographic debate. In pretransition populations, the practice of breast-feeding spaced births naturally. By prolonging postpartum amenorrhea, breast-feeding made mothers infertile for about six months to a year after the birth of a child, depending on when it was weaned. But even when mothers once again became fertile, taboos against intercourse during breast-feeding or the conscious awareness that another pregnancy would threaten the health of both infant and mother discouraged sexual intercourse. In many regions breast-feeding lasted two years or longer. Other external factors independent of conscious fertility control could lengthen birth intervals as well: poor economic conditions, disease, and other circumstances reduced sexual appetite, and seasonal migration interfered with conjugal relations.[28]

Two other factors operated to shorten intervals between births: infant deaths, and the practice of sending children to wet nurses. An infant death increased the chances of another conception by putting a sudden end to breast-feeding. Thus high fertility occurred in populations with high infant mortality. Sending children to wet nurses would have the same effect. French women, especially the bourgeoisie and wage earners, made use of wet nurses far more frequently than other European women.[29]

In the discourse on the fertility transition, the spacing of children and its meaning continue to be debated. Demographers regard fertility as "natural" if intervals between births lengthened because of breast-feeding, poor economic conditions, disease, or temporary migration. The couples' behavior in such circumstances had nothing to do with the conscious desire to limit the ultimate number of children they bore. The basic distinction between natural and controlled fertility thus rests on the couple's intentions. But inferring intentions from statistics on historical populations poses obvious problems. The conscious attempt to limit family size may indeed have assumed the form of having children at more widely spaced intervals as well as stopping after a certain point.[30]

Demographers have tried to solve this problem by devising statistical means of distinguishing between the physiological effects of infant mortality, mentioned above, and "replacement" effects. Mortality could also lead to higher fertility, if parents tried to replace infants and children who died. Such a reaction to death would make most sense if parents had in mind a certain target number of children and thus did make efforts to shape their family structures, either by trying to conceive or by trying to avoid conception. However they responded to infant and child deaths, working-class families suffered them frequently in the nineteenth

Table 6.   Infant and Child Mortality, 1816–1845
(Children born to couples married 1816–1825)

| | 0–1 | | |
	Deaths/1,000 live births	Deaths/1,000 births (w/stillbirths)	1–5
Entire cohort	95	122	95
Nail makers	153	181	93
Ribbon weavers	71	100	147
France, 1780–1820	195	—	—

Source: Data for France are from Michael W. Flinn, *The European Demographic System, 1500–1820* (Baltimore: Johns Hopkins University Press, 1981), p. 135.

century, and demographers are developing new tools for examining how mortality may have influenced family strategies. Apart from measuring how intervals of births after infant deaths diverged from the average length, they have sought to determine whether couples proceeded to have another child after any of their children died, not just the infant preceding a short birth interval.[31]

If fertility rates for Saint Chamond did not demonstrate so clearly that couples had deviated from natural fertility, the relatively long intervals between births would suggest that mothers breast-fed their infants for at least a year, that infant mortality, in part because of this breast-feeding, would be low, and that these mothers did not send their children to wet nurses. At first glance, the mortality rates presented in Table 6 support these hypotheses.

These rates confirm that a strong relationship between fertility and mortality existed in Saint Chamond. At 71 deaths per 1,000 live births, the mortality rate among ribbon weavers' infants fell below that of the whole cohort, just as did their fertility, while that of nail makers' rose far above it. The birth interval after an infant death fell four months below the average length, a difference that also had statistical significance.[32] Clearly, mortality influenced family strategies among these workers; since a significant number of couples in this population did exercise fertility control, it is reasonable to conclude that some families did indeed replace infants and children who had died.

Unfortunately, it is not possible to establish "replacement" with any further precision in this case because death registrations for

Table 7.   Infant and Child Mortality, by Sex, 1816–1845
(Children born to couples married 1816–1825)

	0–1				1–5		
	Births	*Deaths*	*Rate*	$_1q_0{}^a$	*Births*	*Deaths*	*Rate*
Girls							
Whole cohort	574	63	110	195	475	43	91
Nail makers	135	23	170	—	110	15	136
Ribbon weavers	137	8	58	—	119	13	109
Boys							
Whole cohort	570	41	81	227	490	49	100
Nail makers	115	15	130	—	94	4	43
Ribbon weavers	144	12	83	—	126	23	183

[a] Derived from life tables in Ansley J. Coale and Paul Demeny, *Regional Model Life Tables and Stable Populations* (Princeton: Princeton University Press, 1966), p. 8. The rates are taken from model "west," level 8.

these families were not complete. The most remarkable feature about Table 6 is how low the rates are for the entire cohort and for ribbon weavers. Although ribbon weavers earned wages higher than those of nail makers, they suffered more from unemployment. The majority of them certainly did not enjoy a degree of prosperity that could justify the miraculous picture of health their infant deathrates suggest. Saint Chamond's rates as calculated here stood far below those of other parishes throughout France, as well as throughout the Loire. In 1819, J. Duplessy noted that one-fifth of all children born in the Loire died before they reached their first birthday, and only about 60.6 percent of all male children reached twenty years of age.[33] But in Saint Chamond, according to Table 6, fewer than 10 percent of the infants died within the first year of life. The toll rises to 12.2 percent if we include stillbirths in the numbers of births and deaths, which demographers normally avoid in their calculation of infant mortality rates. Not only does this deathrate fall far below what Duplessy found for the entire department, but it is also low in comparison with the findings of other reconstitution studies. In the eighteenth-century rural villages Henry studied, infant mortality ranged from 210 to 286 per 1,000. The Saint Chamond rate is also much lower than the weighted means Michael Flinn calculated for parishes throughout

France, shown in Table 6.[34] The relatively low fertility in Saint Chamond leads us to expect low infant mortality as well. These rates are too low, however, not to give rise to the suspicion that a significant portion of infant death records never found their way to the commune's *état civil.*

Table 7 breaks down mortality rates by sex. Here another statistic startles the eye: not only were infant deathrates low, but they were much lower among boys than girls, a result which goes against the grain of recorded demographic history. For this table, life tables were also used to estimate what infant mortality should have been. Ideally, child mortality rates from Saint Chamond should be used to estimate infant mortality. For reasons that will become apparent below, the registration of child deaths was far more accurate. But if infant deaths were under-registered, the child mortality rate would be underestimated as well, because children who in fact had died in infancy would have been included in the denominator for its calculation. The use of life expectancy, which averaged 36.5 years for women in the Loire between 1816 and 1835, should thus provide us with a closer approximation of what infant deathrates actually were. Based on life expectancy, the table indicates that deaths in Saint Chamond may be under-registered by as much as 44 percent for girls and 64 percent for boys.[35]

On the one hand, the under-reporting of infant deaths and the impossibility of determining the degree of inaccuracy place unfortunate limits on the demographic analysis of these reconstituted families.[36] On the other hand, gaps themselves actually become a source of information. The low infant deathrates provide compelling evidence that a significant proportion of infants in this cohort, particularly those in ribbon-weaving families, died outside Saint Chamond in the care (or lack thereof) of wet nurses.

Women in the Stéphanois region commonly resorted to wet nurses, and for good reason mothers in ribbon-weaving families did so far more frequently than mothers in nail-making families. In his study of Lyon in the eighteenth century, Maurice Garden pointed to two criteria that determined whether parents sent their children to wet nurses: their wealth, and the wife's economic activity. Women in occupations most directly associated with the work of their husbands sent their infants out to be nursed. Garden found the practice particularly pronounced among those who worked on looms beside their husbands and those in the food trades, where traditionally the wife ran the shop.[37]

Study of the wet-nursing business on the receiving end further confirms that silk workers sent the largest number of children to wet nurses. More than 43.5 percent of the nurslings sent to Marlhes, a village above the Stéphanois valley (nineteen kilometers from Saint Etienne and thirty-one kilometers from Saint Chamond), between 1841 and 1865 were the children of ribbon weavers.[38] This percentage reflects Saint Etienne's occupational structure, for 44.7 percent of the population worked in the ribbon industry. But in Saint Chamond, evidence strongly suggests that silk weavers relied on wet nurses more than did metal workers, because their wives provided them with indispensable assistance such as running errands, winding weft threads onto spools, mounting the loom, and removing impurities from the silk ribbon once the weaving was completed. Because weavers had to fill orders at very short notice, the work required such intensity that it could not tolerate the interruptions of infant care. Infants interfered with production far more in these families than they did with the work of nail makers, which afforded fewer opportunities for wives' assistance. The women certainly ran errands such as carrying nails to merchants and negotiating with them, but could provide little help in the actual forging and finishing of nails. Their tasks were less urgent, more flexible, and more compatible with breast-feeding and other demands of infant care. Moreover, nail makers could ill afford the services of a wet nurse even if their wives wanted to avoid breast-feeding.

Garden similarly found a low deathrate among silk workers' infants in Lyon because so many of them had been sent to wet nurses and died in the countryside instead of the city. Sending infants to wet nurses doubled their chances of dying. If they did not fall off the wagon on the bumpy road and get crushed under its wheels on their way to the countryside, the wet nurse's avarice, negligence, or need frequently killed them. To earn more income, she would often take on other nurslings who competed for her meager milk; or she would simply feed them unpasturized cow's or goat's milk, which would result in their illness or death. Even if they survived the wet nurse, returning to the city at the age of eighteen months or two years was frequently more than these poor creatures could bear: "Victims of a change of life, of air, of conditions: the city . . . killed a part of those who survived conditions in the country during their nursing."[39] Barely defined as urban, Saint Chamond did not provide a healthy environment, for children there died at a high rate. But deaths that occurred in the country-side surely accounted for the low deathrate calculated among infants. Mortality rates in Saint Chamond were higher than they are represented here and, since wet nursing was common, may have even exceeded the averages found in other parts of France.

The skewed figures in Table 7 invite further speculation. If indeed these low apparent deathrates resulted from under-registration due to rural wet nursing, the extraordinarily low deathrate among boys and its underestimation by as much as 64 percent suggest that parents sent boys to wet nurses more frequently than they sent girls. We can only guess at why this may have been the case. Girls apparently contributed more to the family economy and for a longer period of time after they started earning wages than boys did. Louise Tilly and Joan Scott have pointed out that "daughters were especially desired for they were useful as spinners and family production needed more spinners than weavers." One daughter "wove at home until her fortieth year, putting all her earnings into the common pot."[40] If it was primarily the mother's decision to send a child to a wet nurse, and it probably was, she may have given priority to girls for other reasons as well. Wives tended to outlive their husbands, and female offspring may have offered more support to a widow than male offspring. If indeed mothers gave preference to the survival of female children, they may have been linking their own futures to those of their daughters.

In the analysis of birth and death patterns, it is the job of statistical averages to focus attention away from individual variation. Though no single family conformed perfectly to the average pattern, a closer look at individual cases illustrates more vividly the differences between the two most important occupational groups in Saint Chamond, nail makers and ribbon weavers. The lives of real human beings provide richer flavor than do numbers, and in them can be found evidence for why family structure varied by occupation even though the actual number of children born into these families did not differ significantly.

In 1817, when he was twenty years old, ribbon weaver François

Boissonna married Catherine Rey, a twenty-one-year-old silk spinner. Between 1818 and 1834, Catherine gave birth to five girls and
one boy. The first child, born only seven months after the wedding, had been conceived prenuptially. The pregnancy had no
doubt pressed this couple into marriage at the groom's very young
age. The second child came only fourteen months later, and the
third child fifteen months after the second. These short intervals
suggest that Catherine sent her first two babies to a wet nurse,
which quickly renewed her fertility but freed her to assist her husband with ribbon weaving.

After having had these three children, Catherine and François
avoided having more children for five years. They then had a
fourth and, two years later, a fifth child. Seven more years passed
before Catherine bore her sixth and last child. She was thirty-eight
years old when she ended sixteen years of childbearing.

It is not possible to determine from this pattern Catherine and
François's intentions in this manner of spacing their children, but
it is possible to guess. Deliberately postponing the births of the
fourth and fifth children until the first three were old enough to
care for them and participate in domestic production would have
made good sense. The last child more than likely resulted from a
failed effort at contraception. The pattern in this family clearly
suggests that Catherine and François tried to control births both
through spacing and by limiting the ultimate family size.

Nail maker Bartholomy Gautier and his wife Margery Vaganay
exhibited a strategy very different from that of Catherine and François. They married in 1822 when Margery, a silk worker, was eighteen and Bartholomy was twenty-four. In the next twenty-three
years, they had nine children. They not only had more children
than the ribbon weaver's family, but the births were spaced very
differently. Margery bore the first child nine months after the wedding. Their next two children were born over a period of more than
five years; the births of the five subsequent children took place
with more regularity than those of the Boissonna family. No two
births were separated by as much as four years, and only three
years passed between the births of the penultimate and the last
child. Moreover, at age forty-one Margery was three years older
than Catherine had been when she gave birth to her last child.[41]

These family formation strategies differed in at least two ways.

First, nail maker Gautier and his wife apparently did not attempt to limit the number of children they had, while François Boissonna and his wife stopped having children twice during their childbearing period. Second, two of Gautier's children died in infancy, one at age six months and the other at nine months, while Boissonna registered no infant or child death in Saint Chamond. The infant deaths in the nail maker's family influenced subsequent births, and most likely for physiological reasons. Spacing between births, especially the first few, suggests that Margery was nursing her babies, particularly since the intervals after the infant deaths, seventeen and eleven months, were significantly shorter than the others. The termination of breast-feeding quickly made her fertile again.

Intervals between births in the Boissonna family suggest that Catherine did not breast-feed her first two children but instead sent them to a wet nurse. The first long interval, five years, came after the birth of their first son. Perhaps a combination of breast-feeding and deliberate contraception lengthened this interval. But suspecting that the Boissonnas sent their infants to a wet nurse also means that some of their children may well have died without record in the Saint Chamond *état civil*. We know that their first and third children survived; they married in Saint Chamond in 1836 and 1850, respectively. But the others left no record of their fate. Thus it is possible that they had a fifth child only two years after the fourth because the fourth had died in the countryside and they wished to "replace" her.

Educated guesses cannot fill archival gaps, but they do help account for the stop-and-go pattern in the Boissonna family and enhance the meaning of statistical averages in these two groups of workers. While silk and iron workers married at basically the same mean age, and their wives' ages were about the same, the way they proceeded to form their families diverged. Age-specific fertility rates among the wives of ribbon weavers were higher until they reached age thirty, and mean and median birth intervals were shorter than those in nail-making families. Wives of ribbon weavers stopped having children at a remarkably young age and bore them for a much shorter period of time than did wives of nail makers. In their family formation strategies, ribbon weavers and their wives exhibited a pattern closer to that of commercial families than to that of their fellow proto-industrial workers. In both commerce and silk, husbands depended on their wives' assistance. The role of women in small shopkeeping and even in some wholesale commerce has been well documented.[42] Both groups relied on wet nurses and tried to limit the size of their families. Because the work of nail makers' wives was more flexible and because they were poorer, they used the services of wet nurses less frequently. Breast-feeding helped lengthen birth intervals throughout their marriages, but they bore children for a longer period of time and ultimately had more of them.

Regardless of varying approaches to family formation, a large portion of families suffered infant or child deaths in Saint Chamond. Nearly one in two families (49.3 percent) registered at least one death of a child under five years old. Interestingly, though nail makers suffered a higher rate of mortality among their children, deaths were not evenly distributed; only 34 percent of their families registered the death of a child, while 52.2 percent of the ribbon weavers' families did. The concentration of multiple deaths in nail makers' families and a higher child—as opposed to infant—deathrate in ribbon weavers' families account for this difference.

Death pervaded these workers' lives. The picture of death not only indicates a low and precarious standard of living but points to the unpredictability entailed in any effort to try to plan a particular family size. Workers in all occupations suffered uncertainty of prolonged illness or sudden deaths in their families. Patterns in age-specific fertility rates and average birth intervals resulted from different responses to death, stemming from different family strategies. The patterns of births and deaths also provide evidence of how these strategies were linked to the work, not just of ribbon weavers and nail makers, but of their wives.

During the period when ribbon weavers in this cohort were having children, they also faced gradual proletarianization. Not only did they suffer the usual cyclical unemployment characteristic of industries based on the whims of fashion, but technological change further divided labor, made looms increasingly expensive, and gave merchants more control over work. And in the space of a single generation—their generation—the bulk of the industry exited from Saint Chamond. Weavers survived by taking on other types of work in addition to ribbon weaving, but rarely did they abandon their craft completely. Instead, family cooperation intensified and wives and children helped absorb many of these pressures. The pride weavers showed in their work and the steadfastness with which they clung to it in the decline of the industry compare with that of handloom weavers in England. These qualities also distinguished a later generation of ribbon weavers in Saint Etienne during the most severe and fatal crisis in the industry, at the end of the nineteenth century.

Between 1816 and 1850, proletarianization and weavers' attachment to their craft influenced the structures their families assumed. Their family formation strategies conformed to the logic of their work situation. Since a wife and children could provide indispensable aid to the ribbon weaver, it made sense to have children early in a marriage and in quick succession so that the period of dependency would pass quickly. But because the wife's aid was so crucial, some of these children were sent to wet nurses. Like other proto-industrial families that have been studied, it appears that ribbon weavers and their wives tried to have enough children to assure the survival of at least two or three into adulthood. From the vantage point of a ribbon weaver, the earlier his children reached adulthood the better, for he would not be able to work much past forty years of age. Ending childbearing early in marriage would assure that very young children would not strain the family budget at a point when the ribbon weaver's work would become less efficient; it would also increase the weaver's chances of relying on the support of his adult children in his early, involuntary retirement.

Nail makers faced a different situation. As a group they suffered a lower standard of living. Few ever tried to leave the status of worker. Their product left little opportunity for improvement or entrepreneurial innovation. Even though many of them owned their own tools, they exercised less skill in their work and thus less control over it than silk workers. In their behavior nail makers exhibited much less attachment to their craft than weavers did to theirs. Their work afforded less opportunity for pride. Their lifestyle, however, appeared more relaxed. Their oral history refers to an important and colorful sociability that developed around their work.[43]

The most important difference between these occupational groups is that iron production was not oriented around the family to the degree and with the intricacy that ribbon production was.

Women and children participated regularly in auxiliary tasks, but not nearly as intensely as they did in ribbon-weaving families. They could supplement the family income with casual jobs associated with the silk industry, which they performed in their own homes or in small workshops when they had time to do so. They did not suffer the same external pressures during the high season and had less incentive as well as fewer funds available to send their children to wet nurses.

Herein lay the key to their respective family formation strategies. It may seem ironic that the occupation that could make most use of children's labor had fewer children. But a child's usefulness had limits: it depended on his or her age and on the number of siblings. It also fluctuated with time. It was women's labor, not children's, that had the decisive impact on family strategy. Nail makers and their wives exhibited fertility that approached the natural level not because they wanted to exploit their children's labor or because they lacked control over their instincts, but simply because the nature of their labor did not demand that they restrict the number of children they had. They exhibited evidence of family limitation only late in their marriages, after they already had large families. It was far from unusual for women who had begun childbearing earlier than age 25 to stop having children later in their marriages.

Ribbon weavers also evinced traits indirectly related to their work that family historians commonly associate with fertility decline: literacy, a propensity to save, and self-discipline. Although using signatures on marriage records as an indication of literacy is problematic, the variation in ability to sign, according to occupation, does reflect cultural differences. Among all couples who married between 1816 and 1825, 65 percent of the men and 45 percent of the women signed their names. Ribbon weavers more frequently acquired some education, because they had to keep records. A marked difference indeed existed between occupations: 85 percent of the ribbon weavers signed their marriage records, while only 29 percent of the nail makers did. Just as interesting is the variation that appeared among the women they married. Ribbon weavers' brides signed their names at a rate (40.2 percent) more than twice as high as that of nail makers' brides (18.2 percent), further reflecting differences in background and in the nature of the wives' contribution to work.[44]

In addition to having a higher rate of literacy, ribbon weavers tried to save money in order to buy looms.[45] This ability obviously varied from family to family, and as looms increased in expense the goal grew less attainable. But more ribbon weavers than any other occupational group had savings accounts. Demographers have associated the ability to save with fertility control, because of the need to plan for the future and to postpone certain forms of gratification. Contemporary observers also noted other values ribbon weavers embraced that might be compared with middle-class values: a desire to own property, an attachment to their families, and a sense of individualism. Finally, the craft of ribbon weaving required great discipline. Not only did setting up a loom and weaving itself demand patience and precision, but cycles of underemployment or unemployment meant that weavers had to work in great bursts, not only to earn enough income, but to meet the deadlines of unrelenting *fabricants*. In short, certain cultural elements associated with the craft of ribbon weaving better equipped these workers to exercise some control over their fertility.[46]

Most of the cultural traits associated with fertility decline are also associated with the urban environment. Indeed, decline that took place prior to the Revolution appears to be closely associated with urbanization. Jean-Pierre Bardet analyzes this trend for eighteenth-century Rouen in exhaustive and fascinating detail . Many of his results agree with suggestions of other studies that the middle and upper classes manifested most extensive fertility control; they are followed by artisans and then by unskilled workers. He posits that fertility decline is a function not just of urbanization but of the degree of urbanization and the values of individualism that it fostered. The comparison of Saint Chamond with Rouen can only be a rough one. The population of Rouen grew from 63,904 in 1700 to 80,000 in 1800.[47] As of 1851, Saint Chamond remained fairly small, with a population of only 8,887. Though it had grown by nearly 50 percent since the 1816–1825 cohort married, it was hardly a Rouen. And yet the artisans and proletariat of Saint Chamond had families slightly smaller than the Rouennais had between 1760 and 1792.

On a broad level, to be sure, workers experienced urban conditions often associated with lower fertility. But when the couples who married between 1816 and 1825 began building their families,

Saint Chamond still had many rural qualities. Urbanization alone cannot explain fertility control. Workers in this town shared something far more specific than values with the urban, upper-class leaders of fertility decline: they shared the practice of sending their babies to wet nurses. Upper-class women began taking contraceptive measures precisely because sending their children to wet nurses instead of breast-feeding meant that they quickly became fertile after each birth. Fertility control among the group in Saint Chamond who most obviously sent their children to wet nurses supports this thesis. But this mutual experience is in part mere coincidence, because workers resorted to wet nurses for reasons very different from those of the middle classes. The conflicting demands of wife- and motherhood prevented working-class women from breast-feeding and also motivated them to try to have fewer children. Family formation among workers reflected and contributed to a distinct culture of their own. How they formed their families conformed to the demands of their work lives and pivoted especially on the activities of women.

More compelling than the diffusion downward of upper-class values as a motive for fertility control among workers were the dictates of their own culture. In a system of domestic production in which most workers did not own or have access to land for the production of food, skills themselves became a type of property; in many cases they assumed a role similar to that of property with regard to people's perceptions of their futures and the family formation strategies they adopted. Participation in a craft from an early age—the acquisition of delicate ribbon-weaving skills or the more physically demanding skills of nail making—in principle shaped a child's future in much the same way as the inheritance of landed property. A particular skill eventually influenced the choice of a marriage partner and permitted the establishment of a new household. The ability to transmit skills easily from one generation to another and the opportunity for husbands, wives, and children to pool their efforts toward a common goal made early marriage and high fertility a possibility, if not a necessity. But unlike landed property, the skills parents could pass on to their children did not diminish in inverse proportion to the number of children they had. Only technological or economic change would modify the value of any particular skill.

Workers' family lives supplied traditions, values, and ideas; they provided a context within which workers experienced productive relationships. French workers on the average continued to bear more children than many peasants or the middle class, but when they did so, data here suggest it was because they had no reason not to do so. When they had smaller families, as did ribbon weavers, they tried to stop conceiving at least in part because the logic of their work lives required it of them.

For the upper classes, peasants, rural artisans, and urban workers, fertility control afforded more individual control over personal and family lives. Commercial and industrial capitalism helped foster the mentality necessary for fertility control, which the scientific revolution and the Enlightenment in turn sanctioned. Capitalism did not develop in a linear fashion, and so its impacts could not be linear. But where it did transform economic activity, it also helped promote the individualism Bardet associates with urbanization. Industrial capitalism affected the upper and the lower classes very differently; among the latter, it often promoted collective strategies for survival. Some workers also adopted a deliberate family strategy, which implies individual action as well as logic and intent. The specific circumstances that pressed workers into contraceptive practices differed from those of their predecessors and, no doubt, from their rural contemporaries as well. But some cultural and psychological factors that provided it as an option— particularly relative liberation from ecclesiastical control and the accompanying notion that one could empower oneself in this life— may have been the same.

Nowhere was secular fertility decline mechanistic. Many ribbon weavers, middle-class merchants, and notables in Saint Chamond had large families between 1816 and 1850, while some nail makers had small families. Moreover, even for those who did try deliberately to shape their families, mortality and unintended births too often made a mockery of planning. But evidence in this small, industrializing city does demonstrate that, for whatever reason, the bulk of residents, including workers, limited family size.

When in 1798 Malthus published his famous treatise on population, upper- and middle-class parents throughout France, and particularly urban France, had been practicing contraception for nearly a century. They adopted this practice, which Malthus himself condemned, as they began to cherish the child and center their lives around it. As they kept their own families smaller than those of earlier generations, they wondered all the more why those who could ill afford it would bear many children. In this regard, the nineteenth century marked a time when middle-class family goals and values diverged completely from those of the working class. Workers could not center their lives on the child, for labor itself continued to dominate as the organizing principle of family life. Though much of the working class did attempt to shape the structure of their families, the premature death of a parent or a fundamental shift in the local economy could easily throw a family over the threshold to poverty, where the middle class viewed them as irrational and animalistic for the apparently numerous children they brought to life in crowded urban slums.[48]

Although middle-class perceptions of high fertility among workers remained constant through the nineteenth century, the conditions surrounding that fertility changed in fundamental ways. Full-scale industrialization would transform the logic behind workers' survival strategies and force workers to restructure their families around new forms of work. For families in Saint Chamond, industrialization, more than early industrial capitalism, created new imperatives for limiting reproduction.

3

Mechanization and the
Reorganization of Work, 1840–1895

As the generation who married in Saint Chamond between 1816 and 1825 bore and raised children and entered middle and old age, most of them continued to work in traditional occupations even when they changed jobs. The continuity they exhibited belies several dramatic changes that occurred prior to the end of their lives. From the 1830s and 1840s, the development of braid production and large-scale metallurgy began to reshape the economy and labor force of Saint Chamond. Nail making and ribbon weaving declined and domestic industry began to disappear. Work that had once been performed in the home either left Saint Chamond or became mechanized. By the 1860s, most of the workers in Saint Chamond—both men and women—had to leave their homes and go into factories in order to earn wages. While this new labor force included some artisans and their offspring from the earlier generation, its largest constituency had migrated from the countryside. In its conversion from small shop and domestic production to mechanized factory labor and in its urbanization, Saint Chamond offers a classic example of industrialization.

Recent literature has emphasized the continuities rather than the changes that industrialization brought to the everyday lives of workers, particularly the ability of families to adjust to new work structures and to the effects of migration. In some respects the experience of workers in Saint Chamond suggests that they did not suffer severe disruption from industrialization. For many native Saint-Chamonais and migrants alike, economic development and the new organization of work offered new opportunities. Gabriel Fond and his family offer one example of how workers at once became absorbed into the new economic structure and yet retained many of their traditional skills. The son, the husband, and the father of silk-ribbon weavers, Gabriel Fond had become a master in his craft and a property owner by 1856, when, at age fifty-eight, twenty years of life remained for him. Four of his eight children settled in Saint Chamond with occupations that bridged the artisan and factory worlds. Two of them became highly skilled readers who punched designs in cardboard for the Jacquard looms. One daughter became a warehouse girl in a braid factory. Fond's eldest son abandoned the silk trade for locksmithing. He later used his metallurgical and mechanical skills to become a braid tagger (*ferreur de lacets*). He began his own business making metal ferrules— bands for the ends of braided cords—and employed other workers, including his brother-in-law.[1]

The Fond family thus demonstrated at once a remarkable continuity in adhering to their traditional trade and a capacity for acquiring new skills necessary to stay within the textile industry. Fond enjoyed his success in large part because his wife also wove ribbons. Despite the difficulties of learning new technologies, two of his sons mastered the innovations of the Jacquard loom. Yet another carved out a profitable niche for himself in the new braid industry.

But most families in Saint Chamond did not survive technological change with such apparent ease. Fewer than 21 percent of the children born to couples married between 1816 and 1825 remained in Saint Chamond long enough to marry there. At least 46 percent had not even survived to adulthood; despite the demand for labor new industries brought to Saint Chamond, the remainder chose to leave.[2] A detailed look at the family economy among those who remained in or migrated to Saint Chamond suggests that industrialization forced workers to restructure their family lives in ways more fundamental than the recent scholarship has argued.

The key change came with the removal of work from the home and its reorganization outside the context of the family. Industrialization posed the greatest challenges to working women, for it made coordinating productive and reproductive activities in traditional ways impossible. Except among the most highly skilled workers, men were not able to support their families, and married women had to earn wages. But work that could be performed in the home, and particularly work that commanded a sufficient wage, became rare. Many married women had no choice but to leave home for the braid factories.

While factory work had its most obvious impacts on women's roles, it changed men's relationship to the family in fundamental ways as well. Women had always assumed more responsibility for raising children, but men played an important role, not only by their very presence in the home but in the training they provided their children. Factory work for the most part eliminated that element of parent-child relations and thus eliminated one of the foundations of working-class culture.

Finally, while migration patterns to Saint Chamond manifested many of the continuities historians have uncovered in other industrializing towns, a close examination of marriage records reveals that the move to the city nonetheless placed stress on family life and contributed to its redefinition. Migrants in the 1860s came from slightly further distances than they had in the past, and frequently from farming rather than industrial backgrounds. Although they followed fellow villagers to Saint Chamond, it is clear that stressful situations pushed them there. In general, migrants had fewer resources than natives and their social networks could not always meet the challenges posed by the new urban life.

The fundamental transformation in Saint Chamond's economy rested on the transfer of capital resources from domestic, small-shop production to large-scale, mechanized factory production. This transfer first occurred in the textile industry, and the story of how it happened is classic. Saint Chamond's ribbon industry had suffered from the Revolution and from imperial wars, in part because of sudden fashion changes. In the effort to recover from the period of crisis, ribbon *fabricants* sought to make production more efficient and less expensive. The ribbon industry had not succeeded in adapting the production of *galons* (gold braids) to the Zurich loom. When Jean-François Richard-Chambovet brought his three braid looms back from Paris in 1807, he hoped to use them to manufacture *galons* more cheaply and efficiently. The mechanisms had spindles that braided threads by twisting them back and forth, eliminating the warp and weft that constituted weaving. They thus fabricated a material far sturdier than ribbons.[3]

Though the looms could not produce the fancy *galons*, they did make *lacets*: products ranging from simple shoelaces to flat and round cords, ornamental ribbons, yarn for imitation lace, metallic thread, and decorative borders for men's and women's clothing.

Herein lay a key to this industry's success: the production of ordinary as well as fancy objects enabled it to survive the sudden fashion changes that plagued the ribbon industry. Unlike delicate ribbon looms, braid mechanisms adapted well to steam. Steam-run looms, of course, encouraged manufacturers to organize braid production in factories rather than relying on traditional home production. Richard-Chambovet became the first entrepreneur in the Loire to use a steam engine outside of the mining industry. By 1817, 300 looms brought fortune to six *fabricants*. These looms also lent themselves to new products. In 1843 they produced the first forms of elastic, braiding "rubber covered with silk fabric."[4]

Braid production expanded rapidly in Saint Chamond, in part as a result of the exodus of the ribbon industry to Paris and Saint Etienne. Its decline left available "an abundant labor force, above all female, careful and rendered capable by long tradition," which in turn attracted more *fabricants*.[5] Descendants of the original houses developed the industry through the century. Richard-Chambovet's grandsons carried on the pioneer firm as Richard Frères. The Balas firm became established in 1830 and later became Balas Frères. Irenée Brun founded his firm in 1841. Many ribbon merchants also contributed to the growth of braids by choosing to remain in Saint Chamond, transferring their capital, and converting their workshops to braid production. As early as 1843, the *Bottin* of Saint Chamond listed thirteen braid *fabricants*; even during the harsh years of the 1840s, this number grew threefold. In 1854, Benoît Oriol, a "simple builder of looms," began manufacturing braids. Emile Alamagny joined him shortly thereafter and they quickly became Saint Chamond's largest and most famous firm (see figures 4 and 5).[6]

In 1860 Saint Chamond had twenty-five braid firms, making the city the most important braid producer in France. Its houses monopolized 90 percent of the national and international markets. Braids from Saint Chamond found their way to North and South America, Italy, Spain, England, and even Germany, the home of their stiffest competition. Not only did each of these manufacturers become extraordinarily successful in his own right, but most of them and some of their descendants became major figures in the paternalistic and Catholic community of Saint Chamond. They also played a large role in local politics. Brun, Bergé, and Reymond all

served on the municipal council; Benoît Oriol *fils* took over his father's firm and served as mayor; at one time or another, almost all
these manufacturers served on the powerful administrative commission of the Saint Chamond hospice. The Balas brothers and two
other braid manufacturers, François Gillet and Ivan Grangier, were
numbered among the founders of the the Association of Catholic
Employers, which grew to over 100 members.[7]

Braid factories housed anywhere from 20 to 300 looms and employed 25 to 600 workers each. Production involved three general
steps similar to ribbon fabrication. The first operation consisted of
preparing the silk or, increasingly often, the cotton, wool, mohair,
and linen. Depending on the material, preparation entailed skeining, milling, and doubling threads and winding them onto bobbins
and spools, just as women had done in their own homes and workshops during the first half of the century. Braiding, the second
stage, simply required that workers supervise machines. Each
laceteuse walked up and down rows of ten or fifteen mechanically operated looms. She reattached broken threads and replaced
empty bobbins with full ones (see figure 6). The third stage of production involved finishing the braids: removing knots, correcting
unevenness, placing metal bands on the ends of the cords, folding
them, and packaging them. Altogether, the production of silk
braids required twenty-two different operations. Three-fourths of
the factory labor force devoted itself to preparatory and finishing
stages.[8]

Some braiding continued to rely on domestic labor. When J. Valserres studied the industry in the early 1860s, domestic handlooms
produced almost half the braids for the firms of Saint Chamond.
He pointed out, however, that

> since the equipment in the large factories is better perfected, and
> since the looms operate with steam and the supervision is more in-
> timate, it appears that they are preferred. One is assured that the
> products are better made. . . . The family workshops will not be able
> to stand against the vast factories run with steam. With the compe-
> tition that they have between them, the industries seem destined to
> abandon the putting-out form that still distinguishes them today and
> to become concentrated in the vast factories.[9]

Valserre's prediction proved accurate: by 1872 the family workshop
had completely disappeared.[10]

Manufacturers had good reason to concentrate production in

factories: one steam-powered loom could produce 150 meters of braid in twelve hours. In the best-run factories, a single worker supervising eight looms, with one hundred spindles, could oversee the production of 1,200 meters of braid each day. Steam-run looms not only produced braids more efficiently but gave them a higher quality. The cost of braid looms to workers, 500 francs, became prohibitive and helped end home production.

The Chevalier-Cobden Treaty of 1860 provided a great impetus to braid production in Saint Chamond, which in turn pressed manufacturers into further modernization. Prior to the treaty, manufacturers could only import spun and polished wool from England with a stiff tariff of 8 francs per kilogram, while it entered Prussia at a cost of only 75 centimes per kilogram. After the treaty, large amounts of English wool and linen—already prepared—poured into Saint Chamond. At the same time the manufacturers received spun cotton from Rouen and linen from Lille. These prepared materials replaced some of the home-prepared silk that had been used for braids, thus further reducing domestic industry. The production of ordinary, factory-prepared goods expanded.[11]

The ribbon *fabrique* had provided a convenient prototype for the organization of work in braiding, but braid manufacturers took centralization much further. Like their predecessors, they increasingly brought the processes of reeling and warping into their own workshops, especially as these steps of production became mechanized. Cotton, linen, and wool not only required less preparation than silk prior to braiding, but since they were also less delicate, they were more easily prepared by steam-run machines. Even some stages of silk preparation became mechanized. In the past, silk millers had worked as jobbers for ribbon *fabricants*; the braid industry, with steam-powered silk mills, transferred even this process to its own factories (see figures 7, 8). Already by about 1860 three steam engines in the factories of Oriol and Alamagny powered the silk mills as well as the looms. The finishing stages—picking out knots and impurities (*émouchetage*), folding, pressing, and packaging—also took place in the braid workshops (see figure 9). The market for braids increased sharply in 1873 and 1874, which further necessitated more efficient production and increased the demand for female factory workers.[12]

Similar to its predecessor but on a far more massive scale, the braid industry relied on young women who migrated from the surrounding countryside. Nineteenth-century observers offered contradictory testimony about whether the new work organization constituted an improvement or a deterioration in the conditions to which women workers were subjected. On the one hand, Valserres, for example, lamented the disappearance of the home-based industry in Saint Chamond: "Putting-out [*morcellement*] has its advantages: first, it does not pile workers on top of one another in the often narrow factories; it makes braids a family industry. Under the double viewpoint of hygiene and morals, the division of looms merits recommendation."[13] Entrepreneurs and apologists for large-scale industry, on the other hand, hailed the braid factories as offering the perfect kind of employment for young women. Audiganne contrasted it with the physically debilitating ribbon work. He noted how "the ingenious apparatuses assume all the difficult part of the labor and leave to women only the [tasks] that are not tiring, either for their eyes or their arms."[14] Employers and their publicists also described pristine, well lit, and well ventilated factories, as they are portrayed with neat geometrical lines in figures 6–9. Employers assumed the role of fathers to the young women who left families behind in the countryside to come and work in the factories.[15]

Before a commission of inquiry in 1869, Ennemond Richard, grandson of Richard-Chambovet, described ideal living conditions and the "perfect morality" among the young women in this industry. They had iron beds with mattresses, feather pillows, and linen sheets, as well as running water. The dorms were well protected from "the public," meaning young male workers in the steel industry. Three times a day the employers provided workers with bouillon with butter and seasonal vegetables. According to Richard's account, the young women returned to their families in nearby villages on Saturday evenings and then came back to the city with four days' supply of food. Their mothers would give them additional food on Thursdays when they came to town for the market. Each worker had her own cabinet to store food, and kitchens provided ample space for cooking.[16]

The factory system did offer some advantages to women. It put an end to their exploitation by fathers and husbands, offered more regular and steady employment, and in some ways indeed demanded less physical exertion. Although most women turned their wages over to their families, for others factory labor offered new opportunities for material and psychological independence.[17] But in other respects, the factory system made new demands on workers. When emphasizing how well machine-tending suited women because it did not require physical exertion, employers thought nothing of the twelve-hour work shifts they imposed. Since 1831 when gas lighting first made night work possible, braid factories operated twenty-four hours per day. Until 1893, when legislation forced a reduction in the number of hours women could work, the majority of braid workers had shifts from noon to midnight and from midnight until noon.[18]

In his study of Loire industries published in 1862, J. Valserres offered an analysis more balanced than those of the braid industry's publicists. He noted the obvious: "the loom does not require much force; but over the long run [the work] must be tiring because the workers remain standing continually." Contrary to what Turgan later wrote, Valserres found the factories very poorly ventilated.[19] Until 1869, the workers ate standing up while supervising their looms; they had no breaks during the twelve hours. After 1869 they had two breaks of one-half hour each in order to eat, and they were then forbidden from taking food with them onto the floor of the factory. The duration of the work itself was reduced by one-half hour, but this schedule still meant that workers had to remain in the factory for twelve and one-half hours each day.[20] Finally, while artisans in their own homes had frequently worked for sixteen hours at a time, they could interrupt their own work at will and intersperse it with meals, child care, and housekeeping chores. For both married and single women, factory labor made family responsibilities more difficult to meet.

Author M. Fournier witnessed life in Saint Chamond in the late nineteenth century as a schoolteacher. A self-appointed spokesperson for workers, he also supplied a picture of the braid industry that contrasted sharply with that of its apologists.[21] The braid workers inspired in him a profound pity that pervaded his works. In the introduction to *La vallée ardente*, he addressed himself to the "poor girls" whose workshops and dormitories he had visited. The freezing, humid dorms "choked the flight of dreams and left shadows over their minds." Loom spindles "danced an infernal saraband,"

and oil left workers' clothing blotted and soiled. The humid factories enclosed poisonous air and mildew covered their walls.

Fournier's characterization of Mélanie Crozier merits quotation: she and her companions were

> linked . . . to these tireless machines, in an eternal servitude. She had suffered the lowest wages, having lived for a long time on three soups per day. . . . The roses of her cheeks, brought fresh from her village, had become discolored, withered. Strand after strand had fallen from her opulent head of hair. The skin of her face, satin and soft, had precociously been invaded with wrinkles. Under the poisonous oil of the machines, her chest had collapsed. Her arms, made to cradle a child or satisfy a husband, were now scrawny, angular and hard.[22]

For Fournier, Mélanie Crozier served as the archetypal *laceteuse*. She arrived young and innocent from a mountain village and sacrificed her youth and beauty at the hands of the exploitative braid industrialists. Unlike the image Richard Ennemond presented of braid workers' relations with their rural parents, Mélanie's mother never came to town with extra food from nearby La Valla; and when Mélanie returned there during periods of unemployment, her parents greedily supervised every crumb she ate. She never married but, like other *laceteuses*, lost her virginity in an ephemeral liaison with a metal worker.[23] Though this testimony lacks the detachment necessary for complete objectivity, it offers another eyewitness account that contradicts Turgan's and Audiganne's descriptions. Factory inspection reports, moreover, lend more credibility to Fournier's descriptions than to those of the other observers.[24]

Despite the advantages of the factory system, conditions there were miserable, both in the physical environment and in the strict supervision that prohibited personal freedom. Contemporary observers and historians alike have played down these disadvantages by emphasizing that the women who worked there did so only for a few years prior to marriage and childbearing, after which either they found some form of productive labor that they could perform in the home or their husbands' wages could support them. Fournier, for example, portrayed braid workers in one of two ways: either as young and sexually vulnerable or as old, barren, and withered. The "little old ladies, twisted and pale," "dressed in black, broken down, all wrinkled [and] tottering," pervade his works.[25] Young or old, these women were unmarried. The image stemmed in part from the sexual imbalance the braid industry had created in Saint Chamond. Census reports indicate that the number of women exceeded that of men throughout the last half of the century. In 1876, for example, single or widowed females outnumbered single or widowed males by 1,580.[26] Unmarried girls and women worked in braid factories because they needed the wages and because their relative freedom from familial responsibilities made them available for labor outside the home.

Other factors helped create the image of braid makers as unmarried. Public opinion frowned on female factory labor, particularly that of wives and mothers. Manufacturers' reports thus usually stressed that most braid workers were young, single girls who came to Saint Chamond from the countryside and lived safely in factory dormitories. According to employers' reports, they stopped working after getting married, usually in their early twenties.[27] In practice, however, braid manufacturers encouraged women to stay on the job as long and as continuously as possible. Oriol and Alamagny, owners of the largest braid factory, offered annual cash bonuses, graduated according to workers' seniority. One year on the job awarded a worker ten francs, while five or more years brought annual bonuses of fifty francs, increasing the yearly wage by 14 percent. The employers recognized this practice as a "good way to attach the personnel to the company, to keep them as long as possible and consequently to make them familiar with the firm's concerns and desires."[28]

Married women and mothers participated extensively in this labor force. By 1885, the braid industry in Saint Chamond employed 1,866 women over age twenty-one, 1,253 between sixteen and twenty years old, and 658 girls between twelve and sixteen.[29] Women over twenty-one constituted nearly 50 percent of the factory labor force. No available record provides precise ages or marital status, but one report estimated that "after age twenty-one, three-fourths to nine-tenths of women workers are married."[30] The law of 1874, ironically, encouraged more extensive employment of married women and mothers by forbidding women under twenty-one from working at night. This law provoked a twenty-year battle between the braid manufacturers of Saint Chamond and the government. Some factory owners circumvented the problem by continuing the twenty-four-hour shifts, but rescheduling them from

6 A.M. to 6 P.M. and from 6 P.M. to 6 A.M. and confining women under twenty-one to the former. Most employers kept the half-day and half-night shifts, believing that all-night work "exceeded female strength."[31] Since factory inspections took place during the day, many manufacturers ignored the law, and did so blatantly.[32] Nonetheless, the legislation eventually forced employers to substitute older women for younger ones. By 1890, the proportion of women over twenty-one exceeded 60 percent.[33]

The law of 1892 finally prohibited the employment of any women at night; braid employers' battle over this new regulation pointed to the important place married women held in their labor force. One manufacturer's report implied that their "half day and half night" shifts had been organized precisely for the benefit of married women and mothers, so that they "could tend to household chores, especially the mid-day meal, as well as contribute to the family income."[34] Although manufacturers put them up to it, women signed and submitted a petition similarly conveying how these shifts accommodated the conflicting demands on their time: "Married women take the night shift so that they can do housework at home in the morning, take care of their children, prepare food at noon for the whole family, and then . . . earn a salary."[35] Saint Chamond's braid employers complied with the 1892 law; they reduced the length of shifts and reorganized them from 4 A.M. to 1 P.M. and from 1 P.M. to 10 P.M., with married women concentrated in the latter so they could coordinate their household chores with wage earning.[36]

Their own testimony thus reveals that many women did not stop working in braid factories once they began raising families. These women also found their way into Saint Chamond's literary legacy. Local poet Antoine Roule earnestly described a warper racing to deliver her cartons to the folding mistress so that she could rush home to feed her husband and children, "feeling fortunate that the grocer always had cooked vegetables."[37]

If during their years of bearing and raising children women worked only sporadically, widowhood forced them back to the factory. They continued to work well into their seventies and eighties, or until they died. Twenty-two of the women who married between 1816 and 1825, and who survived past age fifty and died in Saint Chamond, expired as silk or braid workers. Their ages ranged from fifty-two to eighty years old, with almost half of them in their mid-seventies.[38] As in Fournier's portrayals, the ubiquitous *vieilleuse* was, in Saint Chamond, the old braid maker.

Although the decline in ribbon production and the growth in braid production resulted in a textile-labor force that was mostly female, not all work in the braid industry could rely on the hands of women. The use of steam engines required machinists; the thousands of braid looms also demanded more loom mechanics, a job most suitable for ex–ribbon weavers. Men thus composed 5 to 13 percent of the work force in braid production. Elastic production, moreover, became the only factory-based textile industry that employed more men than women in mechanical weaving.[39]

The production of cords and shoelaces also created a new specialty for men: *ferrage*, the placing of metal bands on the cut ends. Braid manufacturer M. Simon invented four small machines to perform this operation. The first machine cut the brass into tiny pieces, the second placed it on the cord, the third cut off the frayed ends, and the fourth rounded out and pointed the metal. Tagging cords, the trade Gabriel Fond's eldest son adopted, became an enterprise unto itself. Manufacturers employed a small team of workers that included ten- to fourteen-year-old children who operated the machines with foot pedals, pumping them forty times a minute.[40]

Through its growth alone, the braid industry caused considerable expansion in the dye works, especially after 1860. New chemicals, moreover, increased the amount of silk from Lyon dyed in Saint Chamond, because they required purer water which the Gier River alone could supply. By the 1880s, 1,000 people worked in the Saint Chamond dye industry; one of the dyeworks employed more than 300. The industry hired men primarily, but women assumed unskilled positions in it as well. In 1890, for example, Gillet and Sons employed 295 men, 46 women, and 12 girls between sixteen and twenty-one years old.[41]

Modernization in metallurgy, however, changed the work of men far more than did textiles. It also provided the primary magnet for young male migrants. As in the braid industry, mechanization in metallurgy began in the early nineteenth century. Rolling mills and English forges were installed in Saint Chamond between 1815 and 1825. Hippolyte Petin and Jean Gaudet started the making of their fortunes with the establishment of a machine construction workshop in Rive-de-Gier in 1839. In 1840, Petin acquired a steam hammer from Le Creusot and became the first in France to put it to use. Between 1840 and 1842, the steam hammer completed the revolution that the rolling mill had begun. Henceforth, wrought iron could replace cast iron in the fabrication of large pieces.[42]

The economic and political turmoil in the late 1840s cut off orders and forced Petin and Gaudet to look for new market outlets. They began to make iron cannons for the navy, and then armor plating for warships. The government recognized their accomplishments in 1852 by awarding them the medal of the Legion of Honor. Their armor plating first appeared in 1853 for warships destined to attack Kinburn during the Crimean War. Shortly thereafter they applied the rolling mill to thicken and enlarge armor plating.[43]

Petin and Gaudet manifested an even stronger entrepreneurial spirit than the braid manufacturers did. They ceaselessly and successfully sought ways to improve armor plating in the 1850s and 1860s. They also contributed inventions which improved the puddling process, resulting in seamless railroad wheels and *frettes,* or gun tubes, to reinforce artillery pieces. Added to the cannons and armor plating, these products soon brought Petin and Gaudet to the head of the French metallurgical industry. In 1854 they formed an association with the Jackson Brothers, sons of the James Jackson who had first introduced English metallurgical methods to the Loire. They also joined with Parent, Shaken, and Goldsmith and Company of Paris and bought the forges of Neyrand, Thiollière, and Bergeron and Company—all long-established forge masters and nail *fabricants* in Saint Chamond. Petin and Gaudet thus assumed direction of the new Compagnie des Hauts Fourneaux, Forges et Aciéries de la Marine et des Chemins de Fer. The company, which came to be known as Petin and Gaudet, owned four factories in the Loire, blast furnaces in Corsica and Berry, and a factory in Persans. By 1862, it employed 8,000 workers, half of whom labored in factories. The remainder extracted and shipped iron minerals and shipped finished goods. Three of the company forges operated in the Gier valley—in Saint Chamond, Rive-de-Gier, and Assaily—employing 6,000 workers.[44]

The forges in Saint Chamond were for a time the most important in the industrial basin, enjoying a monopoly in the production of cannons, *frettes,* and armor plating. In 1856, a year of crisis, Petin and Gaudet employed 600 workers in Saint Chamond. By 1862, this number had nearly tripled, to 1,600. The Petin-Gaudet forges alone took up an entire faubourg (see figures 10 and 11). In addition to unskilled laborers with no specialties (*manoeuvres*), they employed forty-two different categories of workers distributed throughout eight different workshops: one each for armor plating, seamless wheels, puddling, rails, and sketching, two for adjusting, and one for maintenance and construction. Each category of work included a foreman, journeymen, and helpers. Similar to the braid industry, shifts ran on a twelve-hour basis, from 6 P.M. to 6 A.M. and from 6 A.M. to 6 P.M.[45]

In addition to the Petin and Gaudet forges, Saint Chamond had another large forge owned by Dubouchet, and a number of smaller ones that produced hardware. After selling their forges to the Petin and Gaudet company, Neyrand and Thiollière specialized in the production of very thin nails (*pointes*) and other forms of hardware. By 1858, Saint Chamond also had three machine construction workshops.[46]

Marriage records from weddings celebrated between 1861 and 1870 bear the mark of the profound change that had occurred since the days of the generation who married between 1816 and 1825. As Table 8 shows, occupations for both men and women reflect the nearly complete shift from domestic industry to large-scale manufacture. The proportion of men who worked in textiles declined precipitously. Of those who did declare occupations in this sector, only 25 percent wove ribbons; one-third were dyers, and the remainder performed skilled and unskilled work in various branches of the braid industry. The largest number of men in this cohort worked in heavy metallurgy. Indeed, their proportion multiplied eight times over that in the first cohort. Despite the diversification of labor, the overall occupational distribution among men became more concentrated in the metal industry than it had been in the past.

Women's occupations also reveal striking changes. In the first group of marriages, 69 percent of the brides declared occupations; between 1861 and 1870, this proportion rose to 83 percent. Of those who worked, the same proportion of women declared occupations in textiles as they had in the past, but the vast majority of those in

Table 8.   Occupations of Men and Women Married 1861–1870

	Men			Women		
	No.	%	Index of change[a]	No.	%	Index of change[a]
Agriculture	6	0.6	− 1.1	1	0.1	0
Mining	44	4.4	+ 2.7	0	0	0
Small metallurgy	29	2.9	−16.0	0	0	0
Large metallurgy	414	41.6	+36.6	1	0.1	+ 0.1
Textiles (dyeworks, braids)	112	11.3	−13.4	472	47.5	0
Construction	109	11.0	+ 0.9	1	0.1	+ 0.1
Clothing	31	3.1	− 3.6	200	20.1	+10.3
Misc. crafts	64	6.4	− 0.7	3	0.3	− 3.4
Land transport	33	3.3	+ 1.6	4	0.4	+ 0.4
Shopkeeping and food	91	9.2	− 6.4	28	2.8	+ 0.6
Misc. services	61	6.1	− 0.8	110	11.1	+ 5.7
None declared	0	0	0	174	17.5	−13.7
Total	994	100.0		994	100.0	

[a]Proportion of individuals in each occupation 1861–1870, minus the proportion from 1816–1825.

the later generation worked in braid factories rather than in their own homes or in small workshops. Industrialization had expanded opportunities for women in the clothing industry and the service sector: their proportion more than doubled.

Thus work organization in both metal and textiles became fundamentally restructured after 1840. The removal of the work from the home, separating it from the family, is perhaps the most important change that occurred in Saint Chamond in the nineteenth century. Two interrelated issues demand careful consideration in this regard: the capacity of male wages to support a family, and the degree to which productive labor really did leave the home.

Determining the buying power of wages among workers during the second half of the nineteenth century is exceedingly difficult and remains a subject of debate. Prices and wages varied by region; only a few workers' budgets exist, and their reliability is questionable. The family needs of a dyeworker were estimated in 1872 at 1,780 francs per year if he had a wife and two children.[47] Full-time employment at an average daily wage of 4f50 would yield an annual income almost 400 francs short of this budget. An analysis of the budgets further indicates that workers continued to spend up to 60 percent of their income on food, a sign that their overall standard of living remained mediocre.[48] Even Louis Reybaud's own estimates suggest a picture more humble than the one he portrayed. In 1874, a family with two adults and two children in the Gier valley, he said, required 584 francs per year for food alone. This figure did not include meat or wine. Rents in Saint Chamond amounted to about 120 francs per year. Clothing, mutual assistance, laundry, and heating expenses, as well as a family size that usually exceeded four, amounted to a yearly budget greater than most male wages could cover.[49] Lequin concluded that wages in the Lyonnais region rose, but so did the price of food. Wages in metallurgy increased 20 percent, while the price of bread rose 30 percent. The condition of the worker from the Second Republic to the Great Depression, he notes, was no longer one of permanent poverty, but it "remained precarious and occasionally miserable."[50]

Reports on wages vary by year and by source, but they clearly indicate that the average male wage in all occupations could not support a family. Skilled positions in metallurgy were certainly known for their high wages, and it was indeed the promise of these high wages that drew so many migrants to Saint Chamond. But the reality did not fulfill this promise. Between 1860 and 1865, daily wages for metal workers averaged 3f43 per day, or just under 900 francs a year if they worked the average 260 days. In 1874, annual earnings ranged from 800 francs for beginners to 1,200 francs for skilled workers. Depending on the quality and quantity of their work, puddlers could earn up to 12 francs per day. Some workers in the fitting shops earned that much as well, but most remained at wages of 4 or 5 francs per day. Those who worked rolling mills and steam hammers needed less skill, since machines performed most of the labor. Workers in these shops earned 3 francs to 3f50 per day.[51]

In 1880, salaries in the nine foundries, forges, and steelworks of Saint Chamond amounted to a maximum of 6 francs and a minimum of 3 francs per day. In 1881, maximum and minimum wages in steel were 10 francs and 2f75, respectively; in adjusting, 6f50 and 3 francs; in the foundries, 5f75 and 2f75; and in the forges, 10 francs and 2f75. Children's wages ranged from 1 to 2 francs. Throughout the second half of the century, the majority of those who worked in metal averaged wages closer to the lower end of the scale, usually about 900 to 1,000 francs per year.[52]

Of the 414 metal workers who married between 1861 and 1870, only 5.8 percent held skilled positions at the time of their marriages.[53] Starting out in an unskilled or semiskilled position did not mean that the worker would always remain at that level; but the opportunity to earn higher wages declined with technological change that eliminated skilled positions, especially after 1880.[54] The occupational histories in reconstituted families indicate that only a minority obtained skilled positions. For the majority, wages in metal could adequately support a single man, but not a family with two or more children.

Male textile work was not as skilled as the most demanding of the positions in metallurgy, but more workers in textiles performed labor that demanded expertise than did those in metal. Dyeing, especially silk dyeing, required considerable proficiency. Mixing precise measures of dyes and chemicals and knowing the exact moment to remove materials from the chemical baths called for concentration and practice. Dyers, weavers, elastic makers, and loom mechanics earned an average of 4 to 5 francs in the 1860s and 1870s.[55] Elastic workers in Saint Etienne, who had a growing number of counterparts in Saint Chamond, earned an average of 4 francs per day in the early 1870s. They testified that workers with two children could barely survive if the mother could not earn wages. The only possible way to save any money was to have the wife working.[56]

Even if real wages did rise, cyclical unemployment remained a problem. Crises continued to occur frequently in the silk industry: in 1861, 1866, 1867, between 1877 and 1879, and again in the early 1890s. In the crisis year of 1894, dyers and male braid workers only earned an average of 3f50, a 12 to 30 percent reduction from what they had earned in the 1860s and 1870s.[57] Metal workers suffered a similar cut, earning an average of only 3f97. Layoffs in metal production occurred in 1871, 1872, 1874, and in the early 1880s and 1890s.[58]

Cyclical unemployment, coupled with the coexistence of two very different industries, resulted in another phenomenon that further complicates the task of interpreting living standards: workers changed jobs frequently. Of the metal workers married between 1861 and 1866, fifty-five, or 34.4 percent, left metal working and declared seventy-seven different professions. Of those who changed, twenty-three assumed occupations in textiles: braids, passementerie, elastic, ribbon weaving, dyeing. Some continued to perform the same tasks they had in metallurgy, such as work as a stoker in a dyeworks. Other jobs ranged from miner, nail maker, or gardener to entrepreneur or merchant of ovens, grain, or coal.[59] In the considerable variety they demonstrated, many took unexpected paths in their search for different livelihoods. Jean Marie S., a machinist at the Petin forges in 1856, was selling food (*marchand de comestibles*) in 1872 and became an itinerant porcelain merchant five years later. Bartholomy P., a shearer's assistant (*aide cisailleur*) in the Petin forges in 1863, worked as a weaver in an elastic fabric factory by 1867 and called himself a master *passementier*. François F., a "furnace boy" at the forges in 1866, worked as a carpenter sixteen years later. After taking on a variety of unskilled jobs at the Petin forges over a period of twelve years, Jean G. had become a gardener by 1880. Skilled and unskilled workers alike sought escape from metallurgy.[60]

That so many men left metallurgy for work in textiles certainly suggests that the process of choosing jobs did not end with entry into adulthood. But it was not just cyclical unemployment or dissatisfaction with wages that inspired metal workers to leave their jobs. The work was taxing—especially the better-paid work. When Louis Reybaud's inquiry into the "moral, intellectual, and material condition" of workers in the metal industry brought him to Saint Chamond in the early 1860s, he noted that the father "sends the most robust [of his sons] to work in the foundry and rolling mills; the others continue to make braids and passementerie with the girls and the mother."[61] Reybaud did note that puddling "alters the organs and shortens life," but he characteristically understated the amount of endurance metallurgy required and its long-term insalubrious effects on workers.[62] Health risks and injury had even more influence on occupational changes among the most highly skilled workers. Pierre Perrin and his son-in-law, for example, each abandoned puddling for shopkeeping, illustrating the common tendency among puddlers to leave the industry as soon as they had

1. Church of Saint Ennemond (1978)

2.   Grande rue Saint Ennemond (1978)

3. Bar loom with a Jacquard mechanism (circa 1860)

4. Oriol and Alamagny Factories on place Notre Dame (circa 1885)

5. Oriol and Alamagny Factories on the Gier River and rue Vignette (circa 1885)

6. Braid looms in the Oriol and Alamagny Factories (circa 1885)

7. Warping, skeining, and bobbin-winding in the Oriol and Alamagny Factories (circa 1885)

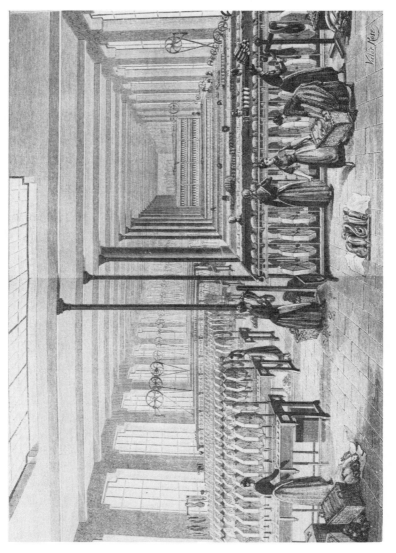

8.   Silk-throwing in the Oriol and Alamagny Factories (circa 1885)

9. Folding in the Oriol and Alamagny Factories (circa 1885)

10. The factories of Saint Chamond (circa 1890)

11.   Naval steelworks: assembling workshop (circa 1900)

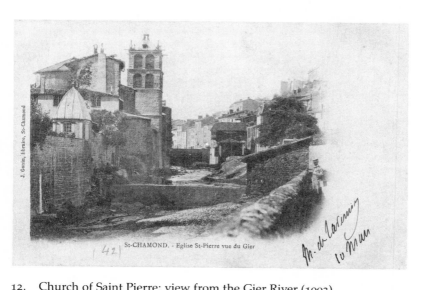

12.   Church of Saint Pierre: view from the Gier River (1903)

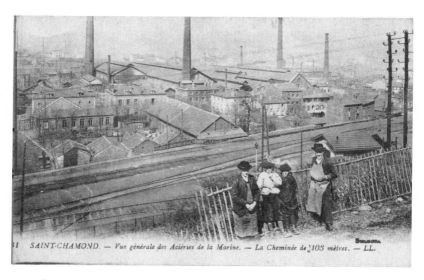

SAINT-CHAMOND. — *Vue générale des Aciéries de la Marine.* — *La Cheminée de 103 mètres.* — LL.

13.   General view of the steelworks (circa 1900)

St-CHAMOND - Cantonnements ouvriers de la Compagnie des Forges et Aciéries de la Marine et d'Homécourt

14.   Worker dormitories of the steelworks (circa 1900)

15. Worker dormitories of the steelworks: interior (circa 1900)

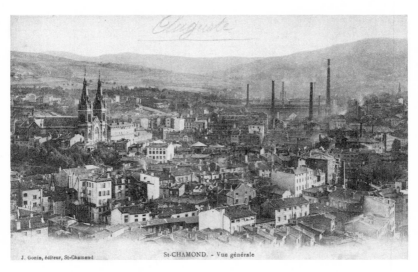

16. General view of Saint Chamond (circa 1900)

Aciéries de la Marine - Usines de Saint-Chamond
Atelier d'usinage - Rayage des Canons de petits calibres

Mme Gonin, éd., St-Chamond

17.   Steelworks: machine workshop (circa 1900)

746. SAINT-CHAMOND. — Rue de la Gare

P. Martel, édit., Lyon

18.   The bourgeoisie of Saint Chamond (1905)

enough savings to start their own businesses. Many, however, could not wait for that point and abandoned puddling for lower-paying jobs. Puddlers did not suffer alone. In 1884, in response to a parliamentary inquiry, molders in Saint Etienne complained of frequent rheumatism. They stated, no doubt with some exaggeration, that their average life span was only thirty-three to thirty-five years, and if they survived beyond that point, few remained capable of working after age forty-five. Accidents in the foundries, especially burns, occurred frequently.[63]

Whether or not workers suffered periodic unemployment or frequent job changes, few could support a family without the help of their wives and children. Only the more skilled metallurgists, earning 12 francs per day, could support a family of four—provided that unemployment, injury, or sickness did not interrupt their work. A woman working in braids could contribute about 350 francs per year to the family economy, if she worked all year. Without the help of children, this contribution could bring the average family income to about 1,350 francs per year, if men averaged the standard 260 workdays per year.[64] Even this combined income stood 430 francs below the estimated necessary family budget for four in 1872.

Working-class families, unable to live on the adult male wage alone, became caught in an ever-tightening vise of decline in domestic work available to women and stiffer regulation of children's labor. Laws regulating child labor excluded them from factories. With the exception of one step in braid production—tagging cords, which employed children as young as ten—the employer class in Saint Chamond generally respected laws prohibiting children under the age of twelve from working in factories. Their commitment to education motivated them to respect the law, and an adequate labor force of adult females and adolescents between twelve and sixteen enabled them to do so. But in 1874, the French government placed further restrictions on employing those under age sixteen. The law prohibited them from working at night and limited the total number of hours they could work to six per day unless they had a *livret* or a certificate of primary education.[65] Given the demand for the labor of adolescents, as well as the working-class family's need for their wages, employers, with the cooperation of the mayor, often shut their eyes to the latter two requirements.[66]

Nonetheless, few children contributed to the family income prior to age twelve, a practice which broke with the past.

Mechanization and laws regulating the factory labor that it created generally extended by six years the period during which children consumed family resources without producing any. Compulsory education further strained the family because it made older children unavailable for the care of younger siblings in the mother's absence. The arrival of children in the families of even the more prosperous workers could upset family budgets by at once creating new costs and removing the mother from the labor force. Once children started working, however, they could sometimes earn as much as their mothers did. In the 1870s, they were paid from 1 to 2 francs in metallurgy, and from 80 centimes to 1f70 in silk.[67] But the extended period during which young people could not work made most working-class families more dependent, at least for part of the family life cycle, on the work of the mothers.

The extent to which married women worked for wages during the last century has become notoriously difficult to determine. For tax purposes and other reasons not entirely understood, women or their husbands commonly did not report their occupations to census takers or to officers of the *état civil*. The situation in Saint Chamond clearly indicates that for the majority of the working class, the adult male's wages could not support the family. Either wives and mothers had to contribute to the family income, or the family had to rely on charity. Many families did adopt the latter solution.[68] Most women, however, must have worked, at least sporadically, throughout their lives. But the facility with which they did so depended on the availability of domestic labor. Certainly some garment making took place in the home. Laundering employed many women in Saint Chamond, but even this very demanding and time-consuming occupation brought them out of the home to the riverbanks. The standard textile-related home industries declined in Saint Chamond during the second half of the century, but just how much industry remained in the home is unclear. The hand production of passementerie, mainly gold braid, persisted through the 1860s. Ribbon weavers continued to produce these novelties—elastic fabric, galloons, and special fabrics for buttons—on Zurich looms equipped with Jacquard mechanisms. Little by little, however, the looms "followed the exodus to Saint Etienne" and by the 1890s they had all but disappeared.[69]

Available evidence suggests that to some extent the preparation of raw materials and of finished products for marketing continued to take place in the home. In the 1880s and 1890s *fabricants* claimed that one-third to one-fourth of their labor force consisted of mothers at home reeling silk, doubling threads, winding bobbins, and picking knots out of finished braids.[70] After 1872, however, manufacturers had good reason to exaggerate the number of workers they employed outside their factories. In their petitions opposing the laws regulating women's work, they resorted to questionable arguments. They claimed, for example, that night work benefited women under twenty-one because it reduced illegitimacy. But the manufacturers also pointed to the unemployment that the suppression of night work would cause for nonfactory as well as factory workers. They argued that to eliminate the night shift in braid factories would so reduce production that mothers at home would be thrown out of work and hundreds of families would be unable to make ends meet.[71]

The government so distrusted manufacturers' claims regarding the number of home workers they employed that it requested proof in the form of receipts for wages that had been paid. Unfortunately, braid employers' petitions to the government seem to be the only source for these figures. Home workers were never counted or surveyed by inspectors. Even if the numbers are accurate, they refer to workers employed in the braid industry throughout the Gier valley and not just in Saint Chamond. Most of the domestic workers were employed in the rural areas surrounding Saint Chamond, since in the city itself auxiliary tasks could be performed more efficiently in the factories.

Workers themselves testified that most work for married women lay outside the home. Respondents to the government inquiry of 1884 stated that almost all women were employed in textiles. "Many women are employed in their own homes, but the largest number work in the factories as warpers, doublers or bobbin winders, and those who have no one at home during the hours of work, prepare meals in the morning for the entire day." Further evidence that mothers worked in factories can be found in their complaints about the insufficient numbers of *crèches* in a questionnaire of 1884.[72]

No doubt some women were able to continue to work in their own homes, picking floss from braids and folding them. In his

novels Fournier portrayed these tasks as the type that aged spin-
sters and widows performed. Because inspection reports concerned
themselves with factory labor, we have no information about the
wages this work brought to the family economy or believable figures about the actual number of women, particularly in the city
itself, who had access to such work. Surely it paid very poorly:
Fournier noted a daily income from this labor of only 15 to 20 centimes—a small fraction of the 1f20 or 2f wages women earned in
twelve-hour factory shifts.[73] Moreover, even to earn that meager
amount would require that a woman put in a full workday, unin-
terrupted by attention to children and household chores.

The importance that factory work held for married women and
employers became articulated in protests against the laws regulating their work. Braid *fabricants* noted in 1886 that since the metallurgical crisis had begun in 1882, a "large number of households
with metal workers, dyers, and miners had no other resource than
women's labor, that is, the labor of our [factory] workers." In another petition the following year they stated:

> The effects of this crisis have been to reduce a large number of
> households to destitution bordering on misery; to attenuate the sad
> consequences, many wives of workers have not hesitated to solicit
> night work, an option that is better paid and that their age permits.
> We have thus often seen the singular spectacle of the woman work-
> ing outside in order to bring in some small resources for the house-
> hold while the husband, confined to the house by lack of work, is
> occupied in the preparation of food and child care.[74]

The workers themselves sadly echoed this statement again in 1893
when they protested the 1892 law that reduced their workday
to eight hours and eliminated night work for all women. They
stressed the importance of their work outside the home, especially
during their husbands' unemployment.[75]

Employer and worker protests against legislation came at a time
when high unemployment coincided with more efficient factory
work inspection. But in fact married women had worked in braid
factories since the earliest days of the industry. As domestic industry disappeared, they had to rely increasingly on factory work.
Family survival came to depend on wives' and mothers' wages; yet,
to earn those wages in Saint Chamond, they had to work outside
the home.

Unfortunately, apart from petitions reacting to legislation regulating factory labor, workers in Saint Chamond left no record of a direct verbal response to changes in the organization of work, and particularly its removal from the home. However, workers outside Saint Chamond who experienced similar changes did leave a record. In the series of annual workers' congresses that began in 1876, "women's work" always assumed a high place on the agenda. Men and women delegates commented extensively on the ways factory labor had interfered with family life. Mothers did indeed leave the home to work, depriving their children of a proper moral and physical upbringing and subjecting themselves to the unhealthy conditions in factories. Since pregnant women worked until they gave birth and then resumed work shortly thereafter, workers blamed factory labor for the high rate of maternal and infant mortality. Men also expressed concern that their wives and daughters were subjected to immoral conditions in factories, which suggests that the departure of women from the home threatened their own power of patriarchy. The domestic labor that remained available did not pay adequate wages and yet required that women devote full time to it. While never questioning the need or right of women to earn wages, the debates make it clear that women earning wages outside the home had a demoralizing impact on the working class.[76]

The new work organization in Saint Chamond not only removed work from the home, segregated it by gender, and organized it into twelve-hour shifts, but required a much larger labor force—one that exceeded what Saint Chamond's population could, or would, provide. The new industries brought to Saint Chamond a new population. This migrant population, with its more shallow social, familial, and economic roots, stood at a distinct disadvantage in dealing with the new organization of work. The success of Gabriel Fond's family, mentioned above, resulted largely from the fact that his wife was also a weaver and they were able to pass valuable skills on to their children. In establishing their own occupations and families as adults, their children relied on stable family resources. Migrants to the city did not enjoy such advantages.

Marriage records in the Saint Chamond *état civil* between 1861 and 1870 supply far more information about the wedding celebrants than do earlier ones. Although the added detail does not permit further comparison with the earlier cohort, it does make

possible a richer examination of those who experienced industrialization most directly, and marks the 1860s as a period of decisive
cultural and social change. It is not surprising that of those who
married in Saint Chamond during the 1860s, few had been born
there. Only 25 percent of the men and 29 percent of the women
declared themselves to be natives. These figures contrast with the
51 percent and 47 percent, respectively, of those who married between 1816 and 1825. Even in the 1850s, 30 percent of the men and
38 percent of the women who married had been born in the city.
The male and female migrants to Saint Chamond arrived from
sixty-seven departments, several French colonies, and more than
eight foreign countries.

For the most part, the geographical origins of these migrants
replicated those of their predecessors in the 1850s: most of them
came from the Gier valley and adjacent departments. But in the
1860s, more migrants came from greater distances. As Table 9 indicates, proportionately fewer men came from the Loire and more
came from other neighboring departments, especially the Rhône
and the Ardèche. A larger proportion came from the more distant
departments. The proportions of men and women who came from
the Gier valley dropped, respectively, from 35 and 39 percent to 26
and 27.6 percent.[77]

That most of the migrants came from the same regions as their
predecessors confirms what Lequin and other researchers have established about "chain migration." Residents of a single village or
commune, decade after decade, followed their predecessors to the
same town.[78] Departments primarily to the east and south, the
Puy-de-Dôme and the Haute-Loire, favored Saint Chamond. The
Puy-de-Dôme continued to send the largest numbers. Migrants
came from fifty-nine communes in this department, and nearly 40
percent of them came from only three villages. The canton of Saint-
Amand-Roche-Savine alone sent twenty-nine men and women to
Saint Chamond. Those from more distant departments, however,
tended to come alone.[79]

As this clustering suggests, even if people did not migrate as
a family unit, sisters, brothers, and cousins, friends and neighbors followed one another. Chain migration provided networks for
many new to the city. Jean Faure and Antoinette Goutebessis, for
example, were born in the same commune in the Puy-de-Dôme.

Table 9. Geographical Origins of Nonnative Women and
Men Married in Saint Chamond 1851–1860 and 1861–1870

| | 1851–1860[a] | | | | 1861–1870 | | | |
| | Men | | Women | | Men | | Women | |
	No.	%	No.	%	No.	%	No.	%
Loire	281	64.6	279	62.7	379	51.2	420	60.2
Haute-Loire	24	5.5	26	5.8	44	5.9	39	5.6
Puy-de-Dôme	30	6.8	69	15.5	69	9.3	106	15.2
Subtotal	335	77.0	374	84.0	492	66.5	565	80.9
Other departments[b]	44	10.1	45	10.1	139	18.8	89	12.7
Rest of France	47	10.8	25	5.6	95	12.8	41	5.9
Foreign countries	9	2.1	1	0.2	14	1.9	3	0.4
Total	435		445		740		698	

[a]Data for 1851–1860 are from Yves Lequin, *Les ouvriers de la région lyonnaise*. Vol. 1: *La formation de la classe ouvrière régionale* (Lyon: Presses Universitaires de Lyon, 1977), p. 215.

[b]Rhône, Drôme, Ardèche, Saône-et-Loire, Allier.

When Jean moved to Saint Chamond, he lived with Antoinette's brother. Antoinette arrived six years later, and they married two years after her arrival. Louis Fournioux, also from the Puy-de-Dôme, had a married sister in Saint Chamond with whom he lived until his marriage. Jean Antoine Caillet joined his older brother in Saint Chamond when he moved north from the Ardèche. His brother lodged in the home of Sophie Rouchouse, whom Jean Antoine eventually married. Though she, too, had come from the countryside, Sophie had two married sisters with whom she lived. She and Jean Antoine continued to share a residence with her sisters and brothers-in-law until their first child was born.[80]

Though networks of family and friends clearly eased the stress of migration, we must not lose sight of two important points: first, not all migrants—especially not those who came from greater distances—had access to such networks. Marriage records rarely yield evidence of such extensive contacts. Second, disruption, if not trauma, often precipitated a move to the city. Many migrated as a result of broken families and lacked resources in the city. In-

formation in the marriage records suggests that a death often precipitated a migration. For example, when Marie Vallet's husband
died in 1847, she was living in Rive-de-Gier. A mining and glassmaking town, Rive-de-Gier offered little or no work for women.
Shortly after the death, she and her four-year-old daughter moved
to Saint Chamond, where Vallet found work in a braid factory.
Similarly, Marie Valla and her mother arrived in Saint Chamond
five years after her father had died, when she was just old enough
to work in a braid factory. They moved from Chambon, a village in
the Haute-Loire. Marie became a skeiner and her mother continued
work as a lace maker. Many other young women came to Saint
Chamond alone. Jenny Dufour left Saint Etienne at age thirteen,
when her father died. In Saint Chamond she labored in a silk mill
and lived in a factory dormitory, while her mother remained in
Saint Etienne. Françoise Tiodet migrated from a small village in the
Puy-de-Dôme at age sixteen, just after her mother died; her father
had abandoned the family eight years earlier.[81] Such examples
are repeated frequently among male and female migrants; death
clearly placed families under new economic pressures and hence
forced people to seek opportunities elsewhere.

These impressionistic patterns gleaned from the marriage records are confirmed in a statistical analysis of parental death among
migrants and natives. As Table 10 indicates, many more migrants
than natives had suffered the death of a parent. Local sons and
daughters enjoyed the advantage of having a larger number of parents alive when they married. Among the parents who were still
alive, the poor, propertyless, or ill certainly imposed extra burdens
on their children. But the older generation in town had often been
able to accumulate resources in contacts if not in property. Just
as parental death sometimes provoked migration, it also could
deprive young couples in an urban, industrial situation of support—such as housing and child care—that their peers could not
provide.

Whether they came from remote mountain villages in adjacent
departments or from the neighboring industrial towns of Rive-de-
Gier and Saint Etienne, migrants faced a severe housing problem.
Between 1851 and 1856, the population of Saint Chamond grew by
more than 30 percent, from 8,897 inhabitants to 11,626. During the
following two decades it grew by another 20 percent, to 13,713.

Table 10. Parental Death among Migrants and Natives Who Married 1861–1870

	Brides				Grooms			
	No. native	%	No. migrant	%	No. native	%	No. migrant	%
Fathers								
Alive	178	62.7	345	49.9	129	52.4	366	50.1
Dead	106	37.3	347	50.1	117	47.6	364	49.9
Total	284	100.0	692	100.0	246	100.0	730	100.0
Mothers								
Alive	208	73.2	435	62.9	163	66.3	400	54.8
Dead	76	26.8	257	37.1	83	33.7	330	45.2
Total	284	100.0	692	100.0	246	100.0	730	100.0

Housing became inadequate in the 1850s and remained so through the end of the century. Since many of the houses in Saint Chamond had been built to accommodate tall ribbon looms, they had very high ceilings. Their large size made them too expensive for workers to buy. The narrowness of the Gier valley limited expansion in Saint Chamond; lack of space prevented the building of new, inexpensive lodgings for workers. In the 1860s and 1870s, on the average each house contained more than three households and more than thirteen people. To keep rents affordable for workers, landlords crowded as many as ten into each room. In 1858, one investigator found twelve beds in a single room, "touching each other and destined to receive two men each."[82]

As in any city with housing shortages, family and friends gained great importance in the search for a place to live. Living arrangements among those who married between 1861 and 1870 speak to the value of having family members in town. The above examples of Jean Faure, Antoinette Goutebessis, Louis Fournioux, Jean Antoine Caillet, and Sophie Rouchouse illustrate the role that village networks could play here. But natives enjoyed a clear advantage. Some examples among offspring from the first sample of marriages illustrate this point. Originally a forge worker when he married in 1825, Pierre Perrin became a puddler, then a wine merchant by the 1850s. He owned a house on the place Notre Dame. His sons became shoemakers, dye workers, and shopkeepers, and relied extensively on one another for employment and housing. Joseph, the oldest, employed his younger brother Jean Benoît in his dyeworks. After his marriage in 1856, Jean Benoît continued to live in his deceased parents' house, sharing it with his sister Marie Gabrielle and her husband, Jean François Fayolle. Fayolle, like his father-in-law Perrin, abandoned puddling and became a grocer. He took over his father-in-law's wine business after the latter died. He and Marie Gabrielle continued to live in the Perrin house, but Jean Benoît and his wife eventually moved, into the same house Fayolle and his parents had lived in prior to Fayolle's marriage.[83]

Family and friends often facilitated residence changes. Jean Baptiste D.'s pattern appeared frequently: over a period of twenty years (1861–1881), his family moved at least four times. One of the houses they inhabited belonged to a friend who had been a witness at Jean Baptiste's wedding; a witness to the birth of his child later moved into Jean Baptiste's former residence. Jean Baptiste's brother lived in yet another house that he had vacated.[84]

No matter how many links in the chain migrants could boast, natives enjoyed the advantage of more extensive family and friendship networks. Of both men and women native to Saint Chamond, 96 percent had at least one parent living in the city. In contrast, only 25 percent of the migrant men and 46 percent of the migrant women did. The importance of having parents live in the city becomes apparent in living arrangements: 70 percent of the native men and women lived with parents or another relative, while only 27 percent of the migrant men and women did. Newly married couples who did have family in town typically lived with either the husband's or the wife's parents or in the home of a brother or sister during at least the first year of marriage, and frequently much longer.[85]

That more men and women born in Saint Chamond had parents living there and indeed tended more often to live with their parents is hardly surprising. These data do show, however, that the vast majority of migrant workers had to survive independently of close family ties. Residing apart from parents and family did not signify independence or relative affluence. Workers without families lived in overcrowded apartments and factory dorms.

Migrants, not surprisingly, also concentrated in Saint Chamond's newest industries, adding to the geographical break with their pasts a cultural one. For example, less than one-fourth of men in heavy metallurgy and only 28 percent of women in braid production had been born in Saint Chamond or had lived there for twenty years prior to marriage, while more than half the men working in textiles were natives or long-term residents. Fewer male metal workers (29.5 percent) lived with their parents in Saint Chamond than male textile workers (43.8 percent).[86] Despite the fact that so many of them had migrated, 41 percent of the braid workers lived with their fathers or mothers, and only 17 percent lived in factory dorms prior to their marriages.[87] The effects of migration also appear in what little traces remain of the social relations these workers developed. Textile workers had a greater tendency to include family members as witnesses to births, marriages, and deaths, and a relatively high proportion also asked neighbors to assist them. The pattern among metal workers reflects not just the uprootedness of migration but the greater concentration of workers in factories: they relied more heavily on friendships developed on the job. Construction workers, in contrast, exhibited much deeper geographical roots than metal workers but used fewer family members as witnesses and relied on neighbors more frequently.[88]

Although migrants concentrated in Saint Chamond's new industries, the majority of all its inhabitants labored in factories and thus experienced a generation gap. Data about occupational inheritance, more dramatically than any other, point to the 1860s as a watershed for the way industrialization transformed family life. Among all the men who married between 1816 and 1825, more than half followed their father's profession. Data from marriages in the 1850s suggest that occupational inheritance generally remained steady: more than 50 percent of marrying couples in all occupations inherited their father's profession, and approximately one-third of them had fathers-in-law who shared the same profession.[89] But among the men who married between 1861 and 1870, occupational inheritance fell by about half (Table 11). In the 1860s, only 26 percent practiced the same occupation as their father did, and only 18 percent shared an occupation with their father-in-law.[90] Moreover, as many as 30 percent had fathers in agriculture, a sharp increase from the 18 percent in the cohort that married between 1816 and 1825.[91] Though the geographical origins of migrants had not changed much over the century, their occupational roots had changed: the pressures to leave the land and the demand for urban labor had extended beyond rural industrial workers and dipped into the pool of families devoted more exclusively to farming.

Measures of occupational inheritance and occupational endogamy indicate a distinctly weakened capacity for marriage and family formation to reinforce occupational identity. Conversely, the influence occupation exercised on marriage and family formation grew weaker. Among all workers, generational disparity in choice of occupation weakened the bonds of shared experience between parents and children. Where workers did inherit their occupations, inheritance usually had a meaning different from that which it had had in the first half of the nineteenth century, especially among metal workers. Beyond the raw materials, nail making and other forms of traditional metal working had little in common with heavy metallurgy. Fathers who did work in the latter most often did not

Table 11.   Sons Who Inherited Father's Occupation, 1861–1870

	Fathers who declared	Inherited No.	%
Mining	24	7	29.2
Small metallurgy	16	9	56.3
Large metallurgy	211	48	22.7
Textiles	58	18	31.0
Construction	50	12	24.0
Clothing	15	3	20.0
Furniture	9	3	33.3
Land transport	13	2	15.4
Railroad	10	2	20.0
Shopkeeping and food	43	10	23.3
Misc. services	34	13	38.2
Total	483	126	26.1

have skills to pass on to their sons. Transmission of skills from father to son played a minor role in the 1860s, if it played one at all.

Certainly fathers and sons did sometimes work together in the same plant. Pierre Duc from Vienne (Isère), Pierre Dubost from Roanne (Loire), and Maurice Antoine Baujolin from Saint-Heand (Loire) all worked as turners at the Petin forges and also had fathers there who worked as turners. Denis Giron, a puddler in the Petin forges, had a son who worked there as an assistant puddler. Maritte Aurore and his father worked as stokers in the Thiollière *pointe* factory.[92] These examples, however, constitute only a handful of the 414 metal workers who married between 1861 and 1870. The few others who exhibited occupational inheritance either worked in a different plant from that of their father or worked at different, unrelated, unskilled tasks. Jean Benoît Peyrieux was an apprentice brazier when his sixty-four-year-old father was simply a *manoeuvre*. Etienne Belland, a puddler's assistant, and Jean Antoine Berne, a "taker" (*preneur*), also had fathers who declared their occupation as *manoeuvre* in the Petin forges.[93]

In some cases, sons clearly had developed more skill than their fathers. Jean Fayolle was a puddler in the Petin forges, while his father worked there as a weigher. Master puddler Jean Claude Desmartin's father worked as a boiler feeder (*alimenteur de chaudière*).[94]

Though it would be misleading to assume that fathers and sons who worked in metal during the century shared no experiences or values, they did lack the traditions that had previously served as an important bond between generations. As metallurgy expanded, becoming more mechanized and less skilled, it drew men of all ages and all occupational and geographical backgrounds. Fathers who were weavers, dyers, and builders saw almost as many of their sons go into metal work as into their own professions.[95]

To try to analyze direct occupational endogamy—the rate at which men married women in their own professions—would be pointless for the 1860s. As work became more gender-segregated, the context of direct endogamy changed; even if a husband and wife both worked in textiles, they did so outside the home, apart from one another, and their respective activities differed considerably. Rates of female occupational inheritance do, however, reveal interesting and significant changes through the nineteenth century: the proportion of women textile workers whose fathers also worked in textiles dropped from 41 to 10 percent; at the same time, the proportion who had fathers working in agriculture more than tripled, to 31.6 percent.[96] Work bonds between men and women— daughters and fathers as well as wives and husbands—broke apart in the course of the century.

In their geographical origins, their cultural inheritance, the separation of work and family, and the segregation of work by gender, couples in the 1860s differed markedly from those in the first quarter of the century and even from those who had married in Saint Chamond in just the preceding decade. This break in tradition influenced their everyday lives. Other historians have documented the separation artisans felt from factory workers, as well as the difficulty of organizing newcomers into mutual aid societies, political clubs, and other worker associations. Community ties served as a prerequisite for the development of worker associations.[97]

Workers' reticence to associate stemmed from more than the simple fact of migration or the new experience of factory work. It also resulted from the cultural disruption that both migration and factory work produced. Transmission of skills through the family had always been the source of pride in work. It had also defined standards. When young men took on jobs with which their parents were so unfamiliar, they had no standards against which to compare work conditions or rates and methods of pay. Old definitions did not fit new situations. Several historians have suggested that occupational inheritance provided workers with a basis for independence, self-discipline, and resistance to demands of industrial employers. Removal of control over skills in Saint Chamond is symbolized by the creation of a school for apprenticeship in October 1889 that was run by the Association of Catholic Employers. Its purpose was to form "intelligent workers who could later become foremen."[98] With the creation of institutions such as this, workers further lost collective control over labor. The geographical separation and the sharp decline in occupational inheritance created a gap between generations whose implications have barely been explored.

The cultural break with the past certainly did not make adjustment to the new family economy in this later generation any easier. The need to work outside the home created conflicts with other household responsibilities, particularly that of childrearing. Migration had reduced the number of relatives, especially those in the older generation, who might have assisted with child care. Yet, as workers testified, if the woman did remain in the home to meet household needs, her family could not survive. The greater difficulty in combining household responsibilities with wage earning constituted a further hardship for the generation of workers in the new industries. Certainly artisans in the past had suffered periods of unemployment. But by working together, as the Fond and Perrin families illustrate, the family could pool its resources more effectively. The geographical and cultural dispersion of families in the second half of the century made meeting these needs more difficult. The mechanized labor these workers performed imposed new rhythms on their everyday lives; it ruptured the link between home life and work life that had been so fundamental among artisan workers. By removing work from the home, industrialization further segregated it according to age and gender and made it impossible for family members to work together. Wage earning, which had previously been a family enterprise, instead came into conflict with family needs. The new industrial workers—and the families they began to form—placed artisans such as the Fonds well in the background of the urban tableau.

Most workers in Saint Chamond survived. The combination of textiles and metallurgy—whose respective crises usually did not coincide—made it easier for men and women to alternate jobs and for married women especially to work sporadically. Those who could not earn a sufficient wage to support their families—either because they fell ill or because wages simply could not meet their needs—received charity from numerous Saint-Chamonais institutions.[99] Men's wages became family wages only among a minority of skilled and talented workers who knew not just how to command a high wage but how to spend it and save it as well. Women thus continued to do what they had always done: to supplement their husband's wages in whatever manner they could with extremely meager compensation. What changed from the past was not simply the removal of most work from the home but the fact that women could no longer contribute to the family income by assisting their husbands. The reduction in the contribution that children could make placed further pressure on mothers. Simultaneously, the removal of work from the home made it impossible for men to contribute to household and childrearing tasks during their twelve-hour shifts, placing still greater burdens on women.

The decades between 1860 and 1890 marked a turning point in the formation of the working class in Saint Chamond. Some disruptive tendencies continued past the turn of the century. Saint Chamond continued to be a city of newcomers. Between 1902 and 1911 only about 25 percent of the men who married in the city had been born there. This rate contrasts sharply with those of Lyon, Givors, Vienne, and Saint Etienne, where up to 42 percent of the grooms married in their native towns.[100]

Significantly, however, the generation of males born to workers married between 1861 and 1866 began as adults to restore some cultural and family continuity. Of the fifty-two sons of metal workers whose occupations appeared in birth, marriage, or death registers, twenty-five (48 percent) worked in metallurgy. This second-generation sample is, of course, biased toward those who also manifested geographical stability by remaining in Saint Chamond. But this trend is a noteworthy one. Molders in Saint Etienne responding to the parliamentary inquiry of 1884 noted that they had learned their skills from their fathers. About thirty years later the Compagnie des Forges et Aciéries de la Marine of Saint Chamond boasted of multiple generations working in their factories just after the turn of the century.[101] Data from marriages between 1902 and

1911 confirm this trend: instead of trailing behind the other cities as it did in native marriages, Saint Chamond's rate of occupational inheritance excelled: more than 50 percent of all workers who married inherited their father's profession. Metal workers, notably, shared their father's profession at an even higher rate than other workers—nearly three out of five.[102]

In rates of occupational inheritance, the population of Saint Chamond thus came full circle from 1816 to 1911. Work did reenter family relationships, or at least those between fathers and sons. But by no stretch of the imagination did occupational inheritance in the large-scale industrial context assume the meaning it had in the artisanal world. Even when fathers and sons worked in the same trade they did not necessarily work together, and parents certainly had fewer opportunities to train their children, especially since the technology continually changed. Among artisans, the passing on of skills constituted a family experience that combined apprenticeship with childrearing. Parents trained their children in discipline and morality as well as in skills. Not only did industrialization remove this process from the home, but it removed from working-class parents a measure of authority and control over their children and placed it in the hands of the manufacturers.

The historian can imagine either of two divergent developments resulting from this change. On the one hand, the working-class family became less patriarchal as fathers exercised less control over sons and as wives and daughters worked more frequently outside the home. As work and social traditions ceased to center in the home, they became based more in the community, in such locations as cafés and factories. The loss of the father's authority, in addition to new forms of sociability, may have encouraged young workers to develop lateral forms of solidarity with fellow workers in the community rather than vertical solidarity within the family. Occupational differences in witnesses to marriages suggest that this was the case: textile workers exhibited much stronger family bonds, while metal workers developed social relations with co-workers. In other words, the separation of work from family life may have helped to promote class consciousness and class solidarity. On the other hand, certain forms of authority clearly became transferred from parents to manufacturers. The paternalism of factory owners, particularly as exhibited through such institutions as schools of apprenticeship, replaced family patriarchy in a manner that reinforced hierarchical relationships outside the family. Community relations and class consciousness in Saint Chamond, as we will see, reflected both tendencies in complex ways.

Before they could benefit from any roots the second generation of workers may have reestablished in Saint Chamond, they first had to survive—a task more difficult than it had been for the proto-industrial generation. A comparison of data from the 1850s and from the first decade of the twentieth century suggests continuity. But the simultaneous mechanization in textiles and metallurgy during the 1860s, combined with the stress of migration, forced the working-class family to reorganize in fundamental ways. This re-organization left its mark on the Saint Chamond working class socially, politically, and demographically. Nowhere is the traumatic side of industrialization more apparent than in its effect on family structure.

4

Family Formation, 1861–1895

The reproductive behavior of ribbon weavers and nail makers in Saint Chamond during the first half of the nineteenth century demonstrates that the organization of artisanal work strongly influenced family structure itself: the demands of ribbon production, coupled with the professional aspirations of ribbon weavers and their wives, led them to exercise considerable control over the number of children they had and when they had them. Nail-making skills required less family cooperation and did not shape family structure as much as textile skills did. Nail makers' wives did not need to resort to wet nurses and could not easily afford them anyway. They thus had more "natural" spacing between the births of their children and exercised deliberate control only later in their lives. While textile and metal workers exhibited different patterns in the formation of their families, in both cases domestic work organization clearly influenced those patterns.

The removal of work from the home during the course of the nineteenth century dramatically transformed the relationship between the family and wage-earning activities. It put women in a particularly difficult bind because they could not combine household responsibilities with wage earning in the same manner as they had in the past. Even if they continued to perform productive labor in the home, this labor brought such meager compensation that they had to work longer hours. Men's absence from the home, furthermore, meant that fathers had a much reduced role in the socialization of their children, particularly with regard to passing on work skills and work-related values. Finally, the removal of work from the home also transformed the roles of children. They too had less opportunity to contribute to the family income, especially once legislation barred them from factories and compelled them to attend school until the age of twelve.

The dissolution of the traditional relationship between productive labor and family life among workers inevitably influenced the

111

structure of their families. Indeed, the removal of young children from the labor force, the greater difficulties women met in bearing and rearing children and earning wages, and the inadequacy of the male wage for supporting a family provided compelling reasons for workers to limit family size with a new deliberateness. Interestingly, however, contemporary observers and historians alike have frequently pointed to the large number of children workers continued to have during the period of industrialization.[1] This perception has helped build the case for continuity in working-class family life from the proto-industrial era and implies that industrialization did not transform family structure. It has also promoted an image of workers hopelessly doing themselves in by producing more children than they could afford to support and keeping themselves bound to a precarious standard of living.

But while working-class families remained large in comparison to those of other classes, workers actually began to have fewer children, a fact that contemporaries and historians have largely ignored. So too have they ignored the implications of fertility decline among workers. Did families become smaller as a result of ill health or mortality? Or did they shrink because workers, like the bourgeoisie, resorted to contraception? If the latter was the case, did deliberate fertility control mean that workers had begun to adopt bourgeois family values? Or did it mean that workers began to limit family size for reasons of their own, and particularly as a means of reclaiming a measure of control over their own lives that they had lost with industrialization? Did smaller families help workers adjust to industrialization?

Family formation during the period of industrialization has not received the kind of detailed attention demographers have devoted to preindustrial and proto-industrial populations. Specifically, urban industrial populations have not been the subject of the precise analysis afforded by the technique of family reconstitution. Applying this technique to the population of Saint Chamond in the second half of the nineteenth century confirms that industrialization marked a break with the working-class past: it unmistakably inspired new family formation strategies among workers in Saint Chamond.

The first visible indication that workers adopted new behavior and attitudes toward the family appears in the circumstances sur-

Table 12.   Age at First Marriage, by Occupation, 1861–1866

Husband's occupation	Husbands			Wives		
	No.[a]	Mean age	Median age	No.[a]	Mean age	Median age
Agriculture	1	33.3	33.3	1	38.1	38.1
Mining	9	25.5	27.6	13	24.4	22.8
Small metallurgy	12	26.4	26.2	12	26.1	22.9
Large metallurgy	163	27.3	27.3	174	24.1	23.2
Textiles	35	29.7	28.5	40	25.2	24.4
Construction	38	27.9	27.4	41	25.6	25.9
Clothing	10	32.8	30.5	10	28.4	27.6
Furniture	9	27.9	25.6	7	23.3	22.3
Leather	2	27.5	27.5	1	19.5	19.5
Misc. industries	2	29.7	29.7	2	31.4	31.4
Misc. crafts	2	23.6	23.6	4	26.0	25.7
Land transportation	16	30.1	30.6	15	25.9	25.3
Railroad	5	29.0	29.5	5	21.9	20.6
Shopkeeping and food	19	28.1	26.7	24	25.7	24.1
Misc. services	9	30.8	30.1	11	30.8	30.0
Unknown	3	25.7	26.0	4	20.0	20.0
Total	335	28.0	27.6	364	24.8	23.9

[a]The numbers of husbands and wives differ because only first marriages are included here. The data here are from marriages used for family reconstitution only.

rounding marriage. Average age at first marriage suggests that couples in this generation of the 1860s faced more complex if not more difficult social, economic, and cultural conditions than did their proto-industrial predecessors. A comparison of Tables 12 and 2 shows that the mean age at first marriage rose by 1.3 years and the median age by 2.6 years for the entire cohort of men. By demographic standards, this rise is a significant one. Moreover, age differences between the artisan workers in the early-nineteenth-century cohort and new metal workers between 1861 and 1866 extended to about two years. Wage labor in an industrial context thus did not promote earlier marriages as it had among proto-industrial workers.[2]

Migration was no doubt primarily responsible for delaying marriage during the 1860s. Three-quarters of the men who married in

Saint Chamond had not been born there. Metal workers manifested even less stability; only one groom out of five was native to the city. Migration made amassing the minimum economic resources necessary for marriage more difficult for men. Among those born in Saint Chamond, 70 percent married at age thirty or below; only 45 percent of the nonnatives were wedded that young.

The disappearance of domestic industry and, with it, the ability of men and women to combine skills fruitfully may also have caused men to postpone marriage, since they could not as readily rely on women's assistance to meet family needs.[3] But migration and industrial reorganization apparently did not force women to postpone weddings, for age at first marriage differed minimally from that of women earlier in the century. According to manufacturers' claims, factory work enabled young women to build dowries more readily than in traditional industries.[4]

Illegitimacy and premarital pregnancies provide a further index of increasing social hardship since the first half of the century. The rise in illegitimacy rates throughout Western Europe during the course of the nineteenth century, as well as the urbanization of Saint Chamond, would lead us to expect more illegitimate births. In addition, the population structure of Saint Chamond should have helped promote premarital activity and its unfortunate consequences. Though new industries attracted migrants of both sexes, the braid industry created a "surplus" of women in the second half of the nineteenth century. In 1876, for example, single and widowed women outnumbered single and widowed men by a ratio of 1.25 to 1. The braid industry produced a "marriage squeeze" by attracting so many young women to Saint Chamond, and many remained unmarried. The local bourgeoisie blamed this sexual imbalance for what they perceived as loose behavior. Braid workers' morality became the focus of poets, employers, and the republican press. Characterizations ranged from immodesty to outright licentiousness.[5]

Ironically, these women did not merit their unfortunate reputation. Braid industrialists noted that between 1869 and 1871 their workers had sixty-three illegitimate babies. Based on rough estimates of the number of unmarried women they employed, those who gave birth out of wedlock constituted no more than about 5 percent of their labor force. Among all Saint-Chamonaises, crude illegitimacy rates rose from an average of 5.8 per 100 births between 1824 and 1830 to 8.1 between 1861 and 1870. During roughly the same period, rates of illegitimacy reached 21 per 100 births in Strasbourg and 18 in Mulhouse.[6] Given its large migrant population and the imbalanced sex ratio, that the Saint Chamond rate remained as low as it did is surprising. The Saint-Chamonaises indeed exercised relative prudence.

Prenuptial conceptions, however, did rise dramatically. More than one in five of the women who married between 1861 and 1866 were pregnant on the day of their wedding. Nearly one-fourth of the metal workers' brides gave birth within the first eight months of their marriage, a fraction twice as large as that of their counterparts earlier in the century.[7] The fact that rates of prenuptial conception rose so much more than crude illegitimacy rates underscores the relatively conservative nature of this apparent "sexual revolution": sexual relations clearly anticipated marriage. That pregnancy preceded a wedding more often than it had in the past suggests that courtship customs had become more lax; but it also indicates that once courtship began, marriage came less readily to these wage earners than to proto-industrial wage earners. Either the acceptability of premarital intimacy slowed their way to the altar, or economic conditions obstructed it.[8]

Couples who conceived or bore children prior to marriage defy generalization, but many cases suggest that insufficient resources had forced them to postpone marriage. Jeanne Ogier, a braid worker, had lived in Saint Chamond with her parents for four years when she became pregnant at age twenty-one. She married Jacques Bruyas, a twenty-year-old assistant laminator at the Petin forges, eight months after becoming pregnant. Unable to set up their own household, they lived with Jeanne's parents for the first two or three years of their marriage. Jeanne Marie Rosalie Doitrand gave birth to an illegitimate child at age twenty-five, seven years after moving to Saint Chamond from a village in the Loire. The child's father, Michel Louis Badard, a machinist in the Petin forges, was only twenty-one and living with his parents. They did not marry until their baby was seven months old and Rosalie was two months pregnant with their second child. They finally had their own household by the time their second child was born.[9]

Some examples of illegitimacy fit the stereotype of young, naive girls coming from the countryside or from families broken by death, and falling victim to urban morals. Jeanne Marie Doitrand, mentioned above, came to Saint Chamond at age eighteen with no family or relatives. Her father had died when she was three, and her mother died just prior to Jeanne's departure from her village in the Loire. Josephine Samuel had come to Saint Chamond from a rural commune near Rive-de-Gier in 1865 to work in one of the Alamagny silk mills when she was seventeen. Both her parents had died when she was very young, and her grandmother, a wool spinner, had raised her. She became pregnant within only a few months of her arrival in Saint Chamond and married four months before the birth of her child. Like numerous other silk workers, Jeanne Dupouhait had left her farmer parents and come to Saint Chamond from the mountain town of Tours (Puy-de-Dôme) when she was about nineteen. She gave birth to her illegitimate daughter when she was about to turn twenty-three and married when she was twenty-five.[10]

In several cases it is not at all clear that the groom had fathered the child he legitimized at the wedding. François Charles Barbeaux gave his name to Jeanne Chambe's eleven-month-old baby when they married in August 1862, but the child had been born three months prior to his arrival in Saint Chamond, where he moved from the Vosges. Jeanne had lived in Saint Chamond all her life. When they married in 1865, Joseph Marie Barles, an adjuster at the Petin forges, declared Jeanne Dupouhait's two-and-one-half-year-old child to be his own. Yet Joseph had still been married to his first wife at the time of this child's birth, and he did not marry Jeanne until two years after his wife had died.[11]

According to addresses recorded in the marriage registers, none of the couples mentioned above lived together at the time of their wedding. But nearly 20 percent of all brides and grooms who married between 1861 and 1870 gave the same address. A larger proportion of metal workers—23.8 percent—shared the address of their bride. Living in the same house, however, did not necessarily mean these couples cohabited, for an average of 3.5 households shared each building in Saint Chamond. Common addresses also indicate the role residential proximity played in the choice of marriage partners—a factor more important for metal workers, who had fewer roots in the city. Among those couples who clearly did cohabit were Jeanne Marie Milliat, a twenty-four-year-old widow with one child, and Jean Claude Bailly, aged twenty-three. The two had come from the same village in the Isère, and both were pork butchers. Jeanne Marie had lived in Saint Chamond for five and one-half years, and Jean Claude for two years, when they married. Jean Claude arrived in Saint Chamond around the time that Jeanne Marie's first husband died; it is impossible to know whether he arrived in response to her being widowed. But it is clear that he assumed his predecessor's place in more than the pork butchery business. When they married in 1864, Jeanne Marie was six months pregnant.[12]

Untimely pregnancies and births came to a large variety of men and women in Saint Chamond during the 1860s. Some were young, recently arrived rural migrants; others were more mature and had well-established roots in the city. Many pregnancies did not result from the stable relationships that cohabitation would imply. In most cases, the little information available about these men's and women's lives indicates instead that family life had at some point, in some manner, been disrupted—either through the death of a parent or a spouse or through migration. The conception or arrival of children, if marriage followed, began family life anew.

If these couples demonstrated a lack of restraint prior to their wedding, many of them manifested considerable control as they proceeded to build their families. Couples who married in the 1860s contrast even more with those who married between 1816 and 1825 in their postwedding behavior than in their premarital activity. As Table 13 indicates, fertility rates dropped significantly from the first half of the century to the second. The decline in fertility appears most obviously in the total marital fertility rates, which measure the number of children women would have had if their marriages lasted throughout their childbearing years.

Fertility rates fell at all ages, but particularly in the twenty-five to twenty-nine age group and after age thirty-five. Women who married at age twenty-five or younger exerted more control over their fertility than either the cohort as a whole or their counterparts in the first half of the century. Regardless of age at marriage, family size dropped by two through the course of the century. The value of m from this table provides a standardized measure for comparison of the two cohorts as well as for comparison with the results

Table 13.   Age-Specific Marital Fertility of Women Married 1861–1866

Age group	Years at risk	Children born	Rate/1,000	Rate cohort married 1816–1825	Index of change
Women married at all ages					
20–24	476	166	349	438	80
25–29	834	240	288	398	72
30–34	905	215	238	319	75
35–39	874	116	133	205	65
40–44	798	57	71	105	68
45–49	645	3	5	8	63
Total marital fertility rate			5.4	7.4	
Women married 25 or younger					
20–24	474	166	350	438	80
25–29	645	169	262	395	66
30–34	585	114	195	283	69
35–39	525	56	107	177	60
40–44	451	28	62	81	77
45–49	342	2	6	4	150
Total marital fertility rate			4.9	6.9	

Note: Marriages backdated to include prenuptial conceptions and rates corrected for under-registration of births. See Appendix A. For index of fertility control m among women married at all ages (.4578), see Appendix B, Table B-18. See Table B-8 for m of first cohort.

Index of change = (2d cohort rates/1st cohort rates) × 100.

from other studies of fertility decline. This value rose from .3378 to .4578, demonstrating a clear trend of increased fertility control over the first half of the nineteenth century (see also Tables 3 and 4).

Given the facts that Saint-Chamonais couples had begun limiting family size in the first half of the nineteenth century and that most of France had made the transition to lower fertility by the middle of the century, it is not surprising that the Saint Chamond population manifested a further decline in the number of children produced between 1861 and 1890. But two characteristics of this population make the decline noteworthy: first, close to 75 percent of the men and women who married in Saint Chamond in the 1860s had migrated. Among those migrants, the majority came from rural villages in the Loire or neighboring departments, where families continued to lag behind most of France in the transition to lower fertility. Between 1851 and 1891, most villages in the region shifted from uncontrolled to controlled fertility, though the shift was anything but simultaneous. Certain villages such as Marlhes, studied by James Lehning, continued to produce large families. Fertility remained especially high in the southern part of the Loire, where Saint Chamond is located.[13] Indeed, the calculation of total marital fertility rates according to the parents' geographical origin does result in higher rates among those who came from rural areas: parents from rural areas had a rate of 5.5, while those who had urban origins had only a rate of 4.5.[14] But even though men and women of rural origin had on the average larger families, they too exercised fertility control in the city and thus diverged from the broader regional pattern.

The second characteristic that makes low fertility in Saint Chamond noteworthy is the occupational composition of its population. Workers in heavy metallurgy constituted 49 percent of this cohort. Other studies have stressed metal workers' propensity to have large families.[15] Crude birthrates in the French metallurgical centers of Alsace, Creusot, Decazeville, Guérigny, Hayange, and Commentry rose substantially after 1851, while those for France declined. Rates in these areas ranged from thirty-three to fifty-two births per 1,000 inhabitants in 1861 and averaged forty-one. Between 1851 and 1855, the crude birthrate in Le Creusot more than doubled the national average of twenty-five. Crude birthrates must, however, be interpreted with caution, since they do not take into account the age structure of the population; it is likely that these industrial centers had a high concentration of young couples who were starting families. Yet studies using more accurate measures have come to similar conclusions; one, for example, has shown that as late as 1911, iron and steel workers had about 20 percent more children than the French national average.[16]

The analysis of reconstituted families from Saint Chamond offers a distinctly different portrayal of fertility among metal workers, and one that should be more accurate. While total marital fertility rates yield numbers larger than the actual births per family, they measure fertility more accurately than census data and crude birthrates because they take into account marriage duration and the total number of children born. Census data can only measure the

Table 14.   Age-Specific Marital Fertility among Metal Workers'
Wives Married 1861–1866
(Married under age 25)

Age group	Years at risk	Children born	Rate/1,000	Cohort rate	Index of difference[a]
20–24	236	86	365	350	104
25–29	326	81	248	262	95
30–34	294	62	211	195	108
35–39	265	28	106	107	99
40–44	224	11	49	62	79
45–49	173	0	0	6	—
Total marital fertility rate			4.9	4.9	

[a] Equals (rate of metalworkers' wives/rate of cohort) × 100.

number of children living with their parents at the time of the enu-
meration. Table 14 supplies age-specific marital fertility rates of
metal workers' wives married below age 25. In only two age groups
are the rates higher than that of the whole cohort, and in the rest
they are lower, resulting in the same total marital fertility rate. Occupational groups other than metallurgy are too small to analyze
with statistical confidence, particularly when fertility rates are broken down by age. Total marital fertility rates do, however, reveal
interesting differences (see Table 15). Metal workers did have
higher fertility than some of the other occupational groups, particularly shopkeepers and textile workers. The most significant
point here, however, is not that they had slightly larger families but
that the total marital fertility rate of 4.9 for women who married
under age 25 clearly indicates that they exercised control over their
reproduction.

The lengths of the intervals between births and the mother's age
at the birth of her last child provide further means of detecting
deliberate fertility control.[17] Table 16 supplies these measures for
the entire cohort, as well as for the wives of metal workers. A comparison with the first cohort in Table 5 shows that mothers' average
age at the last birth dropped by more than two years, clearly indicating that these women tried to avoid further pregnancies at an
earlier point than their predecessors had. Metal workers' wives
stopped having children almost three years earlier than the previous generation had. The average length of penultimate intervals

Table 15.   Total Marital Fertility Rates,
by Husband's Occupation, of Women Married 1861–1866

	Married under age 25	Married under age 30
Mining	6.3	5.9
Small metallurgy	6.4	6.8
Large metallurgy	4.9	5.2
Textiles	4.0	4.2
Construction	5.3	5.3
Clothing	4.3	4.3
Furniture	5.4	5.6
Leather	4.0	4.0
Misc. crafts	6.6	6.3
Land transportation	5.8	6.9
Railroad	2.9	2.3
Shopkeeping and food	3.6	4.0
Misc. services	5.7	6.2

Table 16.   Intervals between Births, and Mother's Age at Birth
of Last Child, among Women Married 1861–1866
(Median intervals in parentheses)

	Intervals between births (months)					Mother's age at birth of last child
	Marriage to 1st	1st to 2d	2d to 3d	2d to last	Last	
Entire cohort	15.9	31.8	33.7	31.7	48.6	
	(12.2)	(24.8)	(27.1)	(29.6)	(38.6)	34.8
Metal workers	20.0	30.8	29.2	33.6	45.9	
	(13.5)	(25.2)	(26.3)	(30.2)	(33.5)	34.2

further confirms this tendency. These last intervals were often the longest precisely because women were trying to avoid pregnancy, and they grew longer in the second half of the century.

Intermediate intervals over the two cohorts also lengthened. This slower pacing of births further suggests an effort to avoid pregnancies. Yet another, more traditional factor may have lengthened intervals as well: a return to breast-feeding. Women who migrated from the countryside most likely brought with them more traditional practices which they continued in the city. Their breast-feeding would have delayed the return of ovulation after birth and

Table 17.   Birth Intervals in Families of Rural and Urban Origin,
Couples Married 1861–1866
(Median intervals in parentheses)

	Intervals between births (months)			
Origin	*1st to 2d*	*2d to 3d*	*2d to last*	*Last*
Wife urban	30.6	31.6	33.7	54.3
	(25.8)	(27.0)	(26.9)	(42.5)
Wife rural	27.5	28.9	30.3	45.0
	(22.1)	(26.7)	(29.6)	(35.1)
Husband urban	28.7	31.4	32.3	49.3
	(24.4)	(28.4)	(28.8)	(38.0)
Husband rural	29.2	28.1	31.9	46.9
	(25.0)	(26.1)	(30.6)	(38.4)
Both urban	31.4	31.1	37.1	48.5
	(24.0)	(27.0)	(26.8)	(38.8)
Both rural	28.9	26.2	31.6	39.5
	(21.4)	(22.6)	(30.6)	(35.0)

thus have helped lengthen the intervals between births. The removal of work from the home might also have made a return to breast-feeding more possible for all women, regardless of their geographical origins. The supposition that women did breast-feed more than their early-nineteenth-century counterparts also implies either that they did not work or that the work they performed did not conflict with the demands of motherhood. As Table 17 shows, women with rural origins actually had shorter intervals between births than women native to cities. Their intervals, in fact, are similar to those in the first cohort, suggesting a more traditional approach to family formation yet also indicating some presence of fertility control even if they were breast-feeding.

Fertility rates, birth intervals, and the termination of childbearing at a younger age all demonstrate that the working-class population of Saint Chamond, including metal workers and their wives, deliberately attempted to have fewer children by the 1860s and 1870s. While family size remained relatively large when compared with that of the bourgeoisie, it clearly shrank, and it did so during the period of intensive industrialization and migration. The concurrence of economic and demographic change does not, of course, automatically imply cause and effect. Such explanations are the bane of demographic historians. At the same time that working-class fertility declined, peasant and middle-class fertility also declined, not only in France but throughout Europe. Such a general decline suggests that these diverse social and national groups may have been responding uniformly to some broader phenomenon or set of phenomena, ranging from concrete demographic factors such as a drop in infant mortality to opaque cultural constructs such as an increased sense of individualism, the development of a consumer economy, or new attitudes toward children and family life.

But the detailed information from family reconstitution clearly argues that workers responded to a set of circumstances specific to the logic of their own lives. Workers did not begin to have smaller families because they shared values of individualism and domesticity with the middle classes—they could hardly afford to adopt these values, particularly in the last third of the nineteenth century. Nor had the family economy among these workers become a consumer economy, as is typically associated with fertility decline. Wage and budget estimates indicate that most workers continued to spend the major portion of their income on food and shelter, not on consumer items that would suggest an improvement in their standard of living.[18]

It was because of their own material situation and the values they associated with it that workers began to limit the number of children they had. The mothers in this later generation of Saint-Chamonaises faced a situation similar to that of the ribbon weavers' wives earlier in the century who sent their babies to wet nurses: work and child care conflicted. But women's work had changed by the 1860s. No longer did wives assist their husbands at home. Not only had men left the home to work, but the whole array of auxiliary tasks women had performed for the textile industry had become mechanized. Even productive labor that women could continue to perform in the home presented obstacles to household responsibilities that their early-nineteenth-century counterparts had not experienced: the work was so poorly paid that to earn any meaningful income required longer hours. At the same time, most men were not paid wages that could support a wife and children. The disappearance of the ribbon industry, and along with it most lucrative employment that could be performed in the home, forced married women and mothers to leave the home to work in braid factories. Women's work after marriage continued to play a crucial role in the working-class family economy, even though their employment may have been sporadic.[19]

The decline in the availability of lucrative wage labor that could be performed in the home undermined the ability of wives and children to contribute to the family economy. The departure of men from the household increased the childrearing burdens on women. Moreover, children who consumed without producing strained family budgets. In this situation children could easily become a liability, threatening family survival. Family limitation among workers thus developed as a response to the contradictions and conflicts between work and family life stemming from the separation between the two. Mechanization further undermined workers' control over the work process and their self-determination in family life. Unable to change or control work organization, women attempted to reduce the responsibilities surrounding their reproductive roles.

An examination of mortality rates further suggests that industrial conditions forced changes in family structure among the working class. Deathrates in Saint Chamond tellingly defy the standard demographic explanation that fertility declined when infants and children had greater chances of surviving. Table 18 shows measures of infant and child mortality that indicate a substantial rise in deaths over the course of the century. We must recall, however, that rates in the first cohort were underestimated because so many deaths occurred outside Saint Chamond. If deathrates in the second cohort cannot establish a rise in mortality, the figures of 149 infant deaths and 130 child deaths per 1,000 births nonetheless portray a bleak state of health.

At the same time, mortality rates in this second cohort do fall below those in other industrial cities. Abbé Cetty, for example, cited infant deathrates in Mulhouse between 1861 and 1870 as 330 per 1,000 legitimate births, and 450 per 1,000 illegitimate births.[20] Mulhouse, of course, was a much larger city than Saint Chamond and harbored worse conditions. But this disparity does not necessarily result from better health among the population of Saint Chamond. Once again, as in the first cohort of families, infant deaths in the second were under-registered or misregistered. Some miscarriages and many live births were incorrectly reported as stillbirths.[21] Mortality rates here are also underestimated because

Table 18.   Infant and Child Mortality
(Comparison of rates in both cohorts)

	Aged 0–1			Aged 1–5		
	Deaths/ 1,000 births 1861–98	*Deaths/ 1,000 births 1816–45*	*Index of change[a]*	*Deaths/ 1,000 children 1861–98*	*Deaths/ 1,000 children 1816–45*	*Index of change[a]*
Entire cohort	200	122	164	130	95	137
Metal workers	190	—	—	142	—	—

[a] Equals (2d cohort rates/1st cohort rates) × 100. For purposes of comparison between the two cohorts, stillbirths are included in the infant mortality rates. Using live births only, the infant mortality rate for babies born to the cohort married between 1861 and 1866 was 149/1,000; for those born to metal workers it was 154/1,000. The index of change does not apply to workers in large metallurgy, because there were very few of them in the cohort that married from 1816 to 1825.

mothers in Saint Chamond, like their predecessors and their counterparts in other industrial cities, continued in the second half of the century to send their infants to wet nurses.[22] Many of these infants died in the countryside, and their deaths went unrecorded in Saint Chamond.

An 1874 hygiene report on the arrondissement commented on the frequency of this practice in the Stéphanois region. Women continued to rely heavily on wet-nursing through the 1880s. In 1887–1888, 47.9 percent of the babies in Lyon and 24.1 percent of those in Saint Etienne were sent to wet nurses outside the city. Figures are not available for Saint Chamond, but they no doubt fell somewhere in this range. The hygiene report lamented that "at the end of five or six months [infants] would be returned in a deplorable state of health and their parents would only find out . . . too late to remedy it."[23] Surely some of the babies from Saint Chamond died before their parents could retrieve them from the countryside. As Table 19 shows, the differences between Saint Chamond's deathrates and death probabilities from life tables (values of $_1q_0$) suggest that the infant deaths may be off by as much as 19 percent for girls and 25 percent for boys. That these rates are more accurate in the second half of the century than in the first nonetheless suggests that the practice of wet-nursing was declining.

In addition to causing higher mortality and reducing the accuracy of deathrate figures for Saint Chamond, the practice of wet-

Table 19.   Infant and Child Mortality, by Sex, 1861–1898 (Children born to couples married 1861–1866; stillbirths not included)

	Aged 0–1				Aged 1–5		
	Births	*Deaths*	*Rate*	$_1 q_0{}^a$	*Births*	*Deaths*	*Rate*
Girls							
Whole cohort	410	59	144	177	313	39	125
Metal workers	182	26	143	—	139	17	122
Boys							
Whole cohort	398	62	156	207	310	42	135
Metal workers	175	29	166	—	135	19	141

[a] Probable mortality rates taken from life tables in Ansley J. Coale and Paul Demeny, *Regional Model Life Tables and Stable Populations* (Princeton: Princeton University Press, 1966), p. 10. These rates are taken from model "west," level 9.

nursing tells us something about working-class life-style, just as it did for ribbon-weaving families in the first half of the century. Though the practice did begin to decline, the alternative to wet-nursing unfortunately did not offer a happy solution. The 1874 report on public health for the arrondissement remarked that women in Saint Chamond and other industrial cities, in order to "return to lucrative occupations" which were "incompatible with nursing," weaned their infants prematurely.[24] Mothers who worked outside the home had their children bottle-fed with unpasturized cow's and goat's milk. From the age of two or three months, they fed them paps and bread soups. The effects of early weaning left their mark on seasonal mortality. Artificial feeding became particularly lethal during the summer months, when warm weather fostered bacteria associated with intestinal disorders.[25] The graph of infant mortality (opposite) demonstrates that infant deaths rose during the summer months more dramatically in the second cohort than in the first, suggesting that toward the end of the century, mothers more frequently weaned their children prematurely. The need to earn wages, inside or outside the home, competed with infant care and contributed to high deathrates.

The examination of birth intervals establishes a link between fertility and mortality: women conceived an average of eleven months earlier following an infant death than they did if the infant survived. Mortality also tended to concentrate in families with a larger

% Infants who died

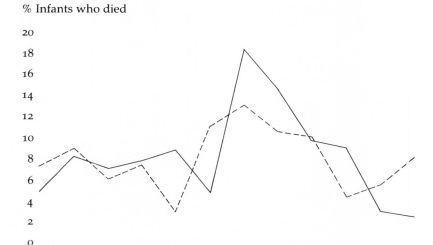

Infant Mortality by Season

Dotted line represents infant deaths from cohort married 1816–1825. Solid line represents infant deaths from cohort married 1861–1866.

number of births, but this concentration may simply have resulted from that fact that larger families had a greater statistical probability of suffering more deaths.[26]

Significantly, as Table 20 indicates, later-born children ran greater chances of early death, perhaps because their arrival stretched family resources beyond the threshold necessary for survival. We must keep in mind, however, that a number of infants died outside Saint Chamond, leaving no clue to their birth order. Evidence regarding which children parents sent to wet nurses is lacking, but it would seem logical that they sent the earlier-born more frequently than the later-born, since older siblings could bottle-feed their younger brothers and sisters. If children in earlier ranks did go to wet nurses more frequently, this practice would have artificially lowered their mortality rates, since a larger portion of their deaths would have gone unrecorded in Saint Chamond. Breaking down mortality by birth rank, as in Table 20, in fact suggests that earlier-

Table 20.   Infant Mortality by Birth Rank, 1861–1898
(Children born to couples married 1861–1866; stillbirths included)

Rank	No. born	No. died	Rate/1,000
1–3	813	140	172
4–6	269	51	190
7–14	107	25	234

born children may have been sent to wet nurses more readily, since rates in the later birth ranks approach those more typical of other industrial cities.

Infant ill-health and deaths in and around Saint Chamond caused deep consternation among middle-class observers. In 1872, one Dr. Fredet formed a "Société Protectrice de l'Enfance" modeled on similar societies in Paris and Lyon. Its purpose was to encourage maternal nursing among working-class women, to prevent premature weaning, to regulate wet-nursing, and to protect children from the negligence of wet nurses. The society was short-lived and never functioned effectively because "it was welcomed by the population with indifference," no doubt reflecting the impossibility of resolving the conflict between wage earning and infant care.[27] The problem remained an acute one as late as 1907, when the Union of Mutual Aid Societies in the Loire blamed working-class women for 75 percent of all infant deaths. "Rather than quit their jobs," mothers either sent their infants to wet nurses or made them "the victims of poor feeding and . . . deprivation of mother's milk. The dangers of bottle-feeding are . . . the worst during the first months of life."[28] But while these reports legitimately linked work outside the household, wet-nursing, artificial feeding, and infant mortality, a middle-class perspective prevented their authors from making a distinction between symptoms and causes. They did not understand, nor would they have accepted, that women simply continued to do what they had in the past—contribute to the family economy—only this contribution took a more exacting toll than it had in the context of domestic industries such as ribbon production.

Beyond feeding practices, we need not look far for the causes of infant mortality. With stillbirths included, nearly 58.5 percent of infant deaths recorded in Saint Chamond from the second cohort were endogenous, that is, they occurred within the first month of life, which suggests that they resulted from the mother's poor health or complications from pregnancy. Endogenous deaths among these infants remained high at a time when they were declining in France; from 1855 to 1913, they declined nationwide from 50 percent to 21 percent.[29] Maternal mortality—the number of mothers who died within a month after the birth of a child—more than doubled in Saint Chamond through the nineteenth century, rising from 7.4 maternal deaths per 1,000 births to 16.2.[30]

A number of factors new to Saint Chamond between 1850 and 1890 contributed to the poor health of its population. Close to half of the women who married after 1860 worked in braid production. Although women only supervised looms or performed other supposedly effortless tasks, attendance to braid-making, reeling, and spinning machines required that workers stand for at least four hours at a time with no break; until 1869, braid workers in the Oriol and Alamagny factory worked for twelve hours with no break and ate their meals while standing up and supervising looms. In 1878 workers complained of a thirteen-and-one-half-hour day with no rest or interruption.[31] Particularly when combined with poor nutrition, this work was harmful for pregnant women who, if they followed the same practice as their counterparts in other textile cities, worked until shortly before giving birth and often returned to work soon afterward.[32]

The work shifts in braid factories, moreover, always included night work. When employers changed the length of the workday, they eliminated the hours from midnight to 4 A.M., but many women, especially married women, continued to work during the night hours. Wages for night work were somewhat higher and, more important, the night shifts made it easier for married women to coordinate wage earning with household responsibilities. Legislation barring women under age twenty-one from night work also inadvertently forced more married women into these shifts. A report on the effects of night work based on workers' testimonies indicated that it caused fatigue, headaches, eye strain, and, because it made workers lose their appetites, serious nutritional problems. One twenty-five-year-old woman had to stop working because she could no longer eat. The author of this report stated that the effects of night work came on very gradually but concluded that it "causes serious problems with nutrition," resulting in "a weakening of the race."[33] In 1886, 415 workers signed seven petitions requesting an end to night work because it was "very demanding, very toilsome, it hinders the development of their physical forces, impairs their vision and does considerable harm to their overall health."[34]

The large proportion of endogenous infant deaths, the rise in maternal mortality, and the high rates of infant and child mortality bear testimony to the more brutal conditions industrialization brought to these workers' lives. Though records in the *état civil* do not list causes of death, the description of women's work conditions suggests that they contributed to a decline in health. Hygiene reports generated by middle-class observers were not the only source to link women's industrial work with their poor health and infant mortality. In this same period, working-class women and men throughout the industrial centers of France themselves complained bitterly that industrial work ruined women's health, that it caused increased miscarriages and stillbirths, and that their infants were dying because mothers could not breast-feed them.[35]

Mothers, infants, and children were not the only victims of industrialization. Adults of both sexes in the second cohort died earlier than those who married between 1816 and 1825. Among the latter, 8.7 percent of all first marriages ended before the tenth anniversary; 14.5 percent of those celebrated between 1861 and 1866 ended that early.[36] Other ailments associated with industrializing and urbanizing society—hazardous work conditions, pollution, and diseases such as tuberculosis—further debilitated workers and contributed to their mortality.

The issue of hazardous work conditions merits attention because so often a relatively high pay rate among skilled workers is taken to suggest that standards of living rose with industrialization. Dyeworkers, for example, frequently became afflicted with stomach ailments, convulsive coughing, and spitting up blood as a result of breathing the sulfuric acid gas used for dyes. Many of the dyeworks in Saint Chamond specialized in dyeing silk black, the process that required the largest number of chemical substances. Direct contact with chemical solutions also ate away at the skin, injured cuticles, and dried up nails.[37]

Metal production took place in an even more hazardous environment; its accident rate ranked among the highest of all occupations in France.[38] Working with masses of molten iron and steel and using machinery that weighed up to 12,000 tons necessitated a high level of organization, discipline, coordination, and alertness. Operation of the steam hammer, for example, required that forty workers act as a single man. A few seconds' lapse of attention could and did cause fatal accidents and major catastrophes.[39] More minor mishaps occurred regularly. A glance at hospital records in the 1860s rivets attention on the influence of industrial accidents: burns, abscesses, fractures, dislocations, and amputations filled the "surgical category." In 1864, 104 men entered the hospital to be treated for injuries resulting from accidents. This category accounted for more than 25 percent of the male patients.[40]

Outside their places of work, the working-class population of Saint Chamond risked illness on the streets and inside their homes from conditions typical of all rapidly growing and industrializing cities. As migrants poured into the valley after 1850, rents rose and lodgings frequently became overcrowded. Inspectors had noted the problem by the late 1850s: "ground floors [of houses] are true cesspools . . . insufficient air and light penetrate rooms. Almost every staircase is indescribably filthy and poisoned by [the] stench of cesspools with which they are always in direct communication: hallways have neither tiles nor boards, and their [dirt floors] are soaked with rain and household waters filled with debris of all kinds that [residents] throw out."[41] Their valley setting made lodgings extremely damp: waters drained from the hillside and accumulated on the ground floors. The wetness and humidity exacerbated the rheumatism that so often crippled workers. Overcrowding further aggravated problems of filth and dampness. One investigator discovered a room in which each tenant had four cubic meters of air instead of the legally required twelve to fourteen. These conditions fostered the spread of tuberculosis and other contagious diseases.[42]

Industrial pollution also threatened workers' health. As early as 1841, inhabitants complained of black smoke from the coal and steam engines that permeated the city. They claimed it inhibited the growth of vegetation and caused "serious illness" in people.[43] The amount of smoke increased with the growth of the braid industry and metallurgy through the 1860s and 1870s. So too did another type of pollution. The number of dyeworks in the city increased as a result of the braid industry's growth. Dependent on water for washing silks, cottons, and other textiles, dyeworks by 1865 stretched along the riverbanks of the Gier for a distance of two kilometers. The river became a receptacle for dye solution wastes: pewter salts, iron sulfate, and sulfuric acid poisoned its waters. An engineer's report expressed fear that the water feeding the entire city would soon be poisoned. As middle- and upper-class residents of the city had access to public baths and washhouses, this pollution affected the working class most immediately. The report stressed that "the dyeworks industry . . . has for the working class intolerable inconveniences, to the point of making it almost impossible to do their laundry and satisfy the most urgent needs of domestic life."[44] Mayor Jules Duclos expressed sympathy for the material conditions workers suffered when he wrote to the prefect in 1865 of their special burden: "Having fewer clothes and jobs that soil their clothes, they have more need to wash." Washing became impossible during the day; workers had to wait until nightfall, after some of the chemicals had washed away, to use the river.[45] Elsewhere, use of similarly polluted waters was thought to have effects far more serious than laundry problems. A medical report in 1877 attributed infant deaths in Condrieu, along the Rhône River, to chemical pollution.[46]

Between 1867 and 1876, the quantity of textiles processed through the Saint Chamond dyeworks multiplied fifteen to sixteen times as more extensive mechanization increased braid production. The water of the Gier was compared with that of the Seine and the Thames, having been transformed into a main sewer. The construction of a dam, completed in 1870, was meant to improve the situation, and the municipality backed off. But unfortunately the new dam made little difference. The river had become so polluted by 1879 that the inhabitants of Saint-Julien-en-Jarrez, the commune just downriver from Saint Chamond, complained they could no longer use the water even for their meadows or animals.[47]

An engineer's report in 1884 admitted that during periods of good business a single dyeworks could dump as much as 1,000 kilograms of chemical substances into the river per day. In this year of economic crisis, the dye industry as a whole dumped 11,000 kilograms of chemicals daily—a quantity well below that of normal times. But the report pointed out that other industries polluted the river as well. Manufacturers of *pointes* dumped sulfuric acid in the river. In addition, twenty washhouses discharged soap, and three manufacturers of gallic acid sent their wash waters into the river. Mines contributed their share of the pollution with acid water. In addition to industrial pollutants, the engineer reminded his readers, raw sewage from Saint Chamond, Izieux, Saint Julien, and Rive-de-Gier also found its way to the river. Amazingly, he concluded that chemicals from the dyeworks operated as disinfectants and actually helped purify the water.[48]

The effects of occupational hazards, poor housing, and industrial pollutants were reflected in Saint Chamond's hospital records. In the second half of the nineteenth century, 500 to 600 men, women, and children entered the hospital annually. Diseases listed in the records do not perfectly reflect their incidence in the community, but they do provide a sense of what ailed the Saint-Chamonais. Bronchial and pulmonary catarrh and phthisis—which the medical profession later learned to recognize as stages of tuberculosis—as well as recognized consumption accounted for nearly one-third of the adult diseases. Typhoid and rheumatism also numbered among the most common illnesses. Other serious ailments that struck the Saint-Chamonais did not always send them to the hospital. One doctor commented that the most frequent afflictions in Saint Chamond were contagious eye infections—scrophulous ophthalmia—from which children as well as adults suffered.[49]

Industrial, urban conditions and hospital records offer only an indirect and imperfect explanation for the mortality rates in Saint Chamond. Rates alone, however, complete the demographic profile of Saint Chamond's workers and, sad to say, demonstrate that middle-class values such as a new devotion to motherhood and "modern" concerns for the health and well-being of women or a decline in infant and child mortality could not have been responsible for the pronounced decline in family size.

Mortality rates also further enhance our understanding of fertility, for they suggest that breast-feeding—a factor that not only would have helped lengthen birth intervals but would have preserved infant health—was not widely practiced. Indeed, birth intervals lengthened in the second half of the century despite continued high infant mortality; infant deaths in a traditional population would have caused shorter birth intervals. Although mortality concentrated in families with higher fertility, infant and child death pervaded family life in Saint Chamond: more than one out of every two families (52 percent) suffered at least one child's death.[50]

Fertility and mortality patterns in this cohort point clearly to the large number of couples who did not "replace" infants and children who died or who "replaced" them very slowly. Antoine Marie R. and Margaret C. had a third child only three years after their first two had died. Marie P., married to a metal worker, waited five years before giving birth to her third child after the second had died at the age of fourteen months. Others simply stopped having children despite child deaths and small family size. Françoise G. and shoemaker Jean Baptiste L. had only one child who survived to adulthood. Their second child was stillborn and the third died at ten months. Though Françoise was only twenty-eight when their last child died, she had no more pregnancies.[51]

Given the relatively low rates of fertility and high rates of infant death, women clearly used artificial means to space births or try to stop them. But decline in family size did not result from contraceptive efforts alone. Recent studies have argued convincingly that women in the second half of the nineteenth century resorted far more frequently to abortion than has previously been suspected. Married working-class women, moreover, may have been most responsible for the increase. But since it was criminal and therefore practiced surreptitiously, the extent of abortion as a form of limiting family size remains largely undocumented. A recent study of crime during the nineteenth century in the arrondissement of Saint Etienne suggests that the urban proletariat frequently resorted to abortion, but the guilty knew how to hide their crime. One known case occurred in Saint Chamond: in 1861, a widow died in the hospice from an abortion performed, using poultry feathers, by a forty-one-year-old silk reeler, mother of four, born and residing in Saint Chamond. Other Saint-Chamonaises no doubt went to Lyon, a relatively easy train ride, to have their pregnancies terminated. This city reportedly had 10,000 abortions to 9,000 births in 1906.[52]

In his study of working-class fertility in France, Angus McLaren has made several observations about the absence of abortion as a consideration in demographic history, as well as the role it played in working-class women's lives. In addition to the fact that the prevalence of abortion cannot be measured, historians may have ignored it because it assigns to women the initiative for fertility control. McLaren argues, first, that the apparently increased incidence of abortion suggests that in fact fertility decline among the working classes resulted from female rather than male motivation.[53]

Second, McLaren links abortion to specific conditions in urban industrial society and particularly to the nature of women's work. More women in cities worked outside the home. The option for abortion derived from the same mentality as did the option of sending infants to wet nurses: pregnancy threatened to deprive the family of the woman's income. McLaren notes: "It is likely that those working-class husbands who supported their wives' decision to abort did so for the same reason they accepted the putting out of their babies to nurse in the country—so as not to lose the wife's contribution to the family income or her participation in the small family enterprise so characteristic of French capitalism."[54] Factory work also provided a network for information about the means to terminate pregnancies. It is quite likely that many women resorted to abortion with neither the support nor the knowledge of their husbands.

The apparent frequency with which working-class women, particularly in an urban industrial context, resorted to abortion leads to a reassessment of family limitation in Saint Chamond. Terminated pregnancies would have had a statistical impact on measures of fertility control, for they would have lengthened the intervals between births. Nor, unfortunately, can we dismiss the practice of infanticide. The Ministry of Justice noted and deplored a sharp rise in infanticides between 1855 and 1860.[55] Abbé Cetty cited twenty-two infanticides in Alsace-Lorraine. He also referred to a report published in England in the late 1870s stating that many infants declared as stillborn had actually been slain.[56] Similarly, a medical report to the French Ministry of the Interior in 1877 noted an alarming rate of one "stillbirth" out of every seven illegitimate births in Marseille and suggested that one cause for these deaths was infanticide.[57]

The pervasiveness of death and illness in Saint Chamond would make it foolish to assume that smaller family size resulted from voluntary control alone. Increased numbers of stillbirths, miscarriages, and temporary sterility also prolonged the intervals between births. Poor diet and overcrowded and unsanitary housing that spread diseases such as tuberculosis caused chronic ill health in parents and children.[58] Stress, fatigue, and conflicting work schedules interfered with conjugal relations. A report on night work in another city applies to many Saint-Chamonaises. It describes the life of a plasterer and his wife. The couple had only one child, and the wife specifically requested night work in order to be able to care for him. Her husband would return home from work after his wife left for the factory. "She literally sees [her husband] only on Sunday, and from Sunday to Monday," the report states.[59] To attribute low fertility in Saint Chamond to the effects of night work would be extreme, but it surely did interfere with conjugal relations among a large number of workers. Metal workers, it must be recalled, also worked at night and alternated day and night shifts every two weeks. The work both women and men performed depleted their energy. In seeking reasons to explain overall population decline in France, one medical report cited "weakness of constitution" among couples resulting from their life-style, as well as the "genital inertia" that derived from it.[60]

The demographic profile of Saint Chamond provides two contradictory images of the working-class family. On the one hand, a logical family formation strategy of voluntary fertility control— whether through coitus interruptus, abstinence, or abortion—enabled the working class, and particularly working-class women, to cope with the new organization of work which had decidedly usurped from them a degree of power they had once exercised. Important here was not just the space in which they performed work, but the regulation of its hours. The introduction of inanimate sources of energy clinched the separation of work and family, home and factory, for which proto-industry had set the stage. To regain some control over their lives, workers adjusted their family strategies. Since children could earn wages only after some years of dependency and their care interfered with the mother's ability to contribute to the family income, fewer children posed less of a relative burden. These workers did not simply try to stop having children after their families had reached some sort of "target size." They also had children far more slowly than had workers in the past.

On the other hand, these workers' demographic profile also

presents quite an opposite image. Work schedules interfered with conjugal relations and proper feeding practices, poor diets and disease inhibited fertility and caused infant and child deaths, and early adult deaths put an abrupt end to family formation. This profile hardly affords an image of more freedom or control in family life. Among these workers, low fertility was involuntary. Small families in Saint Chamond resulted from some couples consciously limiting births, as well as from other couples suffering ill health— and some may have fitted into both categories. In any case, having smaller families preceded having healthier children.

Not all couples who married between 1861 and 1866 exhibited control over their lives by having fewer children. Some had very large families. Just as in the first cohort, certain individuals in the second did not show any sign of pursuing a strategy of family limitation. But male occupations had no apparent influence on family size. Nothing about occupation per se motivated these workers to have large families, nor did it motivate them to have small families, as it had for ribbon weavers. Family formation ceased having anything to do with occupation. Workers in Saint Chamond, and no doubt in other industrial cities as well, began to produce fewer children as a response to an environment that threatened the survival of their families. In this respect the way their pattern of family formation differed from that of ribbon weavers has particular significance: rather than limiting births after attaining a certain family size later in marriage, metal workers and their wives hesitated to have children even at the outset of the marriage.

For most workers in Saint Chamond, restrictions on children's labor and the competition between household responsibilities and employment for women outside the household provided sufficient motivation to delay having children or to have them more slowly. The disruption of the family wage economy, rather than the desire to consume more goods or to preserve a way of life centered on the relationship between family and work, drove couples to have fewer children in whatever manner they could. A key element in this behavioral change was the transformation of female and child labor. The economy in Saint Chamond had depended on the nimble fingers of women and children since the introduction of silk milling in the sixteenth century. Although child labor came to be restricted in the second half of the nineteenth century, the braid industry was built upon female labor and continued to depend upon it. The role of women's labor in the local economy no doubt helped prevent most male wages from becoming "family wages." At the same time, mechanization changed the relationship between women's labor and family life. Women in the second half of the century experienced greater difficulty earning wages inside or outside the home, and they had to cope with the absence of their husbands from the household. Smaller family size, whether it was due to deliberate effort or to ill health and death, reflected an adjustment to the new relationship between family and work.

Testimony from worker congresses in the 1870s and later indicates that industrialization had similar effects in other working-class communities, and it required some form of family adjustment. Beyond male occupations, numerous factors contributed to the logic of a family economy and family formation strategies, or lack thereof, among workers: most important, perhaps, is the nature of a local economy and the specific ways men's and women's work complemented or competed with family life. The effects of mechanization in Saint Chamond were particularly intense because in addition to eliminating most domestic industry, mechanization simultaneously transformed two major sectors, textiles and metal, and thus restructured the work of men, women, and children all at once. Finally, this examination of urban demography, in support of others that have preceded it, suggests that beyond work, less tangible factors associated with urban living—such as miserable living conditions and disease—discouraged large families. Just as with the first cohort, the logic of any strategy could become useless in the face of death, disease, and economic fluctuations—experiences far more familiar to industrial workers after 1860 than to their proto-industrial predecessors.

PART 2

CLASS RELATIONS

5

Elite Response to Social Problems

Changes in the working-class family structure in Saint Chamond reflect some of the fundamental transformations that capitalism and industrialization brought to workers' lives. Proto-industrial artisanal work in the first half of the nineteenth century accommodated family life but nonetheless subjected it to commercial cycles and the growing power of merchants. Among some workers, particularly those in the ribbon industry, family planning became a strategy to control unpredictable material and trade conditions. Full-scale industrialization, by removing work from the home and from the rhythms of family life, forced more workers to limit reproduction. They delayed marriage and childbearing or they slowed the pace of births by avoiding conception or resorting to abortion. In many cases smaller families resulted from ill health and high deathrates.

Couples who produced more than two children often stretched the family economy beyond its capacity, particularly since industrialization changed the system of family wages. In Saint Chamond, the decline of domestic industry, the monopolization of textile production by factory labor, and restrictions on female and child employment from the 1870s on limited wage-earning opportunities. The adult male wage could not yet support a family, especially a large one. Throughout the century, most workers in domestic and factory industries faced frequent unemployment or underemployment. Low standards of living, combined with sometimes dangerous work and industrial and urban pollution, resulted in untimely deaths, injury, and illness.

The challenges workers faced in their family lives not only reflected their material conditions but also helped to define class relations. The plight of the working-class family became a focal point for interaction with the elite. Employers and municipal officials could hardly ignore working-class hardships. Abandoned, ill, and dying infants and children became a source of public concern and shaped elite attitudes toward workers. Humanitarian, and particularly Christian, sentiments as well as a pragmatic desire to preserve the labor force produced a strong charitable impulse among the employers and notables of Saint Chamond. Attention to children as the most helpless victims naturally extended to women as reproducers, to men as the fathers of families, and, by the second half of the nineteenth century, to single men as future heads of families. Class relations cannot be understood without an examination of elite attitudes, which will be a primary focus of this chapter.

In their stance toward the working class, employers in Saint Chamond were certainly not unique in France, but they were unusual, particularly for the Stéphanois industrial basin after 1850. A profound commitment to Catholicism and to Legitimism—loyalty to the deposed Bourbon monarchy—distinguished them. Even the new industrialists who embraced economic liberalism espoused Old Regime values or at most a very conservative and Catholic republicanism after 1870. These traditional values lay behind extensive material assistance the local elite provided to workers.

Industrialization in the second half of the century brought new challenges to social peace in Saint Chamond, and elite responses to these challenges engaged workers and employers in a complex set of relationships. Not only did the working-class family experience new forms of stress and indeed become structurally weakened, but republicanism and socialism offered workers a new vision of themselves in relation to their employers. The latter answered this challenge by continuing to offer extensive material assistance, but also by combining that assistance with a systematic effort to educate and moralize workers according to their own vision. While traditional values continued to inspire employers' behavior, industrialization forced them to accommodate their strategies to the new organization of work, the challenge of anticlerical, republican government, and their own commitment to economic liberalism. Material assistance became a means to discipline as well as to preserve the labor force, and Social Catholicism became a means to moralize it.

The collective mentality of Saint Chamond's merchant manufacturers and industrial entrepreneurs had historical roots, for the city's most important families had shaped the local economy and politics over a number of generations. By the end of the eighteenth century, the Saint Chamond elite—about 10 percent of the population—was composed primarily of wealthy forging and silk-merchandising families and petty nobles, whose prominence continued through the nineteenth century. They included names such as Dugas, Praire, Thiollière, Neyrand, Chaland, Grangier, and Flachat.

Their attachment to Old Regime values can in part be explained by their experience with the Revolution of 1789. Prior to the Revolution, this town enjoyed status as the capital of French ribbon production. The ennoblement of the Dugas brothers and other ribbon manufacturers for their innovations brought local renown and strengthened the commercial elite's loyalty to the Bourbon monarchy. In addition to abolishing noble privileges, the Revolution brought an end to Saint Chamond's proud commercial status. The price of raw materials became exorbitant and the "revolutionary excesses" of the Terror brought a virtual halt to commerce. Throughout the period of revolution, merchants in Saint Chamond met with economic disaster from numerous sources: the depreciation of *assignats*, the revolutionary paper money based upon the wealth of the church; the siege of nearby Lyon; the loss of taste for luxury items; and, most important, the wars that paralyzed commerce and cut off markets. During the period of stagnation, foreign ribbon production progressed rapidly, and Berlin in particular became a dangerous rival.[1] Though competition from Saint Etienne caused the ultimate decline of the Saint Chamond ribbon trade, manufacturers could more easily blame their plight on the Revolution.

The Revolution also caused local political turmoil and destroyed part of Saint Chamond's cherished religious heritage. Silk millers and ribbon merchants identified with the counterrevolutionary federalist cause, pitting them against most of the local workers, who sympathized with Jacobinism.[2] Vandals came from the nearby mountains of the Haute-Loire and destroyed the château, the tombs of its seigneurial lords, and the old church of the original parish, Saint Ennemond. This parish would remain without a priest for nearly sixty years. Most of the Saint Chamond clergy refused to take the oath to the constitution and fled, while anticlerical revolutionaries drove out three of the town's religious orders. The Revolution attacked and nearly destroyed a heritage dear to Saint Chamond's very identity.[3]

The prolonged commercial crisis, the struggle between the merchants and Jacobin workers, and the banishment of the religious orders left their mark on the merchant manufacturers and petty nobles of Saint Chamond: they emerged from the period of war and revolution with a distinct commitment to restoring the old order and everything for which it had stood. Most important, their vision of social peace rested upon a permanent association among divine monarchy, the church, and commercial prosperity. They saluted the restored monarchy as a "deliverance" and expressed joy that "France returns to this dynasty under which she saw eight centuries of prosperity flow for her." Part of the municipality's registered proclamation declared, "Inhabitants of Saint Chamond, your industry will once again find the means to become developed, workshops will reopen for you; peace . . . will renew social [and commercial] relations; young and old, rich and poor, reunite in sentiments of gladness and hope, of love for your legitimate sovereign."[4] Many other municipal governments in the Loire proclaimed their support for the restored monarch in April 1814, but the vast majority that did so were those of small, rural communes. Already Saint Chamond distinguished itself from the two industrial cities on either side, Rive-de-Gier and Saint Etienne, whose acceptance of the restored monarchy manifested less enthusiasm than quiet cooperation.[5]

The association among authoritarian government, religion, and economic prosperity articulated in 1814 would be echoed in Saint Chamond throughout the rest of the century. The memories of 1789 and each subsequent upheaval that threatened to repeat its events renewed the elite's attachment to the past, particularly to divine monarchy and the power of the church. The wealthy merchant class continued to associate anticlericalism and revolution with commercial stagnation. Their legitimism and devotion to Catholicism were also an inherent part of a larger worldview that included a belief in a rigidly hierarchical society and a profound sense of noblesse oblige, attitudes which informed their stance toward workers and the laboring poor.

The laboring poor, however, were less easily reconciled to the restored monarchy, and class relations throughout the region became tense after Napoleon's defeat. Long-term unemployment fostered deep discontent among workers. The prefect noted that troubles brewing in Lyon passed along the route through Givors into the Stéphanois valley, to Rive-de-Gier, Saint Chamond, and Saint Etienne, contaminating each city along the way.[6] But Saint Chamond remained remarkably peaceful. Indeed, more than one observer attributed the relative social peace that prevailed in Saint Chamond during the Restoration and the July Monarchy to the particular nature of the local elite. In the crisis year of 1818, for example, J. Duplessy suggested that a spirit of altruism in Saint Chamond inspired the reconciliation, noting that inhabitants distinguished themselves by "a harmony, ordinarily very rare among persons for whom the practice of the same profession too often gives birth to distressing rivalries. [In Saint Chamond], as soon as it is a matter of doing good works, everyone is in agreement. The *collège* rebuilt, the almshouse enlarged, the churches repaired, decorated, and richly maintained attest to the qualities which distinguish [the Saint Chamonais]."[7] A few years after the 1834 riot in Lyon which spread to the Stéphanois valley, a military observer compared the upper classes in Saint Chamond and Saint Etienne. He complimented the former as "truly aristocratic" while calling Saint Etienne's elite "bourgeois" because it "only cared about money."[8]

The merchant and noble classes of Saint Chamond were not unique in their ultra politics, their attachment to Catholicism, or their charitable spirit toward workers.[9] But the persistence of ultramontane sentiments suggests that this elite remained organized and exerted considerable influence for an especially long period of time. And while municipalities elsewhere certainly distributed material assistance, Saint Chamond retained a reputation for being particularly charitable.

The nature of the ribbon industry itself had long made material assistance a necessary element of the local economy. In addition to its dependency upon capricious fashions, nature itself—the health of silkworms and mulberry trees—often determined its fate. While the Revolution diminished commercial fortunes and produced political rifts between merchants and workers, charity continued and helped to ease tensions. The capacity of the hospice to distribute material aid became urgent in the early years of the new century.

In 1803, ribbon production only employed one-tenth of the workers it had in 1790, and daily wages had fallen by one-third. By 1806,
according to the prefect of the Loire, mendicity had made "humiliating progress" as "day laborers, charcoal burners, nail makers and
ribbon weavers" could no longer make ends meet; their wages continued to fall, and as they aged they lost the ability to work. The
prefect duly noted the importance of charity, for male workers often
died young, leaving widows and children.[10] In 1807, a disastrous
winter devastated the silkworm's staple diet, mulberry leaves. The
resulting dearth of silk reduced the work force in ribbon production by 75 percent.[11]

After substantial cutbacks due to revolutionary upheaval, private donations beginning in 1804 permitted Saint Chamond to expand the services of its hospice. Relief went first to orphans and
the children of indigents, who received food and shelter. With the
crisis of 1807, the hospice began distributing bread to the unemployed in the amount of 2,000 francs' worth per year, and their
offer of shelter extended from children to the old and incurable. In
1810, war and further tariffs on ribbons reduced exports another 75
percent; by 1811, ribbon weavers in Saint Chamond worked an average of only one week per month. Of the inhabitants throughout
the arrondissement, 24,000 had to rely on assistance.[12]

The economic situation during the Restoration called on charitable institutions to do far more than provide assistance to the unemployed. A sharp increase in the number of abandoned children
(*enfants trouvés*) offers sad testimony to the inability of the economy
to absorb overall population growth, even as many couples began
to have fewer children. Those who could no longer care for their
children began to abandon them at an alarming rate. Though providing no statistics, the General Council of the Loire reported a
constant rise in the number of abandoned children between 1819
and 1821, and the number of children brought to hospice charities
grew enormously in the 1830s and 1840s.[13]

Although it was certainly not the only charitable institution, the
hospice best symbolized and most abundantly documented the
meaning of charity in Saint Chamond. This institution first became
established sometime prior to 1561.[14] Within its walls, various religious orders cared for the sick, the old, and the incurable, and
raised abandoned, orphaned, or indigent children. Three major

sources of funding provided it with comfortable profits: extensive landholdings which were rented and farmed, the investment of profits from those lands in bonds, and private donations. The customs tax (*droit d'octroi*) contributed a lesser amount.[15]

Local notables staffed the administrative commission of five which decided all budgetary questions as well as policy matters relating to admissions, releases, rules within the hospice, and the distribution of outside aid. The commission met weekly or fortnightly to decide which individuals would be admitted or would receive outside aid, as well as to formulate social policies for the entire community.[16] The provision of aid by local notables and wealthy bourgeois defined the nature of their relations with workers almost as much as wages did. For example, forgemaster and nail merchant Antoine Neyrand and ribbon *fabricants* F. Grangier and J.-M. Estienne were among those who sat in the offices of the hospice and deliberated the fates of those who needed aid. They also were the employers or former employers of many of these poor. Their alternate roles of benefactor and *patron* personalized the administration of charity during times of need.[17]

No explicit effort to moralize the laboring poor and unemployed accompanied the charity they received. The hospice administrative commission overtly concerned itself with molding good workers, but members directed their attentions primarily toward children, both inside and outside the hospice. They gave orphaned or abandoned children a "useful and moral" upbringing. The commission's goal, as stated in 1806, was to "accustom children to a regulated and sober life, such as it must be for workers, but with enough abundance to give them a trade so that they can subsist and be useful to society."[18]

Boys were taught to make nails, in the hope that as adults they would return to the countryside and combine forging with farming. The hospice taught girls to reel silk, to sew, and to run a household, so they could work as domestics in the city or the countryside. Girls were provided with clothing when they left the hospice, and the Dames de Charité, wives of the elite, continued to supervise them after their departure. The nails and silk that children produced in the hospice brought to it a profit of 474 francs in 1804, which grew steadily to 6,566 francs in 1838.[19]

The hospice made every effort to reach children beyond its doors as well. In 1806 they established a primary school for girls and boys from poor families, directed respectively by the Sisters of Saint Charles and the Brothers of the Christian Schools. These two religious orders enjoyed a great resurgence during the Restoration and received considerable support from notables who financed their educational and charitable activities. Instruction focused on instilling religion and work habits from a young age. In their successful religious instruction, Saint Chamond's school became a model for the rest of the Loire department.[20]

While religious instruction for children and material assistance for the poor expanded in Saint Chamond during the Restoration, the July Revolution of 1830 that overthrew Charles X inspired elite goals of moralizing and preserving the labor force with new impetus. The revolution not only challenged divine monarchy but broke the alliance between throne and altar that had profited religious orders during the Restoration. This illegitimate regime gave the Catholics of Saint Chamond, as it did those throughout France, cause to redouble their attachment to the altar. In response to the relaxation of press censorship that in turn gave rise to an anticlerical campaign, a substantial number of Saint-Chamonais formed a Carlist party in opposition to the new Orleanist regime of Louis Philippe.[21] They also drew more religious orders to the town and gave them solid financial backing. Private donations helped to establish the Society of Saint Vincent de Paul in 1834, which joined the Sisters of Saint Joseph, the Sisters of Saint Charles, the Ursulines, the Brothers of the Christian Schools, and the Marists in administering charity.[22]

Religious instruction became the most important target of reform for the government and, consequently, of resistance among its conservative opposition. The Guizot Law of 1833 on education required the establishment of an elementary school in every commune. It was also intended to raise teaching standards. By providing more incentives for lay teachers, the government hoped to reduce the influence and power of the clergy. But in areas strongly Catholic and Legitimist, the Guizot Law resulted in a mobilization of old and new wealth behind the religious orders that offered instruction.[23]

In Saint Chamond, the Brothers of the Christian Schools "multiplied themselves" during the 1830s; by 1839 they had established two new schools and taught 210 students in the parish of Notre Dame and 130 in Saint Pierre. In the entire canton of Saint Chamond this teaching congregation reached no fewer than 600 children.[24] During the July Monarchy, instruction extended beyond children to adults. Forge masters Antoine Neyrand and Antoine Thiollière established an adult school in 1846. The Brothers of the Christian Schools became known not just for their superior teaching skills but for their attempts to instill virtue in parents by insisting that they have marriage contracts.[25]

While elite solicitude toward workers served as a defense against the anticlerical July Monarchy, it also reflected a broader awareness of the potential of working-class discontent—another hallmark of the 1830 revolution. Up to this point Saint Chamond had had little direct experience with worker protest, but the elite had good reason for concern. Even in the best of times, ribbon weaving was a precarious trade, and now, increasingly, *fabricants* and *commis de barre* cheated the weaver of his just wage.[26] By the beginning of the July Monarchy, ribbon weavers were experiencing deep frustration and anger. In 1833, weavers in Lyon and Saint Etienne began to demand fixed prices for patterned fabrics and ribbons. *Fabricants* refused; workers held meetings that "threatened to trouble public order," and authorities intervened. The prefect had been right in 1814: trouble did spread from Lyon westward, and the railroad built in 1827 hastened its progress by facilitating travel and communication. Ribbon weavers in Saint Etienne and Saint Chamond rioted in March 1834, and the national guard had to be called in. In the following month, protest became full-scale insurrection in Lyon and Saint Etienne, with workers calling for a republic. This time, however, the trouble bypassed Saint Chamond.[27]

The discontent among workers in Lyon and the Stéphanois region reflected a growing consciousness among French workers of their rights, sparked by the revolution of 1830. To the bourgeois elite who profited from this revolution, "liberty" meant freedom of expression and freedom to pursue economic gain. For many among the popular masses, this slogan, coupled with the economic hardship they had suffered, came to mean the "right to work."[28] At the same time, the "dangerous classes" and their social problems became more visible. The government of the bourgeois monarchy, as Armand Audiganne pointed out, began "to preoccupy itself with an anxious concern over the fate of workers, whether by seeking to create new sources of work, by multiplying schools, by developing the institution of savings accounts, kindergartens, etc."[29]

This new attention directed toward the laboring classes reflected the influence of liberal economists. Officials attempted to shift emphasis from direct material assistance to self-help. In the 1830s, for example, Jean-Baptiste Say insisted that the unemployed and destitute had no right to charity. Only the "deserving poor"— abandoned and orphaned children, the aged, and the infirm— could rightfully receive assistance. Liberal economists viewed even the right to work, a demand that became increasingly important during the July Monarchy, as a violation of liberty. Only economic expansion, not the government, could supply more work opportunities. The health of any economy, this logic argued, depended upon individualism and self-reliance.[30]

The establishment of savings institutions thus became a key means to try to foster individual responsibility, independence, and self-sufficiency among workers. The "doctrine of savings" would strengthen the family and make it autonomous. Individual savings would make workers independent of state assistance and, just as important, independent of their own associations. Jacques Donzelot has suggested that those who wanted to instill these habits in the poor deliberately intended to undermine workers' associations. Government officials and liberal economists hoped the habit of saving would "reduce the organic, festive, transfamilial forms of solidarity so as to eliminate the risk of dependence as well as the parallel risk of insurrection."[31]

The thinking of liberal economists became incorporated into official government policy, but with few positive results. Efforts to address the growing problem of abandoned children and to rationalize charity in the department of the Loire failed during these years. The cyclical crises in the industrializing economy of the Stéphanois region made barring the able-bodied from charity senseless. In 1840, the subprefect of the arrondissement of Saint Etienne lamented to the General Council, "It is indispensable to shelter the proletariat from need in a region where commercial crises occur several times a year."[32] In Saint Chamond, the spirit of noblesse oblige persisted even as the elite assumed more of an entrepreneurial character with the development of large-scale metallurgy and mechanized braid-making. Private assistance frequently accompanied that which the hospice and religious orders already provided.[33]

Local response to the commercial crisis of 1837 provides the best and most thoroughly documented example of attitudes in Saint Chamond toward the laboring poor. The crisis hit ribbon weavers hardest, but workers in other trades eventually suffered as well. Though their use of the term is not recorded, the municipality of Saint Chamond revealed a commitment to the "right to work." It provided subventions to employ 1,000 people—a substantial portion of the city's adult male population—in public works such as road building and street sweeping. Firms tried to continue to employ workers even when they received no orders. Dames de la Ville opened charity workshops and shelters to aid poor families and single women.[34] A second *salle d'asile* was created whose double purpose was charity and education.[35]

The existence of direct charity did not, however, preclude self-help institutions. The hospice administrative commission in 1839 established savings accounts for children living there to "encourage the love of work" and good habits. Every six months they put one-tenth of each child's earnings into an account which the child received upon leaving the hospice. As the century progressed, education began to play a greater role in moralizing children than did work. At the same time, the commission began to give exiting orphans larger sums of money, often the gifts of benefactors.[36] Adults saved as well. The district council of the arrondissement (*conseil d'arrondissement*) established savings institutions in 1837 in Rive-de-Gier, Saint Etienne, and Saint Chamond. By the end of 1839, the bank in Saint Chamond had 148 accounts amounting to a total of 69,350 francs—"remarkable results at the end of three years of existence in a town of 9,000 souls." The number of accounts, of which ribbon weavers held about one-third, multiplied to 780 by 1846.[37]

Despite these partially successful efforts to inspire self-help, most workers could not save. Economic downturns regularly obliterated the accounts of those who did. The crises of 1807, 1810, 1816, and 1837 hit most ribbon weavers and forced many of them to rely on material assistance. Nail makers and their families suffered chronic poverty; most could not weather a family or economic

crisis alone. Thousands of workers received aid over two generations. In 1844, out of 3,600 inhabitants in one of Saint Chamond's
parishes 2,200—more than 60 percent—received material assistance of some kind.[38]

The economic and political upheavals of 1848 resulted in further
community aid. The administrative commission of the hospice decided on 2 May to ask all property owners to make contributions
in proportion to their wealth in order to "subsidize the needs of
the moment." Victor Dugas urged that the hospice commission allocate 3,000 francs to help the unemployed. The commission would
pay them to farm uncultivated domains owned by the hospice.
Because the property lay some distance from Saint Chamond,
the hospice would provide two servings of soup per day to each
worker, in addition to a daily wage. Within a month the project
was fully implemented, and on 10 June the commission decided to
allocate an additional 5,000 francs to extend it. Such efforts to provide aid during times of crisis certainly did not conform to Louis
Blanc's vision of "social workshops," but neither did they fall victim, as did national workshops in Paris, to political conflicts.[39]

Municipalities and the wealthy merchant classes in Lyon, Rive-
de-Gier, Saint Etienne, and other industrial cities of the Stéphanois
basin also provided material aid to workers and tried to moralize
them through religious instruction. But in those cities, class relations assumed a form quite different from that in Saint Chamond.
In the former, the riots and insurrections of the early 1830s were
followed by intense revolutionary activity in 1848, while Saint Chamond remained relatively untouched by turmoil. Given that the
town lay among cities with similar industries and politically conscious workers, its quiescence is difficult to explain.

The nature of the elite and the manner in which charity was
distributed to some extent explain the relative social harmony in
Saint Chamond. If the merchant elite was more "aristocratic" than
the bourgeoisie in neighboring towns, as observers claimed, class
relations remained somewhat more "feudalistic." A military observer in 1837 noted that, in contrast to Saint Etienne's workers,
"The working-class [of Saint Chamond] has no opinion. It mimics
all the *fabricants* who make it work, is subordinate to them and has
respect for them because they make use of loyalty . . . and they
never leave their rank, as in Saint Etienne."[40]

"Subordinate," "loyalty," and "rank" are all words that apply to the hierarchical, authoritarian society in which Legitimists in Saint Chamond believed. The spirit of Christian charity and noblesse oblige may have softened the edges of exploitation ribbon weavers experienced at the hands of avaricious *fabricants* on their way up.

And yet this charitable élan seems incongruous, given that these bourgeois were reaping the benefits of industrial capitalism. *Fabricants'* treatment of ribbon weavers and nail makers could in most cases hardly be described as altruistic; indeed, relations became more antagonistic as aspiring middlemen and merchants extricated more profits from workers. But two factors account for the spirit of charity that prevailed. First, much of it came from old commercial wealth, from individuals whose families had been established in Saint Chamond for several generations. Private donations to the hospice reflect their influence. Between 1812 and 1848, the hospice budget more than tripled, from 18,466 francs to 68,036 francs. The Dugas, Thiollière, Neyrand, Chaland, Grangier, and Flachat families—whose wealth was based on forging and silk merchandising—featured prominently among the donors. These families had made their fortunes prior to the Revolution, and their descendants continued to identify with Old Regime values of noblesse oblige.[41]

A second factor in this charitable spirit was pure self-interest. Providing direct assistance and employment in public works helped keep the local labor force in Saint Chamond. The ribbon manufacturers had particular cause for concern. During the 1830s their industry began to face insurmountable competition from Saint Etienne. Indeed, the crisis of 1837 marked a point of no return for many. In the hope that this crisis, like others, would pass, they had a keen interest in preventing weavers from moving to Saint Etienne, Lyon, or Paris.[42]

More concrete factors specific to the local working classes also help to explain the development of political consciousness or the lack thereof. In Lyon, for example, convent workshops that housed indigent and orphaned children provided direct competition to silk workers and engendered considerable hostility. As Jardin and Tudesq describe it: "Better organized and more conscious of their condition, these workers were the first to claim that justice rather than charity was the basis of social relations." These workers thus provided the first socialist critique against Social Catholicism.[43] In Saint Etienne, where workers also exhibited class consciousness in 1848, ribbon weavers had formed their own highly successful mutual aid society which made them independent of charity.[44] Workers in Saint Chamond faced a different situation. Only the hospice put children to work making nails and processing silk, and their production did not threaten workers. Ribbon weavers organized a mutual aid society in 1833 which attracted 140 members. But it was dissolved during the insurrection of 1834.[45] It never revived, probably because the declining industry could not support it. Given the local economy, workers in Saint Chamond had greater need for material assistance and it was provided more directly than in other cities.

The workers of Saint Chamond posed no threat to order throughout the short-lived Second Republic or during the events that ended it. Even as the city's elite became more industrial, it continued to commit itself to traditional authoritarian government. Legitimists supported Louis Napoleon, who increasingly seemed to stand for order, religion, and commercial prosperity. The coup d'état of 1851 received widespread upper-class support in the city. The police commissioner confidently assured the prefect that the principal property holders marveled at the "change that occurred in the high levels of power." M. Richard, a ribbon manufacturer who had spent 1,300 francs to help get Louis Napoleon elected in 1848, promised a unanimous vote from Saint Chamond in his support during the plebescite of November 1852.[46] Historian Condamin captured the reaction accurately when he said of the coup d'état that it "imposed silence on the improvised orators of tumultuous meetings and rendered to our city security and peace, for which [its commerce] always had an imperious need." Just as they had in 1814 and 1830, the industrialists of Saint Chamond saw in authoritarian government the promise of commercial prosperity and social peace.[47]

In the 1850s and 1860s, it would appear, this promise was fulfilled. Saint Chamond and the entire Stéphanois valley experienced intensive industrial growth. The year 1853 in particular marked an important turning point. Petin and Gaudet at this time established forges in Saint Chamond where they began producing naval artillery and armor plating for battleships. This event coincided, not accidentally, with the outbreak of the Crimean War—a conflict that provided these captains of industry with a new outlet for products and modes of production. The war united upper class and workers in the patriotism it inspired; of more lasting importance, it played a major role in the expansion and success of these forges. In 1854 Benoît Oriol, later joined by Emile Alamagny, contributed further to industrial expansion in the city by establishing the largest braid factory.[48]

Together, the braid and steel industries transformed Saint Chamond and redefined the parameters and meaning of charity. During the 1850s, the new metalworks and the braid factories continued to attract migrants in ever-growing numbers. By 1856, inhabitants numbered nearly 11,000. These new industries also left their mark on the city's physical appearance. Developers tore down the old, picturesque buildings that lined the squares of Saint Pierre and Notre Dame and ripped up plants and trees to make more room for large factories. In his travels through Saint Chamond in 1862, journalist J. Valserres called the city a miniature of Manchester and Birmingham and noted how smoke from its tall chimneys made the sky forever gloomy.[49] "In this industrial conglomeration," another observer wrote, "All is somber, all is black, everything carries the imprint of fire and smoke, of dust or continuous jolts [of steam hammers,] . . . piles of rock, slag, debris of all kinds, houses or factories partly demolished, presenting a lugubrious and sad countenance as if war and fire had just happened in this region."[50]

Industrialization in Saint Chamond did more than create an eyesore. The problems it caused for the workers placed increased demands on the charitable impulse of its elite. In the first place, not only did industrialization create new strains on family life, but the dangers of the workplace now lay in the domain of the employer rather than in the worker's own home. Second, though the population growth in Saint Chamond did not compare to that of Saint Etienne, the valley location made expansion difficult. Housing became crowded and unsanitary. Poor housing combined with industrial pollution of both air and water made for noxious living conditions that contributed to the deterioration of workers' health. Third, the republican politics that reemerged in the 1860s and became permanently installed in French life during the 1870s undermined the very basis for class relations. Republicanism challenged both the concept and the reality of a hierarchical society. Even more threatening to the Catholics of Saint Chamond, it began systematically to dismantle the elite's primary tool of working-class moralization: religious instruction. The elite's response to these challenges imaginatively combined their devout Catholicism and monarchism with their own commitment to free enterprise.

Employers and public officials could not ignore problems of housing, pollution, and overt signs of deteriorating public health such as the large number of stillbirths and the high rate of infant mortality that came with industrialization. At the same time, however, belief in the principles of private property and a free market economy predisposed official policies toward problems of public health. For example, owners of dyeworks, some of whom sat on the municipal council, in the name of free enterprise effectively blocked any effort to prevent or even limit the appalling river pollution. They claimed that use of the river waters had become their right and that to force them to move would interfere with their freedom of work and private property. While the municipality recognized the problem this posed for the workers of Saint Chamond, it also acknowledged the dye industry's importance to the city economy, particularly because it served the Lyon silk industry as well as their own braid industry. As long as owners of the dyeworks and braid manufacturers continued to serve on the municipal council, the river would continue to receive pollutants.[51] Local author M. Fournier lamented that "the frolics of young children were carried on in the midst of limitless refuse [and] carrion, bathing their nude feet in water which drains all the blemishes of a city!" The municipality finally covered the river in the 1890s, and today it still flows below concrete.[52]

In its stance on the housing problem, the local government of Saint Chamond similarly demonstrated its preference for preserving rights of private property over preserving workers' health. The municipal council established a health commission in 1859 to address problems of unsanitary housing. But in 1864, Mayor Jules Duclos still noted the "large number of lodgings that are far from offering all the guarantees necessary to health."[53] He formed yet another commission to improve the situation but, like its predecessors, it accomplished nothing and stopped meeting after 1875, under the mayorship of Claude de Boissieu. Evidence that conditions remained deplorable persists through the 1870s, with no hint of any later improvement.[54] The commissions remained impotent because any regulation they tried to enforce interfered with the rights of private property.

Profit motives also determined industrialists' response to legislation in 1874 and 1892 that sought to protect the health of women and children by restricting their labor. In most cases the directors of large plants did not employ children under the age of twelve. But the conservative municipality participated in the illicit hiring of youths between the ages of twelve and sixteen by providing the requisite *livrets* and unearned certificates of instruction. Unlike their counterparts in the Nord and the Allier, manufacturers in Saint Chamond saw nothing wrong with employing women—even married women and mothers—in factory labor and night work.[55] Legislation restricting night work had the ironic effect of encouraging employers to hire a larger number of older and hence married women. Between 1874 and 1893, braid manufacturers used every argument they could imagine to preserve their right to employ women in "traditional" work shifts. They claimed, for example, that night work helped prevent unwed motherhood and permitted married women more opportunity to care for their families during the day.[56] One could argue that their desire to keep women and youths employed did reflect a genuine sympathy for the working-class family's need for wages. But self-interest lay behind the braid manufacturers' rhetoric. Cutting back shifts to comply with the laws would, they believed, destroy the edge the braid manufacturers of Saint Chamond enjoyed over their domestic and foreign competition.[57]

The behavior of industrialists in Saint Chamond toward the problems of housing, pollution, and night work underscores their commitment to the free market economy. And yet while this new generation of employers devoted itself to economic liberalism, it also, paradoxically, continued to practice traditional noblesse oblige as well as new forms of paternalism.[58] To the government survey shortly after the events of the Paris Commune, the local Consultative Chamber of Arts and Manufacturers responded, "the best way of avoiding conflicts is for the employer to have a relationship with his workers, to concern himself with them, their morals, and their material welfare."[59] Twenty-five years later, Louis Jury, president of the Saint Chamond Association of Textile Employers, suggested that this policy had become pervasive: "The directors of the shops (and this is characteristic of the employer spirit in Saint Chamond) are generally paternal; most of the employers consider themselves moral substitutes for the father of a family and treat their men and women workers with justice." [60] Like their fore-fathers, Saint Chamond industrialists built reputations on their generosity toward workers. Influenced by "tradition . . . and reli-gious faith," Charles Neyrand demonstrated "sentiments of re-sponsibility and paternity toward his personnel." [61] He performed a "mass of charitable works" and was known as "father of the poor." Braid manufacturer François Gillet earned a reputation for his "works of charity, assistance, and familial organization." Ad-rien de Montgolfier, successor to Petin and Gaudet, "interested himself generously in all charitable works which solicited his sup-port" and was known for his "paternal devotion." [62] Jules Duclos, silk miller and mayor in the early 1870s, opened a restaurant for workers where they could obtain substantial meals at a low price. He also arranged to have his money distributed among the poor after his death. Ladies bountiful—the wives of Oriol, de Boissieu, Jury, Alamagny, and many others—regularly supplied financial as-sistance to workers' families. [63]

As in the past, employers offered large donations to the hospice. Oriol, Alamagny, and Brun were among those who donated hun-dreds of thousands of francs for aid to the old and infirm, the sick, and orphaned children. The annual budget tripled from an average of 66,033 francs between 1844 and 1848 to 194,396 francs between 1884 and 1886. During this same period the population of Saint Chamond grew from 8,000 to 14,000 inhabitants. The amount that the hospice spent annually per inhabitant grew from 8f25 to 13f50. The hospice also provided direct material assistance during the economic crisis of the 1880s, just as it had during the crises in the first half of the century. [64]

This continuity with the past exhibited in charitable activities stemmed in part from the ruling elite's own heritage. Many of them were descendants of old Saint-Chamonais families—for ex-ample, banker and investor Charles de Boissieu, notary Victor Louis Finaz, Ennemond Richard, grandson of the pioneer braid manufacturer, and the Balas, Neyrand, and Thiollière families.

The very prevalence of traditional attitudes and the belief that they maintained class harmony in Saint Chamond attracted like-minded newcomers: Petin, Gaudet, Montgolfier in the steel industry, Louis Jury, and many others in the braid industry embraced monarchist politics as well as Catholicism. Although some of the newer industrialists—Oriol, Alamagny and forge master Chavanne-Brun—professed cautious republicanism after 1870, they nonetheless joined with the Legitimists in their strong attachment to Catholicism, which helps explain their disposition toward material assistance.

But while the material aid that employers offered through religious orders, private charity, and the hospice might at first appear a simple continuation of the Old Regime spirit of noblesse oblige, in fact the "fatherly" concern for workers necessarily assumed new qualities during the second half of the century. Changes in the work force and the environment brought about two key transformations in the manner that charitable institutions administered material assistance. First, more extensively than in the past, in Saint Chamond the employers assumed family functions in the care of the children, the sick, and the old. Second, the commission no longer provided aid indiscriminately. Despite the prolonged depression of the 1880s and early 1890s, the sort of indiscriminate aid that had been typical during the many crises in the first half of the century was given only once during the second half.

As industrial labor became more dangerous, and living conditions brought further detriment to workers' health, the need for material assistance increased. The fact that work took place on the premises of the employer rather than in the worker's home extended the employer's guardianship over the latter's physical welfare. The noxious industrial environment, the increased threat of work-related accidents, and the employment of mothers outside the home forced elites to assume greater responsibility in the care of workers' health and in the upbringing of their children. Employer-sponsored mutual aid became established from at least the 1870s and provided workers the security of assured medical care.[65] Workers usually contributed part of their wages to these funds, but employers supplied the major portion and sometimes the total amount. In any case, employers retained the power over its administration. Mutual aid in particular became an instrument they used to meet the needs of their labor force and still maintain control over the workplace, for it substituted for raising wages or improving conditions. Industrialists also established child-care institutions, administered by religious orders. Employers in Saint Chamond staffed the hospice administrative commission, the *bureau de bien-faisance*, and the municipal council and used these institutions to govern workers' behavior. Faced with the need to preserve a labor force, charitable institutions, rather than shoring up the working-class family, assumed some of its functions.

Whether or not this policy was a conscious one, it became particularly apparent in employers' stance toward women. Significantly, while other French industrialists were slow to provide mutual aid for female workers, employers in Saint Chamond did so readily. By the 1870s, Oriol and Alamagny, who employed 800 women in their factories, supplied medical insurance free of cost to workers. In cases of accidents, they paid for all medical and pharmaceutical expenses and even paid full wages during absence from work. Sick workers received half their wages. The company also established retirement pensions for women after they reached sixty years of age.[66] In 1895, industrialists' wives formed La Prévoyance Féminine, in which they became "honorary" members. Regular contributions from Louis Jury and other braid manufacturers sustained it. Annual fairs were held to raise funds for all the mutualist associations.[67]

Because the braid industry removed women from the home, the need for child care became urgent. So dependent on women's labor were these industrialists that it never occurred to them that women's factory labor should be regulated, much less eliminated. Women had always worked, had always contributed to the family income. Thus instead of encouraging them to stay in the home as paternalists in other parts of France did, they addressed the needs that labor outside the home generated. Petin and Gaudet established a *salle d'asile* for young children in their factory. In 1864 Ennemond Richard founded a *salle d'asile* in Saint Chamond's poorest parish, Saint Ennemond. The Sisters of Saint Charles administered both these kindergartens, and in the latter thus supplemented catechism with 2,500 to 3,000 francs yearly in food and clothing. Between 1867 and 1869, the Alamagny family also created a *crèche* and on the street that bore their name constructed a hospital for children. Alamagny's widow established yet another kindergarten, attended by 250 children in 1884, as well as one in the adjacent commune of Saint Martin, where braidworks also employed women extensively.[68]

But it was more than ill health, work-related accidents, or need for child care that made the working-class family more dependent on employer aid than it had been in the past. The inability even to keep children or to care for the old in their families also forced workers to rely on private charity and municipal aid. A few examples will illustrate this point. Three times during the last two decades of the century, Jean-Marie R. sought aid for his family from the Saint Chamond hospice. Born in the countryside near neighboring Rive-de-Gier, Jean-Marie R. had lived in Saint Chamond ten years prior to his marriage in 1864. Over the next nineteen years he held several semiskilled jobs at the Petin forges while his wife, Marie-Anne G., worked as a braid maker and then as a silk reeler. Marie-Anne bore a child every two years until she died, three days after giving birth to her tenth. She left Jean-Marie with an infant who needed to be breast-fed, a two-year-old, a ten-year-old boy, and a seventeen-year-old daughter with the unlucky name of Marie-Antoinette. The rest of their children had died in infancy. Marie-Antoinette assumed her mother's household responsibilities. But soon the family encountered further misfortune. Less than two years after Marie-Anne's death, Marie-Antoinette entered the hospice to give birth to an illegitimate child whom she named after her own mother. Marie-Antoinette died in the hospice five days after the birth; the baby died a day later.[69]

Infant death had already become a familiar experience for Jean-Marie R. Whatever grief he felt for his first grandchild's misfortune may have been mixed with some sense of relief that he would not have to assume single-handed responsibility for a third child under age five. The loss of his daughter, just two years after his wife had also died from childbirth, posed a more overwhelming challenge.

The subsequent history of this family can be sketchily reconstructed. Jean-Marie could not raise his children alone; in 1892 he placed his last son, then aged ten, in the hospice, where the boy remained for the next seven years. The absence of his other young son from the 1891 census suggests that he, too, may have been placed in the care of a religious order. No one in this family had

good fortune; Jean-Marie's oldest surviving son died in a peniten-
tiary at age twenty-seven.[70]

The history of this family encapsulates many of the structural
changes that occurred in family life over the nineteenth century:
increased illegitimacy, maternal mortality, increased infant and
child death, and the inability of urban workers' families to survive
independently of institutional aid. Hospice records provide an
abundance of such examples. Though each case was unique, together they form a pattern. A mother of five brought her nine-year-
old boy to the hospice because her husband had died; she could
not work since she had to nurse her youngest. A widower who
received a daily wage of 3f50 and "aid allocated to him from diverse
sources" (such as the *bureau de bienfaisance*, Saint Vincent de Paul,
and private charity) could not support his five offspring and so
brought one of them to the charity. Being childless could also act
as a liability. Marie Anne L. married late in life and had no children. She became widowed at sixty-five. Like numerous other widows in Saint Chamond, she survived as a braid worker until age
seventy-five, when, "without family and without resources," she
presented herself to the commission asking to be admitted to the
home for the aged.[71]

François C.'s experience represented that of many Saint-
Chamonais, for it derived from a common work-related illness. He
worked as a stoker at the Petin forges in the 1860s and then at the
Richard and Puthod dyeworks in the 1870s and 1880s. Eventually
he became ill from breathing the sulfuric acid gas used for dyes. In
June 1885, François presented his case to the administrative commission of the hospice. Unable to support his wife and four children because of "frequent ill health that sent him to the hospital,"
he asked that his ten-year-old daughter be admitted to the orphanage. The commission admitted her. François C. died five years
later, at age fifty, in Saint Etienne.[72] The administrative commission
considered several such cases every week; in each case, illness,
death, too many children, or lack of children pressed families into
dependence on the charity of religious orders and the municipality.

The need to seek aid from the hospice touched hundreds of
working-class families in Saint Chamond through the period of
full-scale industrialization. Fertility and mortality rates provide
only one clue to the adverse material conditions workers faced in

their daily lives. Behind the statistics lay countless stories of how individual families, in coping with these conditions, had to open the most intimate details of their lives to the will of the ruling elite. Life in the hospice bore similarity to that in a prison. Grilled windows and locked and guarded doors restricted and regulated the visits of friends and relatives. All inmates assumed the status of children and had to submit to strict discipline. They retired in the evenings and rose in the mornings at specified times; food and wine were carefully rationed. The able-bodied were expected to work. The old especially lost their personal freedom, since they often went there to spend the rest of their lives and had to relinquish any savings or pensions they had earned. On numerous occasions old men and women requested release and tried to live on their own, only to return weeks, months, or years later to subject themselves once again to the humiliating scrutiny of the administrative commission and the religious orders.[73]

Entering the hospice became more complicated in the later decades of the nineteenth century; it was in the admissions to the hospital, the orphanage, and the home for the aged, as well as in releases from these institutions, that employers exerted considerable power over the inhabitants of Saint Chamond. As was the case throughout France, in Saint Chamond there were more candidates for admission to the hospice than there were places for them. The administrative commission had to turn away many of the old, the young, and the sick.[74] In the second half of the nineteenth century, admission became more discriminating, not only because the numbers needing assistance rose but because the economics of admissions changed. Originally, founders of hospices intended that they provide aid for indigents. Because *d'octroi* impositions and other local taxes supported hospices, the law of 7 August 1851 stipulated that communes with no hospice could send their indigents to neighboring communes that did have a hospice, provided that the former paid a daily rate fixed by the prefect. This law had the inadvertent effect of encouraging hospices to give priority in their admissions policy to those who could pay or be paid for. Thus they admitted first the sick for whom an employer, a relative, a society of mutual aid, or the municipality of another commune paid the expenses. They then considered those sick who could pay for themselves. This practice spread in the second half of the nineteenth century, even though it violated the fundamental principle that hospices were meant to aid precisely those who could not pay.[75]

In cities such as Saint Chamond, the hospice admittance policy increased workers' dependence on the mutual assistance provided by employers. In principle, any resident of the commune of Saint Chamond, Izieux, and Saint-Julien-en-Jarrez could enter the hospice at a cost of 1f50 per day, about one-half to one-third a day's wages for employed workers. The hospice would assume the cost for indigents, and industries with insurance policies would pay for their workers. Though the hospice continued to accept indigents, they admitted them only after a thorough investigation that determined whether a candidate had relatives who could come to his or her aid. Workers supported by mutual aid societies or pensions had priority. Their fate too, however, depended on an investigation and on the employer's judgment.[76]

Sick workers funded by company insurance could enter the hospital only on their employer's recommendation. In order to make such a recommendation, employers had to become personally familiar with workers' circumstances. Thus, for example, Grangier and Reymond, whose braid factory employed about 100 workers, wrote to the administrative commission of the hospices in June 1876: "One of our workers is from the department of the Vaucluse and consequently has no family here who can take care of her. We ask that you take her in and give her your best care." She spent forty-two days in the hospital. On one occasion the Petin and Gaudet Company refused to pay the expenses of a worker because he had come to the hospital against the wishes of a doctor whom they had consulted. They intended to prevent workers from availing themselves of this benefit too freely.[77]

Personal knowledge of clients also influenced entry into the orphanage and home for the elderly and incurable. The administrative commission frequently made decisions favoring or opposing admission on the basis of recommendations from prominent members of the community, such as Louis Jury, head of the Association of Textile Employers, or members of the long-established and notable de Boissieu family. One elderly widow entered the hospice on the recommendation of the foreman at the Petin forges where her husband had worked prior to his death many years earlier. Those who donated large sums of money to the hospice also influenced admissions. They could, and almost always did, specify to what use their gifts would be put. Braid manufacturer Irenée Brun wanted the annual interest from his 3,000-franc donation to be used for the support of three new beds in the home for the aged. He also reserved the right for himself and his family to determine which individuals would be admitted for those places.[78] The ability—and need—for the administrative commission to exercise increased discrimination in admissions to the hospice increased over the course of the century. Despite the enormous expansion in this institution's budget, demands for care outpaced the growth of resources to meet them.

The release of children from the orphanage also required a scrutiny of family circumstances. The hospice invested time and money in the children they raised, so the commission released them only when they felt confident that circumstances warranted the release. After they received a certificate of instruction, children could leave if they were returning to a family in proper moral and economic circumstances. In 1894, for example, the commission granted a woman's request to have her daughter returned because she had remarried and her new husband had a stable income.[79]

If parents took their children prior to the time the commission judged suitable, which they frequently tried to do, they were expected to pay 12f50 for each month the child had lived in the hospice. One miner, for example, "stole" his ten-year-old daughter from the hospice on the occasion of a visit with her. The commission decided that this father had to pay for the two-and-one-half years she had lived there, as well as return the dress she was wearing when she left. In another instance, a Mme L. removed her ten-year-old daughter without authorization. When she refused to return her, the administrative commission sought the aid of the police. A couple of months later, Mme L. asked once more for her daughter. The commission finally asked Mme de Boissieu to take moral responsibility for both mother and daughter.[80]

Having Mme de Boissieu assume "moral responsibility" in this case offers but one example of how the request for assistance provided ample opportunity for the administrative commission and their associates to intrude upon the privacy of family life. Regarding the admission of two children to the hospice in 1898, the commission recorded in its registers:

> The father is an inveterate drunk; all the efforts made, notably by [braid manufacturer] M. Jury, to lead him back to better sensibilities have failed. He mistreats his wife and children, and it is a social work to protect them from his influence. . . . The wife, on the contrary, is valiant and expends a superhuman energy to meet the needs of her large family, but cannot assure them the barest necessities.[81]

Though most workers did not experience the direct personal intervention of elites such as Louis Jury, assistance from the hospice, the *bureau de bienfaisance*, and religious orders pervaded their lives. If they did not receive aid, they anticipated that one day they might, or they clung with great pride to their independence from it. Fournier portrays this aspect of their lives in his novels about Saint Chamond's working class. His character Rosine Aubert, a former braid maker, had in her old age only "the interest from a small sum placed in the savings bank, fifteen or twenty sous she earned each day in pulling floss from finished braids, and one hundred francs the curé Verdier paid her at the end of the year for sweeping the church and maintaining the altars." To this she added profits from candles she sold at pilgrimages to Saint Ennemond. "Never had she wanted to register herself at the *bureau de bienfaisance* and [she] had refused with a smile the aid offered her by Sister Gabrielle of the Order of Saint Vincent."[82] Another character, Stéphanie Cointe, "would not know the humiliation of having herself admitted 'to the ranks of the old,' to the sinister hospice of the city, built on the filthy Gier, where the indigent of [Saint Chamond] came to end their lives." But *père* Briquet put himself in quite a different situation. After he had borrowed 2,000 francs to buy a house, his wife chastised him:

> So you want to become a property owner! Look what will happen to you! Have you only thought of the taxes that are going to overwhelm you at the end of the year? [You will be] stricken from the *bureau de bienfaisance*, the free distributions, the Bread of Saint Antoine, the works of Saint-François-Régis! And that's not all! When you become sick and you're taken to the hospital, you'll be put in the ranks of the paying![83]

Old Briquet ended by selling the house and returning the 2,000 francs to his friend. Even if this last vignette lacks credibility, it does suggest, as do examples throughout Fournier's books, that charity pervaded the lives of Saint-Chamonais and that assistance frequently came from the hands of clerics.

Significantly, the lines between charitable institutions of all kinds in Saint Chamond (the *crèches*, the *salles d'asiles*, the *bureau de bienfaisance*, and the hospice) became blurred: the same group of people—employers, their wives, and clerics—staffed all the administrative bodies and discharged the aid. An employer who one day dismissed a worker from his factory might encounter him at the *bureau de bienfaisance* or the hospice the following week. From the worker's viewpoint, not only was this charity inseparable from the employer, but it was inseparable from the clerical orders which administered it. In the operation of the hospice itself, moreover, it becomes apparent that the disciplining of the working class, as well as its preservation, had become a goal of its administrators.

Industrial employers' position toward the material distress of the poor reflected their experience in large-scale, capitalist industry, as well as their roots in Saint Chamond's charitable past. Even though they created and perpetuated the conditions that undermined workers' health, they also sought to preserve workers by providing material assistance and medical care. If their behavior appears paradoxical, it reflects the complexity of their own economic position and sentiments. Their entrepreneurial activity and faith in free enterprise prevented them from treating the true causes of distress among workers, while their Old Regime values—Catholicism, authoritarian government, a belief in a hierarchical society—inspired them with genuine concern for workers' material conditions.

But material assistance to working-class families, in whatever form, did not suffice in the face of new challenges to traditional sensibilities—republicanism, anticlericalism, and socialism—each of which encouraged workers to find their own solutions independent of paternalist employers and the church. The new industrialists continued to associate economic prosperity with authoritarian government. They thus sought to prevent liberalism—whose economic forms they embraced—from invading the political arena. They wanted Christianity to become a moral substitute for republicanism. The paradox of their position arose from the difficulties inherent in trying to promote Christian values of deference in a

society whose economic well-being depended upon aggressive individualism. Their mission, moreover, became much more difficult
in the context of Third Republic anticlericalism. A speech Petin
gave to workers in 1877 well illustrates the stance they assumed:

> All our large factories, which today make the glory and wealth of
> our region, have been founded by men who came from our Christian
> schools. . . . All the positions of accountants, clerks, and foremen
> have been taken exclusively by them. Their aptitudes and above all
> their conduct have made them sought out for the most delicate
> jobs. Why? Because they not only have instruction, but also possess
> these religious principles which give them consciousness of their
> duties. . . . One can say that primary and religious instruction is the
> application . . . of the principle of equality in our society, and when
> I see that our Christian schools, so popular, so veritably democratic,
> and so useful to the laborious class, are attacked so arduously, I can
> only conclude one thing: that those who attack them do not like the
> working class.[84]

Petin thus portrayed Christianity as a medium for social action
and even a means of upward mobility for the worker. Religious
instruction was the only way to establish and spread Christianity.
In attacking religious instruction, he argued, the Third Republic
attacked the true interests of workers. At the same time, in making
his appeal Petin went far beyond the language of Catholicism and
borrowed the republican language of democracy and equality. Yet
he clearly sought to convey that only Christianity, not republicanism, provided the true foundation for human freedom and equality.
Thus, more than ever, in the industrial period employers in Saint
Chamond reinforced and extended the influence of Catholicism.

A campaign to integrate workers into this Catholic community
began to intensify just as industries expanded in the 1850s and
migrants flocked into Saint Chamond from the countryside. At this
time the quality of schools depended heavily on the sentiments
and finances of the municipality. Local government also determined whether lay or religious instructors taught in the schools.
Legitimists dominated the Saint Chamond municipal council at this
time, and they duly shaped local instruction in their own image.[85]
During these same years, legislation on education further empowered Catholic monarchists. The law of 14 June 1854 established
cantonal delegations to supervise both lay and congregational-
ist schools. Throughout France and in Saint Chamond, these
delegations gave reactionary forces influence comparable to that

which they had enjoyed during the Restoration. In the 1850s and 1860s, religious orders increasingly replaced lay teachers. Catholic and monarchist notables and industrialists such as Benoît Oriol, Hippolyte Petin, Victor Finaz, and Charles de Boissieu staffed this delegation and controlled education in the canton of Saint Chamond.[86]

Though most nonnative workers came from the nearby country-side where Catholicism was widely practiced, the values of an industrial society were foreign to them. Even if they had previously engaged in cottage industry, workers from rural areas were unaccustomed to the supervision and regimentation of twelve-hour shifts. Nor had they learned the work ethic of their employers. Even the French language was often unfamiliar to them. A large portion of migrants to Saint Chamond came from the mountains of the Haute-Loire and the Puy-de-Dôme, where they spoke an Auvergnais patois. Teachers faced great obstacles substituting French for the migrants' native tongue. Local pride and children's embarrassment over speaking a language different from that of their parents discouraged them from learning French. Schools in the Stéphanois basin began making substantial progress in conversion to French by the mid-1850s, and in 1860 they formally forbade patois.[87] Being forced to abandon their former language and adopt standard French had an important psychological effect on workers as they became integrated into urban life. Giving up the language of their parents and adopting that of the urban middle class completed a cultural break with their pasts of which migration itself had been but the first step. Speaking French may also have encouraged an identification with the bourgeois elite rather than with fellow workers.[88]

By the mid-1850s, efforts to bring children into the schoolhouses—and under the influence of religious orders and the industrial elite—proved fruitful. Education became more religious as congregationist teachers increasingly replaced lay teachers. In 1857 only 273 boys in the arrondissement between the ages of seven and thirteen, or 1.9 percent, had received no education.[89]

With the changing urban environment and work structure in the city, adults became a focus of instruction and moral education. To the free adult schools that forge masters Charles Neyrand and Camille Thiollière had established in 1846 were added in 1856 night courses for miners. By the 1860s subscriptions from various private donors supported several adult classes, and workers attended them at night free of cost. Between 1864 and 1871, a course taught by Antoine Cara averaged about 150 students per year, and for his excellent teaching he received an imperial medal. Emma Canel ran a course for adult women with an enrollment of 95, but she complained of irregular attendance because so often the women had to work at night. She did note that all the women who took her course knew how to read and write. By 1872, voluntary gifts and subscriptions amounting to 600 francs helped support five instructors who taught 581 adults. Educational trends in Saint Chamond reflected those throughout much of the arrondissement, and particularly Saint Etienne. But Saint Chamond distinguished itself by the substantial private donations that supported religious orders, kindergartens, and, especially important, adult education.[90]

Instilling workers with religious sentiment became at once more difficult and more urgent as the Third Republic began its anticlerical attacks and as republican and socialist ideologies offered alternatives to employer paternalism and Catholicism. As in the July Monarchy, new challenges to religious influence mobilized Catholics to extend their efforts and finances beyond instruction. Laicization of schools and other legislative efforts to restrict religious orders obliged Catholic employers to assume personal responsibility for strengthening religious sentiment among their workers. Several prominent employers in Saint Chamond joined the Social Catholic movement that enjoyed resurgence after the Paris Commune of 1871. Inspired by distaste for bourgeois individualism and fear of a working-class revolution, Albert de Mun, La Tour du Pin, and their followers wanted to substitute a "Christian social order" for the liberal bourgeois social order. They sought an alliance between the nobility—or what was left of it—and the working class, forming associations for both workers and employers.[91]

Camille Thiollière and Charles Neyrand apparently established the first *cercle* in Saint Chamond, in 1872, but its statutes were not registered until 1876, when it had forty-seven members. Its purpose was "essentially moralization, in that it seeks to separate the worker from places where he will spend his family's money, ruin his health by debauchery, [and] have his morals corrupted, and to attract him to and maintain him in an honest and Christian milieu, where his savings will run no risk, and his health will suffer no damage from excesses, and where his morals will remain pure."[92] By 1880, the *cercle* had seventy-eight full members and thirty-four associates, with a ribbon weaver serving as president and Claude de Boissieu as president of the directing committee. Other members of the ruling class, especially Montgolfier, Victor Finaz, and Oriol, participated in the *cercles* and other more centralized Social Catholic institutions such as the Catholic Committee and the Industrial Commission. Both Thiollière and Neyrand became nationally prominent in the movement.[93]

The *cercles* in Saint Chamond functioned in a manner similar to others in France, reflecting a paradoxical attitude toward workers. Leaders encouraged workers to assume responsibilities within the *cercles* but insisted that they remain subordinate in an authoritarian and rigidly structured hierarchy. Because Social Catholics equated workers with children, the rules instructed the director to behave as a "loving father" and "give them the appearance of having great independence" while reserving for himself the role of "discreet but all-powerful guardian."[94] The *cercle* engaged workers in religious and social activities. They also provided a *caisse de famille* to supply aid to members in times of sickness or unemployment.[95]

In contrast to the national movement, Social Catholic institutions in Saint Chamond enjoyed comparative success. They received support from employers, persisted beyond the turn of the century, and by 1903 could boast 665 members, the majority of whom were reportedly workers.[96] This success can be attributed to a predisposition toward Catholicism in this town, but the talents of Camille Thiollière and Charles Neyrand also played a key role in shaping the local movement. These forge masters went beyond Albert de Mun's model of worker *cercles* and attempted to imitate Léon Harmel, the *bon père* known for his successful experiments in giving workers some control over his factory in Val-des-Bois (Nord). Neyrand set up a "union" in his factory, administered by a council of six employers and six workers. The union created a cooperative, subsidized by nuns who would care for sick workers in their homes. Neyrand's *cercle catholique* encouraged workers "to take a preponderant influence in the life of the factory."[97] While Neyrand and Thiollière did not succeed as well as Harmel, they received credit for averting the "hostile influence of anarchists, . . . pulling together the different elements of work in Saint Chamond and contributing to maintaining there an atmosphere of social peace."[98]

The Association of Catholic Employers was another institution through which employers of all ranks sought to reinforce Catholicism among workers, a purpose they could not state in their statutes, for it violated civil liberties. The exact relationship to Social Catholicism was made deliberately unclear, and the precise date of its formation is unknown. More than likely it first organized in the early 1870s and served as the employer organization which directed the workers' *cercles*. In 1889, its statutes indicated its professional purpose: to group together Catholic businessmen to defend themselves against enemies of the Church who might sabotage their economic interests.[99] The true goal of this organization, however, was to reinforce Christian belief among workers. The association's earlier statutes instructed members to develop religious principles and good morals among their workers. Each member had to conduct himself as a "good father of the family with workers" and promise never to assign work on Sundays. Employers had to enforce strict discipline in the workplace, for discipline provided the "basis of . . . prosperity and [the] source of well-being for the family of the worker." No fewer than one hundred employers belonged to this association. Members ranged from the large braid manufacturers—Chavanne and Brun—to foremen in the forges and small shopkeepers.[100]

The zeal with which employers in Saint Chamond pursued these duties in some cases violated workers' civil liberties and thus drew the attention of the public prosecutor's office in Lyon. Braid factory owners forced women workers who lived in their dormitories to attend mass twice a week, say prayers in common morning and night, go to confession, and receive communion. Although in principle these workers could choose not to participate in these religious exercises, "they all believed they would be fired if they refused."[101] Most employers did not house their workers and thus had less opportunity to instill religious habits in them, but other members of the association behaved in a spirit similar to that of the braid manufacturers.

Through the nineteenth century, but particularly during the industrial period, moralizing and preserving the labor force remained the dual goal of the local notables and employers in Saint Chamond. While their attention to the working classes reflected traditional values of noblesse oblige in a rigidly structured social hierarchy, the ruling elite were forced to adapt their strategies to the changing physical, political, and moral environment. The successive generations of employers demonstrated continuity in their adherence to Catholicism and authoritarian government; the most prominent bourgeois industrialists of Saint Chamond continued to mobilize themselves against anticlerical attacks, and some professed monarchist politics into the twentieth century. But the new elite in braid manufacturing and large-scale metallurgy, unlike their predecessors, found themselves in the position of having to defend a free market economy. Their strategies for dealing with the moral and physical well-being of the working class accordingly changed: they no longer administered charity indiscriminately to those who needed it. Instead, they exercised a paternalism in which they assumed more responsibility for instilling Catholic values in workers and used material aid as a means of disciplining them.

A variety of observers, inhabitants as well as travelers, suggested that efforts to reinforce Catholicism and discipline workers succeeded.[102] In addition to the testimonies referred to above, parish reports based on the number of parishioners receiving sacraments indicate that the workers of Saint Chamond practiced Catholicism more than those in neighboring towns through the turn of the century. And yet we must wonder if the perceptions of a military officer in 1843 may have held true for the rest of the century. He noted "more appearance than reality in this religious disposition . . . and the morality is very far from having any relationship to this exterior devotion and ostentation in which priests delight."[103]

If indeed there was more appearance than genuine piety in workers' religious activities, it no doubt resulted from the fact that the administration of material aid was, in the eyes of the Saint-Chamonais, as much a function of religious orders as was the administration of sacraments. Economic factors in the last two decades of the century exercised a more fundamental influence over their lives than religion did. Whether or not workers became indoctrinated with Catholicism, many of them did become recipients of charity and other sources of material aid through the hospice, all administered by employers and run by religious orders.

If this care did not help much to stem the rise in deathrates, it did become a factor in defining class relations. But while the relative quiescence among workers may have resulted in part from employer solicitude, it did not mean the elite had succeeded in shaping the working class in its own image. Indeed, beginning in the 1860s, a substantial number of workers in Saint Chamond began to articulate a political, if not moral, posture independent of their employers, which became more distinct by the end of the century.

6

Workers and Politics

Situated in the arrondissement of Saint Etienne, Saint Chamond is surrounded by cities with similar industries and economic conditions and which produced militant labor movements during the nineteenth century: Rive-de-Gier to the east, and Saint Etienne, Le Chambon-Feugerolles, and Firminy to the west. The entire industrial basin, as police agents and prefects were quick to point out, became vulnerable to political and social radicalism from Lyon. Saint Chamond, however, remained relatively tranquil in a region that suffered most of France's political and social storms. When the labor movement brought turmoil to neighboring cities, the ruling elite of Saint Chamond bragged complacently of their well-behaved workers. In one of his local histories, Fournier boasted, "Troublemakers, agitators, preachers of revolt do not hold our . . . peaceful, calm, and ordered city in much esteem. It is too wise or too intelligent for them. Our workers—sober, economical, thoughtful, attached to their homes—raise their small families there in complete quietude, in an atmosphere of harmony."[1]

This same author later reminisced, "Without any complaints, anger, fights . . . the four police agents did not know what to do with their time."[2] Series M in the departmental archives at first glance supports the complacent self-portrayal that local historians have offered. One must wade through numerous reports of contention in other cities before coming across the often slim accounts of events in Saint Chamond. Officials reported "the greatest tranquility" even during the tumultuous years of the early 1830s, 1848, 1851, and 1870–1871. During the Third Republic, the proclerical, antirepublican right wing in Saint Chamond attracted more attention from the police than did workers.

If political life in Saint Chamond remained relatively harmonious, another series in the departmental archives—registers of births, marriages, and deaths in Saint Chamond—affords a less

175

happy picture of this city. Material conditions brought considerable misfortune to the family lives of workers. Mortality and fertility rates suggest that Fournier's "small families" resulted as much
from horrible material conditions, poor health, and abortion as
from prudence. Without question, high rates of infant and child
mortality helped to minimize family size. In addition to a precarious family structure, workers experienced the complete restructur-
ing of industrial organization, the effects of cyclical economic crises
and the resulting unemployment or underemployment, the uprootedness of migration, inadequate housing, industrial pollution,
and chronic disease. The workers of Saint Chamond—natives and
migrants—suffered the same disruptions as workers in other industrializing cities but suffered them in a silence uncharacteristic
of the region. These two sides of Saint Chamond—social tranquility and harsh material conditions—are not easily reconciled.

It would be tempting to resolve this anomaly by concluding that
material assistance and Catholic moralization reduced class tensions in Saint Chamond. This conclusion, however, would do in-
justice to the complexity of class relations, particularly from the
viewpoint of workers, for we have said little about their responses
to elite solicitation. Moreover, it would not explain why paternalism was relatively successful in Saint Chamond when workers elsewhere rejected it. Examining workers' responses to charitable and
religious efforts in this city is exceedingly difficult, however, precisely because its "quiet" population left little record of its reac-
tions. But the absence of direct, documented response to employer
efforts at exerting hegemony over workers must not simply be
taken to mean that these efforts were successful.

A close examination of local politics reveals that workers appeared "tranquil" only in contrast to those in neighboring cities.
Though the Saint-Chamonais voted more conservatively than other
working-class populations in the Stéphanois region, they nonetheless supported republicanism rather than the monarchism of their
employers. The labor movement in Lyon, Rive-de-Gier, and Saint
Etienne, moreover, helped inspire and sustain a labor movement
in Saint Chamond. Not only did this population call its share of
strikes, but it elected socialists to its municipality and hosted a
sizable group of anarchists. Strike activity and the development of
independent working-class politics provide indirect evidence that

workers did not submit docilely to a reactionary, Catholic world-view; indeed, they assumed a posture quite distinct from that of their employers.

A number of critical factors did, however, limit the extent of the labor movement, the degree of militancy, and ultimately the mass basis of support necessary for socialists to gain the upper hand in local politics. The organization of work itself and the geographical and cultural uprootedness among workers inhibited independent associational life among them. In addition, and perhaps more important, the reactionary politics among the bourgeoisie and their charitable and moralizing activities did influence worker consciousness. Though workers exhibited cultural and political independence from the employer class, paternalism can be credited for preventing them from realizing their full potential for militancy. The anticlericalism of the left in particular divided workers, and the majority remained loyal to local priests for reasons other than religious sentiment. The vulnerability of working-class families and material assistance from religious congregations and employers help to explain the limits to militancy.

Like those in other Stéphanois cities, during the Second Empire workers in Saint Chamond began to develop a political consciousness independent of the elite. The silence of the 1850s stemmed more from repression than detachment, as the prefect signaled in 1858 when he assured the minister of the interior that new repressive measures brought into law that year kept anarchists in the Loire "living in fear."[3] Just a few years later more liberal constitutional reforms opened the dike for opposition to Napoleon III's regime. Industrialist Agamemnon Imbert, a machine constructor and former worker who employed 300 men, helped to organize Saint Chamond's first republican club and spread propaganda. The legislative elections of 1863 became the first sign, and a dramatic one, that workers in Stéphanois cities had become politically conscious. Despite a booming economy this consciousness translated into a rejection of the Empire. Just under 50 percent of the voters in Saint Chamond joined other Stéphanois in voting for opposition candidates.[4]

Stéphanois workers soon expressed further dissent after the legalization of strikes in 1864. In the summer of 1865 the prefect anxiously argued that "the nature of the industrial population"

required doubling the strength of the garrison in the arrondissement of Saint Etienne. Strikes broke out the following fall among
miners, masons, and velvet makers in Saint Etienne, which then
spread to the miners in Saint Chamond.[5] Dormant tensions revived
in 1869, a year of widespread strike activity in much of France.
Miners throughout the Loire coal basin went on strike in early
June. While prolonged and violent in Saint Etienne, the strike
among coal miners in Saint Chamond was short-lived. But it did
assume political overtones. Through the night of 14 June, workers
at the Saint Chamond pits sang the "Marseillaise," caused "tumultuous scenes," and boisterously proclaimed their support for the
republican candidate in their circumscription.[6]

By 1 July the police commissioner of Saint Chamond reported
that miners there had resumed work, and while it appeared that
the working classes were less hostile, he expressed concern that
the democratic press, by which he meant the *Eclaireur* of Saint
Etienne, had influenced workers in Saint Chamond: they had in-
contestably become more concerned with politics than previously.
But most workers, he reported confidently, would not follow the
leaders for very long. They "will conserve the cult of the great Na-
poleonic principle which responds so well to [their] aspirations and
genius."[7]

Just the following month, however, Saint-Chamonais metal workers went on strike. Repeating the pattern of workers throughout
the Lyonnais region, those in the Petin forges demanded a reduction in the workday from eleven to ten hours and a bonus of 50
percent for overtime. The company compromised and granted
them a one-half-hour reduction in the workday and a 40 percent
bonus for overtime. The workers peacefully accepted these conditions. In the spring of 1870, another wave of strikes hit Saint
Etienne and Rive-de-Gier. Workers in Saint Chamond did not
strike, but in August several hundred loudly protested their state
of unemployment by running through the city's streets and singing
the "Marseillaise." To this song they added the line, "and the Republic will reign in France."[8]

Strike activity during the 1860s in Saint Chamond thus not only
stemmed from demands for higher wages and shorter hours but
also became a vehicle through which workers began to demand a
republic—a political sentiment quite distinct from that of the em-

ployer class. Soon workers in Saint Chamond organized a more direct means of political expression, the Cercle des Travailleurs. Upon its creation in 1870, the club stated its purpose: to "propagate progressive and fraternal ideas" and "to assist in the development of intelligence," through a library, through readings of newspapers and other materials, and through lectures. Their office would also serve as a labor exchange. The police soon pointed out, however, that the club was composed of radical republicans whose true purpose was to combat the influence of the Saint Chamond monarchist club, the Cercle de la Ville, whose origins dated back to 1831.[9]

The 177 men who joined the Cercle des Travailleurs came from "workers of all categories." But the handful of leaders who merited close police scrutiny had primarily petit-bourgeois and even middle-class origins. These included the president, Deigas, who was a merchant tailor; Deschamps, a pharmacist; Jean Charvet, a laborer and former letter carrier; his brother Claude Charvet, a journeyman shoemaker; Pouget, a junk merchant; Gauthier, a café keeper; Jamet, a gallic acid manufacturer; Bergé, a braid manufacturer; Ollagnier, a wine merchant; and Loubet, Chanson, Payre, and Veyre, "simple workers living with much difficulty from the product of their work."[10] Some industrial workers no doubt numbered among the rank and file, but it is noteworthy that they provided no impetus or leadership for the club. As in Rive-de-Gier, Lyon, and Saint Etienne, radicalism came, not from industrial workers, but from artisans and small merchants.[11]

With notable exceptions such as Agamemnon Imbert and Paul Bergé, bourgeois industrialists in Saint Chamond did not share the republican sentiments developing among workers. Indeed, the growing republicanism deepened bourgeois commitment to the regime of Napoleon III. As believers in authoritarian government, these industrialists did not welcome the reforms for a more liberal constitution in 1860. As devout Catholics, they were offended by Napoleon III's support for Italian independence and the partial annexation of the papal states to the kingdom of Italy. Yet they clearly preferred the relatively authoritarian imperial government to any republican alternative.[12]

In this posture, the industrial bourgeoisie of Saint Chamond diverged from its counterpart in Saint Etienne, who helped mobilize republican opposition to the government. There industrialists opposed economic measures the government had taken, particularly the Cobden-Chevalier Treaty of 1860 establishing free trade with England. Republican opposition among the industrialists, moreover, provided leadership and impetus for a working-class republicanism that eventually turned against the middle class.[13] The industrialists of Saint Chamond, however, supported most of the government's economic policies. The Cobden-Chevalier Treaty had been a boon to braid makers. The metallurgical firms were large enough to escape its negative impacts. The Petin and Gaudet Company indeed owed its growth and prosperity to government orders. They no doubt also felt a personal loyalty to the emperor, for he had awarded them the medal of the Legion of Honor. Profit from economic policies and abhorrence for republicanism thus inspired the Saint-Chamonais Catholic, monarchist elite to continue its support for the Empire during its liberal phase in the 1860s.[14] In the plebiscite of May 1870, 60 percent of the voters in Saint Chamond endorsed the Empire. This vote, which was essentially a vote in favor of order and in opposition to republicanism, demonstrated that the city's conservative and reactionary elite still held a good deal of influence over voters. In contrast, voters in Saint Etienne and Le Chambon-Feugerolles overwhelmingly rejected the Empire.[15]

The Franco-Prussian War and the fall of the Second Empire, however, jolted the Legitimist elite from its monopoly of power in Saint Chamond and brought republicans into the municipal government. As soon as Napoleon III met with humiliating defeat in September 1870, the Cercle des Travailleurs quickly mobilized itself, presented candidates for the municipal council, and spread electoral propaganda among workers. The members of the new municipal council constituted on 24 September 1870 came from this group, including Deschamps, Deigas, Chanson, Gauthier, Jamet, Loubet, Payre, Pouget, Veyre, and Imbert.[16] These elections and subsequent prefectoral action deprived Catholic monarchists of control over Saint Chamond and unseated such figures as Emile Alamagny, Irenée Brun, Dugas-Vialis, Victor Louis Finaz, Henri Neyrand, Louis Zavier Pascal, Ennemond Richard, and Henri Thiollière.[17]

In contrast to workers in Rive-de-Gier, Saint Etienne, and Lyon, radical republicans in Saint Chamond remained relatively moderate. The Paris insurrection that began on 18 March 1871 sparked militant activity in these other cities, and workers in Saint Etienne and Lyon even established communes. The Saint Chamond municipal council contented itself with making an official commitment to republicanism. On 4 April 1871 it sent an address to the National Assembly expressing fear that this body was preparing "a restoration of the monarchy," which the country did not want. "The Republic is above all discussion, above universal suffrage itself. No one has the right to alienate his liberty, still less that of his descendants." [18]

But the appointed mayor, Deschamps, soon alienated a substantial number of Saint-Chamonais over issues other than republicanism. Legend has it that upon entering the city hall he put a symbolic end to the Empire by throwing the bust of Napoleon III out the window. More offensive to the Saint-Chamonais was his anticlericalism and that of his colleague, César Pouget, an "enemy of priests and religion." The latter appointed himself cantonal delegate of primary instruction and laicized Saint Chamond's communal schools. To this measure Saint Chamond's Catholics responded with substantial enough donations to reestablish the teaching congregations. In May, the clergy still received nearly three-fourths of the city's 1,047 children. [19] Even if the majority of Saint-Chamonais parted company from the monarchist elite in their support of republicanism, anticlericalism turned many against the municipality. In the same month, conservative former mayor Jules Duclos was returned to the office by proclamation. [20] The issue of anticlericalism confused republican sentiment in Saint Chamond, as it would on many future occasions.

Through most of 1873, the members of the Cercle des Travailleurs numbered about 200 and remained well organized. According to the police, they propagated "doctrines of the commune" and "spread revolutionary electoral propaganda" among workers in Saint Chamond and the surrounding region. Apart from promoting anticlericalism, it seems their main preoccupation was to prevent monarchists from regaining power. In any case, this group forced a political realignment in the city. In response to their activity, 148 middle-class conservative republicans established a Cercle de l'Industrie et du Commerce in January 1872. In the previous elections to the General Council, the conservative candidate had backed down in favor of the Legitimist, but the latter lost to the radical republican. The moderate republicans thus realized that they had to organize their own political group to combat the "radical democracy which grows worse every day in the spirit of the worker population."[21] In requesting from the prefect the requisite official sanction, both the mayor, Jules Duclos, and the police commissioner stressed that this group included only "men of order and honor." Even though it was illegal for *cercles* to discuss politics or religion, both the mayor, himself a member of the club, and the commissioner emphasized that the club should be sanctioned despite its political intent, for it would help to establish social peace in Saint Chamond.[22]

Industrialists, entrepreneurs, businessmen, merchants, and master workers composed the club's membership. Among them numbered several braid manufacturers—including Emile Alamagny as president and Benoît Oriol—numerous dye masters, and forge master Chavanne-Brun. In their paternalism, Catholicism, and fear of democracy, these conservative republicans shared much with the Legitimists. Indeed, radical republican César Pouget said of Alamagny that he would give "100,000 francs to be . . . received in the great Legitimist families."[23] They differed principally in their social origins and in their reluctant but pragmatic acceptance of republicanism. It was through pressure from this group that the prefect finally dissolved the Cercle des Travailleurs in August 1873, for violating the law against political activity, the same law the Cercle de l'Industrie itself broke with sanction from the police, prefect, and mayor.[24]

The dissolution of the radical republican group in Saint Chamond came at a time when monarchists on both the national and local level had begun to regain power and establish the "moral order," the conservative reply to the "sins" of the Paris Commune. This label refers specifically to the period beginning with MacMahon's replacement of Thiers as chief executive in May 1873 and extending to the legislative elections of October 1877. During these years proclerical monarchists dominated the National Assembly. The humiliating defeat to the Prussians made them believe that France had become sinful and frivolous, diseased by the virus of freethinking and irreligion. Concrete manifestations of their sentiments abounded. It was during these years that Albert de Mun attempted to address the problems of industrialization with the establishment of Social Catholic institutions meant to moralize both workers and employers.[25] Paris built its Sacré Coeur to atone for its sins; Lyon, Limoges, and many other cities erected comparable structures.

Saint Chamond rebuilt its beloved Notre Dame, and Neyrand and Thiollière founded their *cercles catholiques*. Social Catholicism established itself in this city with some degree of coercion. One resident wrote that "since the foundation of the *cercle catholique* our city is turned upside down and we no longer understand what is happening." "The Jesuits" apparently forced people to join, threatening them with a fall from grace if they did not. Marists and Brothers of the Christian Doctrine supported the *cercle*, but some of the parish priests opposed it and were forced to leave.[26]

Employers in Saint Chamond established other social, economic, and political institutions which manifested their solidarity. Their spirit of cooperation is best symbolized in the Association of Catholic Employers formed sometime in the 1870s. The twenty-two founding members included Adrien de Montgolfier; braid manufacturers Gabriel, Florian, and Jules Balas, François Gillet, and Léon Chaland; forge masters Camille Thiollière and Charles, Eugène, and André Neyrand; notables Charles de Boissieu and Victor, René, and Louis Finaz; and eight other industrialists and notables. In addition to the founders, the association numbered more than one hundred members, most of whom were small-scale employers and shopkeepers, although other major industrialists in addition to the founders also joined. Among them, for example, were Irenée Brun and his sons, whose factories in and around Saint Chamond employed nearly a thousand workers.[27]

No institution could better represent the spirit of cooperation between the old elite and the new. The association's ostensible purpose was "to find all the possible means for supporting and fostering small local commerce" and "to cooperate in the professional prosperity of other members . . . by according them preference [in] purchases and orders." Their pretext for such cooperation lay in their fear that the "enemies of the church" were trying to "destroy the influence of Catholics by impoverishing them and by closing their activity to all the roads that lead to an independent situation."²⁸ As we have already seen, they had as another purpose to wean their workers away from republicanism by reinforcing their Catholicism.

The Catholic elite also organized itself politically. In 1873 Victor Louis Finaz formed a Catholic Committee or monarchist-clerical party which included some of the most important industrialists in the Stéphanois, such as Charles Neyrand, Camille Thiollière, Hippolyte Petin, and forge master J. Euverte from Rive-de-Gier.²⁹ Adrien de Montgolfier proved to be the most important and most influential figure among them. In 1874, at age forty-three, Montgolfier assumed the directorship of the Petin-Gaudet forges, the Aciéries de la Marine et des Chemins de Fer. Prior to his takeover of the steelworks, he had served as chief engineer of roads and bridges, as cantonal delegate of instruction, and since 1871, as a monarchist deputy to the National Assembly.³⁰ It is ironic that for nearly forty years the very defense of the Republic rested in part on a company whose director vehemently opposed republicanism. In his own mind, of course, Montgolfier was helping to defend the nation, not the government which he detested. The military importance of the steelworks combined with Montgolfier's own political shrewdness gave him considerable influence in Paris, which in turn brought him renown and brought economic profit to Saint Chamond.

In the discourse of the Catholic Committee one can detect its fundamental principles: Christian morality and economic liberty. Each had to be defended against the anticlericalism and political liberalism of the fledgling Third Republic. These industrial monarchists feared that universal suffrage would result in legislation that would compromise the freedom of the marketplace. Charles Neyrand's statement during the 1876 legislative elections looked to an authoritarian government to assure the preservation of these two principles:

> I will defend religion against the attacks that revolutionary atheism and this so-called liberal hypocrisy are preparing to wage against it. I will defend property against the endeavors of dangerous utopians who, under the pretext of distributing equitably the burdens on each and every one of us, will fatally arrive, by the theory of progressive taxation, at the absolute negation of the right of ownership and, in so doing, will ruin private and public fortune.³¹

In the years following the formation of the Catholic Committee, many of its members and their sympathizers regained power. Notable Claude de Boissieu became mayor in 1874, and Henri Neyrand, Victor Louis Finaz, Camille Thiollière, and the director of the Company of Mines, de Beauvais, all served on the municipal council.[32] Shortly after they returned to power, a return sanctioned by the national atmosphere of "moral order," they witnessed a degree of class conflict hitherto unknown in their once peaceful community.

Workers in Saint Chamond had lost their political power base through the dissolution of the Cercles des Travailleurs and the ousting of radical republicans from the municipality. But the republican and communard ideology had changed their view of employers and had made it impossible for politically conscious workers to embrace the same moral vision. For the first time since 1869, strikes broke out in 1875. Dye workers, who had replaced ribbon weavers as the largest male occupational group in textiles, fought for their autonomy and independence. In May 1875, almost all the city's 500 dyers went on strike to reduce the length of the workday. They also agitated for the right to name their own foremen, directly challenging the authority of employers. In the employers' view, each concession would only result in further demands. They were willing to concede the reduction in the workday, but only on the condition of a promise to stay overtime when necessary. The dye workers reluctantly agreed to accept overtime work with bonuses. Although the strike ended peacefully, the police commissioner warned that dye workers expressed "extreme jealousy" for the wealth of others and a "profound hatred of the rich." Significantly, more than half of the dye masters against whom workers struck belonged to the conservative Cercle de l'Industrie et du Commerce.[33]

Employers could not rest easy with the strikers' success, particularly because it had challenged their authority over workers. In an effort to reinforce deference and discipline, the Richard and Puthod dyeworks posted a warning that any insult, disobedience, or unauthorized absence gave the foreman the right to fire workers. The dyers took this notice as a violation of their liberty and an insult to their dignity. In a clear assertion of their moral independence, 200 walked out. The strike ended quickly with a compromise. Employers established more equitable guidelines for the dismissal of workers; the latter had to pledge that they would in the future give three days' notice prior to any work stoppage, in order to avoid damaging the silks.[34]

Insubordination then spread to the metal industry. The following month, June of 1875, 286 of the 1,600 workers in Montgolfier's steelworks, the Aciéries de la Marine, protested the temporary elimination of the night shift because it meant the layoff of nearly 50 percent of the plant's work force. The protesters would accept a reduction of hours so that layoffs could be avoided. They circulated petitions in the workshops of smaller forges throughout the city, hoping to set off a major strike. Unable to believe that his workers could be at once so disloyal and so well organized, Montgolfier assumed that outside agitators had instigated the movement. In the end he succeeded in thwarting the strike, in part because he had more than the police behind him. Since the production of cannons for the military was at stake, concern over this possible strike extended well beyond Saint Chamond. The central government prepared the army to intervene, a measure that ended the movement.[35]

The strike and strike threats of 1875 were followed by legislative elections in 1876 that eroded Legitimist power in Saint Chamond. The Catholic Committee mobilized all its resources for this election. Montgolfier, who became a senator after the passage of the Wallon Amendment of 1875, used his power and prestige to back monarchist candidates, particularly Charles Neyrand. Neyrand posed a serious threat to the republicans, for as a leading industrialist and member of a long-established family in the region he enjoyed widespread popularity.[36] The republican newspaper did what it could to undermine him: "You disguise your clerical and Legitimist opinions under an insipid phraseology; your manner of walking like a common man, your patois, the social and democratic pipe that you smoke incessantly in the street, fool no one, for each knows that under this appearance [of simplicity] hides a zealous, intolerant, ruthless reactionary."[37] Neyrand lost to the radical republican candidate Richarme by a wide margin in the arrondissement of Saint Etienne. Although Saint Chamond gave a higher portion of its votes to Neyrand than did any other canton—even the previously reactionary rural ones—it too favored Richarme with 58 percent of the vote.[38]

Local conservatives suffered further setbacks after President MacMahon's ill-fated coup of *seize mai* in 1877. Part of MacMahon's effort to manipulate the legislative elections had consisted of ordering prefects to revoke republican mayors and municipal council members. In this same year, the paternalist and Catholic braid manufacturer Benoît Oriol had been elected mayor. Despite his very conservative republicanism, the prefect dissolved the entire municipal council on 24 August, replacing Oriol with the former mayor, Legitimist Claude de Boissieu. The usual Legitimists returned to the council. But this tampering with the municipal government had unfortunate consequences for conservatives and reactionaries after the ultimate republican victory over MacMahon. Saint Chamond responded to the coup in the same manner as most of France, giving 66 percent of its votes to the republican candidate in the legislative elections of October 1877. The city elected into office a municipal council and a mayor, Marius Chavanne, who proved sympathetic to the labor movement.[39]

The new municipal government elected early in 1878 overtly encouraged workers to organize and gave particular inspiration to dye workers. The police complained that Marius Chavanne granted "official consecration" to militant speakers by permitting them to use municipal halls for their speeches.[40] Workers took advantage of this support. In the summer of 1878 dye workers once again went on strike, this time demanding standardized pay and pay raises for both skilled and unskilled workers. In violation of the pledge they had made in 1875, the dyers gave no notice of their work stoppage, and at 2 o'clock in the afternoon quit the dyeworks, leaving silk in acid baths. The prolonged soaking in acid resulted in an alleged 100,000 franc loss for the owners of the dyeworks.[41]

As 400 workers in Saint Chamond and 300 in the neighboring communes of Izieux, Saint-Martin-en-Coallieux, and Lavalla joined the strike, dyeworks shut down completely; their closure in turn interfered with ribbon, braid, and silk fabric production. Mayor Chavanne had already incurred the anger of police and employers by leaving the city to take a water cure just as the strike broke out. Far more serious were the allegations that his adjunct, Claude Raymond, had been the principal organizer of the strike. A former master dye worker himself, Raymond not only supported the strike but referred to employers (his former competitors) as exploit-ers and encouraged workers to leave the silk in the acid baths.[42] Class consciousness became more pronounced as dye workers appealed for assistance from Lyon. The Trade Union Committee of Dye Workers wrote that they waged their strike "in the name of the social principles and of solidarity. . . . We can finish this battle victoriously with the cooperation of all the colleagues and citizens guided by fraternal love which must make us succeed in the liberation of the proletariat."[43]

This strike had a massive and unforgettable impact on Saint Chamond when female braid makers joined the dyers; nearly 5,000 workers in and around the city stopped working. Yet these numbers are deceptive. A coalition between dye workers and braid makers might have been a powerful weapon against the employer class, not only because dyeing was a "collaborator with weaving in the silk industry" but because members of the same family often worked in the two branches of the industry, which might have facilitated organization and strengthened solidarity among workers. Police indeed referred to an "alliance" between those two groups of workers in 1878.[44] The respective strikes had no direct relationship, however. Dyers neither encouraged nor helped braid makers. Instead, a certain Mlle Finet from Lyon, a "habitual orator on women's rights," gave a speech in Saint Chamond that provoked braid makers to leave their work.[45] The ability of this feminist, an *étrangère* no less, to inspire a strike testifies to the double exploitation braid makers felt as workers and as women. But even before the 300 women in the Oriol and Alamagny factory threatened to stop working, Oriol engineered an agreement with the other braid manufacturers to close all the factories if a strike began in one of them. It was the shutdown, not the strike, that put 4,200 women out of work. It also locked a substantial proportion of them out of factory dormitories and virtually threw them into the streets.[46]

In contrast to the dye workers' month-long effort, the women stayed away from the factories for only one week. Their employers made no concessions. But the dye workers' strike failed completely as well. Rather than giving workers the advantage, the occupational structure in Saint Chamond may have helped to prevent their success. The interdependency of dyeworks and braiding gave employers, rather than workers, the advantage in quelling strikes. To the extent that dye workers themselves depended on women's industrial employment, they would suffer if their wives and daughters went on strike. The double interdependency of male and female workers on the one hand and the braid industry and dyeworks on the other may have hastened the failure of both strikes in 1878.

Industrialists in Saint Chamond thus succeeded in resisting the strikers' demands despite support from the municipality for the dye workers. Indeed, the radicalism of Marius Chavanne played an important role in forging a common front between dye masters and braid manufacturers. Chavanne nonetheless continued to assist workers in organizing. In 1880, the municipal council gave metal workers the use of the town theater to establish a union; they met two or three times with a delegate from the workers' congress of Lyon. Despite this municipal support, the meetings attracted the interest of only about six metal workers, a clear sign that they did not yet have the basis for a sustained labor movement.[47]

In 1881, Chavanne, like his predecessor Deschamps ten years earlier, incurred further animosity when he suppressed congregational schools. The monarchists finally succeeded in ousting him from the municipal government in 1882 when the deputy mayor and secretary were discovered to have embezzled money from the city. Adjunct Paul Bergé, a braid manufacturer, radical republican, and former member of the Cercle des Travailleurs, served as mayor for about two years. But in 1884, Benoît Oriol, whose Catholicism carried more weight than his conservative republicanism, returned to office as mayor.[48]

The labor movement and working-class politics in Saint Chamond suffered serious setbacks in the 1880s. Not only did workers lose municipal support but they suffered a severe economic crisis which undermined their leverage with employers. At the same time, monarchists regained influence, particularly through the divisive issue of clericalism. The economic difficulties primarily hit the metallurgical industry and thus affected a majority of the adult male workers. The crisis stemmed from the implementation of the Thomas-Gilchrist process, first developed in 1878. Until that time only choice minerals could be used for cast iron in steel production. This new process permitted the use of lower-quality minerals. Prices plummeted. This major innovation also came just when the demand for steel rails dropped. Annual steel production in the

Loire suddenly fell by 60,000 tons. Some of the steelworks were forced to close completely; others moved. The number of workers in neighboring Terrenoire dropped from 14,000 to 6,000.[49]

In part because it had government contracts, but also because of skilled direction, the Saint Chamond steel industry survived this crisis relatively intact. Montgolfier's Aciéries de la Marine, for example, converted to the production of fine steel and developed new specialties.[50] Nonetheless, the 1880s required considerable adjustment that resulted in high levels of unemployment and worker-employer tension. Two days before Christmas in 1882, management at the Aciéries de la Marine informed workers that 80 to 100 of them would be dismissed at the end of the month. The company claimed the layoffs resulted from a decline in orders. In fact, they had just received a substantial order for cannons from the Mexican government. Their true purpose was to eliminate the night shift because maintenance of certain equipment and the detection of malfunctioning during the night hours had become too difficult.[51]

Within a few months the company again used the excuse of a slowdown in orders to change from day wages to piecework for turners and molders. The latter found piecework particularly onerous and unjust. The issue was not simply that they would earn less but that they lost control over their work. With piecework, the company paid workers for every 100 kilograms fabricated. But if a cast mold did not succeed, workers would receive nothing for a month's work unless the company guaranteed them a minimum salary. One hundred molders and turners went on strike in June and July 1883, when the company agreed only to guarantee 35 percent of the daily wage instead of the requested 90 percent. Montgolfier expressed astonishment, for he believed that piecework would profit workers. "All they need do is work a little harder," he protested, "and they will be able to earn as much!" The strikers responded that they already produced as much as they possibly could, and piecework would result in reduced wages. The strike spread to the Neyrand and Thiollière factories in L'Horme.[52]

After two weeks, only four workers returned to Montgolfier's plant, and the company fired the rest of the strikers.[53] As the workers petitioned unions and individuals in the community for funds, the dispute became more political. In August, a meeting to benefit the strikers drew 225 people. Jean Ablemanc of the National Committee of Paris "preached socialism" to the group. Five months later, in January 1884, 400 people attended another benefit lecture over which former mayor Marius Chavanne presided. The lecture addressed "the social question."[54]

Despite this prolonged strike activity and its clear impact on worker consciousness in Saint Chamond, with the help of the economic crisis in the early 1880s and a more conservative atmosphere nationally, reactionary employers regained their political influence. In the elections of October 1885, conservatives throughout France and in the Loire made substantial gains. Three parties presented candidates in the Loire. The Union Républicaine, also called the Alliance Républicaine, consisted of opportunist moderate republicans. Representing the extreme left were the radical-socialists, who included some anarchists and enjoyed substantial support in Saint Etienne. The monarchist party had two elements: families from the old nobility with wealth based in agriculture, considered to be pure monarchists, and newer industrialists, who opposed republicanism but promised to uphold the constitution. The monarchists' final electoral list which, after much deliberation, favored the industrial group included Charles Neyrand, Petin, and Euverte. The prefect predicted that despite the great popularity of these paternalist forge masters, the monarchist list would place third in the arrondissement of Saint Etienne because it lacked support among the workers.[55]

To the prefect's surprise, the radical-socialists lost miserably in the first ballot, and monarchists came in a close second to the Republican alliance, a mere 1,000 votes behind. Joined by radical-socialists in the second ballot, the moderate Republican alliance won easily. But once again Saint Chamond voted more conservatively than the other Stéphanois cities and gave the republicans but a slim victory. Agamemnon Imbert received just 4 more votes than monarchist Neyrand; only 142 votes separated the republican candidate who came in first from the monarchist who came in last.[56]

The monarchists owed the support they received to an issue that had come to divide France deeply in the 1880s: attacks against the church. In their campaign of 1885, conservatives focused most on the threat of anticlericalism. Once again, the attitude of the Saint-Chamonais toward congregations served as a bellwether for their politics. Even though they favored the Republic as a form of government, the majority of residents in Saint Chamond again resisted the anticlericalism of the Third Republic. Their support for clerics became apparent, for example, in 1884, when upon becoming mayor, conservative republican Oriol circulated a petition to reestablish the religious schools and gained the signatures of Saint-Chamonais in every neighborhood, occupation, and social class. The religious schools continued to teach classes with the support of 80 percent of the pupils and their families.[57]

The monarchists exploited this proclerical sentiment in joining with clergy and waging what the prefect later called a "dirty campaign." In their sermons and instruction—even in the confessional—priests attempted to manipulate votes. The special police commissioner reported to the minister of the interior that priests were telling their parishioners to "pray for this poor France which agonizes . . . that these sectarians will be ruined. [Pray] for this poor France from which God and his ministers are chased and [pray] in the churches where soon praying will no longer be permitted." The commissioner pointed out that this was being said in every commune. "When the priest does not say it from the pulpit," he continued, "he whispers it in the ear of his penitents."[58] The curé of Saint Pierre, Father Bouvard, had a reputation for prudence and moderation. But even he exhorted his faithful to pray that the next elections would result in the "greatest good for France."[59] He had no need to tell his parishioners directly that the greatest good for France would be an end to the anticlerical Third Republic.

Exploiting working-class material insecurity, reactionary industrialists added to this spiritual blackmail a more worldly one. Neyrand in particular was accused of bribing workers to vote for the reactionary party and to convince their friends to do so as well. Reactionaries paid their workers to distribute ballots with the conservative list in cafés and to convince their friends that if Neyrand, Euverte, and Petin did not win, the factories would close.[60] Their argument had particular potency for workers during this period of crisis and adjustment in the steel industry. Unemployment remained high, and much of the steel work depended upon government contracts.

During the 1885 electoral campaign, the conservative municipality provided aid for unemployed workers. The hospice, run by the same people who dominated the municipal council, spent

18,000 francs to help those out of work.[61] Monarchists and moderate republicans sat on the administrative commission and decided to support unemployed workers. They joined hands in acknowledging that charity was better than socialism. This aid began seven months prior to the legislative elections.

Though the majority of Saint-Chamonais voted republican in the legislative elections of 1887 and 1888, material assistance from the municipality apparently influenced voters to continue supporting conservatives and monarchists, for they persisted in electing them to the municipal council. Paternalist, reactionary industrialists Eugène Neyrand, Louis Jury, and Jean Pascal received the most votes and shared power on the council only with weak republicans such as Vial and Fabreguettes. The one known radical republican whose name appeared on the list of council members in 1888, Rochefort, garnered the fewest votes.[62] The composition of the municipal government between 1878 and 1882 had clearly been important to workers' efforts at gaining independence from their employers. Thanks in part to the unfortunate corruption of Chavanne and his cohorts, that influence became extinct in the early 1880s—just when steel workers most needed support.

However workers in Saint Chamond felt about charitable assistance, its availability eroded the basis for independent associational activity. Socialists in Saint Etienne, for example, had, with good reason, come to be suspicious of public aid as they witnessed ribbon weavers "suffer in silence and count on public aid to help them." Ribbon weavers in that city remained moderate in their republicanism and avoided radical politics.[63] Why should workers form a union and pay the monthly dues of one franc—which might or might not give them assistance in times of sickness or need—when employers, the municipality, Saint Vincent de Paul, and the Sisters of Saint Charles already provided that protection?

Only in the 1890s did trade unions form in Saint Chamond and begin to offer some of the same protection employers, the municipality, and the church had long been providing for workers. Beginning with miners in November 1889, by the end of 1893 dye workers, elastic weavers, masons, and metal workers had all formed unions. By January 1894, a total of 505 men had unionized and had collected funds amounting to 3,139 francs.[64] This number comprised 7.8 percent of the employed population and roughly 12.6

percent of the employed men.[65] Though still a small fraction of the workers in Saint Chamond, this percentage constitutes a rate far higher than the French average for mining, metallurgy, textiles, and construction for the years 1884–1897.[66]

Workers who unionized not only exerted independence from their employers but became radical in their politics. All the unions that formed in Saint Chamond at this time allocated funds for general expenses to maintain the organization itself as well as to aid sick or needy members, providing a chance for workers to become independent of employer-sponsored mutual aid funds. Just as significant, they allocated a portion of their funds for support of strikes outside their own occupations. Though it numbered only eighty members, the molders' and modelers' union collected the largest amount, 1,140 francs, some of which they sent to metal workers in Rive-de-Gier and to glassmakers in Saint Etienne.[67] The existence of this *syndicat* caused further hand-wringing on the part of the Saint Chamond police commissioner, who noted that most of the unionized molders and modelers from the Aciéries de la Marine professed "revolutionary socialist opinions," while others identified themselves as anarchists.[68]

The revolutionary socialism of the molders and modelers and their example of having obtained a ten-hour day inspired the formation of a union among other metal workers in Saint Chamond. The Saint Etienne Bourse du Travail quickly provided assistance. The union of metal workers in turn professed "very advanced socialist opinions in the meetings of their corporation" and regularly engaged in political activity, especially during municipal or legislative elections. They too supported strikes outside Saint Chamond.[69]

Other unions in Saint Chamond also provided generous support to striking workers elsewhere. Masons and miners sent funds to metal workers in Rive-de-Gier, stonecutters in Dijon, glove makers in Nantes, and miners in Saint Florine (Haute-Loire). These unions, the police commissioner noted, also exhibited "overt participation in politics."[70]

Despite their identification with workers outside their own trades and outside their city, the Saint-Chamonais commitment to the labor movement had limits. Two key meetings took place in January 1893, with molders providing the nucleus. Simmonet, a representative from the Fédération des Chambres Syndicales Métallurgiques de France in Paris, came to urge the Saint Chamond metal workers' unions to federate; representatives from Saint Etienne and Rive-de-Gier came as well, to plead for support for striking metal workers in the latter city. The molders of Saint Chamond considered a sympathy strike but decided against it. They did, however, donate 171f70 to support the Rive-de-Gier strikers. The following week 120 metal workers attended a meeting with union representatives from Saint Etienne. Once again, they gave money at the door to support their colleagues in Rive-de-Gier but exhibited reluctance to federate, apparently because they perceived the leaders as ambitious politicians and distrusted them.[71]

But these workers showed more commitment in their own political activity. Metal workers, all employees of the Aciéries de la Marine, headed the socialist committee in Saint Chamond, which met regularly at the Rouchouse café. They in turn established Cercles d'Etudes Sociales to educate workers even though, according to the police, none of the founders themselves had any education. A group of anarchists also became visible during the 1890s. About 200 of them existed in the arrondissement of Saint Etienne, half of them in the city itself. The police considered only about 40 to be "dangerous" and worth spying on.[72] Saint Chamond's police commissioner felt differently about the anarchists in his own jurisdiction. They met regularly at two cafés, and even though they caused almost no overt trouble they inspired the commissioner to make repeated requests for more police agents. The six agents in Saint Chamond had to oversee a population of 23,000 in the entire canton, which included, the commissioner claimed, around 80 anarchists. The commissioner's anxiety portrays a situation opposite to the one described by local author Fournier, who boasted, "Without any complaints, anger, fights . . . the four police agents did not know what to do with their time."[73]

This apparently sudden radicalization among many Saint-Chamonais coincided with the growth of socialist and anarchist movements throughout France in the 1890s. Militancy in this city indeed pales in comparison with that in some other industrial cities such as Limoges and Saint Etienne.[74] But a number of events occurred during these years that suggested, either through direct resistance or by symbolic gestures, that a critical mass among Saint

Chamond's working class rejected the moral and material hegemony the monarchist and republican bourgeois elite tried to exercise over it. Small gestures, insignificant by themselves, occurred with increasing frequency. Although most political groups in Saint Chamond mourned the assassination of President Sadi Carnot, certain elements, anarchists being among the prime suspects, tried to make a hero of his murderer, Sante Caserio. In July 1894, the month following Carnot's death, during a Bastille Day celebration a small group sang a song claiming Caserio would be avenged; during the most important celebration in Saint Chamond the following September, a woman wanted to display a wax figure of the assassin.[75]

Irreverence extended even into the hospice in the late 1880s and through the 1890s. Nuns reported that insubordination began to increase after—and apparently in reaction to—conservative success in the municipal elections of 1888. Both the young in the orphanage and the old in the home for the aged exhibited disobedience and impiety on numerous occasions. The men became drunk more frequently and their Thursday outings had to be suppressed for eight months. Children became so disrespectful and undisciplined that the nuns had to be replaced with male lay teachers. The administrative commission had to take several measures to increase internal security. In order to make supervision more effective, they decided to keep all but one of the doors locked at all times and to place a guard at the unlocked one.[76]

In the 1890s women, more than any other group, exhibited "complaints, anger, fights." They were the only workers to go on strike. Their strikes have interest not only for the momentary assertiveness they reveal but because they demonstrate clearly the limits of male support among workers as well as among the paternalist employers. At issue was a cutback in working hours and thus a decline in wages. In August and September 1890, the Balas, Brun-Jury, and Castel-Patisseur braid firms reduced the workday by 25 percent, from 11.5 hours to 8.5 hours. They reduced wages by 10 percent. The workers preferred the longer days at their previous wages. Close to 400 women in these three firms went on strike, but after a few days they returned under the employers' conditions.[77] A year later the Brun-Jury firm reduced wages a further 20 percent, and the Levy company followed suit. One of the workers wrote to the prefect, "It's shameful on the part of [employers] who earn millions because of female workers. They recently bought more properties in the Midi as large as the city of Saint Chamond. What are they lacking? They want workers to be their slaves." [78] Braid makers struck in both firms, but once again they returned without concessions and accepted the 20 percent reduction in their wages. [79]

In 1893, 300 workers from these same firms went on strike when employers reduced the workday further by one half-hour and lowered daily wages from 1f80 to 1f70. The law of 2 November 1892 pressed employers to take this action. It required a break of one hour instead of one half-hour. Until then, the women worked at two 8½-hour shifts, one from 4 A.M. to 1 P.M. and the other from 1 P.M. to 10 P.M. Manufacturers could not accommodate the added half-hour break because the law also prohibited women from working after 10 P.M. or before 4 A.M. The strikers submitted a petition to the police commissioner requesting that the law be interpreted more liberally in their case, and that they continue their previous work schedule with one half-hour break. The petition stressed that the old schedule permitted them to combine wage-earning with housekeeping and mothering. [80]

As these women confronted the employers, they also became their pawns. Manufacturers had a keen interest in preserving the two 8½-hour shifts; returning to a single 11-hour-day shift would have been their only alternative, and with that they would have lost four hours of production. The police stressed that in their own opposition to the law of 2 November 1892, manufacturers had deliberately pushed workers to strike. Levy had reportedly prompted his headmistress to organize the strike in his factory. The police affirmed that employers had themselves prepared the workers' petition. Indeed, with refined language, this petition deferentially and compassionately referred to the impossible situation in which foreign competition had placed the women's bosses. But its intent did represent workers' interest, and 200 braid makers converged on the police station to sign it. In the end, the braid manufacturers agreed to comply with the law, and the striking workers had no choice but to return to the factories at 10 centimes less per day. [81] Although they were ever willing to send funds to workers outside Saint Chamond, established unions there gave no assistance to the locally striking braid makers.

A further incident involving braid makers illustrates the limits of any moral hegemony the industrial and Catholic elite had tried to extend over workers. In October 1895, in the Levy braid factory, three female workers raped a fifteen-year-old girl with a loom spindle while fifty others looked on with amusement. Her youth, physical attractiveness, naiveté, and virginity had reportedly inspired jealousy and malice on the part of others.[82] This incident caused turmoil far beyond the factory and produced descriptions of common morality in Saint Chamond found nowhere else. The radical press in Saint Etienne, *L'Eclaireur*, exploited the incident as an occasion to expose industrialists' mismanagement of the workplace and to decry the miserable situation in which factory work had placed women. The press also revealed in no uncertain terms their own views toward these workers. *L'Eclaireur* referred to the women as "female animals" and as "unfortunates who seek pleasurable satisfactions among themselves because men are a minority in Saint Chamond." The article continued:

> It is well known that in Saint Chamond the braid factories are not convents, and the workers are not even half-virgin. . . . In their excess of nymphomania, the workers go to the point of using their spindles and other implements. . . . The worst practices are common among these poor, veritably possessed girls. . . . This is a dreadful sickness which can easily be remedied by facilitating early marriage.[83]

The account implied that this incident, far from being isolated, resulted from sexual excess among the women. The incident itself and its depiction in the newspapers suggest that the Association of Catholic Employers had failed in their efforts to moralize workers. As a Jewish employer, Levy did not participate in Social Catholicism, but the newspaper attack generalized the "woman problem" to all of Saint Chamond's young female workers. The braid manufacturers united against the slander in *L'Eclaireur* and eventually avenged themselves. The newspaper described the incident in such explicit detail that the braid manufacturers successfully sued the editors for publishing pornography. The latter had to pay a fine of 50 francs. The three attackers received five-month prison sentences which were later reduced to three months.[84]

The formation of workers' unions, the growing visibility of socialists and anarchists, the braid makers' strikes, and other gestures of insubordination occurred during years of economic crisis that reached a peak in 1894. Foreign competition forced cutbacks in braid production, which, along with a crisis in the Saint Etienne ribbon industry, caused slowdowns in the dyeworks. By February 1894, dyers worked only five days per week.[85] All the industries, but especially metalworks and braid factories, had to lay off an increasing number of workers through the year. Between May and July, the Aciéries de la Marine had to lay off 262 men. During these months the number of people who registered themselves at the *bureau de bienfaisance* increased daily.[86]

This time the economic crisis did not strengthen the old authority of the Catholic party as it had done in the 1880s. Monarchists ceased to dominate the municipal council, and instead bourgeois moderate republicans assumed control. In 1893, for the first time, the council included at least one worker: Lerme, an officer in the metallurgists' union.[87]

Ultimately, however, the economic crisis prevented the fledgling labor movement in Saint Chamond from gaining further strength. Dyers self-consciously curbed their union activities and their political rhetoric for "fear of reprisals."[88] The republican municipal council, moreover, turned out to be no friend of workers. Moderate or opportunist republicans in Saint Chamond reacted to working-class militancy as they did throughout France: they became more conservative and used their power on the municipal council to thwart the labor movement. In October 1895, the municipality unanimously rejected a request from the unions in Saint Chamond for an annual subvention of 2,500 francs to support a Bourse du Travail. Four days later the unions requested a room in the municipality for socialist lectures and for their Bourse du Travail. "Tired of being accosted in the town hall every day by the politicians of socialism," opportunist Mayor Vial suggested they request a subvention to rent a room somewhere else in the city. It took almost a month for the municipal council to vote on the request, and it was unanimously rejected. In the meantime, the Cercle d'Etudes Sociales voted to censure Vial for the successive refusals and to have the censure published in the socialist newspaper *Peuple de la Loire*.[89] These workers must have wished that Saint Chamond had had a socialist municipality, like those in Carmaux and Limoges, that would lend its support to workers.

Catholic monarchists experienced their own metamorphosis in

reaction to the new worker militancy. But theirs was also a response to other key events: the death in 1883 of the Comte de Chambord, pretender to the throne; the moderate path that republicanism had assumed; and the encyclicals of Pope Leo XIII, *Rerum novarum* in 1891 and *Au milieu des sollicitudes* in 1892. The latter encyclical called for acceptance of, or *ralliement* to, the Republic. Most monarchist Catholics in Saint Chamond henceforward tacitly accepted republicanism. In 1893, M. Heville, accountant for the Société Industrielle, addressed 100 members of the Catholic Committee: "True Catholics do not concern themselves with the form of government: they like a republic as much as a monarchy, but on condition that the government respects the liberty of conscience."[90]

The other encyclical, *Rerum novarum,* asked that Catholics pay more active attention to the problems of the industrial working class. It generally divided conservative Catholics into two groups: "noninterventionists," who adhered to a belief in economic liberalism and charity, and "interventionists," who believed that social justice had to precede charity and that the state could be used as an "arm of progress."[91] As industrialists, conservative Catholics in Saint Chamond fell into the former category. In keeping with their city's charitable and religious past, they viewed the spirit of Christianity and Christian charity as the only means to ameliorate the workers' lot. This position was hardly new to them. Only Catholics could resolve the "social question," Heville contended, for they alone could feel true compassion for the workers' condition.[92] Their concern for working-class material conditions was genuine, and in addressing material needs they also attempted to address workers in a language with which they could identify. Just as they had borrowed the words of liberty and equality in the 1870s, in the 1890s they appropriated the very language of socialism to lure workers from its godless and dangerous solutions to their problems.

The discourse of the Catholic elite appeared regularly in the newspaper *La Croix de Saint-Chamond*, a weekly edition of the national *La Croix*. Begun in Saint Chamond in 1897 with considerable financial and editorial support from Charles Neyrand, the newspaper became a major organ through which the elite tried to reach workers. It self-consciously addressed them in both its contents and its price. Its circulation grew from 1,200 to 2,800 by 1902, reaching close to half of the adult population.[93]

In addition to reporting on events and issues of concern to workers, essays appeared regularly to explain why Catholicism provided the only alternative to socialism. While allowing for the "necessary stimulus of private ownership, indispensable to the march of scientific, material, intellectual, and moral progress," Catholicism, if practiced scrupulously, would inevitably result in "the social ideal of 'every man assured bread to the end of his life.' How could a practicing Catholic excuse himself from coming to the aid of his less fortunate brothers, he to whom Jesus Christ made it a strict duty to love his neighbor as himself?"[94] At least one article or editorial commentary in each weekly issue devoted itself to the social goals of Catholicism and to the weaknesses of socialism. One issue, for example, contained a "letter from a worker" describing how he had come to understand the iniquity of socialism. Another article portrayed a priest explaining to a worker laboring over his garden that under socialism, he would have to turn the products of his garden over to his neighbors who were too lazy to cultivate their own food. Upon this revelation, the worker ceased believing in socialist ideals and came to understand the moral: "Each time a socialist becomes a property owner, he no longer wants to share."[95]

It is noteworthy that the Saint Chamond elite began its concerted newspaper campaign in the 1890s, when further economic crises had made socialism and anarchism so appealing to a substantial number of workers in the Stéphanois region. The Christian rhetoric accompanied further attempts to meet workers' economic needs. Louis Jury and the wives of several braid manufacturers established the Prévoyance Feminine, a mutual aid society for women workers, in 1895; in 1896, the Catholic Committee established another mutual aid society for workers, La Caisse de Famille de Notre Dame du Travail. In 1899, Montgolfier decided to have the Aciéries de la Marine, which employed 95 percent of the Saint Chamond metal workers, assume total financial responsibility for mutual aid, further undermining workers' motivation to provide independent protection for themselves. The decision "produced an excellent effect among the personnel of these establishments," who were "already animated by a better spirit than in certain other working-class towns."[96]

Although reactionary Catholics in Saint Chamond responded to the papal encyclicals with greater solicitude toward workers and reluctant toleration of republicanism, they did not become completely reconciled to the government of the Third Republic, particularly because it did not, in their view, permit freedom of conscience. From 1899 the attention of the Catholic party necessarily became riveted to the Waldeck-Rousseau cabinet's renewed efforts to limit the power of the church.[97] The anticlerical assault targeted the private schools of teaching congregations, an issue dear to the hearts of the Saint Chamond right wing. It was also around this cause that the right wing had always succeeded in mobilizing popular support. After the laicization of 1881, teaching congregations continued to conduct religious classes in the communal schools.[98] However, the law of 30 October 1886 had prohibited congregations from teaching in these schools. The congregations, with the financial support of private donations, then proceeded to establish congregational schools (*écoles libres*). The Catholic party collected subscriptions to open two new private schools in the parishes of Saint Pierre and Notre Dame in 1897 and 1899, respectively. Montgolfier in particular played an instrumental role in the construction of these schools.[99]

The reactionary Catholic party also exercised their influence over instruction through the cantonal delegation, which they continued to dominate. In 1901, republicans complained that "no friend of lay education, [no] firm republicans, [no] declared enemies of the right-wing alliance" ever appeared on this list. The delegation contained only "the remains of the Oriol committee." It was thanks to their efforts that congregational schools had enjoyed considerable development.[100]

The Waldeck-Rousseau government sought to reduce the powers of the teaching congregations further with the Associations Law of 1901. By requiring that congregations seek authorization from municipalities, the law empowered local governments to prevent them from teaching even in their own schools.[101] Like many local governments throughout France, that of Saint Chamond had become distinctly left-wing in the municipal elections of 1900, seating five socialists. They would surely try to remove the congregations from the local private schools. But before the Associations Law passed, the Catholic Committee waged a citywide campaign to garner support for the religious congregations.[102]

A key issue highlighted in *La Croix* articles and in speeches, meetings, and demonstrations was not simply the clergy's importance to instruction but, notably, the material aid they distributed. In April 1901, the Catholic Committee sponsored a lecture on "The Liberty of Association." More than one thousand voters attended the lecture, and according to *La Croix* the majority of them were workers. In this meeting Charles Neyrand held forth: "The religious render services freely to this immense country. If England is burdened with 250 million in poor taxes, and if France, Paris excepted, spends only 14 million on public assistance, it is because congregations supply the French state with this service. What is going to happen to the sick, the old, the orphans welcomed by these congregations?"[103]

La Croix calculated that if the Sisters of Saint Charles did not administer the kindergarten in the parish of Saint Ennemond, the cost of its administration would rise from 3,420 francs per year to 5,920 francs. Moreover, the Dames Patronesses, who annually raised 2,300 francs for this kindergarten, would not do so if it were a lay school. Thus the kindergarten would require 4,800 francs more if the Sisters of Saint Charles could not administer it. This article pointed out that 165 children attended the kindergarten and all but 10 of them received aid in the form of food and/or clothing.[104]

These words might appear hollow if workers did not in fact face a material plight that forced many families to rely on assistance. The election results for the General Council of the arrondissement two months later measure the impact of such arguments and indicate the degree to which this campaign stirred proclerical feeling. Anticlerical republican candidate Janon received the fewest votes, the socialist candidate came in second, and the clerical party's candidate won—a sharp reversal of the municipal elections of 1900.[105] Saint Chamond again distinguished itself by its conservative reaction in the April-May legislative elections of 1902. Socialist Aristide Briand ran and was elected in the circumscription to which Saint Chamond belonged. But he lost by 300 votes to the clerical candidate in the city of Saint Chamond itself.[106] Despite the militancy of the 1890s and the temporary success of the socialists, the church-state issue forced a critical portion of voters to abandon the left.

Nationally, the elections of 1902 gave the left a big victory and forced the resignation of Waldeck-Rousseau. His replacement, Emile Combes, brought further intensity to the struggle to defend teaching congregations in Saint Chamond. More anticlerical than his predecessor, Combes tried to make the Associations Law ruthless. A decree in July 1902 ordered the closure of all congregations that had not requested authorization from their municipality. The following month the Catholic Committee of Saint Chamond in just four days collected 14,000 signatures in support of the city's congregations. The meeting they held to discuss the issue attracted 4,000 to 7,000 people, an enormous number out of a population of 14,000.[107]

Anticlericalism played a strong role in preventing the Saint-Chamonais from expressing a stronger socialist commitment. The battles between the socialists and the republicans strengthened the power of the Catholic right wing. Despite the support many workers gave to the left during the 1890s, a critical mass remained loyal to religious congregations. Workers who felt little sympathy for anticlericalism fell under right-wing influence, especially since the Catholic party argued that material assistance would end with the repression of the congregations. The anticlerical legislation after the turn of the century thus provoked a political shift in Saint Chamond that favored the reactionary elements.

As widespread support for the religious congregations breathed new life into the local right wing, the influence of unions and socialist clubs in Saint Chamond waned. A frustrated organizer complained in March 1901 that unions in Saint Chamond were "mere embryos."[108] Union membership among metallurgists swelled to 400 when an economic crisis two months later resulted in layoffs. But just one year after the crisis, a union meeting drew only sixty people.[109] Several strikes broke out between 1906 and 1914, especially among masons, joiners, and plasterers. Strikes also broke out in some of the newer factories—manufacturers of chains and bicycle accessories and agricultural tools. Most of these strikes were settled in favor of the workers. Those among construction workers, which occurred most frequently and spread beyond Saint Chamond to Rive-de-Gier, succeeded because workers were so unified and employers lacked any common front.[110] But workers in the large industrial establishments such as the steelworks remained inactive.

Though workers at the Aciéries did not strike, their behavior during these years is telling. They continued to donate substantial sums of money to other strikers, especially masons. On two occasions—1906 and 1911—masons working within the Aciéries supported their striking colleagues outside the steelworks but did not join them. Once the strikes were settled in the workers' favor, masons in the steelworks requested a pay raise. These requests came independently of the metal workers' union. To reward non-unionized workers for their good behavior, the directors not only granted their request but extended a pay raise to other workers.[111] Unionism and the left-wing politics associated with it thus lost impetus among the bulk of the industrial workers in Saint Chamond during the years prior to World War I.

From the 1860s on, strike activity, the formation of the Cercle des Travailleurs, the socialist Cercle d'Etudes Sociales, unions, and anarchist and socialist groups all indicate that workers in Saint Chamond were hardly docile recipients of material aid, Catholic instruction, and the sacraments. Indeed, workers in the newest industrial groups, metallurgy and braids, were often the most militant and highly organized. And yet, socialists did not succeed in winning consistent support, and the majority of workers remained loyal to their employers. Though militancy in Saint Chamond came primarily from skilled workers in the steel plant, most metal workers remained aloof. In his statistical analysis of the relative power of strike activity in Saint Chamond between 1880 and 1914, Michael Hanagan demonstrates that these workers had the least tendency to express grievances. Construction workers lost 22,434 workdays; textile workers, 9,669 workdays; and metal workers, only 1,986 workdays through their respective strike activities. This measure of strike intensity appears the more remarkable because construction workers comprised only about 3 percent of the male labor force in Saint Chamond, while metal workers accounted for nearly half of it.

Contrasting Saint Chamond with Rive-de-Gier and Le Chambon-Feugerolles, Hanagan stressed the important role that artisans played in the industrial labor movements of the latter two cities. The weak presence of artisans in Saint Chamond inhibited the development of an independent working-class culture. Loss of control over work and over apprenticeship, relatively lower wages resulting from less skilled work, and the difficulty of forming on-the-job friendships explain the relatively low rate of strike activity among metal workers. The nature of the work itself and financial difficulties in sustaining union funds created overwhelming obstacles for workers in the mechanized textile and steel industries.[112] In comparison, construction workers retained more control over their work and did succeed in creating a solidarity through their jobs. They replicated this solidarity in the community by concentrating slightly more in certain neighborhoods.

But construction workers exhibited other characteristics as well. Among those married in the 1860s, more had been born in Saint Chamond than had metal workers. Among the witnesses to births, marriages, and deaths in their families, construction workers included a larger portion of neighbors than did either textile or metal workers, which suggests that they had developed more extensive community bonds. They also tended to show more job stability than metal workers: 26.3 percent changed occupation, while 34.4 percent of the metal workers left metallurgy.[113] Metal workers also suffered more than others from the uprootedness of migration and the decline of occupational inheritance. The consequent disappearance of patriarchal authority from the family may have made workers more vulnerable to the patriarchal and paternalistic authority within large industry.

Yet if we use these criteria to try to understand strike patterns, dye workers present an anomaly. Their work remained fairly skilled and they exhibited geographical stability, strong family ties, and a relatively high rate of occupational inheritance. Despite severe crisis years after 1878, they did not strike until after 1900. Ironically, female braid makers, who had far more obstacles to organized activity, accounted for the workdays in textiles lost to strike activity. Clearly, occupations themselves—and the family and social relations generated from them—informed worker consciousness. But occupation alone does a poor job of explaining working-class political radicalism and labor militancy, or the lack thereof.

Nor did occupation especially determine workers' material reality. The analysis of family formation in Saint Chamond demonstrates that families became smaller among all workers, and infant and child mortality did not discriminate by occupation. Similarly, the effects of ill health, disease, physical debilitation, and the sudden deaths of wage earners crossed occupations, as did the need among families to rely on private, municipal, and clerical aid.

Material reality and the acceptance of material assistance influenced worker consciousness as much as the social relations of production. It was not just the lack of cultural and economic resources but the offer of aid from employers, the church, and municipal officials that made it difficult for workers to establish their own independent mutual aid associations. This assistance militated against workers viewing employers or priests as class enemies. It also presented a further barrier to their independence in that aid was administered on the basis of personal familiarity with workers, and a degree of moral blackmail often accompanied it.

A further look at workers in one of Saint Chamond's neighborhoods, the parish of Saint Ennemond, gives us yet another portrayal of consciousness, one that falls between militancy and docility. While it had the same proportion of metal workers as other neighborhoods, Saint Ennemond housed a larger proportion of braid makers and workers in older trades: nail makers, miners, and stonecutters. Most remarkable was its residential stability in contrast to the rest of Saint Chamond: more than twice as many of its residents, including workers in the new industrial trades of steel and braid production, were natives or had lived in the city for at least twenty years prior to marriage in the 1860s. Also noteworthy about the inhabitants of this parish was the reputation they had earned for their irreverence and impiety.[114]

Author Fournier made workers in this neighborhood the subject of his factually based novels. Central to his portrayal was their sociability and associational life, and a culture quite separate from the middle class. They drank copious amounts of wine in cafés, organized activities through their *boules* clubs, and engaged extensively in telling stories about themselves and previous generations of Saint-Chamonais. They expressed class-consciousness in their contempt for the bourgeois municipal council and their support for the "social and democratic Republic" and for the candidacy of Aristide Briand. The inhabitants of this neighborhood also, insofar as it was possible, rejected charity. So great was their aversion to material assistance that some of Fournier's characters literally preferred dying in the streets to entering the hospice. An informal mutual assistance through neighborly generosity permitted the inhabitants of this parish to avoid, or at least postpone, accepting aid from the dreaded hospice.[115]

Fournier thus portrayed these workers as fiercely independent, proud, defensive of their dignity, and conscious of themselves as a class. But this mentality never translated into confrontation or even effective political resistance. While they shunned religion, they expressed affection for the parish priest because he had genuine concern for the poor. They never uttered a negative word about the director of the forges, foremen, or engineers. Employers' treatment of workers had indeed won some degree of loyalty on their part. And if we are to believe Fournier, their love for drink diverted them from serious political activity.[116]

Fournier wanted his fiction to recapture the authentic working-class past in Saint Chamond. Although we cannot assume that it represents reality, archival evidence supports the general thrust of his portrayal. The majority of workers in Saint Chamond did not become militant and did remain outwardly loyal to their Catholic, conservative employers. They also remained loyal to the lower clergy, even when they did not practice Catholicism. What Fournier witnessed and put into print for posterity was the independent culture of these workers—artifacts of which never became documented in archives. His portrayal provides insight into a worker independence from bourgeois hegemony—an independence that did not become translated into any enduring or systematic political opposition or militant confrontation. By his own account, paternalism from both the clergy and employers in part explains their stance. To this explanation can be added a lack of education and a sociability that actually became escapist.

Despite an independent culture among workers, factors enumerated above such as migration, the decline of occupational inheritance, barriers to the formation of independent mutual aid, the reality of material need on the part of families, and loyalty to employers and the clergy together help explain why socialists could not consolidate power once they became elected to the municipality. Hence they could not, in turn, take control over the institutions that administered so much aid—the hospice, the *bureau de bienfaisance*, schools, and congregations. As the history of other cities has demonstrated, such municipal control had key importance for the effectiveness of working-class institutions such as the Bourse du Travail and the labor movement in general.[117]

Conclusion

The pronounced fertility decline in Saint Chamond over the course of the nineteenth century belies the image of workers as having large families that is presented in both current studies and those of nineteenth-century observers. The disparity, however, is more apparent than real. On the average, couples in the lower classes did have larger families than those in the middle and upper classes. For modern scholars and nineteenth-century social scientists, this fact has obscured the more noteworthy one that workers practiced family limitation. Fertility control among workers needs to be understood in its own context, both for what it can contribute to our knowledge about the fertility transition of the nineteenth century and for what it can tell us about the experience of industrialization among workers.

The terms *demographic revolution* and *fertility transition* imply a relatively sudden event resulting from a cause or set of causes which should be identifiable. In addressing this phenomenon, demographic research has thus far provided more description than explanation. Fertility control began in cities among the upper and middle classes. In France, the Revolution of 1789 accelerated a process that had already begun and helped make it a general phenomenon. The reasons for this spread remain unclear. Family historians generally link decline in family size with new attitudes toward children. Though they note that family life varied enormously by social class, they implicitly share the assumption that among all groups it changed in the same direction: emotional functions replaced economic ones. The lower classes have been considered "laggers" in making the transition to fertility control. Scholars assume that once they did begin to limit fertility, they did so for the same reasons the middle class did. Yet general causes for fertility decline among the European population as a whole have yet to be established empirically, and they remain elusive. The timing of decline among various populations defies generalization. No single factor can explain why urban dwellers, upper classes, peasants, workers, and, most puzzling, the French nation as a whole began to limit family size when they did.

Though the concepts of revolution and transition continue to compel researchers to seek general causes, community studies speak instead to varying, particular causes. Ostensibly, the fertility decline in Saint Chamond corresponds to the broader demographic transition throughout France and Western Europe. Workers behaved like the middle and upper classes in having fewer children. But their reasons for doing so were quite different. The way workers in Saint Chamond experienced decline in family size bears no relationship to factors demographers and historians have, up to this point, associated with the general demographic transition: higher standard of living, lower infant mortality, middle-class professions, and changes in the emotional nature of family life. Indeed, these workers continued to suffer a low standard of living, and infant mortality remained high.

The experience of the Saint-Chamonais demonstrates that fertility control did not spread as a result of upper-class values "filtering downward." It was for reasons of their own that workers tried to avoid having numerous children, and through the nineteenth century those reasons changed. Artisans in the early nineteenth century controlled reproduction because women's work conflicted with childbearing and childrearing. Though wives in families of both nail makers and ribbon weavers assisted their husbands, the work that women performed in ribbon-weaving families was at once more demanding and required more precise timing. Women coped with these demands by sending their children to wet nurses. The avoidance of breast-feeding made these mothers more fertile and thus necessitated more deliberate contraceptive measures. While metalwork made different kinds of demands on the wife's time, it too compelled some women to send their children to wet nurses and to avoid numerous births.

In the industrial context of the second half of the nineteenth century, family formation strategies changed. Birth control—whether through contraceptive efforts or through abortion—became more rigorous and more generalized throughout the population. Although the population of Saint Chamond continued to be a mixed one with regard to reproductive behavior, on the average couples delayed having children at the outset of their marriages and had them more slowly than in the earlier part of the century. They also ended their childbearing at an earlier point in their marriages. Fertility strategies in the industrial context still derived from the organization of work. No longer, however, did strategies have anything to do with work activities per se that earlier had created different patterns among metal and silk workers. The role of women in family formation remained pivotal during the period of large-scale industry: mothers had to leave the home to work in factories for the sake of family survival. But even where women could continue to perform labor in the home, the new organization of work conflicted with childbearing and childrearing because most men left the home to perform labor in rigid twelve-hour shifts. The absence of men from the home rendered the labor women performed there more difficult. While labor had always been divided sexually, the lines between men's and women's work in domestic industry had been far less distinct. Men and women shared tasks associated with both reproduction and production.[1] In the industrial period, the tasks in both these categories became more distinctly gender-segregated and the lines between work and family life hardened. Until working-class women no longer had to earn wages, the new organization of work increased their burden. Since family survival depended on their continued contribution to production, the strategy they adopted to resolve the conflicting demands on their time was to reduce the tasks associated with reproduction.

Examination of the physical, economic, and political environment within which the Saint-Chamonais began to have fewer children demonstrates that smaller families resulted, not from new attitudes toward children, but from an environment that proved socially, economically, and physically hostile to traditional goals centered on a tight relationship between work and family. The logic behind decline in fertility among workers thus diverged completely from that of the middle class. It was, moreover, this very difference in the logic of family formation that governed bourgeois perceptions of working-class family life. Though workers' average family size continued to be larger than that of the middle class, it was not size itself that informed bourgeois perceptions. What disturbed the bourgeoisie was that workers formed their families in the context of poverty and an incomprehensibly different way of life: the need to earn wages, rather than emotional gratification, continued to govern working-class families.

Middle-class value judgments changed over the course of the nineteenth century, and their transformation contributed to the dynamic of class relations. In the first half of the nineteenth century, liberal economists such as Jean-Baptiste Say and Simonde de Sismondi referred to high fertility among the lower classes as dangerous. It caused poverty, demoralization, and crime and hindered the progress of capitalistic development. Solutions to the problem necessarily had to rest with the individual. Charity should be limited, and workers should be encouraged to abstain from sex outside of marriage and to marry only when they could afford to have families.[2] Observers in the second half of the nineteenth century continued to comment upon high fertility among workers, but the tone of their commentary changed. In 1881, Claude Tillier referred to the "luxury" of large families that "only the poor can permit."[3] When juxtaposed with Malthusian condemnations of the poor for their high fertility just half a century earlier, this remark does more than lend a sense of irony to middle-class perceptions. It also underscores the profundity and significance of the French experience with decline in fertility.

Just as France's disastrous defeat to the Prussians in 1870 marked a turning point in political life, so too did it help reverse the moral climate. Although fertility control became more pervasive, almost no one publicly condoned it, and many spoke out against it. Tillier and others who expressed concern over the natality problem thus made their observations in the midst of moral debates over the causes and implications of *dépopulation*. Bourgeois and petit-bourgeois women replaced the poor as objects of blame for decadence and selfishness. Where poor women of the past had lacked foresight in having too many children, bourgeois women after 1870 lacked patriotism because they desired too few.[4] For reasons of national defense, large families became valued.

The problem of *dépopulation* inspired observations about the laboring poor that were imbued with a moral purpose. A highly developed sense of family among the middle class, combined with concern over *dépopulation* and the welfare of children after the disaster of 1870, reinforced elite concerns over the well-being of working-class children.[5] While attitudes had changed, the fundamental social problem had not: those who did have large families could not support them. Unwilling to have large families of their own, patriotic social observers felt compelled to assist workers in managing their families. Concern for children extended to workers. Indeed, the middle class viewed workers as "children." The conditions of workers' family lives indicated to employers and their philanthropic wives that workers could not take full responsibility for themselves. Images of working-class family life inspired both "maternalist" and "paternalist" responses. Employers and local charities assumed family functions in their care of children, the sick, and the old. Through administering aid, the middle class tried to mold workers in their own image.

The behavior of Saint Chamond's industrialists does not closely fit the stereotype normally associated with the entrepreneurial class of the nineteenth century, whose views the likes of Jean-Baptiste Say represented and articulated. The French Revolution was supposed to have established the legal framework for the principles of liberalism and individualism. The Declaration of the Rights of Man and the Le Chapelier Law should have paved the way for an exploitative, liberal-minded bourgeoisie. But throughout the nineteenth century, the Saint Chamond elite diverged from the path which the political and industrial revolutions apparently paved for them. Their paternalism was not just an anachronistic reaction stemming from Old Regime values. It was a deliberate strategy that helped shape workers' material and moral lives, as well as their relations with employers. This elite, moreover, was not idiosyncratic; many other French industrialists shared its views and practices.[6]

Just as the practice of paternalism in France was more common than is generally realized, so was its acceptance by workers. The working class in Saint Chamond helps us to understand this acceptance. Though workers exercised control over their fertility, this did not always give them more control over their lives. The high infant, child, and maternal mortality in Saint Chamond and a decline in the duration of marriage demonstrate that the family became more physically vulnerable over the course of the nineteenth century. Chronically poor health, disease, an accident, or a premature death in the family placed the workers in situations where they had no choice but to accept aid.

As the need for assistance increased, migration and mechanization of labor made it more difficult for families to meet their own needs. "Chain migration" eased the stress of uprootedness but could not eliminate it. Crises that provoked the move from village to city, such as the death of a parent or a spouse, also made settling in an urban context more difficult. Migration also created a gap between generations that mechanization deepened. In the 1860s, more men and women had parents working in agriculture than their artisanal predecessors had had. Even when the older generation did work in industry of some kind, they could no longer transmit useful skills to their offspring. Children ceased adopting the same occupation as their parents; parents stopped teaching children work skills and passing on traditions associated with work. Certainly, in some cases industrial change opened new doors to the children of these workers, and the break in generational bonds meant upward mobility. But for most workers in the second half of the nineteenth century, industrialization meant fewer opportunities to learn skills. Unskilled work in a continually fluctuating industrial economy forced people to change jobs and residences frequently. Occupational and geographical instability made the establishment of new cultures and associations centered on work difficult at best.

Abbé Cetty labeled this process a "decline of paternal authority" in the working-class home. Whether or not the working-class father lost status among his children, the authority and power of the family vis-à-vis employers did decline. Mechanization of work gave employers, the owners of machines, a greater measure of control over the workplace as well as over the worker. The workplace became an arena for discipline and training, as well as for reinforcing morality through such organizations as the Association des Patrons Catholiques and *cercles catholiques*.

Both physically and culturally, the working-class family became more permeable to middle-class attentions. The experience of industrialization in Saint Chamond conforms to the model of industrial discipline Michelle Perrot formulated: the worker family had in fact served as the original source of industrial discipline. Mechanization transferred the paternalistic set of social relationships from the family to the factory. The "fatherly" presence of the employer in the place of production, the treatment of workers as "children," and acceptance by workers of these social relationships constituted three main elements of industrial paternalism.[7]

Though effective, paternalism in Saint Chamond had limits. The republicanism, strike activity, unions, and socialist and anarchist clubs indicate that the elite did not succeed in exerting complete hegemony over workers. Yet class relations did remain relatively harmonious. On a material basis alone, the effort to help workers, combined with the real need for assistance, helps to explain why class relations in Saint Chamond differed from those in neighboring cities. Whether or not paternalism "succeeded" is less important than understanding how and why it operated.

The study of Saint Chamond demonstrates that paternalism in employer-worker relations cannot be understood without an examination of workers' family lives and material conditions. Mechanization, urbanization, migration, and the values of the bourgeois elite placed workers in a vicious cycle. The uprootedness of moving to the city, the removal of work from the home, and the devaluation of labor resulting from mechanization made it impossible for many workers to meet their own needs. The lost ability to pass knowledge from one generation to another, frequent job and residence changes, and insufficient wages made it difficult for workers to form associations that would sustain them both materially and politically. At the same time, the industrial elite of Saint Chamond provided the needed material aid and accompanied it with their own moral and political indoctrination. The provision of aid served as a further obstacle to the formation of independent workers' associations.

The religious orders in Saint Chamond meanwhile enjoyed extensive visibility. They had been an intricate and highly praised part of local history ever since Archbishop Ennemond ventured into the Gier valley in the seventh century. Their alliance with the elite had always been powerful, but it became especially crucial with industrialization and the movement toward democracy. Because clerics administered charity, the Catholic industrialists could manipulate local political sentiment. They equated anticlericalism with the disappearance of material assistance. Anticlericalism thus turned many workers away from support of radical republicans and socialists. As a result, the left wing could not sustain electoral support in local government. Without control over the municipality, the left could not control charitable institutions such as the hospice and the *bureau de bienfaisance*. Lacking municipal support, workers faced yet more obstacles in establishing such key institutions as a Bourse du Travail. They had little choice but to accept help from their reactionary employers.

In Saint Chamond, the specific combination of industries, their simultaneous mechanization, and the Catholicism and monarchism of its industrial bourgeoisie distinguished the experience of its working class during the nineteenth century. The microscopic examination possible only in a local study uncovers mechanisms from which generalizations may be made. From both a demographic and a cultural perspective, where industrialization developed intensively and rapidly, it destabilized the working-class family. Change in family structure constituted a response to, as well as a symptom of, the distress workers experienced. Material conditions among workers, as mortality rates indicate, made family survival more difficult. Workers had two alternatives: they could develop independent mutual aid, or they could depend on employers and the local elite for assistance. Numerous factors determined which route workers followed. In communities that continued to have artisans, independent workers' associations developed more readily. Workers in communities with factory work and many recent arrivals to the city faced more difficulty in forming associations. Provision of employer-sponsored mutual aid and the availability of care from hospice institutions and *bureaux de bienfaisance* in such situations filled a need that workers could not, or did not, meet themselves. Whether workers became militant or passive through this process depended on their opportunities or abilities to become self-reliant as a class.

Appendix A:

Birth, Marriage, and Death Records

THE *ETAT CIVIL*

Birth, marriage, and death records in the *état civil* contain a wealth of information for the social historian. Each marriage record contains the date of marriage, the dates of birth for both spouses, occupations, names of witnesses and their occupations, signatures of the spouses (or indication of their inability to sign), an indication as to whether parents were present, and if not, whether they had died. The detail of information in the records for Saint Chamond changed over the course of the nineteenth century. In addition to the information mentioned above, marriage records of the 1860s and 1870s also contained more precise detail about the brides' and grooms' domiciles, such as the street address, whether they were living with parents or relatives or on the premises of their employers, names of employers, and how long they had lived in Saint Chamond prior to their weddings. Addresses and occupations and, if relevant, place of death were provided for parents of the brides and grooms. Information about witnesses also became more detailed in the middle of the century. Records more frequently indicated what relationship the bride or groom had with each witness—relative (uncle, cousin, brother, grandparent), coworker, neighbor, proprietor, employer, and so forth. The addresses recorded for the witnesses were also very precise. Unfortunately, the richness of detail declines once again from the 1880s.

The core of this study begins with all the marriages that took place in Saint Chamond between 1816 and 1825, and those that took place between 1861 and 1870. Marriage records thus included information about 4,312 individuals who lived in Saint Chamond between 1816 and 1825 and information about 12,264 individuals who lived there between 1861 and 1870. The records for the latter cohort provided far richer detail. Information from all the marriages in each of the two cohorts was coded and computerized. Two of the codes, those for occupations and birthplace, are complex and require explication.

Occupations are divided into the following twenty categories: agriculture, mines and quarries, traditional (small) metallurgy, large (mechanized) metallurgy, glassmaking, pottery, textiles, construction and public works, clothing, furniture, books and printing, paper and cardboard, leather and animal skins, divers industries (undesignated workers or manufacturers, or miscellaneous ones such as "manufacturer of gallic acid"), miscellaneous handicrafts (watchmaker, candle maker, carriage maker, blacksmith), land transportation, railroads, water transportation, shopkeeping and food, miscellaneous services (domestic service, school-teachers, clerks, midwives). These categories comprise the first two numbers, 01–20, of a five-digit code. The third number of the code ranges from 1 to 4 and refers to the rank in the particular occupation, with 4 as the least skilled. The final two digits, ranging from 1 (01) to 14, refer to the particular task the individual performed. Thus, for example, domestic servants were coded 20-4-02, puddlers were 04-2-03, stokers in the steelworks were 04-4-01, and master ribbon weavers were 07-1-04. The majority of the workers in Saint Chamond fell into the status ranking of 3 and 4. This system of coding is the same that Yves Lequin employed in his work *Les ouvriers de la région lyonnaise*, which makes my comparisons with the results of his investigation systematic. Not only did he provide me with the coding itself, but he helped me apply it to the enormous detail of occupational descriptions that emerged in the Saint Chamond marriage records, especially between 1860 and 1870.

The second category of coding that requires some explication is that of birthplace. Once again I owe gratitude to Yves Lequin, not only because he provided me with a system of coding but because its application makes possible a systematic comparison with his investigation. Birthplaces are coded according to their distance from Saint Chamond in the shape of a spiral. Some communes in the department of the Rhône, for example, are closer to Saint Chamond than are communes in its own department, the Loire. Someone born in Saint Chamond itself received the code of 001. The communes belonging to the canton of Saint Chamond received 002; the thirty-six communes included in the Stéphanois industrial basin received 003. Codes ranged from 001 to 864.

Marriage records were only the starting point of reconstructing a socio-family history of the population of Saint Chamond. The reconstitution of families combined marriage records with births, marriages, and deaths of each couple's children, as well as the death of each spouse. In addition to the demographic goal of this task, the reconstitution of families also makes possible the reconstruction of occupational and residential histories of families and individuals, as well as family and social relations with witnesses to births, marriages, and deaths. Each birth, marriage, or death record provided addresses and occupations of the individuals key to the particular vital event, as well as of the parents and witnesses. Birth and death registers had only two witnesses, and usually they did not provide as much detail about them as did marriage records. Nonetheless, the provision of information, codable as well as uncodable, afforded the opportunity to study occupational inheritance, occupational endogamy, residential changes, and social relations with witnesses for both cohorts throughout the nineteenth century.

FAMILY RECONSTITUTION

The linkage of birth, marriage, and death records has as its primary goal the study of demographic patterns. This study uses two sets of marriages—all those registered between 1816 and 1825, and between 1861 and 1866—as starting points for reconstituting families that were generated from them. This strategy diverges from the traditional method established by Henry and Fleury. According to their method, the researcher records every birth, marriage, and death from every year of the *état civil* or parish registers over a period long enough—at least one century, and most often more—to include several generations. For any geographical entity larger than a small village, this task is formidable for the single researcher. In order to apply this method to an urban population, I began with one decade of marriages each from the first and second halves of the nineteenth century, with the presumption that the cohorts whose marriages I recorded would not be biased. The problem with using such limited cohorts, however, is that their patterns reflect short-term economic fluctuations. But of primary concern to me was how families dealt with those fluctuations, and in that respect the cohort size afforded rich opportunity in the detail it provided.

The two cohorts are numerically comparable. While I made use of marriages that took place between 1861 and 1870, for practical reasons I reconstituted families only from marriages in the first five years of the decade. The number of marriages that took place in those five years equaled those that occurred in Saint Chamond between 1816 and 1825. Of more concern than the equal size of the two cohorts was simply the manageability of reconstituting that number of families.

For the demographic analysis of both cohorts of reconstituted families I applied several standard rules. Second marriages were eliminated. Marriages in which the groom did not live in Saint Chamond were eliminated. Reconstituted families were divided into three basic categories: First, those in which the wife completed her childbearing years, considered in this study to end at age fifty. These families are considered "complete." To enter this category either the marriage had to end with the death of one of the spouses after the wife passed age fifty, or evidence of the couple living in Saint Chamond had to appear in some other document—such as the marriage of a child—after the woman had reached age fifty. A second category is that in which families are not necessarily complete, but they are "closed," as is indicated by the death of either of the spouses. The important point here is that the marriage, "complete" or not, has a known end, and fertility and mortality can be measured accordingly. The third category of families is the "open" one, in which completion of the wife's childbearing years is uncertain. Whether she and her husband moved out of the city is unknown. Record of the death of either spouse was never found. For purposes of sample size, the largest number of families possible was used for each calculation. In some cases, whether or not the family was "closed" or "complete" was not important. For most calculations, "open" families were not used.

One problem with the method of family reconstitution as a measure of demographic change is that its accuracy depends upon geographical stability, yet another reason why urban populations have rarely been subject to it. Invariably, vital events among the families being recorded do not get entered into the registers being used for study. Most important to the study of fertility and mortality are missed births and deaths. Demographers are currently developing methods to correct for missed births and deaths in registers. In this study, we have corrected only for missed births.

This correction method uses "recovered" births to give an estimate of births "unrecovered" in reconstitution.[1] "Recovered" births are children who had no birth record but who did have a marriage, death, or census record in Saint Chamond. The causes of these omissions are temporary residence of the family in another town or failure to register the birth in Saint Chamond. Birthdates can be estimated for these individuals from the information that later becomes recorded on the family *fiche*, such as the death or marriage of a child, the record of which invariably has the child's birthdate as well. But there remains an unknown group of births that were *not* recovered, since some children died before adulthood outside Saint Chamond and others never married.

To estimate this unknown group of births, which should also be included in marital fertility, Louis Henry proposes a method that focuses on the ratio of births to marriages in a reconstituted sample.[2] Using the proportions of known children who eventually married, we can estimate the original number of births that the "recovered" group represents. The first step is to distribute the number of "recovered" births by source of recovery (see Table A-1).

Next, all the births in the families with "recovered" births are tabulated according to whether or not the offspring married. Using these families as the basis of this step means relying on three assumptions: that in their survival and omission patterns the families are essentially representative of the whole sample; that there are no more births in these families that have not been "recovered"; and that family migrations that could have led to unrecorded births were generally short enough to result in a reasonable chance of children appearing in some later records in Saint Chamond. There are no reasons to reject any of these assumptions for Saint Chamond. The distributions of the experience of children in families with "recovered" births is shown in Table A-2.

There are marriage records for 30.3 percent (83/274) of children in the first cohort and 40.5 percent (77/190) in the second cohort. Dividing the numbers of births "recovered" from marriage records by these marriage rates produces the estimated "pool" of births that led to the marriages:

First cohort: 37 "recovered" marriages/.303
(marriage rate) = 122 births

Table A-1.   Missed Births Recovered from Other Sources

	First cohort	Second cohort
Death record	17	14
Marriage record	37	30
Census	—	19
Total	54	63

Table A-2.   Experience of Children in Families
with "Recovered" Births

	First cohort	Second cohort
Died unmarried	76	72
Married	83	77
Fate unknown	115	41
Total	274	190

Table A-3.   Correction for "Lost" Births in the First
Cohort (couples married 1816–1825)

Mother's age	"Unfound" births added to sample	Correction to fertility rate
15–19	—	—
20–24	11	5.1%
25–29	14	4.3
30–34	12	4.4
35–39	9	5.8
40–44	3	5.0
45–49	—	—
Total births	49	

Second cohort: 30 "recovered" marriages/.405
(marriage rate) = 74 births

Of these "pools," 54 have already been found, using all sources combined for the first cohort and 63 for the second. The 11 "unfound" births for the second cohort are less than 1 percent of all births in the cohort, and adding these births would have virtually no effect on fertility rates. However, the figure of 68 "unfound" births for the first cohort is not negligible and has been used to adjust fertility rates in the first cohort.

Adjusting this cohort's fertility is done by extending Henry's procedure and distributing "unfound" births in the same way as "recovered" ones are distributed. First, the 68 "unfound" births are split between "open" and "closed" families, because fertility rates in this study are based only on "closed" marriages. Just under 73 percent of all births in the first sample are in "closed" families, so 49 of the 68 "unfound" births are assigned to those marriages. Then, to assign these births to maternal age groups for age-specific fertility, the 49 "unfound" births are distributed by the mother's age in the same way as all the "recovered" births were actually distributed (estimating the birthdate of a "recovered" child allows an estimate of the mother's age at the birth as well). Finally, the percentage by which the addition of the "unfound" births raises such an age-specific fertility rate is used as a correction factor to adjust all fertility rates for the first sample. The estimated distribution of "unfound" births and the correction factors are shown in Table A-3.

Appendix B:

Supplemental Tables

Table B-1. Indirect Occupational Endogamy: Fathers-in-law and
Brides of Ribbon Weavers, 1816–1825

| | Fathers-in-law | | Brides | |
Occupation	No.	%	No.	%
Agriculture	13	9.8	0	0
Small metallurgy	1	0.8	0	0
Textiles (ribbon weaving & silk work)	22	16.5	79	59.4
Construction	3	2.3	0	0
Clothing	7	5.3	8	6.0
Misc. industries	4	3.0	4	3.0
Misc. crafts	1	0.8	0	0
Shopkeeping and food	3	2.3	2	1.5
Misc. services	2	1.5	7	5.3
None declared	77	57.9	33	24.8
Total	133	100.0	133	100.0

Table B-2. Occupational Inheritance: Occupations of
Ribbon Weavers' Fathers, 1816–1825

Father's occupation	No.	%
Agriculture	10	7.5
Small metallurgy	1	0.8
Textiles (ribbon weaving)	39	29.3 (65.0)[a]
Construction	2	1.5
Clothing	1	0.8
Misc. industries	2	1.5
Shopkeeping and food	3	2.3
Misc. services	2	1.5
None declared	73	54.9
Total	133	100.0

[a] Percentage of those who declared professions.

223

Table B-3.   Occupational Inheritance of Women Who Married 1816–1825

	Bride's occupation					
	No occupation		Silk work		Clothing	
Father's occupation	No.	%	No.	%	No.	%
Agriculture	14	16.9	10	10.0	7	33.3
Mining	1	1.2	2	2.0	0	0
Small metallurgy	5	6.0	13	13.0	3	14.3
Large metallurgy	0	0	1	1.0	0	0
Textiles (ribbon weaving)	12	14.5	41	41.0	8	38.1
Construction	6	7.2	11	11.0	0	0
Clothing	5	6.0	4	4.0	2	0
Shopkeeping and food	32	38.6	2	2.0	0	0
Misc. services	5	6.0	5	5.0	1	4.8
Other	3	3.6	11	11.0	0	0
Total	83	100.0	100	100.0	21	100.0

Table B-4.   Geographical Stability among Couples Who Married 1816–1825 (Based on reconstituted families)

	Ribbon weavers		Nail makers		Construction		Total cohort	
Residence in Saint Chamond	No.	%	No.	%	No.	%	No.	%
No evidence of presence after marriage	10	8.2	6	7.1	6	12.2	44	10.0
Intermittent presence	3	2.5	8	9.5	2	4.1	24	5.5
Marriage ended 1815–1840	24	19.8	10	11.9	8	16.3	65	14.9
Present until at least 1850	52	43.0	51	60.7	24	49.7	219	49.9
Other[a]	32	26.4	9	10.7	9	18.4	87	19.8
Total	121	100.0	84	100.0	49	100.0	439	100.0

[a] Families who may have lived in Saint Chamond in 1850, but left no records of births, marriages, or deaths.

Table B-5.   The Second Generation from the 1816–1825 Cohort:
Sons and Daughters Who Survived and Married in Saint Chamond

Father's occupation	No. born	No. married	% of all born who married[a]	No. known to have survived to adulthood	% survivors who married[a]
Sons					
Nail maker	115	32	27.8	76	42.1
Ribbon weaver	144	33	22.9	82	40.2
Construction	71	10	14.1	29	34.5
Shopkeeping and food	84	7	8.3	45	15.6
Other	156	32	20.5	90	28.0
Total	570	114	20.0	322	35.4
Daughters					
Nail maker	135	33	24.4	84	39.3
Ribbon weaver	137	26	19.0	74	35.1
Construction	73	17	23.3	30	56.7
Shopkeeping and food	88	12	13.6	36	33.3
Other	141	35	24.8	72	51.1
Total	574	123	21.4	296	51.6

[a]The numerator of both these rates is the number of offspring who married in Saint Chamond. Since infant and child mortality varied by occupation, the percentage of survivors who married provides the more accurate reflection of tendency to settle in Saint Chamond. However, since many infant deaths were not recorded in Saint Chamond, both rates are included.

Table B-6.   Occupational Inheritance: Occupations of
Nail Makers' Fathers, 1816–1825

Father's occupation	No.	%
Agriculture	5	4.9
Small metallurgy	17	16.7 (56.7)[a]
Textiles	3	2.9
Construction	1	1.0
Clothing	1	1.0
Misc. industries	2	1.5
Shopkeeping and food	1	1.0
None declared[b]	72	70.6
Total	102	100.0

[a]Percentage of those who declared occupations.

[b]Those for whom no occupation was declared either had died or did not attend the wedding.

Table B-7.   Deaths of Parents of Brides and
Grooms Who Married 1816–1825

	Grooms		Brides		Nail makers		Ribbon weavers	
	No.	%	No.	%	No.	%	No.	%
Fathers								
Alive	260	48.3	299	55.6	47	46.1	70	52.6
Dead	278	51.7	239	44.4	55	53.9	63	47.4
Total	538	100.0	538	100.0	102	100.0	133	100.0
Mothers								
Alive	328	61.0	343	63.8	58	56.9	93	69.9
Dead	210	39.0	195	36.2	44	43.1	40	30.1
Total	538	100.0	538	100.0	102	100.0	133	100.0

Table B-8.   Coale-Trussel Standard Index of Fertility Control,
Table of Residuals, Cohort Married 1816–1825

Age	Observed	Fitted	Diff.	m(a)
20–24	.438	.449845	−.0118447	0
25–29	.398	.383737	.0142631	.206998
30–34	.319	.308242	.0107577	.286372
35–39	.205	.22181	−.0168097	.413437
40–44	.105	.10142	3.58036E−03	.313268
45–49	.008	.0131884	−.18835E−03	.636961

Note: M (intercept) = .978561. *m* (slope) = .337803. Mean square error = .00213.

Table B-9.   Duration of Childbearing, Cohort Married
1816–1825 ("Complete" families)

	No.	Mean	Median	Standard deviation
Ribbon weavers	56	11.0	11.8	6.0
Nail makers	41	14.4	14.0	6.9
Total cohort	198	12.0	12.3	6.5

Table B-10.   Length of Intervals between Births, According to Death or Survival of Preceding Infant (Based on first four birth intervals)

	No.	Mean	Standard deviation	Standard error	Prob > |T|
First cohort (married 1816–1825)					
No death	751	27.6	15.7	0.571139	0.0071
Death of previous infant	106	23.6	13.9	1.346641	0.0128
Second cohort (married 1861–1866)					
No death	423	32.7	16.5	0.797235	0.0001
Death of previous infant	137	21.9	11.1	0.945260	0.0001

Table B-11.   Birthplaces of Brides and Grooms, 1861–1870

	Brides		Grooms	
	No.	%	No.	%
Saint Chamond	286	28.8	246	24.7
Gier valley (cantons of Saint Etienne and Rive-de-Gier)	274	27.6	258	26.0
Region adjacent to Gier valley	104	10.5	83	8.4
Elsewhere, department of the Loire and adjacent part of Rhône	68	6.8	85	8.6
Unknown	9	0.9	6	0.6
All other departments	253	25.5	316	31.8
Total	994	100.0	994	100.0

Table B-12.   Birthplace and Residential Proximity of Parents
of Men Married 1861–1870

Parental residence	Native		Migrant	
	No.	%	No.	%
Same house	38	71.7	34	20.1
Same neighborhood	2	3.8	1	0.6
Elsewhere in Saint Chamond	11	20.8	8	4.7
Subtotal	51	96.2	43	25.4
Another commune in industrial basin	1	1.9	53	31.4
Another department	1	1.9	58	34.3
Another canton or department, with son	0	0	15	8.9
Total	53	100.0	169	100.0

Source: Addresses of grooms and parents provided in marriage records. Data here are from a random sample of all marriage records between 1861 and 1870.

Table B-13.   Birthplace and Residential Proximity of Parents
of Women Married 1861–1870

Parental residence	Native		Migrant	
	No.	%	No.	%
Same house	59	90.8	65	43.0
Same neighborhood	2	3.1	2	1.3
Elsewhere in Saint Chamond	1	1.5	3	2.0
Subtotal	62	95.4	70	46.4
Another commune in industrial basin	2	3.1	41	27.2
Another department	1	1.5	34	22.5
Another canton or department, with daughter	0	0	6	4.0
Total	65	100.0	151	100.0

Source: Addresses of brides and parents provided in marriage records. Data here are from a random sample of all marriage records between 1861 and 1870.

Table B-14. Living Situations among Native and Nonnative Men and Women at Marriage, 1861–1870

	With parent		With other relatives		Other		Unknown		Total	
	No.	%	No.	%	No.	%	No.	%	No.	%
Native men	144	58.5	2	0.8	6	2.4	94	38.2	246	100.0
Nonnative men	135	18.5	13	1.8	46	6.3	536	73.4	730	100.0
Total	279	28.5	15	1.5	52	5.3	630	64.4	976	100.0
Native women	217	76.4	8	2.8	7	2.5	52	18.3	284	100.0
Nonnative women	206	29.8	31	4.5	159	23.0	296	42.8	692	100.0
Total	423	43.3	39	4.0	166	17.0	348	35.7	976	100.0

Table B-15. Duration of Residence in Saint Chamond Prior to Marriage in 1861–1870

		Duration of residence			
		Less than 2 years		More than 20 years	
Occupation	No. in sample[a]	No.	%	No.	%
Men					
Textiles	96	13	13.5	51	53.1
Metallurgy	368	103	28.0	88	23.9
Construction	100	13	13.0	29	29.0
Shopkeeping and food	69	20	32.8	16	26.2
Women					
Braid making	431	64	14.8	122	28.3
All women	908	135	14.6	303	33.4

[a] Excludes those who did not live in Saint Chamond at the time of their marriages.

Table B-16. Occupation and Living Situation of Men and Women at Marriage, 1861–1870

Occupation	Living with parent		Living with other relatives		Other living situations		Unknown		Total	
	No.	%	No.	%	No.	%	No.	%	No.	%
Men										
Textiles	49	43.8	1	0.9	4	3.6	58	51.8	112	100.0
Metallurgy	122	29.5	9	2.2	12	2.9	271	65.5	414	100.0
Construction	28	25.7	0	—	7	6.4	74	67.9	109	100.0
Shopkeeping and food	16	17.6	0	—	6	6.6	69	75.8	91	100.0
All men	272	28.4	15	1.5	52	5.2	645	64.9	994	100.0
Women										
Braid making	194	41.1	17	3.6	115	24.4	146	30.9	472	100.0
All women	434	43.7	40	4.0	167	16.8	353	35.5	994	100.0

Table B-17. Occupational Inheritance of
Women Who Married 1861–1870

Father's occupation	Bride's occupation							
	No occupation		Silk work		Clothing		Misc. services	
	No.	%	No.	%	No.	%	No.	%
Agriculture	22	21.4	80	31.6	21	19.3	23	47.9
Mining	1	1.0	16	6.3	3	2.8	5	10.4
Small metallurgy	1	1.0	24	9.5	5	4.6	0	0
Large metallurgy	14	13.6	41	16.2	23	21.1	1	2.1
Textiles	13	12.6	25	9.9	6	5.5	2	4.2
Construction	3	2.9	26	10.3	12	11.0	4	8.3
Clothing	3	2.9	8	3.2	9	8.3	0	0
Shopkeeping and food	27	26.2	3	1.2	14	12.8	4	8.3
Misc. services	14	13.6	6	2.4	10	9.2	8	16.7
Other	5	4.9	24	9.5	6	5.5	1	2.1
Total	103	100.0	253	100.0	109	100.0	48	100.0

Table B-18. Coale-Trussel Standard Index of Fertility Control,
Table of Residuals, Cohort Married 1861–1866

Age	Observed	Fitted	Diff.	m(a)
20–24	.349	.349689	$-6.88881E-04$	0
25–29	.288	.288479	$-4.78715E-04$	.463747
30–34	.239	.221184	.0168163	.347934
35–39	.133	.15216	$-.0191598$	.586952
40–44	.071	.0665359	$4.46409E-03$	.411869
45–49	.005	$8.38942E-03$	$-3.38942E-03$	.767509

Note: M (intercept) = .760689. *m* (slope) = .457794. Mean square error = .00554.

Table B-19.   Proportion of Endogenous Infant Deaths
in Families from Both Cohorts

Age at death	First cohort[a]		Second cohort[b]	
	No.	%	No.	%
Including stillbirths				
Birth to 1 month	100	52.9	130	58.0
1–12 months	89	47.1	94	42.0
Total	189	100.0	224	100.0
Without stillbirths				
Birth to 1 month	58	39.5	64	40.5
1–12 months	89	60.5	94	58.5
Total	147	100.0	158	100.0

[a] Married 1816–1825.
[b] Married 1861–1866.

Table B-20.   Duration of Marriage, Both Cohorts
(Based on number of marriages ended by death of either spouse)

Length of marriage	First cohort[a]		Second cohort[b]	
	No.	%	No.	%
0–10 years	34	8.7	56	14.5
11–20 years	31	8.0	30	7.8
21–30 years	38	9.8	42	10.9
31+ years	108	27.8	40	10.4
Unknown	178	45.8	218	56.5
Total	389	100.0	386	100.0

[a] Married 1816–1825.
[b] Married 1861–1866.

Table B-21. Frequency of Infant and Child Deaths in
Families of Couples Married 1816–1825 and 1861–1866

	No deaths		1–2 deaths		3 or more deaths	
	No.	*%*	*No.*	*%*	*No.*	*%*
Nail makers, 1816–1825	22	39.3	22	39.3	12	21.4
Ribbon weavers, 1816–1825	33	47.8	26	37.7	10	14.9
Whole cohort, 1816–1825	136	50.8	95	35.5	37	13.8
Metal workers, 1861–1866	54	45.4	52	43.7	13	10.9
Whole cohort, 1861–1866	129	48.0	105	39.0	35	13.0

Notes

INTRODUCTION

1. The Archbishop Ennemond came from Lyon to evangelize the Gier valley. He built a church on the hill that is now the parish of Saint Ennemond, overlooking the Gier River. The clergy and nobility who joined him in turn built a château and a fortress. The legend of Saint Ennemond imbued the city with a cultish identity. The stories of how he rescued the "naive and superstitious" inhabitants of this valley from their oppressors continued to be recounted in the twentieth century, and regional pilgrimages to his statue in the church of Saint Ennemond, which supposedly also contained his remains, persisted until at least World War I. See M. Fournier, *La vallée ardente: scènes de la vie populaire* (Saint Etienne: Librairie Dubouchet, 1938), pp. 254–73. For Saint Chamond's early history, see also James Condamin, *Histoire de Saint-Chamond et de la seigneurie de Jarez, depuis les temps les plus reculés jusqu'à nos jours* (Paris: A. Picard, 1890), and Stéphane Bertholon, *Histoires de Saint-Chamond: notes et souvenirs d'un vieux couramiaud* (Saint Etienne: n.p., 1927).

2. Archives du Ministère de la Guerre, Vincennes, MR1266, "Rapport sur les environs de Saint-Chamond," 1843.

3. See, for example, Michael Mitterauer and Reinhard Sieder, *The European Family: Patriarchy to Partnership from the Middle Ages to the Present*, trans. Karla Oosterveen and Manfred Horzinger (Chicago: University of Chicago Press, 1983), especially pp. 51–53, 59, 80–81, 93–97, 103–15.

4. For example, Yves Lequin, *Les ouvriers de la région lyonnaise (1848–1914)*, 2 vols. (Lyon: Presses Universitaires de Lyon, 1977); Jacques Schnetzler, *Les industries et les hommes dans la région de Saint-Etienne* (Lille: Service de Reproduction des Thèses, Université de Lille III, 1976); Maxime Perrin, *La population de la région de Saint-Etienne, étude de géographie humaine* (Tours: Arrault, 1937); Perrin, *Saint Etienne et sa région économique: un type de vie industrielle en France* (Tours: Arrault, 1937); Michael Hanagan, *The Logic of Solidarity: Artisans and Industrial Workers in Three French Towns, 1871–1914* (Urbana: University of Illinois Press, 1980); Hanagan, "Urbanization, Worker Settlement Patterns and Social Protest in Nineteenth-Century France," in *French Cities in the Nineteenth Century*, ed. John M. Merriman (New York: Holmes & Meier, 1981), pp. 208–29; David Gordon, *Merchants and Capitalists: Industrialization and Provincial Politics in Mid-Nineteenth Century France* (University: University of Alabama Press, 1985); Bernard Plessy, *La vie quotidienne en Forez avant 1914* (Paris: Hachette, 1981).

5. Archives Départementales de la Loire (henceforth ADL), series S, Chambre de Commerce de Saint Etienne, carton 131 dossier 9, Chambre

Consultative des Arts et Manufactures de Saint-Chamond, "extrait de délibérations," 28 Sept. 1805, "Mémoire au sous-préfet sur l'industrie de la région," Archives du Ministère de la Guerre, Vincennes, MR1266, "Mémoire sur les environs de Saint-Chamond," 1843; J. Duplessy, *Essai statistique sur le département de la Loire* (Montbrison: n.p., 1818), pp. 184, 155.

6. Laurent Boyer, *Les élections politiques dans le département de la Loire au temps de l'assemblée nationale et du Maréchal MacMahon* (Paris: Sirey, 1963), p. 12.

7. Louis René Villermé, *Tableau de l'état physique et moral des ouvriers employés dans les manufactures de coton, de laine et de soie*, 2 vols. (Paris: Renouard, 1840); Jules Simon, *L'Ouvrière* (Paris: Hachette, 1891).

8. Frédéric Le Play, *La réforme sociale en France, déduite de l'observation comparée des peuples européens*, 2 vols. (6th ed. Tours: Mame, 1878), 2:9. For a useful discussion of Le Play and his method, see Catherine Bodard Silver, Introduction to *Frédéric Le Play: On Family, Work, and Social Change*, ed. and trans. Catherine Bodard Silver (Chicago: University of Chicago Press, 1982), pp. 3–134.

9. Henri Cetty, *La famille ouvrière en Alsace* (Rixheim: A. Sutter, 1883), pp. 92–95, 170–74.

10. Ibid., pp. 17, 168.

11. Ibid., pp. 92–95, 116–17, 129, 161, 174.

12. Ibid., pp. 74, 104, 122.

13. Ibid., pp. 183–86, 190–91.

14. Cetty cites the following examples: the directors of forges expelled workers from Sunday mass if they lived *en concubinage*. Employers actively intervened in family disorders. They took severe measures if workers were found drunk. In all these moral matters, they threatened workers with dismissal if they did not reform their behavior. He praised other industrialists for forcing women workers to stay at home at least three weeks after the delivery of their babies: ibid., pp. 50–54, 122.

15. Cetty stated, "Broken in its most intimate ties and dearest affections, struck in the very source of life, [the family] has become the theater of such profound miseries that it has been necessary to invent a new word, 'pauperism,' in order to explain the situation that created it": ibid., p. 11.

16. See Armand Audiganne, *Les populations ouvrières et les industries de la France*, 2 vols. (2d ed. Paris: Capelle, 1860); Louis Reybaud, *Rapport sur la condition morale, intellectuelle et matérielle des ouvriers qui vivent de l'industrie de coton* (Paris: n.p., 1863). For an insightful discussion of these inquiries, see William Reddy, *The Rise of Market Culture: The Textile Trade and French Society, 1750–1900* (Cambridge, Eng.: Cambridge University Press, 1984), pp. 230–31, 233.

17. Edward P. Thompson, *The Making of the English Working Class* (New York: Vintage Books, 1963).

18. Neil Smelser, *Social Change and the Industrial Revolution* (Chicago: University of Chicago Press, 1959); Michael Anderson, *Family Structure in Nineteenth Century Lancashire* (Cambridge, Eng.: Cambridge University Press, 1971), especially pp. 136–69; Yves Lequin, *Les ouvriers de la région lyonnaise*, vol. 1. For a study of migration and family relations, see Leslie Page Moch, *Paths to the City: Regional Migration in Nineteenth-Century France* (Beverly Hills: Sage Publications, 1983), especially pp. 123–67.

19. Franklin F. Mendels coined the term; see Mendels, "Proto-Industrialization: The First Phase of the Industrialization Process," *Journal of Economic History* 32 (1972): 241–61. The literature on this topic has expanded ever since. For example, see Charles Tilly, "Flows of Capital and Forms of Industry in Europe, 1500–1900," *Theory and Society* 12 (1983): 123–42; Tilly, "Did the Cake of Custom Break?" in *Consciousness and Class Experience in Nineteenth-Century Europe*, ed. John M. Merriman (New York: Holmes & Meier, 1979), pp. 17–44; Maxine Berg, *The Age of Manufactures: Industry, Innovation and Work in Britain, 1700–1820* (New York: Oxford University Press, 1986), pp. 69–86.

20. Hans Medick, "The Proto-Industrial Family Economy: The Structural Function of Household and Family during the Transition from Peasant Society to Industrial Capitalism," *Social History* 3 (1976): 291–315; Rudolf Braun, "Early Industrialization and Demographic Change in the Canton of Zurich," in *Historical Studies of Changing Fertility*, ed. Charles Tilly (Princeton: Princeton University Press, 1978), pp. 289–334; David Levine, *Family Formation in an Age of Nascent Capitalism* (New York: Academic Press, 1977); Levine, "Proto-Industrialization and Demographic Upheaval," in *Essays on the Family and Historical Change*, ed. Leslie Page Moch and Gary D. Stark (Arlington: Texas A&M University Press, 1983), pp. 9–34; Levine, "Production, Reproduction, and the Proletarian Family in England, 1500–1851," and Tilly, "Demographic Origins of the European Proletariat," both in *Proletarianization and Family History*, ed. David Levine (New York: Academic Press, 1984), pp. 87–127 and 1–85.

21. Louise A. Tilly and Joan W. Scott, *Women, Work and Family* (New York: Holt, Rinehart and Winston, 1978), p. 232.

22. See, for example, Barbara Franzoi, "Domestic Industry: Work Options and Women's Choices," in *German Women in the Nineteenth Century: A Social History*, ed. John C. Fout (New York: Holmes & Meier, 1984), pp. 256–69; Marilyn Boxer, "Women in Industrial Homework: The Flowermakers of Paris in the Belle Epoque," *French Historical Studies* 12 (Spring 1982): 401–23.

23. Jane Humphries, "Class Struggle and the Persistence of the Working Class Family," in *Cambridge Journal of Economics*, 1 (Sept. 1977): 241–58, p. 250; see also Humphries, "The Working Class Family, Women's Liberation, and Class Struggle: The Case of Nineteenth Century British History," *Review of Radical Political Economics* 8–9 (1976–1977): 25–41.

24. Reddy, *The Rise of Market Culture*, p. 311.

25. For example, see Tilly and Scott, *Women, Work and Family*, pp. 99–100, 225–27.

26. A notable exception, though not of the nineteenth century, is the study of Jean-Pierre Bardet, *Rouen aux XVIIᵉ et XVIIIᵉ siècles: les mutations d'un espace social*, 2 vols. (Paris: Société d'Édition d'Enseignement Supérieur, 1983).

27. For an explanation of family reconstitution, see Appendix A.

28. Michelle Perrot has addressed this question in "The Three Ages of Industrial Discipline in Nineteenth-Century France," in *Consciousness and Class Experience in Nineteenth-Century Europe*, ed. John M. Merriman (New York: Holmes & Meier, 1979), pp. 149–68.

29. Michel Foucault, *Discipline and Punish: The Birth of the Prison*, trans.

Alan Sheridan (New York: Pantheon, 1977); Jacques Donzelot, *The Policing of Families* (New York: Pantheon, 1979); Perrot, "The Three Ages of Industrial Discipline in Nineteenth-Century France."

30. Lequin, *Les ouvriers de la région lyonnaise*; Hanagan, *The Logic of Solidarity*; Sanford Elwitt, *The Making of the Third Republic: Class and Politics in France, 1868–1884* (Baton Rouge: Louisiana State University Press, 1975); and Gordon, *Merchants and Capitalists*.

CHAPTER 1

1. L. Turgan, "Les établissements Oriol et Alamagny," in his *Les grandes usines de la France*, 16 vols. (Paris: Michel Levy, 1865–1884), 15:13–16; Stéphane Bertholon, *Histoires de Saint-Chamond: notes et souvenirs d'un vieux couramiaud* (Saint Etienne, n.p., 1927), p. 82; L. Jury, "L'Industrie des lacets," in *L'Association pour l'Avancement des Sciences, XXVIe session tenue à Saint-Etienne, août 1897*, 2 vols. (Saint Chamond: A. Poméon, 1898), 2:8.

2. James Condamin, *Histoire de Saint-Chamond et de la seigneurie de Jarez, depuis les temps les plus reculés jusqu'à nos jours* (Paris: A. Picard, 1890), p. 643; Jury, "L'Industrie des lacets," p. 15; H. Baret, *Manuel de rubanerie, passementerie et lacets* (Paris: Ballière, 1924), p. 16; Bertholon, *Histoires de Saint-Chamond*, p. 80; Turgan, "Les établissements Oriol et Alamagny," p. 12. For the early history of Saint Chamond's braid industry, see Baret, *Manuel de rubanerie*, pp. 55–58; Turgan, "Les établissements Oriol et Alamagny," pp. 13–16; L.–J. Gras, *Histoire de la rubanerie et des industries de la soie à Saint-Etienne et dans la région stéphanoise suivie d'une historique de la fabrique de lacets de Saint-Chamond* (Saint Etienne: Théolier, 1906), pp. 706–9; J. Duplessy, *Essai statistique sur le département de la Loire* (Montbrison: n.p., 1818), p. 339.

3. Maurice Lévy-Leboyer, *Les banques européennes et l'industrialisation internationale dans la première moitié du XIXe siècle* (Paris: Presses Universitaires de France, 1964), p. 335.

4. See Cynthia M. Truant, "Solidarity and Symbolism among Journeymen Artisans: The Case of *Compagnonnage*," *Comparative Studies in Society and History* 21 (April 1979): 214–26; William H. Sewell, *Work and Revolution in France: The Language of Labor from the Old Regime to 1848* (Cambridge, Eng.: Cambridge University Press, 1980), pp. 162–218.

5. Bertholon, *Histoires de Saint-Chamond*, pp. 34, 37, 42, 63–65, 70, 92.

6. Archives Nationales, Paris (henceforth AN), C956, "Enquête sur le travail agricole et industriel," arrondissement de Saint-Etienne, 1848; Armand Audiganne, *Les populations ouvrières et les industries de la France dans le mouvement social du XIXe siècle* (Paris: Capelle, 1854), p. 309; Duplessy, *Essai statistique*, p. 392; Bernard Plessy, *La vie quotidienne en Forez avant 1914* (Paris: Hachette, 1981), pp. 110–18.

7. For a useful discussion of the role of *fabricants*, see Plessy, *La vie quotidienne en Forez*, pp. 101–3. Among other ribbon *fabricants* who gave Saint Chamond so much to be proud of were G. Bertholon, Bertholon-Dulac, A. Thevenon-Roux, Morel, Magnin father and son, Grange, Bonnard, Coste and Co., Granjon-Gougout and Co., Charles Granjon and

Co., and Dubouchet-Fond. See Condamin, *Histoire de Saint-Chamond*, p. 643.

8. ADL 81M 22, letter from the mayor of Saint Chamond to the prefect, 4 Feb. 1835; Duplessy, *Essai statistique*, pp. 396–97; L. R. Villermé, *Tableau de l'état physique et moral des ouvriers employés dans les manufactures de coton, de laine et de soie*, 2 vols. (Paris: Renouard, 1840), 2:47, 345.

9. Villermé, *Tableau de l'état physique et moral*, 2:345. For conditions of silk workers, see also Jules Simon, *L'Ouvrière* (Paris: Hachette, 1891).

10. Descriptions of women's silk work may also be found in Simon, *L'Ouvrière*, pp. 7–40; Bertholon, *Histoires de Saint-Chamond*, pp. 66–69; and Plessy, *La vie quotidienne en Forez*, pp. 107–8.

11. AN C956, "Enquête sur le travail," 1848.

12. Simon, *L'Ouvrière*, pp. 7–40; Plessy, *La vie quotidienne en Forez*, pp. 107–8.

13. AN C956, "Enquête sur le travail," 1848; Plessy, *La vie quotidienne en Forez*, p. 119.

14. Villermé's investigations helped perpetuate the view that domestic industry did not pose the same health problems as did workshops devoted to silk. Citing Villermé's *Tableau de l'état physique et moral*, pp. 233–38, for example, William Coleman notes, "Except for the preparation of the raw silk drawn from the cocoon, the entire industry seemed not less and perhaps somewhat more salubrious than other branches of textile manufacture": William Coleman, *Death Is a Social Disease: Public Health and Political Economy in Early Industrial France* (Madison: University of Wisconsin Press, 1982), p. 223. It is not clear, however, that Villermé ever spent any time in workers' homes. The government inquiry of 1848 portrays conditions in the homes of silkweavers as quite unhealthy. AN C956, "Enquête sur le travail," 1848.

15. It was possible to collect some information for 72 percent of the couples who married between 1816 and 1825. Death registrations were found for one or both spouses in 51 percent of the cases. See Appendix A for a more detailed explanation of the method of family reconstitution. Data on occupations and occupational inheritance here and below are drawn from marriage records in ADL, subseries 3E 208, 1816–1825. One hundred of the silk workers' fathers, or 39 percent, declared an occupation; of those, 41 wove ribbons. For a full representation of fathers' occupations, see Elinor Accampo, "Industrialization and the Working Class Family: Saint Chamond, 1815–1880," Ph.D. diss., University of California, Berkeley, 1984, p. 312.

16. ADL, series S, Chambre de Commerce de Saint-Etienne, carton 141 dossier 7, letter to the prefect from Saint Etienne regarding the law of 1841, no date.

17. See Appendix B, Table B-1, for occupational endogamy. For a discussion of occupational endogamy and other examples, see John Gillis, *For Better, for Worse: British Marriages, 1600 to the Present* (New York: Oxford University Press, 1985), pp. 117, 175. The literacy rates in Saint Chamond are drawn from signatures on marriage records in ADL, subseries 3E 208, 1815–1825. See also Chapter 2 n. 44, and Accampo, "Industrialization," pp. 246–47.

18. See Appendix B, Table B-2, for occupational inheritance. Fifty-two percent of the grooms' fathers had died, and another 12 percent did not attend the weddings. Of the sixty fathers who declared occupations, thirty-nine were ribbon weavers. For more detail, see Accampo, "Industrialization," Table 3.13, p. 122. For occupational inheritance among ribbon weavers' daughters, see Appendix B, Table B-3.

19. Henri Guitton, *L'Industrie des rubans de soie en France: des particularités de son organisation technique, économique et sociale* (Paris: Sirey, 1928), quoted in Plessy, *La vie quotidienne en Forez*, p. 95. See also p. 118.

20. Jury, "L'Industrie des lacets," p. 5; J. Valserres, *Les industries de la Loire* (Saint Etienne: n.p., 1862), p. 285.

21. Valserres, *Les industries de la Loire*, pp. 286–90; see also Lévy-Leboyer, *Les banques européennes*, pp. 130–32; Baret, *Manuel de rubanerie*, pp. 36–54.

22. Audiganne, *Les populations ouvrières*, p. 399; Robert J. Bezucha, *The Lyon Uprising of 1834: Social and Political Conflict in the Early July Monarchy* (Cambridge, Mass.: Harvard University Press, 1974), p. 23; Colin Lucas, *The Structure of the Terror: The Example of Javogues and the Loire* (London: Oxford University Press, 1973), p. 10.

23. Plessy, *La vie quotidienne en Forez*, pp. 107–8.

24. Valserres, *Les industries de la Loire*, p. 389.

25. AN C956, "Enquête sur le travail," 1848.

26. For fancier weaving as a male activity, see Archives du Ministère de la Guerre, Vincennes, MR1266, "Rapport sur la reconnaissance de la route de Saint-Etienne à Saint-Chamond," 1837; Duplessy, *Essai statistique*, p. 393; Audiganne, *Les populations ouvrières*, p. 231. The same phenomenon occurred in Lyon; see Bezucha, *The Lyon Uprising of 1834*, p. 194. For the concentration of plain ribbons in the countryside and patterned ribbons in the city, see Yves Lequin, *Les ouvriers de la région lyonnaise (1848–1914)*, 2 vols. (Lyon: Presses Universitaires de Lyon, 1977), 1:23; Simon, *L'Ouvrière*, p. 75; and Lévy-Leboyer, *Les banques européennes*, p. 131.

27. AN C956, "Enquête sur le travail," 1848.

28. Plessy, *La vie quotidienne en Forez*, pp. 108–11.

29. AN C956, "Enquête sur le travail agricole et industriel," canton of Saint Chamond, 1848.

30. Ibid.

31. Ibid.

32. Ibid. For the noxious effects of breathing silk dust, see Coleman, *Death Is a Social Disease*, pp. 223–24.

33. AN C956, "Enquête sur le travail agricole et industriel," canton of Saint Chamond, 1848.

34. Ibid.

35. ADL 81M 22, letter from the Consultative Chamber of Arts and Manufactures to the prefect, 1813; letter from the Consultative Chamber to the minister of the interior, 27 May 1809.

36. Jury, "L'Industrie des lacets," p. 6; Bertholon, *Histoires de Saint-Chamond*, pp. 81–82.

37. ADL 56M 4, 1824–1847, document 37, report to the minister of manufactures and commerce, 1830s; there were eighteen ribbon *fabricants* in Saint Chamond employing 392 workers in the city, 1,240 in the country-

side; Archives de la Ministère de la Guerre, Vincennes, MR1266, "Rapport sur les environs de Saint-Chamond," 1843. Among the more important *fabricants* of ribbons who converted to braids were Bergé in 1848, Balas-Dubouchet in 1859, and the Grangier brothers (who became Grangier-Reymond) in 1860. See Condamin, *Histoire de Saint-Chamond*, pp. 640–43; Bertholon, *Histoires de Saint-Chamond*, p. 82. See also ADL, series S, Archives de la Chambre de Commerce, carton 139 dossier 1, register of deliberations, 27 Jan. 1840. The government inquiry of 1848 reported that 415 men and 615 women were employed in the ribbon fabrique in the canton of Saint Chamond. This number includes the countryside, and the total of 1,030 compares with 1,632 reported in the previous decade. See AN C956, "Enquête industrielle et sociale des ouvriers et des chefs d'ateliers rubaniers," arrondissement of Saint Etienne, 1848.

38. The calculation of 43 percent underrepresents the geographical stability of ribbon weavers, for those who had died prior to 1850 were included in the denominator. See Appendix B, Table B-4, for analysis of occupations and geographical stability.

39. ADL, subseries 3E 208, births, marriages, and deaths in Saint Chamond, 1816–1865; reconstituted families beginning with marriage no. 27, 13 Jan. 1819, and marriage no. 11, 4 Jan. 1820.

40. See Chapter 2.

41. These rates of marriage are based on the number of children ever born and do not take into account those who died prior to reaching adulthood. Of those who survived, 35.4 percent of the sons married in Saint Chamond and 40.2 percent of ribbon weavers' sons married in Saint Chamond. Because many infant deaths were not registered in Saint Chamond (see Chapter 2), using the total number of births rather than the total number who survived is more accurate. See Appendix B, Table B-5.

42. ADL, subseries 3E 208, births, marriages, and deaths in Saint Chamond, 1816–1865; reconstituted family beginning with marriage no. 392, 20 Sept. 1819.

43. Of those who survived to adulthood, 41.6 percent of all daughters married in Saint Chamond, while 35 percent of the ribbon weavers' daughters did. Again, these figures cannot be taken at face value because, particularly among the children of ribbon weavers, deaths were underregistered (see Chapter 2). For second-generation marriages, see Appendix B, Table B-5. Of twenty-eight ribbon weavers' daughters who married (including those from "open" families), twelve married ribbon weavers or men associated with the industry, eight married metal workers (most of whom were skilled), two married shoemakers, and one each married a hotel boy, a railroad employee, a confectioner, a café keeper, and a pharmacist.

44. Valserres, *Les industries de la Loire*, p. 336.

45. Quoted from the Chambre Syndicale by Plessy, *La vie quotidienne en Forez*, p. 101.

46. Villermé, *Tableau de l'état physique*, p. 401. For the incompatibility of iron and silk, see also ADL, series S, Chambre de Commerce de Saint-Etienne, carton 139 dossier 2, "Extrait du registre des délibérations de la séance," 27 Jan. 1840, and carton 59 dossier 1, Jules Janin, "La ville de Saint-Etienne," 1831.

47. M. Capnophobe, dit Stéphanois la Vérité, *Les machines à vapeur et les grands foyers de combustion à la houille en présence de l'industrie rubanière,* Aug. 1854, quoted by Plessy, *La vie quotidienne en Forez,* p. 91.

48. Duplessy, *Essai statistique,* pp. 148, 155.

49. Audiganne, *Les populations ouvrières,* p. 318.

50. Duplessy, *Essai statistique,* pp. 148, 155.

51. Louis Reybaud, "Rapport sur la condition morale, intellectuelle et matérielle des ouvriers qui vivent de l'industrie du fer, 1866–1871" (Musée Sociale, no. 9920, vol. 4).

52. For the local history of nail making, see L.-J. Gras, *Essai sur l'histoire de la quincaillerie de petite métallurgie à Saint-Etienne et dans la région stéphanoise* (Saint Etienne: Théolier, 1904), p. 51; Duplessy, *Essai statistique,* p. 329; Bertholon, *Histoires de Saint-Chamond,* pp. 107–8; Maxime Perrin, *Saint-Etienne et sa région économique: un type de vie industrielle en France* (Tours: Arrault, 1937), pp. 216–17; Jean-Paul Bravard, "La clouterie dans la région de Firminy," *Notes d'histoire: au pays de cloutiers* (Firminy: Maison de la Culture de Firminy, February 1977): 1–18.

53. ADL, series S, Chambre de Commerce de Saint-Etienne, carton 131 dossier 9, Chambre Consultative des Arts et Manufactures, "Mémoire sur l'industrie," 24 March 1810.

54. Unless otherwise indicated, this and the following discussion are based primarily on the text of interviews with former nail makers and descendants of nail makers in the hamlet of Ouilles, conducted by Jean-Paul Bravard, 22 January 1977; see Bravard, "La clouterie dans la région de Firminy."

55. Gras, *Essai sur l'histoire de la quincaillerie,* p. 104; Bravard, "La clouterie dans la région de Firminy."

56. Gras, *Essai sur l'histoire de la quincaillerie,* p. 104.

57. Sociability around the forge is discussed in the interviews Bravard conducted; see "La clouterie dans la région de Firminy." Of twenty-two brides' fathers who declared their occupation as nail maker between 1816 and 1825, ten had sons-in-law who were also nail makers.

58. Bravard, "La clouterie dans la région de Firminy."

59. Of twenty-two nail makers' daughters who married, thirteen performed silk work of some kind: Accampo, "Industrialization and the Working Class Family," p. 309. For the combination of silk and metal in the same household, see ADL 40M 93, document 238, report on the establishment of a metallurgical factory, 24 March 1841.

60. John Gillis, on the other hand, found occupational endogamy among miners and metal workers in England in the 1840s; see *For Better, for Worse,* p. 118

61. Bravard, "La clouterie dans la région de Firminy." For occupational inheritance, see Appendix B, Table B-6. Out of 102 nail makers, the fathers of 67.6 percent had died or simply did not declare occupations, and another 3 percent did not attend the weddings. Of 24 fathers who declared their occupations as nail makers, 17 had sons in the same occupation.

62. See Appendix B, Table B-4.

63. Bernard Farber, *Guardians of Virtue: Salem Families in 1800* (New York: Basic Books, 1972), p. 97.

64. ADL, subseries 3E 208, families reconstituted from marriages no.

2, 5 Jan. 1824; no. 20, 1 March 1824; no. 23, 15 Feb. 1817; no. 29, 3 July 1816.

65. Quoted in Bravard, "La clouterie dans la région de Firminy," p. 14.

66. Of forty-three nail makers' sons for whom occupations could be found, ten declared themselves to be nail makers, nine declared jobs of varying skill levels in heavy metallurgy, and five were ribbon weavers. The remainder declared the following: cooper (2), tailor (2), miner (3), reader (*liseur* for ribbon weaving), mason, cabinet merchant, apprentice confectioner, plasterer, gardener, dyer, telegraph employee, apprentice locksmith.

67. Of the daughters who survived to adulthood, 39 percent married in Saint Chamond. But because deaths were under-registered (see Chapter 2), this percentage cannot be taken at face value. These calculations are based on "closed" reconstituted families—that is, those in which the recorded death of either spouse had provided a known end to the period of family formation (for a full explanation of family reconstitution, see Appendix A). Among the families of all nail makers, regardless of whether they were "open" or "closed," fifty-two daughters married; of those, twelve married nail makers and twelve married workers in heavy metallurgy. The remainder married stonecutters (4), miners (5), bakers (2), cabinet makers (2), ribbon weavers (6), farmers (2), a locksmith, a loom mechanic, a carriage driver, a blacksmith, a master bootmaker, a shoemaker, and a postal worker.

68. Farber makes this argument in *Guardians of Virtue*, pp. 105–10.

CHAPTER 2

1. For the literature on proto-industrialization, see Introduction, note 19.

2. Charles Tilly, "Flows of Capital and Forms of Industry in Europe, 1500–1900," *Theory and Society* 12 (1983): 129.

3. Hans Medick, "The Proto-Industrial Family Economy: The Structural Function of Household and Family during the Transition from Peasant Society to Industrial Capitalism," *Social History* 3 (1976): 291–315; Rudolf Braun, "Early Industrialization and Demographic Change in the Canton of Zurich," in *Historical Studies of Changing Fertility*, ed. Charles Tilly (Princeton: Princeton University Press, 1978), pp. 289–334; David Levine, *Family Formation in an Age of Nascent Capitalism* (New York: Academic Press, 1977); Levine, "Proto-Industrialization and Demographic Upheaval," in *Essays on the Family and Historical Change*, ed. Leslie Page Moch and Gary D. Stark (Arlington: Texas A & M University Press, 1983), pp. 9–34; Levine, "Production, Reproduction, and the Proletarian Family in England, 1500–1851," and Charles Tilly, "Demographic Origins of the European Proletariat," in *Proletarianization and Family History*, ed. David Levine (New York: Academic Press, 1984), pp. 87–127 and 1–85; John Gillis, *For Better, for Worse: British Marriages, 1600 to the Present* (New York: Oxford University Press, 1985), p. 117.

4. In his study of the female population of France, Etienne van de Walle showed that many regions had reached a low level of fertility by 1801–1810. But this trend did not occur in the region surrounding Saint

Chamond. The Loire had thirty-five to thirty-nine female births per thousand women between 1801 and 1805. These rates remained the same between 1826 and 1830. The measure of marital fertility, Ig, was over .700 in 1831, suggesting that few people were practicing contraception. This rate was very high in comparison to the rest of France. See Etienne van de Walle, *The Female Population of France in the Nineteenth Century: A Reconstruction of Eighty-Two Departments* (Princeton: Princeton University Press, 1974), pp. 170–76. Ig as a measurement of marital fertility was developed by Ansley J. Coale. The rate is based on the marital fertility of the Hutterite population, for whom total absence of fertility control could be postulated. The index Ig represents the ratio of births in any population to that of the Hutterites after the age structure of the female population has been standardized. Prior to the demographic transition, most European populations had 70 to 90 percent of the marital fertility of the Hutterites; that is, their Ig's were .700 to .900. It is commonly believed that ratios this high indicate that there is no fertility control within marriage. Etienne van de Walle notes, "As a rule of thumb, an Ig of less than .500 indicates with quasi-certainty the voluntary control of marital fertility, and an Ig of less than .600 the great probability of such control. There are wide areas of France where such control appears well-established as early as 1831" (pp. 174–76). Ansley J. Coale describes this measure in "The Decline of Fertility in Europe from the French Revolution to World War II," in *Fertility and Family Planning: A World View*, ed. S. J. Behrman, Leslie Corsa, and Ronald Freedman (Ann Arbor: University of Michigan Press, 1969), pp. 3–24.

5. Colin Lucas, *The Structure of the Terror: The Example of Javogues and the Loire* (London: Oxford University Press, 1973), p. 10.

6. See C. Tilly, "Demographic Origins of the European Proletariat"; Levine, "Production, Reproduction, and the Proletarian Family in England"; Levine, "Proto-Industrialization and Demographic Upheaval"; C. Tilly, "Did the Cake of Custom Break?" in *Consciousness and Class Experience in Nineteenth-Century Europe*, ed. John M. Merriman (New York: Holmes & Meier, 1979); Braun, "Early Industrialization and Demographic Change"; Charles Tilly, "Historical Study of Vital Processes," in *Historical Studies of Changing Fertility*, pp. 3–55; Levine, *Family Formation in an Age of Nascent Capitalism*; Medick, "The Proto-Industrial Family Economy"; Franklin F. Mendels, "Proto-Industrialization: The First Phase of the Industrialization Process," *Journal of Economic History* 32 (1972): 241–61; Gillis, *For Better, for Worse*, chapter 4, esp. p. 126.

7. Quoted from Louis Blanc, *L'Organisation du travail*, in Louis Chevalier, *Laboring Classes and Dangerous Classes in Paris during the First Half of the Nineteenth Century*, trans. Frank Jellinek (Princeton: Princeton University Press, 1973), pp. 455–56n.38.

8. Louis Henry first developed the technique of family reconstitution. See Michel Fleury and Louis Henry, *Nouveau manuel de dépouillement et d'exploitation de l'état civil ancien* (Paris: Editions de l'Institut National d'Études Démographiques, 1965). See also Louis Henry, *Techniques d'analyse en démographie historique* (Paris: INED, 1980). The reconstitution of families in Saint Chamond is based on the *état civil* in ADL, subseries 3E 208, births, marriages, and deaths in the commune of Saint Chamond, 1816 to 1865. Those after 1865 are in the Palais de Justice in Saint Etienne, Greffe du

Tribunal de Grande Instance (henceforth GTGI). For a fuller explanation of how I have employed this technique, see Appendix A.

9. For age at marriage, see Louis Henry and Jacques Houdaille, "Célibat et âge au mariage aux 18ᵉ et 19ᵉ siècles en France. II: Age au premier mariage," *Population* 34 (March 1979): 403–41; Louis Henry, "The Population of France," in *Population in History*, ed. D. V. Glass and E. E. C. Eversley (London: E. Arnold, 1965), p. 454; for Lyon, see Maurice Garden, *Lyon et les lyonnais au XVIIIᵉ siècle* (Paris: Flammarion, 1975), p. 56.

10. But interpretation of the complex demographic and cultural factors behind age at marriage requires caution. Historians and demographers have not succeeded in establishing reasons for late age at marriage prior to the nineteenth century with empirical certainty; thus reasons for the drop in marriage age are also based on some speculation. For a recent discussion of factors surrounding weddings, see John Gillis, "Peasant, Plebeian, and Proletarian Marriage in Britain, 1600–1900," in *Proletarianization and Family History*, pp. 129–162; see also John Hajnal, "European Marriage Patterns in Perspective," in *Population in History*, pp. 101–46; Lutz K. Berkner and Franklin F. Mendels, "Inheritance Systems, Family Structure, and Demographic Patterns in Western Europe, 1700–1900," in *Historical Studies of Changing Fertility*, pp. 209–23; Jack Goody, Joan Thirsk, and E. P. Thompson, *Family and Inheritance: Rural Society in Western Europe, 1200–1800* (Cambridge, Eng.: Cambridge University Press, 1976); Jean-Louis Flandrin, *Families in Former Times: Kinship, Household and Sexuality*, trans. Richard Southern (Cambridge, Eng.: Cambridge University Press, 1976), pp. 184–86; Michael Mitterauer and Reinhard Sieder, *The European Family: Patriarchy to Partnership from the Middle Ages to the Present*, trans. Karla Oosterveen and Manfred Horzinger (Chicago: University of Chicago Press, 1983), pp.121–26; Lawrence Stone, *The Family, Sex and Marriage in England, 1500 to 1800* (New York: Harper and Row, 1977), pp. 42–62; Gillis, *For Better, for Worse*, pp. 117–19.

11. Gillis, *For Better, for Worse*, p. 174

12. Even if the children did not view themselves as part of the family economy, their parents did. Emile Zola provides us with a graphic example in *Germinal*: neither La Levaque nor La Maheude wanted her child to marry, even though a child had already been born to the young couple; Philomène's and Zacharie's wages were too important to their respective families for them to be allowed to establish their own household. It was only after Philomène had a second child that her mother wanted her to leave the household. La Levaque then argued with La Maheude, who still did not want to relinquish Zacharie's wages to a new household. See *Germinal*, trans. Stanley and Eleanor Hochman (New York: NAL, 1970), p. 85. Gillis points to a similar example in *For Better, for Worse*, p. 118. See also Joan W. Scott and Louise A. Tilly, "Women's Work and the Family in Nineteenth Century Europe," *Comparative Studies in Society and History* 17 (1975): 36–64; and Louise A. Tilly and Joan W. Scott, *Women, Work and Family* (New York: Holt, Rinehart and Winston, 1978), pp. 32–42.

13. See Appendix B, Table B-7. Interestingly, parental death assumed much larger proportions among the parents of nail makers than ribbon weavers. The fact that there was virtually no difference in age at marriage for nail makers and ribbon weavers suggests that nail makers' fathers died

at a younger age. But, for numerous reasons, the meaning of such rates cannot be determined. Moreover, even if there were a connection between parental death and the timing of marriage, the presence of siblings and birth order would certainly play a role in timing of marriage as well.

14. See, for example, Gillis, "Peasant, Plebeian and Proletarian Marriage in Britain, 1600–1900," pp. 151–57. See also Gillis, *For Better, for Worse*, p. 128, where he argues that in the context of rural industrialization, the willingness of women to bear children outside of marriage may actually have been a sign of family cohesion, as these women and their offspring remained a part of the family economy. For a controversial discussion of the causes for the rise in illegitimacy during the eighteenth and nineteenth centuries, see Edward Shorter, *The Making of the Modern Family* (New York: Basic Books, 1975), pp. 80–98. For another perspective, see Louise A. Tilly and Miriam Cohen, "Women's Work and European Fertility Patterns," *Journal of Interdisciplinary History* 6 (Winter, 1976): 447–76; Levine, "Proto-Industrialization and Demographic Upheaval," p. 30; Peter Laslett, *Family Life and Illicit Love in Earlier Generations* (Cambridge: Cambridge University Press, 1977), chapter 3.

15. Michael W. Flinn, *The European Demographic System, 1500–1820* (Baltimore: Johns Hopkins University Press, 1981), p. 118.

16. Rates of illegitimacy in Saint Chamond between 1824 and 1830 are drawn from ADL, 48M 5, "Mouvement de la population," 1824, 1825, 1826, 1827, 1828, 1829, and 1830. Between 1820 and 1829, Lyon had an illegitimacy rate of 14.3; Rouen, 24.1; and Meulan, 6.1. See Jean-Pierre Bardet, *Rouen aux XVIIe et XVIIIe siècles: les mutations d'un espace social*, 2 vols. (Paris: Société d'Edition d'Enseignement Supérieur, 1983), 1:320. But the number of illegitimate births per 100 births is a poor measure of the level of illegitimacy, because it does not account for the number of unmarried women in their childbearing years: ages fifteen to forty-five. Young women who came from the countryside to do seasonal silk work in Saint Chamond may have inflated the rate. For an alternative way of measuring illegitimacy, see Shorter, *The Making of the Modern Family*, pp. 332–36.

17. The French average is based on data from only 35 parishes, in which rates fluctuated from 9.7 in the southwest to 25.3 in Loumarin (Vaucluse). See Flinn, *The European Demographic System*, pp. 25–26, 122. In large cities the rate was much higher. In Rouen, for example, in 1789 it reached 31: Bardet, *Rouen aux XVIIe et XVIIIe siècles*, 1:324.

18. See David Weir, "Fertility Transition in Rural France, 1740–1829," Ph.D diss., Stanford University, 1982, table 6, p. 30, for rates of illegitimacy and prenuptial conceptions in rural areas that are similar to those in Saint Chamond.

19. In order to determine with certainty the number of years a woman spent in each age group, only "closed" or "MF"-type families were used, that is, families in which the death of one of the spouses provided a precise date for the end of marriage. In this cohort, 269 families were closed in such a manner.

20. Because a large proportion of marriages ended before the wife reached menopause, the number of children actually born is smaller than the total fertility rate. The number of children born to families in this cohort averaged 4.6. For calculations of m used here, see Appendix B, Table B-8. For explanations and examples of m, the index of fertility control, see

Ansley J. Coale and T. James Trussell, "Technical Note: Finding the Two Parameters That Specify a Model Schedule of Marital Fertility," *Population Index* 44 (1978): 203–11; John E. Knodel, "Family Limitation and the Fertility Transition: Evidence from the Age Patterns of Fertility in Europe and Asia," *Population Studies* 31 (1977): 219–49; for a critical analysis, see Weir, "Fertility Transition in Rural France," pp. 47–58.

21. For recent and very interesting critiques of the concept of natural fertility, see Angus McLaren, *Reproductive Rituals: The Perception of Fertility in England from the Sixteenth Century to the Nineteenth Century* (New York: Methuen, 1984), and Judith Blake, "Fertility Transition: Continuity or Discontinuity with the Past?" in *Proceedings of the International Population Conference, Florence, 5–12 June 1985* (International Union for the Scientific Study of Population), 4:393–405.

22. See Weir, "Fertility Transition in Rural France," table 13, p. 65; Levine, "Proto-Industrialization and Demographic Upheaval," p. 20.

23. Both Weir, "Fertility Transition in Rural France," pp. 62–66, and Bardet, *Rouen aux XVIIe et XVIIIe siècles*, 1:268–71, establish a trend of sharper decline in later years of marriage. The question is a complex one, however; see Weir, "Fertility Transition in Rural France," pp. 58–62, for a discussion of the literature.

24. Louis Henry, *Anciennes familles genevoises: étude démographique, XVIe–XXe siècles* (Paris: P.U.F., 1956), established fertility decline among the upper bourgeoisie. For early fertility decline among notables and merchants in Rouen, see Bardet, *Rouen aux XVIIe et XVIIIe siècles*, 1:279–83.

25. Levine, "Proto-Industrialization and Demographic Upheaval," p. 16.

26. Flinn, *The European Demographic System*, pp. 84–85; Weir, "Fertility Transition in Rural France," pp. 68–70. For mean age at birth of the last child by class between 1670 and 1789 in Rouen, see Bardet, *Rouen aux XVIIe et XVIIIe siècles*, 1:282.

27. For duration of childbearing in Saint Chamond, see Appendix B, Table B-9.

28. The literature on this issue speaks to its complexity. See, for example, Etienne van de Walle and Francine van de Walle, "Allaitement, stérilité et contraception: les opinions jusqu'au XIXe siècle," *Population* 27 (1972): 686–701; John E. Knodel and Etienne van de Walle, "Breast-Feeding, Fertility and Infant Mortality: An Analysis of Some Early German Data," *Population Studies* 21 (1967): 109–31; Knodel, "Two and a Half Centuries of Demographic History in a Bavarian Village," *Population Studies* 3 (1970):353–76; Flandrin, *Families in Former Times*, pp. 206–7.

29. Flandrin suggests that taboos against intercourse during breast-feeding motivated French couples to send their children to wet nurses. On this practice, see Flandrin, *Families in Former Times*, pp. 234–35; for effects on fertility, see pp. 201–17; see also C. Rollet, "Allaitement, mise en nourrice et mortalité infantile en France à la fin du XIXe siècle," *Population* 6 (1978): 1189–1203; Bardet, *Rouen aux XVIIe et XVIIIe siècles*, 1:288–96; John E. Knodel, "European Populations in the Past: Family Level Relations," in *The Effects of Infant and Child Mortality on Fertility*, ed. Samuel H. Preston (New York: Academic Press, 1978), pp. 21–45.

30. See Blake, "Fertility Transition"; Bardet, *Rouen aux XVIIe et XVIIIe siècles*, 1:263–64.

31. Knodel, "European Populations in the Past," pp. 21–45; Weir, "Fertility Transition in Rural France," pp. 106–51.

32. See Appendix B, Table B-10.

33. J. Duplessy, *Essai statistique sur le département de la Loire* (Montbrison: n.p., 1818), p. 132.

34. Henry, "The Population of France," pp. 445–48; see also Weir, "Fertility Transition in Rural France," p. 121, for survival rates from the INED data.

35. For life expectancy among women in the Loire, see van de Walle, *The Female Population of France in the Nineteenth Century*, table 8.1. Using life expectancy for the Loire obviously provides only a rough estimate for measuring infant mortality, since we cannot assume that life expectancy in Saint Chamond was the same as that for the entire department. However, it is more accurate than using the Saint Chamond child mortality rates. I am grateful to David Weir for suggesting this approach. If child mortality rates are used, they indicate that infant mortality is underestimated by 25 percent for girls and 55 percent for boys.

36. For a method for correcting the under-registration of deaths (but that cannot be applied to the Saint Chamond data) see Bardet, *Rouen aux XVIIe et XVIIIe siècles*, 1:368–71.

37. Garden, *Lyon et les lyonnais*, p. 62.

38. James R. Lehning, "Family Life and Wetnursing in a French Village," *Journal of Interdisciplinary History* 12 (Spring 1982): 645–56.

39. Garden, *Lyon et les lyonnais*, p. 72; see also pp. 64–72. On wetnursing, see Bardet, *Rouen aux XVIIe et XVIIIe siècles*, pp. 288–96; George Sussman, "The Wet-Nursing Business in Nineteenth-Century France," *French Historical Studies* 9 (1975): 304–28; Sussman, "The End of the Wet-Nursing Business in France, 1874–1914," *Journal of Family History* 2 (Fall 1977): 237–58; Catherine Rollet, "Allaitement, mise en nourrice et mortalité infantile en France à la fin du XIXe siècle," *Population* 6 (1978): 1189–1203.

40. Tilly and Scott, *Women, Work and Family*, p. 111. They quote Theodore Leuridan, *Histoire de la fabrique de Roubaix* (Roubaix: Beghin, 1864), pp. 156–57.

41. These family histories are based on the reconstituted families from marriage no. 49, 28 Nov. 1822 (Gautier-Vaganay) and marriage no. 48, 24 Sept. 1817 (Boissonna-Rey), in ADL, subseries 3E 208, births, deaths, and marriages, 1816–1865.

42. Garden, *Lyon et les lyonnais*, p. 62; Bonnie Smith discusses wives' assistance to their entrepreneurial husbands in the late eighteenth and early nineteenth centuries. Significantly, when they did assist their husbands they had small families, and later in the century, when women became more domestic, they had much larger families. See *Ladies of the Leisure Class: The Bourgeoises of Northern France in the Nineteenth Century* (Princeton: Princeton University Press, 1981), pp. 34–49.

43. Jean-Paul Bravard, "La clouterie dans la région de Firminy," *Notes d'histoire: au pays de cloutiers* (Firminy: Maison de la Culture de Firminy, Feb. 1977): 1–18.

44. Wives of food merchants, shopkeepers, and men in miscellaneous services signed their marriage records at an especially high rate: 77 and 78 percent, respectively. For signatures as evidence for literacy, see F. Furet

and W. Sachs, "La croissance de l'alphabétisation en France, XVIIIᵉ–XIXᵉ siècles," *Annales ESC* 3 (May–June 1974): 714–37; F. Furet and J. Ozouf, *Reading and Writing: Literacy in France from Calvin to Jules Ferry* (Cambridge, Eng.: Cambridge University Press, 1982), pp. 10–18. Because children were taught to read before they were taught to write, being able to write one's name has been considered an indication that one could read. And yet there are good reasons for skepticism. See Eugen Weber, *Peasants into Frenchmen: The Modernization of Rural France, 1870–1914* (Stanford: Stanford University Press, 1976), p. 310. In addition to signatures on marriage records, other sources attest to the relatively high rate of literacy among ribbon weavers. See AN, C956, "Enquête sur le travail," 1848; Armand Audiganne, *Les populations ouvrières et les industries de la France dans le mouvement social du XIXᵉ siècle* (Paris: Capelle, 1854), p. 323.

45. AN, Fⁱᶜ VII, Loire, 1840: report from the subprefect in Saint Etienne to the district council of the arrondissement.

46. For individualism among ribbon weavers, see Audiganne, *Les populations ouvrières*, p. 332. For middle-class values associated with fertility control, see Etienne van de Walle, "Motivations and Technology in the Decline of French Fertility," in *Family and Sexuality in French History*, ed. Robert Wheaton and Tamara K. Hareven (Philadelphia: University of Pennsylvania Press, 1980), pp. 135–78; John E. Knodel, *The Decline of Fertility in Germany, 1871–1939* (Princeton: Princeton University Press, 1974); Philippe Ariès, "An Interpretation to Be Used for a History of Mentalities," in *Popular Attitudes toward Birth Control in Pre-Industrial France and England*, ed. Orest Ranum and Patricia Ranum (New York: Harper Torchbooks, 1972), pp. 100–125; J. A. Banks and Olive Banks, *Feminism and Family Planning in Victorian England* (New York: Schocken Books, 1964).

47. See Bardet, *Rouen aux XVIIᵉ et XVIIIᵉ siècles*, 2:34.

48. For a valuable discussion of the attitudes of political economists toward fertility among the laboring poor and for a useful bibliography, see William Coleman, *Death Is a Social Disease: Public Health and Political Economy in Early Industrial France* (Madison: University of Wisconsin Press, 1982), pp. 59–81. He draws much of his discussion from J. B. Say, *A Treatise on Political Economy; or, The Production, Distribution, and Consumption of Wealth*, trans. C. R. Prinsep, 4th American ed. (Philadelphia: John Grigg, 1830), and J. B. Say, *Cours complet d'économie politique pratique*, 2d ed., 2 vols. (Paris: Guillaumin, 1840). See also Chevalier, *Laboring Classes and Dangerous Classes*, pp. 455–56n38.

CHAPTER 3

1. ADL, subseries 3E 208, births, marriages, and deaths in Saint Chamond, 1816–1865; after 1865, Palais de Justice, Saint-Etienne, Greffe du Tribunal de Grande Instance (henceforth GTGI): *état civil* of Saint Chamond, births, marriages, and deaths. Family history based on family reconstituted from marriage no. 30, 14 Jan. 1819.

2. See Chapter 2 and Appendix B, Table B-5.

3. L. Turgan, "Les établissements Oriol et Alamagny," in his *Les grandes usines de la France*, 16 vols. (Paris: Michel Levy, 1865–1884), 15:28–34; H. Baret, *Manuel de rubanerie, passementerie et lacets* (Paris: Ballière, 1924), pp. 11–12.

4. Archives de la Ministère de la Guerre, Vincennes, MR1266, "Rapport sur les environs de Saint-Chamond," 1843. Cf. Baret, *Manuel de rubanerie*, pp. 55–58; Turgan, "Les établissements Oriol et Alamagny," pp. 13–16; L.-J. Gras, *Histoire de la rubanerie et des industries de la soie à Saint-Etienne et dans la région stéphanoise suivie d'un histoire de la fabrique de lacets de Saint-Chamond* (Saint Etienne: Théolier, 1906), pp. 706–9.

5. Quoted in Bernard Plessy, *La vie quotidienne en Forez avant 1914* (Paris: Hachette, 1981), p. 122. Cf. Turgan, "Les établissements Oriol et Alamagny," p. 13.

6. ADL, series S, Archives de la Chambre de Commerce de Saint Etienne, carton 59 dossier 1; L. Jury, "L'Industrie des lacets," in *L'Association pour l'Avancement des Sciences, XXVI*ᵉ *session tenue à Saint-Etienne, août 1897*, 2 vols. (Saint Chamond: A. Poméon, 1898), 2:8.

7. J. Valserres, *Les industries de la Loire*, pp. 256, 317, 326; Jury, "L'Industrie des lacets," p. 15; Stéphane Bertholon, *Histoires de Saint-Chamond: notes et souvenirs d'un vieux couramiaud* (Saint Etienne: n.p., 1927), pp. 82, 90; for employers' roles in local government and associations, see Chapter 5.

8. Valserres, *Les industries de la Loire*, pp. 322–25; Jury, "L'Industrie des lacets," p. 17; Bibliothèque de la Chambre de Commerce de Saint-Etienne, Association des Fabricants de Lacets, *Question du travail de nuit dans les fabriques de lacets de Saint-Chamond*, petition no. 2, 12 March 1887 (Saint Etienne, 1890).

9. Valserres, *Les industries de la Loire*, p. 322.

10. Ibid., p. 325; Gras, *Histoire de la rubanerie*, p. 734.

11. Valserres, *Les industries de la Loire*, p. 321; Gras, *Histoire de la rubanerie*, p. 711.

12. Valserres, *Les industries de la Loire*, pp. 321–27; Jury, "L'Industrie des lacets," pp. 10–14. Michael Hanagan argues that all domestic industry disappeared by 1872: see *The Logic of Solidarity: Artisans and Industrial Workers in Three French Towns, 1871–1914* (Urbana: University of Illinois Press, 1980), p. 143.

13. Valserres, *Les industries de la Loire*, p. 322.

14. A. Audiganne, *Les populations ouvrières et les industries de la France dans le mouvement social du XIX*ᵉ *siècle* (Paris: Capelle, 1854), p. 311.

15. How factory conditions were described depended on the observer's perspective. Turgan's massive compendium on France's large factories served to document French industrial progress. Factory conditions and women's factory work were thus viewed favorably. For a discussion of how Louis Reybaud's and Armand Audiganne's respective investigations of French industries and working conditions resulted in "masterpiece[s] of political accommodation," see William M. Reddy, *The Rise of Market Culture: The Textile Trade and French Society, 1750–1900* (Cambridge, Eng.: Cambridge University Press, 1984), pp. 229–36.

16. Bibliothèque de la Chambre de Commerce de Saint-Etienne, Association des Fabricants de Lacets, *Question du travail de nuit*, petition no. 2, 12 March 1887, pp. 22–23.

17. For example, see Thomas Dublin, *Women at Work: The Transformation of Work and Community in Lowell, Massachusetts, 1826–1860* (New York: Columbia University Press, 1979).

18. ADL 90M 1, report of August 1869. For persistence of the twelve-hour shifts, see 88M 18, petitions to the Minister of Commerce and Industry, June 1886 and March 1887.

19. Valserres, *Les industries de la Loire*, p. 322.

20. ADL 90M 1, police commissioner to the prefect, 3 Aug. 1869.

21. Fournier rightly complained that the standard history of Saint-Chamond, James Condamin's *Histoire de Saint Chamond*, published by A. Picard in 1890, was written for the bourgeoisie with the intention of flattering them. No one had written about the common people, especially the braid and metal workers on whose shoulders the fortunes of the bourgeoisie had been built. In his capacity as schoolteacher, Fournier had ample opportunity to observe workers in Saint Chamond and to know them well. Most important to him were the stories they had recounted to one another which had been handed down over the generations. In the 1930s, Fournier finally began to put these stories into print. He insists that he printed them unchanged from the way they were recounted among Saint-Chamonais workers. His purpose, moreover, was to preserve local legends so that they would remain a part of popular tradition as the oral tradition of story-telling declined. Though using his works as a source has obvious risks, they do provide rich material about working-class life in Saint Chamond. For his approach to preserving workers' popular culture, see M. Fournier, *La vallée ardente: scènes de la vie populaire* (Saint Etienne: Librairie Dubouchet, 1938), p. 9. His other works include *L'Essor d'une ville ouvrière: l'oeuvre sociale de la municipalité de Saint Chamond* (Saint Etienne: Imprimerie de la Loire Républicaine, 1934); *Tableaux de la vie saint-chamonaise* (Saint Chamond: Bordron, 1949); *Les forgerons* (Saint Chamond: Bordron, 1939); *Les mineurs du Gier* (*Revue Forézienne*, no date).

22. Fournier, *La vallée ardente*, p. 385;

23. Ibid.

24. For factory conditions see Fournier, *La vallée ardente*, p. 13. See factory inspection reports in ADL 88M 18.

25. Fournier, *La vallée ardente*, p. 13; see also Fournier, *Tableaux de la vie saint-chamonaise*.

26. ADL 49M 226, "Dénombrements de la population," 1876. This calculation is based on a sample coded and computerized and given to me by Michael Hanagan. See also 48M 68, "Mouvement de la population," arrondissement of Saint Etienne. Throughout the second half of the nineteenth century, females in Saint Chamond outnumbered males by about 1,500.

27. ADL 88M 18, petition to the Minister of Commerce and Industry, June 1886, and Bibliothèque de la Chambre de Commerce de Saint-Etienne, Association des Fabricants de Lacets, *Question du travail de nuit*, petition no. 2, 12 March 1887.

28. Turgan, "Les établissements Oriol et Alamagny," pp. 37–39.

29. Gras, *Histoire de la rubanerie*, p. 732.

30. L'Association International pour la Protection Légale des Travailleurs, *Le travail de nuit des femmes dans l'industrie: rapports sur son importance et sa réglementation légale* (Paris: n.p., 1903), pp. 176–79.

31. Bibliothèque de la Chambre de Commerce de Saint-Etienne, Association des Fabricants de Lacets, *Question du travail de nuit*, petition no. 2, 12 March 1887, p. 23.

32. ADL 88M 8, letter to the prefect from the Association des Fabricants de Lacets, 1 Feb. 1883; letter from Marc Bethenod, president of the Conseil de Prud'hommes, to the prefect, 2 Aug. 1883.

33. See inspection reports, ADL 88M 16, 1890. Only two firms, Irenée Brun and Antoine Reymondon, employed more girls between sixteen and twenty-one than women over twenty-one, and these two firms experienced the most difficulty with the law of 1892. See Chapter 6.

34. Jury, "L'Industrie des lacets," p. 18.

35. ADL 92M 49, "Pétition au préfet de la Loire des ouvrières au métier des fabriques de lacets de Saint-Chamond," circa 1893.

36. Ibid.

37. Bibliothèque de la Chambre de Commerce de Saint Etienne, Antoine Roule, "Midi," *Petits poèmes et chansons*, 1921.

38. ADL, subseries 3E 208, and GTGI: births, marriages, and deaths in Saint Chamond, 1816–1865. Families reconstituted from marriages 1816 to 1825. See Chapter 2.

39. For the composition of the labor force in braids, see ADL 10M 102, 1894; Bibliothèque de la Chambre de Commerce de Saint-Etienne, Association des Fabricants de Lacets, *Question du travail de nuit*, petition no. 2, 12 March 1887; Turgan, "Les établissements Oriol et Alamagny," p. 36; Valserres, *Les industries de la Loire*, p. 322.

40. ADL 88M 18, 18 July 1888; Valserres, *Les industries de la Loire*, p. 325.

41. ADL 88M 16, 4 June 1890; Condamin, *Histoire de Saint-Chamond*, pp. 21–24.

42. Jean Vial, *Industrialisation de la sidérurgie française, 1814–1864*, 2 vols. (Paris: Mouton, 1967), 1:114–15. For a history of metallurgy in this region, see also L. Babu, *L'Industrie métallurgique dans la région de Saint-Etienne* (Paris: Dunot, 1899); L. Turgan, "Notice sur les hauts-fourneaux, forges et aciéries de Petin, Gaudet et Compagnie à Vierzon, Givors, Toga, Rive-de-Gier, Saint-Chamond et Assaily," in *Les grandes usines de la France*, vol. 4 (Paris: Michel Levy, 1867); Louis Reybaud, *Le fer et la houille* (Paris: Michel Levy, 1874).

43. Valserres, *Les industries de la Loire*, pp. 135–41.

44. Ibid., p. 109. For descriptions of the Petin and Gaudet forges, see Louis Reybaud, "Rapport sur la condition morale, intellectuelle et matérielle des ouvriers qui vivent de l'industrie du fer, 1866–1871" (Musée Sociale, no. 9920, vol. 4), p. 659; Reybaud, *Le fer et la houille*, p. 152; Vial, *Industrialisation de la sidérurgie française*, 1:259.

45. For shifts in metal works, see AN F^{12} 4728, 13 Oct. 1874; Valserres, *Les industries de la Loire*, p. 44.

46. Babu, *L'Industrie métallurgique*, pp. 138–41, 178; ADL, Archives de la Chambre de Commerce, carton 59 dossier 1, *Bottin* of 1858.

47. AN C3022, Loire, and C3021, Rhône.

48. For workers' budgets, see Yves Lequin, *Les ouvriers de la région lyonnaise (1848–1914)*. Vol. 2: *Les intérêts de classe et de la république* (Lyon: Presses Universitaires de Lyon, 1977), pp. 15–22; Michelle Perrot, *Les ouvriers en grève: France, 1871–1890*, 2 vols. (Paris: Mouton, 1974), 1:208–50.

49. Reybaud, *Le fer et la houille*, p. 147. L.-J. Gras estimates the cost of living in *Histoire du commerce locale et des industries qui s'y rattachent dans la région stéphanoise et forézienne* (Saint Etienne: Théolier, 1910), pp. 636–37.

50. Lequin, *Les ouvriers de la région lyonnaise*, 2:92.

51. See AN C3022, "Enquête sur la situation des classes ouvrières, 1872–1875," Loire; F^{12} 4511B, "Situation industrielle de la Loire, 1865–1886"; ADL, 10M 102, 1894. For wages in metallurgy, throughout France as well as in Saint Chamond, see Vial, *Industrialisation de la sidérurgie française*, 1:156, 259; Reybaud, *Le fer et la houille*, pp. 146–52; Valserres, *Les industries de la Loire*, pp. 93, 152–55; Hanagan, *The Logic of Solidarity*, pp. 126–63.

52. AN F^{12} 4511B, 1880 and 1881.

53. ADL, subseries 3E 208, and GTGI, marriages in Saint Chamond, 1861–1870. For the coding of professions, see Appendix A.

54. Hanagan, *The Logic of Solidarity*, pp. 129–35.

55. AN C3022, "Enquête sur la situation des classes ouvrières, 1872–1875," Loire; ADL 92M 14, document 67, 5 May 1875; Valserres, *Les industries de la Loire*, p. 159.

56. AN C3022, "Enquête, 1872–1875," Loire.

57. ADL 10M 102, May 1894.

58. AN F^{12} 4511B, 1870–1871; ADL 92M 13, 19 Nov. 1872; 92M 14, 20 Feb. 1874; 10M 102, reports of police commissioner, March–November 1894; Lequin, *Les ouvriers de la région lyonnaise*, 2:71–75; Maxime Perrin, *Saint-Etienne et sa région économique: un type de vie industrielle en France* (Tours: Arrault, 1937), p. 225.

59. The occupations of 161 metal workers were traced through their reconstituted families. The 55 who changed occupations, many of whom changed more than once, declared the following: textiles (23), day laborer (5), mine worker (5), quarry worker (3), gardener (3), grocer (3), cultivator (2), navvy (2), joiner (2); one each declared himself engraver, nail maker, locksmith, gunsmith, rag picker, plasterer, cookware merchant, carriage driver, coal merchant, plaster foreman, coach commissioner, mail carrier, itinerant porcelain merchant, clog maker, railroad worker, entrepreneur, lodger, flour merchant, egg merchant, and fruit merchant.

60. ADL, subseries 3E 208, and GTGI, births, marriages, and deaths in Saint Chamond: based on families reconstituted from marriages no. 80, 17 Nov. 1865; no. 53, 27 May 1863; no. 85, 26 Sept. 1866; no. 79, 5 Nov. 1864. In abiding by the request of the French government to preserve anonymity of records in the *état civil* for the past one hundred years, I have substituted initials for full names when referring to events after 1875. Abandoning factory work to vend food was apparently common. See Reddy, *The Rise of Market Culture*, p. 272.

61. Reybaud, *Le fer et la houille*, p. 152.

62. Reybaud, "Rapport sur la condition morale," p. 535.

63. AN C3353, "Enquête parlementaire," Saint Etienne, 1884.

64. In 1869, female braid workers earned at most 1f40 per day. In 1894 they earned about 1f90: ADL 92M 12, 4 Aug. 1869; 10M 102, May 1894.

65. AN C3022, "Enquête, 1872–1875," Loire. Regarding children's work, see also Perrot, *Les ouvriers en grève*, 1:314. Laws regulating child labor generally became more effective during the second half of the nineteenth century, though their enforcement was uneven.

66. AN C3022, "Enquête, 1872–1875," Loire; ADL 92M 12, 4 and 6 August 1869; 88M 8, procès-verbaux against Bethenod, Balas, Dubouchet, March 1883.

67. AN C3022, "Enquête, 1872–1875," Loire.

68. See Chapter 5.

69. Jury, "L'Industrie des lacets," p. 16. See also Turgan, "Les établissements Oriol et Alamagny," p. 28.

70. Turgan reported in 1884 that Oriol et Alamagny employed 800 women, 100 men, and 50 children (aged twelve to sixteen) in their factories, and another 100 men and 400 women in their own homes: see "Les établissements Oriol et Alamagny," p. 36. In 1887, a petition from braid manufacturers to the government protesting the prohibition of night work for women under twenty-one claimed they employed 2,500 to 3,000 "mothers working at home" in reeling, doubling, folding, and finishing braids, in addition to the 463 men and 3,759 women they employed in factories: Bibliothèque de la Chambre de Commerce de Saint-Etienne, Association des Fabricants de Lacets, *Question du travail de nuit*, petition no. 2, 12 March 1887, p. 22. In 1897, L. Jury reported that forty firms throughout the Gier valley employed 5,000 to 6,000 men and women and that 2,000 of the women, or one-fourth of the labor force, worked in their own homes: see Jury, "L'Industrie des lacets," p. 8.

71. Bibliothèque de la Chambre de Commerce de Saint-Etienne, Association des Fabricants de Lacets, *Question du travail de nuit*, petition no. 2, 12 March 1887, pp. 24–25.

72. AN C3022, "Enquête, 1872–1875," Saint Etienne, questionnaire C. Although it was workers in Saint Etienne who responded to this questionnaire, their situation was similar to that of workers in Saint Chamond. If anything, women in Saint Chamond were under more pressure to work outside the home; since ribbon weaving continued in Saint Etienne, more domestic industry was available for women there. For complaints about the lack of *crèches*, see ADL 90M 1, "Questionnaire de secours mutuel des passementiers," 1884.

73. Fournier, *La vallée ardente*, p. 64.

74. ADL 88M 18, petition from braid manufacturers, June 1886; Bibliothèque de la Chambre de Commerce de Saint-Etienne, Association des Fabricants de Lacets, *Question du travail de nuit*, petition no. 2, 12 March 1887, pp. 23–24.

75. ADL 92M 49, petition to the prefect of the Loire from braid workers in Saint Chamond, circa 1893.

76. See, for example, *Congrès ouvrier de France session de 1876 tenu à Paris du 2 au 10 octobre* (Paris: Librairie Sandoz et Fischbacher, 1877), pp. 69–106; *Séances du congrès ouvrier de France, Lyon, 28 janvier à 8 fevrier, 1878* (Lyon: Jules Trichot, 1878), pp. 31–76. Summaries of and excerpts from deliberations of the congresses may be found in Tonim, pseudonym of Albert Minot, *La question sociale et le congrès ouvrier de Paris: conditions rationnelles de l'ordre économique, social et politique: état de la capacité morale et politique du prolétariat* (Paris: M. Blanc, 1877); Léon de Seilhac, *Les congrès ouvriers en France de 1876 à 1897* (Paris: A. Colin, 1899).

77. For a more detailed breakdown of geographical origins of those who married 1861–1870, see Appendix B, Table B-11.

78. Lequin, *Les ouvriers de la région lyonnaise*, 1:214–21. See also Leslie Page Moch, *Paths to the City: Regional Migration in Nineteenth-Century France* (Beverly Hills: Sage, 1983).

79. The sex ratio of migrants from the Puy-de-Dôme is noteworthy: 106

women migrated to Saint Chamond from this department, while only 69 men did. The Puy-de-Dôme had long been a silk-producing region, and the decline of the putting-out industry might explain the large number of migrants, as well as the sex ratio.

80. ADL, subseries 3E 208, and GTGI, births, marriages, and deaths in Saint Chamond, 1861–1914; reconstituted families beginning with marriages no. 46, 1 May 1863; no. 58, 5 June 1863; no. 8, 20 Jan. 1863.

81. Ibid., marriages no. 90, 21 Nov. 1862; no. 20, 14 Feb. 1861; no. 3, 4 Jan. 1863; no. 83, 21 Oct. 1862.

82. "Recensement sommaire des villes non chefs-lieux d'arrondissement ayant plus de 10,000 habitants, 1861," in Bureau de la Statistique Générale, *Statistique de la France: résultats généraux de l'enquête effectuée dans les années 1861–1865* (Nancy: Berger-Levrault, 1873); ADL 48M 68, "Mouvement de la population," 1872; 47M 147, "Conseil d'hygiène salubrité de l'arrondissement de Saint Etienne: rapport sur l'application de la loi de 19 avril 1858 sur logement insalubre dans l'arrondissement de Saint Etienne," 4 May 1858 and 23 Feb. 1858.

83. ADL, subseries 3E 208, and GTGI, births, marriages, and deaths in Saint Chamond; reconstituted family beginning with marriage no. 26, 17 July 1825.

84. Ibid., reconstituted family beginning with marriage no. 85, 26 Dec. 1861.

85. See Appendix B, Tables B-12, B-13, and B-14. Adding figures horizontally and vertically in Table B-14 shows that 371 out of 530 native men and women (70 percent) lived with a parent or relative, while 385 out of 1,422 migrant men and women (27 percent) lived with a parent or relative. In Tables B-12, B-13, and B-14, figures for "same house" and "with parent" vary because the data in the first two tables are based on a random sample of addresses provided in the marriage records, while data in B-14 are based on couples' declarations of their living situations, also recorded in the marriage records. Despite variation in data, both sources show a wide divergence between natives and migrants in their relationships with other family members.

86. See Appendix B, Tables B-15 and B-16.

87. In 1891, 25.1 percent of the braid workers lived in dormitories. See Hanagan, *The Logic of Solidarity*, p. 147. For residence patterns prior to marriage, see Appendix B, Table B-16.

88. For the families reconstituted from marriages between 1861 and 1865, 2,306 men witnessed births, marriages, and deaths. Of those, 501, or 21.7 percent, were relatives. The proportions of relatives for textile and metal workers were 25.4 percent and 20.1 percent, respectively. First witnesses, among the four for marriages, were most important. Neighbors served as first witness in 17.6 percent of metal workers' marriages and in 20.6 percent of textile workers' marriages; 8.9 percent of those for textile workers shared the same profession, while 16.9 percent of metal workers' witnesses were coworkers. For fuller detail, see Elinor Accampo, "Industrialization and the Working Class Family: Saint Chamond, 1815–1880," Ph.D. diss., University of California, Berkeley, 1984, pp. 201, 206–8.

89. Lequin, *Les ouvriers de la région lyonnaise*, 1:222.

90. For occupations of fathers-in-law, see Accampo, "Industrialization and the Working Class Family," p. 307. The differences in results between

the 1850s and the 1860s with regard to occupational inheritance cannot be attributed to differences in methodologies or in coding the occupations, since those used here are the same as those Lequin used. I am grateful for his help in providing and implementing the coding I used. For the coding, see Appendix A.

91. For fuller data on fathers' occupations, see Accampo, "Industrialization and the Working Class Family," pp. 302–3, 310.

92. ADL, subseries 3E 208, marriages no. 17, 1868; no. 2, 1870; no. 5, 1866; no. 53, 1865; no. 7, 1865.

93. Ibid., marriages no. 106, 1868; no. 12, 1867; no. 89, 1866.

94. Ibid., marriages no. 59, 1861; no. 99, 1863.

95. See Accampo, "Industrialization and the Working Class Family," p. 302.

96. See Appendix B, Tables B-3 and B-17.

97. For example, David Gordon notes of Saint Etienne in the 1860s, "Divisions between immigrants and long-term residents as well as artisan and factory workers made new organizations difficult to create and maintain." He stresses the importance of strong community ties in the level of popular radicalism. See *Merchants and Capitalists: Industrialization and Provincial Politics in Mid-Nineteenth-Century France* (University: University of Alabama Press, 1985), p. 95. Similarly, John M. Merriman points to the association among skilled positions, geographical stability, and militancy in Limoges, noting that 68 percent of the workers in the most radical factory were natives. See *The Red City: Limoges and the French Nineteenth Century* (New York: Oxford University Press, 1985), pp. 172–73. William H. Sewell offers a much more detailed analysis of the effects of migration on worker morale in *Structure and Mobility: The Men and Women of Marseille, 1820–1870* (Cambridge, Eng.: Cambridge University Press, 1985). This analysis suggests that the disruptiveness of migration depended on distance and on whether it was permanent or temporary. Though migration undermined worker morale in some cases, it did not prevent a radical political vanguard from developing in Marseille.

98. Condamin, *Histoire de Saint-Chamond*, pp. 589–90. For the importance of occupational inheritance, see Michelle Perrot, "The Three Ages of Industrial Discipline in Nineteenth-Century France," in *Consciousness and Class Experience in Nineteenth-Century Europe*, ed. John M. Merriman (New York: Holmes & Meier, 1979), pp. 153–55; Reddy, *The Rise of Market Culture*, p. 168.

99. See Chapter 5.

100. Lequin, *Les ouvriers de la région lyonnaise*, 1:248.

101. "Histoire des forges et aciéries de la marine et d'Homecourt," from the archives of the Forges et Aciéries de la Marine, chapter 2, p. 5.

102. Lequin, *Les ouvriers de la région lyonnaise*, 1:261.

CHAPTER 4

1. See, for example, Claude Tillier, *Mon oncle Benjamin* (Paris, 1881), p. 78, quoted in Angus McLaren, *Sexuality and Social Order: The Debate over the Fertility of Women and Workers in France, 1780–1920* (New York: Holmes & Meier, 1983), p. 125; among the examples of recent scholarship associating the working class with high fertility are Michael Haines, *Fertility and*

Occupation: Population Patterns in Industrialization (New York: Academic Press, 1979); Ellen Ross, "'Fierce Questions and Taunts': Married Life in Working-Class London, 1870–1914," *Feminist Studies* 8 (1982): 575–602.

2. Men and women in Saint Chamond apparently married later than those in Mulhouse. However, Henri Cetty used different measures, saying that more than one-third of the women married under age twenty and one-third of the men married under age twenty-three: see *La famille ouvrière en Alsace* (Rixheim: A. Sutter, 1883), p. 104. John Gillis cites a drop in marriage age with factory production in *For Better, for Worse: British Marriages, 1600 to the Present* (New York: Oxford University Press, 1985), p. 243. For more discussion of age at marriage, see Louise A. Tilly and Joan W. Scott, *Women, Work and Family* (New York: Holt, Rinehart and Winston, 1978), pp. 93–96.

3. Gillis, *For Better, for Worse*, p. 243.

4. Tilly and Scott, *Women, Work and Family*, p. 109.

5. A song entitled "L'Ouvrière saint-chamonaise," which became popular in a working-class singing society around 1900, provides an ambiguous picture of working-class female morality:

> She is the popular elite
> Who suffers and struggles with dignity,
> Whose courage is exemplary
> And her conduct the same;
> If her language and her manners
> Are a little free sometimes,
> She has morals much more strict
> Than many bourgeois girls.

From J. F. Gonon, *Histoire de la chanson stéphanoise et forézienne depuis son origine jusqu'à notre époque* (Saint Etienne: Imprimerie Cooperative, Union Typographique, 1906), p. 102, quoted in Michael Hanagan, *The Logic of Solidarity: Artisans and Industrial Workers in Three French Towns, 1871–1914* (Urbana: University of Illinois Press, 1980), p. 149. Less ambiguous is the publicity surrounding a bizarre incident that took place in 1895. A rape that occurred in one of the braid factories produced lengthy comment about the immorality of Saint-Chamonaises. See Chapter 6, and AN BB[18] 2019–3480A 95, letters to the prefect and the minister of justice, 10 and 11 Dec. 1895, and *L'Eclaireur*, 17 Nov. 1895.

6. Calculations of illegitimacy in Saint Chamond are based on illegitimate and legitimate births in ADL, subseries 3E 208, and GTGI, births, marriages, and deaths, 1824–1830 and 1861–1870. For Mulhouse and Strasbourg, see Cetty, *La famille ouvrière en Alsace*, p. 145.

7. Rates of prenuptial conception are based on fertility calculations from reconstituted families.

8. On this issue see Tilly and Scott, *Women, Work and Family*, pp. 96–98.

9. These personal histories are based on reconstituted families originating with marriages. Births, marriages, and deaths may be found in GTGI, *état civil* of Saint Chamond, marriage no. 81, 12 Sept. 1866, and marriage no. 33, 12 May 1865. See Appendix A for an explanation of how reconstituted families are used for personal histories.

10. Ibid., marriage no. 75, 4 Nov. 1865; marriage no. 53, 15 June 1866.

11. Ibid., marriage no. 60, 21 Aug. 1862; marriage no. 75, 4 Nov. 1865.

12. Ibid., marriage no. 43, 27 June 1864.

13. In the southern part of the Loire, Ig continued to reach the very high level of .800, suggesting the absence of any fertility control. Saint Chamond itself continued the pattern of fertility control it had established in the first half of the century. By 1851, Ig there measured .660. See James R. Lehning, "The Decline of Marital Fertility: Evidence from a French Department," paper presented to the annual meeting of the Social Science History Association in 1978. See also Lehning, *The Peasants of Marlhes: Economic Development and Family Organization in Nineteenth-Century France* (Chapel Hill: University of North Carolina Press, 1980). For a discussion of Ig, see Chapter 2, note 4. For marital fertility differentials by department in France, see Etienne van de Walle, *The Female Population of France in the Nineteenth Century: A Reconstruction of Eighty-Two Departments* (Princeton: Princeton University Press, 1974).

14. These calculations are based on the age-specific marital fertility rates in reconstituted families according to birthplace declared in marriage records. For these purposes, towns with populations of fewer than 10,000 inhabitants were considered rural. In cases where only the wife's birthplace was urban, the total marital fertility rate was 4.8; where only the husband's was urban, it was 5.3.

15. For example, see Haines, *Fertility and Occupation*, and Jean Vial, *Industrialisation de la sidérurgie française, 1814–1864*, 2 vols. (Paris: Mouton, 1967), 1:357–61.

16. Vial, *L'Industrialisation de la sidérurgie française*, 1:357–61. Michael Haines found that among men fifty to sixty years of age who had been married more than fifteen years, iron and steel workers had 309 surviving children per 100 families, while the national average was 261. See Haines, *Fertility and Occupation* pp. 13–14n.11.

17. See Chapter 2 for more detail.

18. See discussion in Chapter 3 and note 48 there for literature on workers' budgets and standards of living.

19. See Chapter 3.

20. Cetty, *La famille ouvrière en Alsace*, p. 132. A medical report to the minister of the interior cited infant deathrates of 240/1,000 and 260/1,000 in 1876 and 1877, respectively, in La Grand Combe (Gard); see ADL 35M 4, Académie de Médecine, *Rapport annuel de la commission permanente de l'hygiène de l'enfance* (Paris: G. Masson, 1878).

21. In some cases the error is clear, such as when the officer of the *état civil* noted that a fetus was only three months old or stated that the infant had lived for fifteen minutes after birth. But because the officers did not always supply such descriptive detail, the degree of inaccuracy is impossible to determine. The enormous discrepancy in stillbirths between Saint Chamond and Saint Etienne provides ample reason to suspect the validity of recordkeeping. Saint Chamond recorded seventy-four stillbirths per thousand live births between 1856 and 1868, while Saint Etienne recorded only thiry-eight. See Bureau de la Statistique Générale, *Statistique générale de la France*, série 2, vol. 21 (Paris: Imprimerie Nationale, 1901, 1902, 1906). In the industrial centers of Alsace between 1877 and 1878, Cetty recorded forty-nine to sixty-five stillbirths per thousand live births. See Cetty, *La famille ouvrière en Alsace*, p. 182. For purposes of comparison between the

two cohorts, the index of change in Table 18 includes stillbirths in both births and deaths.

22. For workers' concerns about wet-nursing, see the proceedings from the Congress of October 1876 in Tonim, pseudonym of Albert Minot, *La question sociale et le congrès ouvrier de Paris: conditions rationnelles de l'ordre économique, social et politique: état de la capacité morale et politique du prolétariat* (Paris: M. Blanc, 1877), p. 105. Women were forced to use wet nurses when they left the home to work. In addition to complaining that the practice caused infant deaths, they believed children also acquired bad morals. For the incidence of wet-nursing, see George Sussman, "The Wet-Nursing Business in Nineteenth-Century France," *French Historical Studies* 9 (1975): 304–28, and "The End of the Wet-Nursing Business in France, 1874–1914," *Journal of Family History* 2 (Fall 1977): 237–58; C. Rollet, "Allaitement, mise en nourrice et mortalité infantile en France à la fin du XIXe siècle," *Population* 6 (1978): 1189–1203; Rachel Fuchs, *Abandoned Children: Foundlings and Child Welfare in Nineteenth-Century France* (Albany: State University of New York Press, 1984).

23. ADL 35M 4, Service d'hygiène, 1871–1886, "Conseil d'hygiène publique et du salubrité: compte rendue 4 October 1874."

24. Ibid.

25. ADL, Archives de la Chambre de Commerce de Saint-Etienne, carton 25A dossier 3, *Revue de la prévoyance de la mutualité forézienne: Bulletin administratif de l'union départementale des sociétés des secours mutuels de la Loire*, 1907, no. 17. One study indicated that between 1873 and 1877 in Besançon, three-quarters of the babies who had died from diarrhea had been bottle-fed; see 35M 4, *Rapport annuel de la commission permanente de l'hygiène de l'enfance*, p. 12.

26. On earlier conceptions after the death of an infant, see Appendix B, Table B-10. The number of children born and the number who died under age five in closed families had a correlation coefficient of 0.72116 with a probability level of 0.0001. This measure, however, cannot be taken at face value. Duration of marriage was not taken into consideration here. Thus, if the infant mortality rate had been constant in all families, those in which marriages lasted a long time would naturally show more deaths as well as births.

27. ADL 28M 1, Société Protectrice de l'Enfance, 1872; 35M 4, "Enquête relative à protection des enfants en bas age," 4 Oct. 1874, p. 67; 28M 4, report of November 1891 on mutual societies, states that this society never functioned.

28. ADL, Archives de la Chambre de Commerce de Saint-Etienne, carton 25A dossier 3, *Revue de la prévoyance de la mutualité forézienne*. In his study of fertility in Germany, John E. Knodel found "abundant evidence connecting early weaning or lack of breast-feeding with high infant mortality during the latter part of the nineteenth century and early twentieth century": see *The Decline of Fertility in Germany, 1871–1939* (Princeton: Princeton University Press, 1974), p. 165. See also John E. Knodel and Etienne van de Walle, "Breast-Feeding, Fertility and Infant Mortality: An Analysis of Some Early German Data," *Population Studies* 21 (1967): 109–31; Rollet, "Allaitement, mise en nourrice et mortalité infantile"; Tilly and Scott, *Women, Work and Family*, p. 132.

29. See Appendix B, Table B-19; for the decline of endogenous deaths in France, and the method of measuring and interpreting them, see Robert

Nadot, "Evolution de la mortalité infantile endogène en France dans la deuxième moitié du XIXᵉ siècle," *Population* 25 (1970): 49–58.

30. This rate is based on women who died within forty-two days after a birth (MF-type families only). In the first cohort, 269 women bore 1,224 children, and 9 of these women died within forty-two days of the birth. One-third of these were first births. In the second cohort, 268 women bore 924 children, and 15 mothers died within forty-two days. Of those, one-quarter died after a first birth. The rate in Rouen between 1640 and 1800 was 11 deaths per 1,000 births. See Jean-Pierre Bardet, *Rouen aux XVIIᵉ et XVIIIᵉ siècles: les mutations d'un espace social* (Paris: Société d'Edition d'Enseignement Supérieur, 1983), 1:365.

31. ADL 90M 1, report of August 1869; J. Valserres, *Les industries de la Loire* (Saint Etienne: n.p., 1862), p. 322.

32. Of industrial centers in Alsace, Cetty noted, "Poor women have been seen to stay in the factory until the day their child is born. Others return to work two days later to avoid lacking bread. Poverty and misery oblige most of them to resume their wearisome occupations": *La famille ouvrière en Alsace*, p. 122. Workers themselves said the same thing at worker congresses. See Tonim, *La question sociale et le congrès ouvrier de Paris*, pp. 104–5.

33. Association Internationale pour la Protection Légale des Travailleurs, *Le travail de nuit des femmes dans l'industrie: rapports sur son importance et sa réglementation légale* (Paris: n.p., 1903), p. 178.

34. H. Rollet, *L'Action sociale des catholiques en France, 1871–1901* (Paris: Bovin, 1947), p. 189. For the effects of night work, see ADL 90M 1, report of August 1869; Valserres, *Les industries de la Loire*, p. 322; Michelle Perrot, *Les ouvriers en grève: France, 1871–1890*, 2 vols. (Paris: Mouton, 1974), 1:320.

35. Tonim, *La question sociale et le congrès ouvrier de Paris*, p. 105.

36. For duration of marriages in both samples, see Appendix B, Table B-20.

37. For the effects of dye chemicals on health, see AN C956, Enquête 1848, Department of the Loire, arrondissement of Saint Etienne, and ADL 40M 118, engineer's report, 30 June 1884.

38. Judith Stone, *The Search for Social Peace: Reform Legislation in France, 1890–1914* (Albany: State University of New York Press, 1985), p. 227n.36.

39. For a detailed description of machines and work in the Aciéries de la Marine et du Chemin de Fer, see Valserres, *Les industries de la Loire*. For the tragic accident of 1901, see *La Croix de Saint Chamond*, 6 Jan. 1901.

40. ADL 24j (H), carton 102, "Enquête sur la mortalité comparative dans les hôpitaux de la France et de l'étranger: hôpital de Saint Chamond," 1861, 1862; "Statistique hospitalière," commune de Saint Chamond, 1864.

41. ADL 47M 147, "Extrait de registres de délibérations du conseil municipal de Saint-Etienne 5 mai 1858: rapport sur les conditions des logements à Saint-Chamond, Saint-Etienne et Rive-de-Gier."

42. ADL 47M 147, Conseil d'Hygiène Salubrité de l'Arrondissement de Saint-Etienne, "Rapport sur l'application de la loi de 19 avril 1850 sur logement insalubre dans l'arrondissement de Saint-Etienne," 4 May 1858 and 23 Feb. 1858.

43. ADL 40M 93, document 255, letter opposing the establishment of the Targe and Hospital metal factory, 24 March 1841.

44. ADL 40M 118, document 79: engineer's report, circa 1866.

45. Ibid., letter from the mayor of Saint Chamond to the prefect, 31 Oct. 1865; document 85, engineer's report, 4 Jan. 1866.

46. ADL 35M 4, *Rapport annuel de la commission permanente de l'hygiène de l'enfance*, p. 7.

47. ADL 40M 118, documents 365 and 369, May and June 1879.

48. Ibid., document 481, engineer's report, 30 June 1884.

49. For diseases, see ADL 24j (H), carton 102, 1861, 1862; the doctor's comment may be found in register 30bis, 12 March 1889. For a fascinating history of the diagnosis and treatment of tuberculosis, see R. Dubos and J. Dubos, *The White Plague* (London: Little, Brown, 1952).

50. See Appendix B, Table B-21.

51. From reconstituted families originating from marriages no. 25, 22 Feb. 1861; no. 32, 5 May 1866; no. 26, 12 April 1862; GTGI, births, marriages, and deaths in Saint Chamond.

52. McLaren, *Sexuality and Social Order*, p. 148.

53. Ibid., p. 136.

54. Ibid., p. 152.

55. Claude Chatelard, *Crime et criminalité dans l'arrondissement de Saint-Etienne au XIXᵉ siècle* (Saint Etienne: Centre d'Etudes Foréziennes, 1981), pp. 90–94.

56. Cetty, *La famille ouvrière en Alsace*, p. 181.

57. ADL 35M 4, *Rapport annuel de la commission permanente de l'hygiène de l'enfance*, p. 8.

58. Bardet also suggests that poor health resulting from illness or malnutrition could cause a decline in fecundity: see *Rouen aux XVIIᵉ et XVIIIᵉ siècles*, 1:358–62.

59. Association Internationale pour la Protection Légale des Travailleurs, *Le travail de nuit*.

60. ADL 35M 4, *Rapport annuel de la commission permanente de l'hygiène de l'enfance*, p. 8.

CHAPTER 5

1. AN F^{1c} V, Loire 1, "Analyse du mémoire du préfet sur l'industrie et des manufactures de ce département, l'an 9" (circa 1801).

2. Colin Lucas, *The Structure of the Terror: The Example of Javogues and the Loire* (London: Oxford University Press, 1973), pp. 39–53.

3. Stéphane Bertholon, *Histoires de Saint-Chamond: notes et souvenirs d'un vieux couramiaud* (Saint Etienne: n.p., 1927), p. 28; James Condamin, *Histoire de Saint-Chamond et de la seigneurie de Jarez, depuis les temps les plus reculés jusqu'à nos jours* (Paris: A. Picard, 1890), pp. 491–502.

4. AN F^{1c} III, Loire 7, "Extrait des délibérations du conseil municipal de Saint-Chamond," April 1814. Four months later the municipal council asked the king for a royal blessing and the Decoration of the Lys, the "honorable and distinctive sign of friends of the Bourbon throne." Saint Chamond was recommended by "its industries, and by the purity of its morals, by its attachment to the religion of our fathers whose *pure religion* never ceased being practiced." See "Discours au Roi, prononcé par le President de la députation de la ville de Saint Chamond," 27 August 1814.

5. AN F^{1c} III, Loire 7, April 1814, and AN F^{1c} III, Loire 8, May 1814. Words of support for this restored monarchy came, not from a displaced

nobility rejoicing in an apparent return to the old order, but from an elite whose wealth derived from commerce and industry. At least nine of the twenty-one members of the municipal council were not only merchants or industrialists in their own right but were the fathers or family members of future industrialists: François Morel, Guillaume Sirvanton, François Magnin, silk merchants; Jean Claude Pascal, Antoine Moret, Simon Pierre Berne, Jean Baptiste Chaland, Grégoire Bertholon, Charles François Richard, all ribbon or braid merchants; Antoine Neyrand, forge master. Many of these same names and those of other industrialists and merchants appeared on the list of "eligibles" just prior to the July Revolution of 1830: Jean Baptiste Chaland, ribbon merchant; Louis Maximilien Finaz, notary; Antoine Flachat, Pierre Joseph Marie Granjon, François Magnin, all silk merchants; Charles François Richard-Chambovet, pioneer braid manufacturer; Antoine Thiollière, nail merchant. In 1830, Saint Chamond had as its mayor Jean Marie Ardaillon, a forge master, who was also a Legitimist. In 1831 he won a seat in the Legislative Chamber, for which braid manufacturer Richard Chambovet also competed. See AN F^{1c} III, Loire 4, list of eligibles for the Loire; and 28 May 1831–27 July 1831 for legislative elections.

   6. F^{1c} III, Loire 8, July and August 1814; 19 March 1815.
   7. J. Duplessy, *Essai statistique sur le département de la Loire* (Montbrison: n.p., 1818), p. 152.
   8. Archives du Ministère de la Guerre, Vincennes, MR1266, "Rapport sur la reconnaissance de la route de Saint-Etienne à Saint-Chamond," 1837.
   9. See, for example, André Jardin and André-Jean Tudesq, *Restoration and Reaction, 1815–1848*, trans. Elborg Forster (Cambridge, Eng.: Cambridge University Press, 1983), pp. 277–78.
   10. AN F^{1c} V, Loire 1, "Analyse du mémoire du préfet sur l'industrie et des manufactures, l'an XI"; ADL G107, Hospice de la Charité, 1792–1868, 31 Oct. 1806. See also F. Raymond, *Les hospices de Saint-Chamond: histoire, administration, origines, agrandissements, biens et revenus d'après les documents conservés dans leurs archives* (Saint Chamond: A. Poméon, 1888), pp. 24, 31–33.
   11. Duplessy, *Essai statistique sur le département de la Loire*, p. 393.
   12. ADL, series S, Archives de la Chambre de Commerce de Saint-Etienne, carton 131 dossier 9, "Mémoire sur l'industrie," 10 March 1810; AN F^{1c} V, Loire 1, report of the General Council to the minister of the interior, Nov. 1811; Raymond, *Les hospices de Saint-Chamond*, p. 33.
   13. AN F^{1c} V, Loire 1, reports of the General Council to the minister of the interior, 1819–1821; VII, Loire, reports of the subprefect of Saint Etienne to the district council of the arrondissement of Saint Etienne, 1840 and October 1848.
   14. F. Raymond, *Les hospices de Saint-Chamond*, pp. 9–14.
   15. Ibid., pp. 101–76.
   16. ADL 24j (E), carton 59 and registers 30bis and 30ter; also Raymond, *Les hospices de Saint-Chamond*, pp. 159–62.
   17. Raymond, *Les hospices de Saint-Chamond*, p. 159.
   18. ADL G107, Hospice de la Charité, 31 Oct. 1806.
   19. Ibid.; for the product of children's labor, see Raymond, *Les hospices de Saint-Chamond*, p. 179.
   20. AN F^{1c} V, Loire 1, report of the General Council of the Loire to the

minister of the interior, 1807; report of the subprefect to the district council of the arrondissement of Saint Etienne, 1819; VII, Loire, General Council of the arrondissement of Saint Etienne, report of the subprefect to the council, meeting in 1836; report of the subprefect of the arrondissement of Saint Etienne to the district council of the arrondissement, meeting of 1839.

21. ADL 10M 21, general report to the prefect, 7 April 1831. According to the author of this report, the local clergy influenced opinion through women, who were "devoted to their priests and thought just like them." These women in turn exercised "an empire over their husbands" who, well educated and enlightened, would otherwise be "liberal." This informant read poorly the depth of Catholic and Legitimist sentiment among Saint Chamond's ruling elite.

22. For Catholic reaction to the July Monarchy on the issue of education, see Robert Gildea, *Education in Provincial France, 1800–1914: A Study of Three Departments* (Oxford: Clarendon Press, 1983), pp. 39–42. For the increase in the presence of religious orders in Saint Chamond, see Bertholon, *Histoires de Saint-Chamond*, p. 150; Condamin, *Histoire de Saint-Chamond*, pp. 550–53.

23. Gildea, *Education in Provincial France*, pp. 39–42.

24. Since the Revolution of 1789, the parish of Saint Ennemond had been joined with that of Saint Pierre. For instruction in Saint Chamond see Condamin, *Histoire de Saint-Chamond*, p. 553, and M. Fournier, *L'Essor d'une ville ouvrière: l'oeuvre sociale de la municipalité de Saint-Chamond* (Saint Etienne: Imprimerie de la Loire Républicaine, 1934), p. 14.

25. Condamin, *Histoire de Saint-Chamond*, p. 553. These schools received attention and praise in AN F^{17} 9327, report on primary instruction, arrondissement of Saint Etienne, 1855. For "blackmail" from Brothers of the Christian Schools, see J. Donzelot, *The Policing of Families*, trans. Robert Hurley (New York: Pantheon, 1979), pp. 33, 77.

26. See Chapter 1.

27. ADL, series S, Archives de la Chambre de Commerce de Saint Etienne, carton 59 dossier 1, 22 Dec. 1833; 27 March 1834; 12 April 1834; 13 April 1834. See also A. Audiganne, *Les populations ouvrières et les industries de la France dans le mouvement social du XIXe siècle* (Paris: Capelle, 1854), p. 328. For the uprising of silk workers in Lyon, see Robert J. Bezucha, *The Lyon Uprising of 1834: Social and Political Conflict in the Early July Monarchy* (Cambridge, Mass.: Harvard University Press, 1974).

28. See, for example, John M. Merriman, "The *Demoiselles* of the Ariège," in *1830 in France*, ed. John M. Merriman (New York: New Viewpoints, 1975), pp. 87–118; and William M. Reddy, *The Rise of Market Culture: The Textile Trade and French Society, 1750–1900* (Cambridge, Eng.: Cambridge University Press, 1984), pp. 113–15.

29. Audiganne, *Les populations ouvrières*, p. 7.

30. William Coleman, *Death Is a Social Disease: Public Health and Political Economy in Early Industrial France* (Madison: University of Wisconsin Press, 1982), pp. 73–82.

31. Donzelot, *The Policing of Families*, p. 66.

32. AN F^{1c} VII, Loire, report of the subprefect to the district council of the arrondissement of Saint Etienne, 1840. Efforts to rationalize charity assumed concrete form in the department of the Loire. The attempt to

reorganize the arrangements for abandoned and orphaned children provides a case in point. Officials assumed that parents who abandoned their children, especially when they were infants, lacked family sentiment. They believed that if they made abandonment more difficult, parents would be encouraged to keep their children, which in turn would promote a stronger sense of family.

Parents gave up their children to charitable institutions in two ways: either they left infants at *tours*, revolving windows which insured anonymity, or they brought their identified children to the hospice with the intention of reclaiming them at some future point. Officials believed parents retrieved their children in order to put them to work. In 1840 the prefect complained that the cost of supporting these children was becoming exorbitant. He and the hospice administrators in Saint Etienne, which took in all abandoned children under age six from the entire arrondissement, had a twofold goal: reducing the costs of keeping the children, and forcing parents to assume responsibility for them.

Eliminating *tours* would, they believed, deter mothers from abandoning their children because they would no longer be able to do so anonymously. A second idea applied to those who brought children to the hospice hoping to retrieve them later: these children would be exchanged with those in distant hospices, on the assumption that geographical separation would discourage parents from giving up their children in the first place. Third, administrators decided that parents who came to reclaim a child would be charged for the expenses that child had incurred during his or her stay in the hospice. These administrators thus took every possible measure to reduce, in Donzelot's words, "the social cost of . . . reproduction" among the poor and "obtain an optimum number of workers at minimum public expense": Donzelot, *The Policing of Families*, p. 16.

These efforts failed completely in the Loire. Exchanges of children with other hospices in order to send them farther away from parents entailed only inconvenience, with none of the desired results. Nor did they eliminate *tours*. "It is difficult," the prefect lamented, "to try to execute these measures in a region where workers live hand to mouth." Hospice administrators did ask for reimbursement from parents who came to reclaim their children but did not demand it of those who obviously could not pay. The prefect concluded that the "true remedy for abandoned children as well as for their illegitimate procreation, which is one of the causes for abandonment, is in the moralization [of the poor], in the organization of savings accounts, in mutual aid [societies], in schools, in mendicity depots, and in the development of industry and commerce." See AN F¹ᶜ V, Loire 1, year IX; F¹ᶜ VII, Loire, report of 1840 and report of 1848.

The imperatives of economic cycles and the harsh reality of periodic unemployment made rationalization of charity along utilitarian principles impossible. Saint Etienne's *tour* finally closed in 1846, when entries to the foundling hospital rose by 50 percent (from 62 to 92) and withdrawals declined by 50 percent (from 42 to 18). Its closure, the prefect noted, hardly inspired "rebirth of family sentiment" at a time of high unemployment; the situation resulted from "misery rather than depravity": AN F¹ᶜ VII, Loire, report of 1848. On abandoned children see also Rachel Fuchs, *Abandoned Children: Foundlings and Child Welfare in Nineteenth-Century France* (Albany: State University of New York Press, 1984).

33. Condamin, *Histoire de Saint-Chamond*, pp. 550–53.

34. ADL, series S, Archives de la Chambre de Commerce de Saint-Etienne, carton 131 dossier 9, Chambre Consultative des Arts et Manufactures, "Situation industrielle," 15 June 1837; carton 59 dossier 1, "Notes de la séance," 14 Sept. 1837; AN F¹ᶜ VII, Loire, report of the subprefect to the district council of the arrondissement of Saint Etienne, 1840.

35. Condamin, *Histoire de Saint-Chamond*, p. 553. A catechism class "for the preservation of young girls" was added to the *ouvroir* of the Filles de la Charité in 1847.

36. ADL G107, Hospice de la Charité, dossier 1, 31 Dec. 1839; see also 24j (E), carton 59 dossier 3, 5 Oct. 1880; 17 May 1884; Feb. 1885; 7 Dec. 1885; registre 30ᵇⁱˢ, April 1884; June 1886; Aug. 1886; June 1887; Oct. 1888; Dec. 1891.

37. AN F¹ᶜ VII, Loire, report of the subprefect to the district council of the arrondissement of Saint Etienne, 1840.

38. Archives Paroissiales du Rhône, diocèse de Lyon, parish report for Saint Pierre by curé Antoine Adolphe, 1844.

39. ADL 24j (E), carton 59 dossier 4, 2 May 1848; see also 3 May 1848; 1 June 1848; and 10 June 1848.

40. Archives du Ministère de la Guerre, Vincennes, MR1266, "Rapport sur la reconnaissance de la route de Saint-Etienne à Saint-Chamond," 1837.

41. Raymond, *Les hospices de Saint-Chamond*, pp. 174–75, 159–61.

42. Peter Stearns makes this argument in *Paths to Authority: The Middle Class and the Industrial Labor Force in France, 1820–1848* (Urbana: University of Illinois Press, 1978); see especially pp. 36–46, 139–40. For problems in the Saint Chamond ribbon industry, see my Chapter 1.

43. Jardin and Tudesq, *Restoration and Reaction*, p. 278.

44. Audiganne, *Les populations ouvrières*, p. 341.

45. ADL 28M 1, letter to the prefect from the police commissioner of Saint Chamond, 31 March 1843.

46. Despite the absence of overt political activity, Saint Chamond did harbor a distinctly left-wing group. In May 1849, the mayor complained to the prefect that the Montagnard party had made unexpected progress and that the "police had closed their eyes to certain meetings." But while popular demonstrations and insurrections occurred on 13–15 June in Paris and Lyon, nothing happened in Saint Chamond. During the following months the government outlawed clubs and police systematically repressed them. The police commissioner of Saint Chamond noted only one republican club and by October still had not succeeded in finding its meeting place. But he assured the prefect that the club exercised "little influence" in the town. He did, however, take the precaution of seizing the writings of Louis Blanc and other socialist and republican materials from a bookstore. See ADL 10M 28, letter from the mayor of Saint Chamond to the subprefect, 18 Sept. 1848; 10M 31, police of Saint Chamond to the subprefect, 29 Dec. 1849; 10M 30, mayor of Saint Chamond to the prefect, 15 May 1849. For repression during the Second Republic throughout France, see John M. Merriman, *The Agony of the Republic: The Repression of the Left in Revolutionary France, 1848–1851* (New Haven: Yale University Press, 1978). The only incident of actual disorder that broke out prior to Louis Napoleon's coup occurred when a priest failed to appear at a forge worker's funeral arranged by the municipality. Rumor spread that the priest did not arrive because the worker was a republican. Whether workers blamed the priest or the municipality is not clear, but they began to riot and several were

arrested. See AN BB³⁰ 361, "Parquet de la cour d'appel, Lyon au garde des sceaux," 20 July 1850. On the presidential elections in 1848, see F¹ᶜ III, Loire 4, letter from the prefect to the minister of the interior, 16 July 1850. Although local officials in Saint Chamond, as in other places of working-class concentration, took precautions to insure peace at the time of Louis Napoleon's coup d'état in 1851, most Saint-Chamonais received the news with apathy, and others welcomed it. Only a few protested. For this and for the reaction of the upper classes to the coup, see ADL 10M 36, police commissioner of Saint Chamond to the prefect, 4 Dec. 1851, and document 20, 6 Dec. 1851.

47. Condamin, *Histoire de Saint-Chamond*, p. 557. Local notables easily found their niche in the emperor's government. Legitimist Victor Dugas was elected to the General Council of the Loire in 1852, and when he retired because of his age the following year, the minister of the interior warmly supported forge master Antoine Neyrand, another champion of Legitimist politics, as his replacement. See AN F¹ᶜ III, Loire 4, elections, 22 April 1853.

48. AN F¹ᶜ III, Loire 8, bimonthly report of the subprefect of Saint Etienne, 28 Oct. 1854.

49. Condamin, *Histoire de Saint-Chamond*, p. 569; J. Valserres, *Les industries de la Loire* (Saint Etienne: n.p., 1862), p. 42.

50. L. Turgan, "Les établissements Oriol et Alamagny," in his *Les grandes usines de la France*, 16 vols. (Paris: Michel Levy, 1865–1884), 15:53.

51. ADL 10M 147, "Extrait du registre des délibérations du conseil municipal de Saint Chamond," Feb. 1864.

52. Fournier, *L'Essor d'une ville ouvrière*, p. 41.

53. ADL 40M 147, letter from the mayor of Saint Chamond to the prefect, 10 March 1864.

54. ADL 40M 147, "Extraits du registre des délibérations du conseil municipal de la ville de Saint Chamond," 1875–1879.

55. AN C3022, "Enquête sur la situation ouvrière," Loire, 1872–1875; ADL 92M 12, 4 and 6 August 1869; 88M 8, procès-verbaux against Bethenod, Balas, Dubouchet, March 1883. For contrasting and more "paternalistic" attitudes toward women, see Nancy Fitch, "The Effects of Capitalist Development on Family Life in Central France," paper presented at the Social Science History Association Meeting, 24 November 1985; see also Bonnie Smith, *Ladies of the Leisure Class: The Bourgeoises of Northern France in the Nineteenth Century* (Princeton: Princeton University Press, 1981), pp. 123–61.

56. Bibliothèque de la Chambre de Commerce de Saint-Etienne, Association des Fabricants de Lacets, *Question du travail de nuit dans les fabriques de lacets de Saint-Chamond*, petition no. 2, 12 March 1887 (Saint Etienne, 1890), pp. 24–25.

57. Ibid., pp. 25–27; see also ADL 88M 18, petition to the minister of commerce and industry from the braid manufacturers in Saint Chamond, June 1886. These industrialists concerned themselves particularly with competition from Germany.

58. Gaudet's treatment of workers provides an early example of what large-scale industrialization would bring to Saint Chamond. In 1848, when the Petin forges were in Rive-de-Gier, Gaudet virtually bribed the workers away from what he considered the "dangerous effects of republican ideas" by providing financial assistance to any who needed it. Apparently these

employers often provided such aid. Gaudet's biographer eulogized, "[These two men] were not alone in their success. How many workers achieved comfort, and can today, in their old age, enjoy a secure rest! How many others, less fortunate, received aid and assistance from [their] generous hands! For these two men, having been workers themselves, knew well the condition and needs of the worker, and knew also how to relieve their miseries." See Jules du Chevalard, *Notice biographique sur M. J.-M. Gaudet, ancien maître des forges de Rive-de-Gier* (Saint Etienne: n.p., 1887), pp. 14–22.

59. Quoted in AN C3022, "Enquête sur la situation ouvrière," 1872–1875, Département de la Loire, arrondissement de Saint-Etienne.

60. L. Jury, "L'Industrie des lacets," in *L'Association pour l'Avancement des Sciences, XXVIe session tenue à Saint-Etienne, août 1897*, 2 vols. (Saint Chamond: A. Poméon, 1898), 2:19.

61. Condamin, *Histoire de Saint-Chamond*, p. 607.

62. Bertholon, *Histoires de Saint-Chamond*, p. 265.

63. M. Fournier, *Tableaux de la vie saint-chamonaise* (Saint Chamond: Bordron, 1949), p. 106.

64. In 1875, Emile Alamagny donated 100,000 francs and the Oriol-Gillier family gave 50,000 francs for the care of the sick and 20,000 francs for the aged. Braid manufacturer Irenée Brun donated 3,000 francs in 1885, and Oriol *fils* provided 150,000 francs for the construction of a new wing for the aged in 1901. See ADL 24j (E), carton 59 dossier 3, 7 Dec. 1885; register 30bis, 18 May 1856 and 18 Aug. 1886; register 30ter, 1898; see also *La Croix de Saint-Chamond*, 30 Jan. 1903; and for a list of other donors through 1888, see Raymond, *Les hospices de Saint Chamond*, pp. 167–73, 176–77.

An example of direct assistance, similar to actions taken in the first half of the century, came with the crisis of the early 1880s. It became so serious that in February 1885 the hospice administrative commission allocated 4,500 francs to hire unemployed workers to cultivate 3,000 square meters of hospice domains at 3f per day. In March they supplied another 4,500 francs to employ workers. In April they distributed 9,000 francs in direct charity. Serving on the commission at this time were Oriol *fils*, conservative republican and Catholic; Louis Jury, president of the Association of Braid Manufacturers, Catholic and monarchist; radical republican Bergé; opportunist republicans Fabreguettes, Imbert, Jean Louis Loubet, and the future mayor, Vial; and radical Charles Rochefort. They rationalized their decision by saying that the hospice would profit from improved lands and that if they did not spend this money on workers' wages, they would have to spend it on charity within the home. See ADL 24j (E), carton 59 dossier 3, 5 Feb. 1885; register 30bis, 6 March 1885; 7 April 1885.

65. For payments from Déplace, Thiollière, Imbert, Gelas, and Garas to the hospital between 1873 and 1876, see ADL 24j (F), carton 106 dossier 2. Receipts for payments from the Aciéries de la Marine, the forges of l'Horme, the Neyrand brothers, the coal mines of Saint Chamond, the Imbert brothers, Joseph Lanet, and Olagnier for the year 1882 are in Series X, Saint Chamond Hospices, 1873–1893. These archives are quite disorganized, and records for other payments are either lost or scattered throughout other cartons, many of which are no longer available to the public. The listing of some mutual aid societies can be found in 28M 4, "Sociétés mutuels, Saint Chamond," Nov. 1891. In June 1896, a group of Catholic

Workers founded a "Caisse de famille de Notre Dame du Travail" for "utilitarian, moral and religious purposes," which was dominated by monarchist employers. See 10M 115, report of the police commissioner, 19 Feb. 1897.

66. Turgan, "Les établissements Oriol et Alamagny," pp. 37–39.

67. *La Croix de Saint-Chamond*, 7 July 1891; 27 Jan. 1901; 3 Feb. 1901; *L'Eclaireur*, 7 July 1891.

68. Bertholon, *Histoires de Saint-Chamond*, pp. 134, 221; Condamin, *Histoire de Saint-Chamond*, p. 569; *La Croix de Saint-Chamond*, 23 Nov. 1902; Turgan, "Les établissements Oriol et Alamagny," p. 39.

69. The history of this family has been reconstructed from ADL 3E 208, marriage no. 69, 28 Sept. 1864, and subsequent births and deaths in the family. For an explanation of family reconstitution see Chapter 2 and Appendix A. Jean-Marie R.'s case can be found in ADL 24j (E), register 30[ter], 1 Feb. 1900.

70. Ibid.; ADL 49M 285, census of 1891.

71. The widower's case is in ADL, 24j (E), register 30[bis], October 1894 and December 1898; the quote about his aid is in the Dec. 1898 register entry. Marie Anne L.'s case has been reconstructed from register 30ter, 22 Sept. 1898, and her reconstituted family beginning with 3E 208, marriage no. 16, 21 Jan. 1862; 49M 285, census of 1891. The quote about her condition is from the 22 Sept. 1898 register entry.

72. This case appears in ADL 24j (E), register 30bis, June 1885. Further information about François C.'s family and their occupational histories are derived from his reconstituted family, beginning with 3E 208, marriage no. 53; 49M 285, census of 1891.

73. An article in *La Croix de Saint Chamond*, 17 March 1901, indicated that someone jumped out "of the only window at the hospices that did not have a grill." M. Fournier had no good words to describe the hospital, "which filled with dread the sick who crossed its threshold": *L'Essor d'une ville ouvrière*, p. 22. The strict "rules of order and discipline" in the hospices may be found in ADL 24j (E), carton 59 dossier 3.

74. Jean Imbert, *Histoire des hôpitaux en France* (Toulouse: Editions Privat, 1982), p. 339. In Saint Chamond, those for whom there was no space in the hospital or charity were sent to Lyon; they also received aid from the *bureau de bienfaisance*, the various religious orders, or the private charity for which Mme. Oriol and other ladies bountiful were so renowned. See Raymond, *Les hospices de Saint-Chamond*, pp. 94–99. See also ADL 24j (E), register 30bis, 11 Oct. 1887 and 26 June 1889, on the lack of beds and the problems of administering medical aid outside the hospital.

75. Imbert, *Histoire des hôpitaux*, p. 344.

76. ADL 24j (H), carton 102; 24j (E), carton 59 dossier 3; 24j (F), carton 106 dossier 4; Imbert, *Histoire des hôpitaux*, p. 339. Records of employers' payment for sick days are scattered throughout the hospice archives, so a systematic analysis of payments is not possible. One sample set of receipts indicates that in 1882, eight employers paid for 970 sick days; see Series X, 1873–1883.

77. ADL 24j (F), carton 106 dossier 2, 23 June 1876; see also dossier 9, 1863.

78. ADL 24j (E), register 30[bis], March 1886; February 1891; June 1894; March 1895; register 30[ter], November 1898.

79. ADL 24j (E), register 30[bis], July 1894. Numerous similar examples may be found throughout these registers. The uncle of two children requested custody, and the investigation of his circumstances took two months; see register 30bis, June 1893.

80. ADL 24j (E), register 30bis, 3 Dec. 1890; 4 Feb. 1891.

81. ADL 24j (E), register 30ter, 18 Aug. 1889.

82. M. Fournier, *La vallée ardente: scènes de la vie populaire* (Saint Etienne: Librairie Dubouchet, 1938), pp. 64–65.

83. Ibid., p. 158.

84. *Le Moniteur de la Loire et la Haute-Loire*, 16 Aug. 1877.

85. AN F[17] 9327, report on primary instruction, arrondissement of Saint Etienne, 1855. Members of the municipal council came from the old, well-established Saint-Chamonais families of Gillier, Richard, Thiollière, Neyrand, and Dugas-Vialis. They adhered to Legitimist politics and practiced Catholicism devoutly. The new braid industrialists who appeared—Oriol and Brun—were equally Catholic and reactionary. For lists of municipal council members, see ADL 6M 20.

86. ADL T718, cantonal delegates for Saint Chamond in 1850; 17 March 1875; T721, 23 Feb. 1872.

87. AN F[17] 9327, report on primary instruction, arrondissement of Saint Etienne, 1855.

88. AN F[17] 9347, inspection of primary schools, arrondissement of Saint Etienne, 1860. Comments here about the psychological effect of abandoning patois are admittedly speculative. Eugen Weber discusses the importance among villagers in the Loire of continuing to speak patois. He quotes an 1864 report on instruction from the Loire: "In villages, anyone who tried to speak French wouldn't escape the jeers of his neighbors. He would be turned to ridicule": *Peasants into Frenchmen: The Modernization of Rural France, 1870–1914* (Stanford: Stanford University Press, 1976), p. 312. It follows that abandoning patois would also have had great symbolic importance for the migrant. In his account of life in a Breton village, Pierre-Jakez Hélias stresses the humiliation of *not* knowing French, the "bourgeois" language. "Every time they had to deal with a city civil-servant and every time they ventured into a city, they were exposed to sly smiles and to jeers of all kinds. They were called 'straw-choppers,' for example, or 'gorse-grinders,' since their language seemed uncouth to those who didn't understand it." It is inconceivable that language and all it symbolized did not play a profound role in the integration of migrants into an urban setting. This subject is certainly one that merits more systematic exploration. As Hélias reminds us, "Like all populations who never express themselves other than orally, [the Bretons] were very sensitive to language, very heedful of it." See *The Horse of Pride: Life in a Breton Village*, trans. June Guicharnaud (New Haven: Yale University Press, 1978), pp. 151–52.

89. AN F[17] 9327, report on primary instruction, arrondissement of Saint Etienne, 1855; 20 Jan. 1857, 1859, 1860; F[17] 9338, report on instruction, arrondissement of Saint Etienne, 1857; F[17] 9347, inspection of primary schools, arrondissement of Saint Etienne, 1860.

90. ADL T883, adult education, 1864–1867; letter to inspector of primary schools from Emma Canel, 13 June 1872; Bertholon, *Histoires de Saint-Chamond*, p. 134.

91. H. Rollet, *L'Action sociale des catholiques en France, 1871–1901* (Paris:

Bovin, 1947), p. 286; Pierre Pierrard, *L'Eglise et les ouvriers en France (1840–1940)* (Paris: Hachette, 1984), pp. 295–356.

92. ADL M244, tr. 427/6.

93. ADL 27M 2, police commissioner of Saint Chamond to the prefect, 28 April 1880; 10M 113, police of Saint Chamond, 15 July 1896; 10M 115, police of Saint Chamond, 13 Jan. 1897; Bertholon, *Histoires de Saint-Chamond*, pp. 176–78; Yves Lequin, *Les ouvriers de la région lyonnaise (1848–1914)*. Vol. 2: *Les intérêts de classe et de la république* (Lyon: Presses Universitaires de Lyon, 1977), pp. 337–41, 468.

94. Rollet, *L'Action sociale des catholiques en France*, pp. 29–30.

95. Ibid. See also Pierrard, *L'Eglise et les ouvriers*, pp. 286–309.

96. Rollet, *L'Action sociale des catholiques en France*, pp. 255, 686–90; ADL 21M 48, police commissioner of Saint Chamond to prefect, 27 June 1903. This report did not state what kind of workers belonged to the *cercles*.

97. Rollet, *L'Action sociale des catholiques en France*, p. 83; Pierrard, *L'Eglise et les ouvriers*, pp. 343–53.

98. Rollet, *L'Action sociale des catholiques en France*, p. 286.

99. AN BB¹⁸ 1932A 96, "Patrons catholiques," 1892.

100. AN BB¹⁸ 1932A 96, "Oeuvre des cercles catholiques d'ouvriers: le Comité de Saint-Chamond, Association de Patrons," 1877.

101. Ibid., "Parquet de la cour d'appel de Lyon," arrondissement of Saint Etienne, 1892.

102. For example, a local notary in 1867 credited the work of religious orders with the city's harmony and implied that workers there shared their employers' beliefs: "It is thanks to them, to their lessons, to the training of youth by the moral and religious education that they have given it, that we owe the truly extraordinary tranquility which our city has always enjoyed, even during the troubled days of 1848." Quoted in Bertholon, *Histoires de Saint-Chamond*, p. 36.

103. Archives du Ministère de la Guerre, Vincennes, MR1266, "Rapport sur les environs de Saint-Chamond," 1843.

CHAPTER 6

1. M. Fournier, *L'Essor d'une ville ouvrière: l'oeuvre sociale de la municipalité de Saint-Chamond* (Saint Etienne: Imprimerie de la Loire républicaine, 1934), p. 8.

2. M. Fournier, *Tableaux de la vie saint-chamonaise* (Saint Chamond: Bordron, 1949), p. 95.

3. AN F¹ᶜ III, Loire 9, prefect to the minister of the interior, 6 June 1858. See also David Gordon, *Merchants and Capitalists: Industrialization and Provincial Politics in Mid-Nineteenth-Century France* (University: University of Alabama Press, 1985), p. 96. Only the economic downturn of 1857 provoked protest. Someone posted a "seditious placard" in Saint Chamond that blamed the government for poverty among the French. While the police admitted "that our working class is in the greatest state of misery," they found the incident unimportant and nonthreatening to peace in the community. See ADL 10M 53, police of Saint Etienne to the minister of the interior, 13 Nov. 1875, and Tribunal of Saint Etienne to the prefect, 27 Dec. 1875. Even workers in Rive-de-Gier and Saint Etienne exhibited no unrest and expressed no overt interest in politics during these years.

4. Election results may be found in ADL 3M 11, May and June 1863;

retrospective details about Imbert are in 3M 21, police commissioner of Saint Chamond to prefect, 20 Sept. 1885. Opposition candidates received an astonishing 81 percent of the vote in Saint Etienne, where the government had even tried to manipulate votes in its favor, and 53 percent in Rive-de-Gier. For a discussion of these elections in Saint Etienne, see Gordon, *Merchants and Capitalists*, p. 96.

   5. AN F¹ᶜ III, Loire 9, 5 July 1865; 30 Sept. 1865; 20 Oct. 1865.

   6. AN F¹ᶜ III, Loire 9, 11–14 June 1869.

   7. ADL 10M 62, police commissioner of Saint Chamond to prefect, document 132, 1 July 1869; 10M 32, police commissioner of Saint Chamond to prefect, 1 July 1869.

   8. ADL 10M 67, police commissioner of Saint Chamond to prefect, document 154, 11 Aug. 1870; 92M 12, police commissioner of Saint Chamond to prefect, document 40, dated 20, 21, 22 Aug. 1869.

   9. ADL 27M 1, "Cercle des Travailleurs," 1870; police commissioner of Saint Chamond to prefect, 11 Jan. 1872.

   10. ADL 27M 1, police commissioner of Saint Chamond to central commissioner, 24 Aug. 1873.

   11. Gordon, *Merchants and Capitalists*, p. 116.

   12. For Legitimist and clerical sentiment toward the Empire in 1869, see AN F¹ᶜ III, Loire 9, 31 Aug. 1869.

   13. See Gordon, *Merchants and Capitalists*, chapter 4 and pp. 110–11.

   14. For conservatives' fear of revolution and their show of support for Napoleon when he traveled through the region, see AN F¹ᶜ III, Loire 9, prefect to the minister of the interior, 31 Aug. 1869; ADL 10M 62, police commissioner of Saint Chamond to prefect, document 133, 30 Nov. 1869.

   15. For this plebiscite, Napoleon III asked the French to approve or disapprove the liberal reforms of the past decade with a yes or no vote. The meaning of those votes inevitably contains paradox. A no vote could come from two contradictory sentiments: liberals cast negative votes to reject authoritarian government, while conservatives voted no to oppose liberal reforms. But many who opposed the liberal reforms—such as the Legitimists—found themselves in the paradoxical position of voting yes because they wanted to demonstrate their support for the Empire since it stood for order and authority. For a discussion of the paradoxes in this plebiscite, see Theodore Zeldin, *Emile Ollivier and the Liberal Empire of Napoleon III* (Oxford: Clarendon Press, 1963), pp. 154–56. The French population overwhelmingly endorsed the emperor. Within the arrondissement of Saint Etienne, rural communes favored the Empire, while the industrial cities opposed it. The vote distribution ranged from a yes vote of 97 percent in rural Bourg Argental to 27 percent in the cities of Saint Etienne and Le Chambon-Feugerolles. Indeed, Saint Etienne cast the largest proportion of negative votes of any city in France. Significantly, Saint Chamond deviated from its neighboring cities. Saint Chamond remained the stronghold of conservatives who dreaded republicanism. For results of the plebiscite throughout the Loire, see Laurent Boyer, *Les élections politiques dans le département de la Loire au temps de l'assemblée nationale et du Maréchal MacMahon* (Paris: Sirey, 1963), p. 27. For Saint Etienne and the Stéphanois, see Gordon, *Merchants and Capitalists*, pp. 112, 153, 154.

   16. ADL 6M 13, prefect of the Loire to the minister of the interior, 14 Dec. 1870; 27M 1, police commissioner of Saint Chamond to central commissioner, 24 Aug. 1873.

17. ADL 6M 13, prefect of the Loire to the minister of the interior, 14 Dec. 1870; 27M 1, police commissioner of Saint Chamond to central commissioner, 24 Aug. 1873; Stéphane Bertholon, *Histoires de Saint-Chamond: notes et souvenirs d'un vieux couramiaud* (Saint Etienne: n.p., 1927), p. 142.

18. ADL 10M 72, "Extrait du registre des délibérations du Conseil municipal de la ville de Saint-Chamond," document 18, 5 April 1871.

19. ADL 27M 1, police commissioner of Saint Chamond to central commissioner, 24 Aug. 1873; Bertholon, *Histoires de Saint-Chamond*, p. 154.

20. James Condamin, *Histoire de Saint-Chamond et de la seigneurie de Jarez, depuis les temps les plus reculés jusqu'à nos jours* (Paris: A. Picard, 1890), p. 572.

21. ADL 27M 1, letter to prefect from police commissioner of Saint Chamond, 11 Jan. 1872.

22. ADL 27M 1, 8 Jan. 1872; 10 Jan. 1872; 11 Jan. 1872.

23. ADL 27M 1, letter from César Pouget to *Le Radical*, 21 March 1872.

24. ADL 27M 1, police commissioner of Saint Chamond to central commissioner, 24 Aug. 1873; central commissioner of police to prefect of the Loire, 25 Aug. 1873; gendarmerie to lieutenant, 25 Aug. 1873.

25. See Pierre Pierrard, *L'Eglise et les ouvriers en France (1840–1940)* (Paris: Hachette, 1984), pp. 259–312.

26. ADL M244 tr. 427/6, *Le Républicain de la Loire et de la Haute-Loire*, 17 March 1877; Bertholon, *Histoires de Saint-Chamond*, p. 135.

27. For the *cercles catholiques*, see Chapter 5; documents concerning the Association of Catholic Employers may be found in AN BB[18] 1932A 96, 1892. The number of employees in the Brun factories is in ADL 88M 16, 1890.

28. AN BB[18] 1932A 96, "Patrons catholiques."

29. ADL 3M 13, gendarmerie of the Saint Chamond brigade to the commanding officer, 4 Oct. 1873.

30. ADL, series T, 721, cantonal delegates for instruction, 23 Feb. 1872; archives of the Forges et Aciéries de la Marine, "Histoire des forges et aciéries de la marine et d'Homecourt," unpublished manuscript, circa 1920; Bertholon, *Histoires de Saint-Chamond*, p. 267; Boyer, *Les élections politiques dans le département de la Loire*, p. 161.

31. *Mémorial de la Loire*, 15 Feb. 1876, quoted in Boyer, *Les élections politiques dans le département de la Loire*, p. 162.

32. Bertholon, *Histoires de Saint-Chamond*, p. 142; ADL 6M 20, 25 Sept. 1877.

33. ADL 92M 14, documents 47 (n.d.); 57, 5 May 1875; 56, 15 May 1875; 55, 11 May 1875; 69, 11 May 1875; 27M 1, "Liste nominatif des membres du Cercle de l'Industrie et du Commerce de la Ville de Saint Chamond," 12 Oct. 1872. For the tendency of dye workers to avoid overtime, see Michelle Perrot, *Les ouvriers en grève: France, 1871–1890*, 2 vols. (Paris: Mouton, 1974), 1:352–66.

34. ADL 92M 14, documents 51, 25 June 1875; 49, 26 June 1875.

35. ADL 92M 14, police commissioner of Saint Chamond to prefect, document 37, 2 June 1875; special commissioner of the police of railroads to the minister of the interior, document 27, 15 June 1875; document 29, 15 June 1875.

36. Boyer, *Les élections politiques dans le département de la Loire*, pp. 161–63.

37. *Républicain de la Loire*, 19 Feb. 1876, quoted in ibid., p. 162.
38. Boyer, *Les élections politiques dans le département de la Loire*, p. 170.
39. ADL 6M 13, prefect of the Loire to the minister of the interior, 14 Dec. 1877.
40. Archives de la Préfecture de la Police de Paris (henceforth APP) B/A 171, document 15, 24 July 1878; ADL 92M 15, document 89, Aug. 1878; Bertholon, *Histoires de Saint-Chamond*, p. 185; M. Fournier, *L'Essor d'une ville ouvrière: l'oeuvre sociale de la municipalité de Saint-Chamond* (Saint Etienne: Imprimerie de la Loire Républicaine, 1934), p. 12.
41. APP B/A 171, documents 24 (n.d.); 15, 24 July 1875; 23, 25 July 1878; 27 July 1878; 9 Aug. 1878; 19 July 1878; ADL 92M 15, 13 July 1878; 54, 19 July 1874; 68, 23 July 1878; 69 (n.d.); 76, 26 July 1878; 88, 6 Aug. 1878; 64, 22 July 1878; 89, 7 Aug. 1878.
42. APP B/A 171, document 15, 24 July 1878; ADL 92M 15, document 89, Aug. 1878.
43. APP B/A 171, document 17, 27 July 1878; *Lyon Républicain*, 9 Aug. 1878.
44. APP B/A 171, 25 July 1878; ADL 92M 15, 6 Aug. 1878.
45. ADL 92M 15, document 66, July 1878.
46. Ibid.
47. ADL 93M 11, police commissioner of Saint Chamond to prefect of the Loire, 4 Sept. 1880.
48. Retrospective comments about Chavanne can be found in ADL, 10M 103, "Situation politique dans le département de la Loire," 11 Oct. 1894. See also Bertholon, *Histoires de Saint-Chamond*, p. 146; Fournier, *L'Essor d'une ville ouvrière*, p. 12.
49. Maxime Perrin, *Saint-Etienne et sa région économique: un type de vie industrielle en France* (Tours: Arrault, 1937), p. 225. See also L. Babu, *L'Industrie métallurgique dans la région de Saint-Etienne* (Paris: Dunot, 1899), p. 156.
50. Babu, *L'Industrie métallurgique*, pp. 159–68.
51. ADL 92M 21, police commissioner of Saint Chamond to prefect of the Loire, 29 Dec. 1882.
52. AN F[12] 4658, 5 Jan. 1883; 30 June 1883; 5 July 1883, 17 July 1883, 24 July 1883; quote is from 17 July 1883. ADL 92M 21, 30 June 1883.
53. ADL 92M 21, police commissioner of Saint Chamond to prefect of the Loire, 9 July 1883. According to the police, fifteen strikers returned to the Haute-Loire, their department of origin, to do agricultural work. The remaining thirty-one stayed in Saint Chamond, "doubtless living off various workers' unions."
54. ADL 92M 21, police commissioner of Saint Chamond to prefect, 17 Aug. 1883; 93M 11, 20 Jan. 1884.
55. ADL 3M 22, prefect of the Loire to the minister of the interior, 25 June 1885; 16 Aug. 1885.
56. ADL 3M 21, Legislative Elections, 18 Oct. 1885.
57. The petition may be found in ADL, series T, 2058; on opposition to laicization of schools in Saint Chamond, see Condamin, *Histoire de Saint-Chamond*, p. 572, and Bertholon, *Histoires de Saint-Chamond*, p. 157.
58. ADL 3M 22, special police commissioner of Saint Etienne to the minister of the interior, daily report, 21 Oct. 1885.
59. ADL 3M 22, police commissioner of Saint Chamond to prefect, 20 Sept. 1885.

60. ADL 3M 22, special police commissioner of Saint Etienne to the minister of the interior, daily report, 21 Oct. 1885.

61. See ADL 24j (E), carton 59 dossier 3, 5 Feb. 1885; and Chapter 5, note 64.

62. ADL 3M 23, legislative elections, 1887 and 1888; 6M 20, municipal elections, 1888.

63. ADL 10M 102, police commissioner of Saint Etienne, reports of 1894.

64. ADL 10M 102, report of 25 Jan. 1894; 93M 67, police commissioner of Saint Chamond to prefect, 19 Jan. 1894.

65. These percentages are calculated on the basis of the Saint Chamond police commissioner's report that 6,437 people were employed in Saint Chamond in April 1894. Union members constituted roughly 13 percent of all men in Saint Chamond between the ages of twenty and fifty-nine and 6.4 percent of the entire adult population: ADL 10M 102, May 1894.

66. Edward Shorter and Charles Tilly, *Strikes in France, 1830–1968* (London: Cambridge University Press, 1974), p. 152.

67. ADL 93M 11, special commissioner in Saint Etienne to the minister of the interior, 6 July 1892; 21M 48, police commissioner of Saint Chamond to prefect, 8 Jan. 1893, 15 Jan. 1893, 31 Dec. 1894; 93M 67, police commissioner of Saint Chamond to prefect, 19 Jan. 1894.

68. ADL 93M 67, police commissioner of Saint Chamond to prefect, 19 Jan. 1894.

69. Ibid.

70. Ibid.

71. ADL 21M 48, police commissioner of Saint Chamond to prefect, 8 Jan. 1893; 15 Jan. 1893; 20 Jan. 1893.

72. ADL 10M 102, 28 March 1894, Sept. 1894.

73. ADL 10M 103, report of police commissioner for month of July 1894; Fournier, *Tableaux de la vie saint-chamonaise,* p. 95.

74. For Limoges, see John M. Merriman, *The Red City: Limoges and the French Nineteenth Century* (New York: Oxford University Press, 1985), chapters 5 and 6. For the victory of the socialists in Saint Etienne, see ADL 10M 103, "Situation politique dans le département de la Loire," 11 Oct. 1894.

75. ADL 10M 103, Saint Chamond police commissioner's reports of July, Aug., and Sept. 1894.

76. ADL 24j (E), register 30bis, May 1885; 11 Jan. 1886; March 1886; 16 Aug. 1888; 23 Oct. 1888; 20 Nov. 1888; 29 Nov. 1888; 12 March 1889; 2 Nov. 1891; 30 Jan. 1899. Men in the *salle des vieillards* were able to drink more than their share of wine when those who did not want their portion gave it away.

77. ADL 92M 39, police commissioner of Saint Chamond to prefect, 30 Aug. 1890; 2 Sept. 1890.

78. ADL 92M 42, letter from a Saint Chamond worker to prefect, 3 Oct. 1891.

79. ADL 92M 42, police commissioner of Saint Chamond to the prefect, 3 Oct. 1891.

80. ADL 92M 49, report of the national gendarmerie, 3 Jan. 1893; 7 Jan. 1893; 10 Jan. 1893; prefect to the minister of the interior, 23 Jan. 1893; 21M 48, police commissioner of Saint Chamond to prefect, 3 Jan. 1893; 5 Jan. 1893; 6 Jan. 1893; 7 Jan. 1893; 8 Jan. 1893.

81. ADL 21M 48, 5 Jan. 1893; 6 Oct. 1893; 92M 49, 3 Oct. 1891.

82. AN BB[18] 2019–3480A 95, article from *L'Eclaireur de Saint Chamond*, 17 Nov. 1895; "Procureur de la République, Tribunal de Saint-Etienne au Procureur Général," 20 Nov. 1895; letter from M. Balet, 10 Dec. 1895; letter from Antonin Massey and André Villers, owners of *L'Eclaireur*, to the minister of justice, 11 Dec. 1895; letter from Balet, 17 Dec. 1895; reports of the minister of justice, 22 Feb. 1896; 30 Dec. 1895.

83. AN BB[18] 2019–3480A 95, article from *L'Eclaireur*, 17 Nov. 1895.

84. AN BB[18] 2019–3480A 95, reports of the minister of justice, 30 Dec. 1895; 22 Feb. 1896.

85. ADL 10M 102, report of police commissioner of Saint Chamond, 1 March 1894.

86. ADL 10M 102, report of police commissioner of Saint Chamond, 30 May 1894; Nov. 1894.

87. ADL 76M 125, Municipal Council of Saint Chamond, 18 Nov. 1893.

88. ADL 21M 48, 31 Dec. 1894.

89. ADL 93M 67, 17 Oct. 1895; 20 Oct. 1895; 18 Oct. 1895; 11 Nov. 1895.

90. ADL 21M 48, police commissioner of Saint Chamond to prefect, 7 Jan. 1893; for a discussion of the papal encyclicals, see Pierrard, *L'Eglise et les ouvriers*, pp. 357–411.

91. Pierrard, *L'Eglise et les ouvriers*, pp. 360–69.

92. ADL 21M 48, police commissioner of Saint Chamond to prefect, 7 Jan. 1893.

93. ADL 21M 48, police commissioner of Saint Chamond to prefect, 7 Sept. 1900; 21 Nov. 1902; also see Bertholon, *Histoires de Saint-Chamond*, p. 186.

94. *La Croix de Saint-Chamond*, 24 Feb. 1910.

95. Ibid., 25 Aug. 1901.

96. ADL 10M 15, police commissioner of Saint Chamond to prefect, 15 March 1897; 21M 48, police commissioner of Saint Chamond to prefect, 28 June 1899.

97. Robert Gildea, *Education in Provincial France, 1800–1914: A Study of Three Departments* (Oxford: Clarendon Press, 1983), pp. 112–13.

98. ADL, series T, 505, laicization, 1 Feb. 1881.

99. ADL 21M 48, 29 Oct. 1900.

100. ADL 21M 48, article in *Tribunal*, 10 March 1901.

101. See Gildea, *Education in Provincial France*, pp. 112–13.

102. *La Croix de Saint-Chamond*, 7 April 1901.

103. Ibid., 26 May 1901.

104. Ibid.

105. ADL 21M 48, 19 Oct. 1900; 29 Oct. 1900; 3 Dec. 1900; *La Croix de Saint-Chamond*, 26 May 1901; 28 July 1901.

106. *La Croix de Saint-Chamond*, 5 May 1902.

107. Ibid., 10 Aug. 1902; *L'Eclaireur de Saint-Chamond*, 30 Aug. 1902.

108. ADL 21M 48, police commissioner of Saint Chamond to prefect, 9 March 1901.

109. ADL 93M 11, commissioner of police of Saint Chamond to prefect, 19 June 1902; Michael Hanagan, *The Logic of Solidarity: Artisans and Industrial Workers in Three French Towns, 1871–1914* (Urbana: University of Illinois Press, 1980), pp. 152–53.

110. ADL 93M 67, 1906–1914; 93M 11, March 1911–Feb. 1913; 92M 190, Jan. 1911–June 1912.

111. ADL 93M 67, 1906–1914; for Aciéries de la Marine, see especially 21 March–10 April 1911. See also Hanagan, *The Logic of Solidarity*, pp. 150–59.

112. Hanagan, *The Logic of Solidarity*, p. 128.

113. See Chapter 3, note 59.

114. Among the men and women who married between 1861 and 1870 and gave addresses in the parish of Saint Ennemond, 58.1 percent and 51.1 percent, respectively, either had been born in Saint Chamond or had lived there for more than twenty years. Among metal workers, 52.3 percent manifested the same degree of stability. These rates contrast sharply with those of the general population, listed in Appendix B, Table B-15. For the irreligiosity of Saint Ennemond, see *La Croix de Saint-Chamond*, 26 May 1901: thirty people in this parish signed a petition complaining about the religious indoctrination of their children in the *école maternelle* of Saint Ennemond. Throughout his works, M. Fournier portrays the indifference to religion and the independence among the inhabitants of this parish. See especially *La vallée ardente: scènes de la vie popularie* (Saint Etienne: Librairie Dubouchet, 1938), pp. 56–59, 216, 223. See also parish reports in the Archives Paroissiales du Rhône, diocèse de Lyon, and Bertholon's characterization of the "Mognods" in *Histoires de Saint-Chamond*, pp. 33–34, 231.

115. Examples may be found in Fournier, *La vallée ardente*, pp. 108–9, 216–17, 331, 351–53, 365; and M. Fournier, *Les forgerons* (Saint Chamond: Bordron, 1939), pp. 11–16, 20–21.

116. Fournier, *La vallée ardente*, p. 31.

117. Merriman, *The Red City*; Joan W. Scott, *The Glassworkers of Carmaux: French Craftsmen and Political Action in a Nineteenth-Century City* (Cambridge, Mass.: Harvard University Press, 1974).

CONCLUSION

1. Hans Medick hypothesized that proto-industry fostered a system of interchangeable roles. See "The Proto-Industrial Family Economy: The Structural Function of Household and Family during the Transition from Peasant Society to Industrial Capitalism," *Social History* 3 (1976): 291–315.

2. J. B. Say, *A Treatise on Political Economy; or, The Production, Distribution, and Consumption of Wealth*, trans. C. R. Prinsep (4th American ed. Philadelphia: John Grigg, 1830), and Say, *Cours complet d'économie politique pratique*, 2 vols. (2d ed. Paris: Guillaumin, 1840); see discussion in William Coleman, *Death Is a Social Disease: Public Health and Political Economy in Early Industrial France* (Madison: University of Wisconsin Press, 1982), pp. 59–81. See also Louis Chevalier, *Laboring Classes and Dangerous Classes in Paris during the First Half of the Nineteenth Century*, trans. Frank Jellinek (Princeton: Princeton University Press, 1973), pp. 455–56.

3. Claude Tillier, *Mon oncle Benjamin* (Paris, 1881), p. 78, quoted in Angus McLaren, *Sexuality and Social Order: The Debate over the Fertility of Women and Workers in France, 1780–1920* (New York: Holmes & Meier, 1983), p. 125.

4. McLaren, *Sexuality and Social Order*, pp. 125–35.

5. See Rachel Fuchs, "Morality and Poverty: Single Mothers and Welfare Inspectors in Paris, 1880–1904," paper presented at the annual meeting of the Society for French Historical Studies, Quebec, 21 March 1986.

6. Peter Stearns, *Paths to Authority: The Middle Class and the Industrial Labor Force in France, 1820–1848* (Urbana: University of Illinois Press, 1978).

7. Michelle Perrot, "The Three Ages of Industrial Discipline in Nineteenth-Century France," in *Consciousness and Class Experience in Nineteenth-Century Europe*, ed. John M. Merriman (New York: Holmes & Meier, 1979), pp. 149–68. Perrot argues that this set of relationships ended when employers ceased being visible in the workplace. For an excellent discussion of how paternalism operated after the employer left the workplace, see Donald Reid, "Industrial Paternalism: Discourse and Practice in Nineteenth-Century French Mining and Metallurgy," *Comparative Studies in Society and History* 27 (October 1985): 579–607.

APPENDIX A

1. Larry Logue, who is the primary author of this section, devised and implemented the program to correct for missed births in the data from Saint Chamond.

2. Louis Henry, "The Verification of Data in Historical Demography," *Population Studies* 22 (1968): 61–81.

Bibliography

PRIMARY SOURCES

Archives Nationales, Paris (AN)

Série BB[18]. "Correspondance des procureurs généraux": 1932A 96; 2019–3480A 95.

Série BB[30]. "Rapports des procureurs généraux sur la situation morale et politique."
    361   "Troubles postérieurs à la Révolution du février, 1848."

Série C. "Archives parlementaires, Assemblée nationale."
    956   "Enquête sur le travail," 1848. Département de la Loire, arrondissement de Saint-Etienne.
    3021   "Enquête sur la situation ouvrière," 1872–1875. Département du Rhône.
    3022   "Enquête sur la situation ouvrière," 1872–1875. Département de la Loire, arrondissement de Saint-Etienne.
    3353   "Enquête sur la situation des ouvriers en France." Département de la Loire, 1881–1885.

Série F[7]. Police générale: 13605.

Série F[12]. Commerce et industrie.
    4476A "Situation industrielle, département de la Loire, 1830–1847."
    4511B "Situation industrielle, département de la Loire, 1869–1886."
    4658   "Situation industrielle, Hérault à Lozère, 1880–1889."
    4728   "Enquête relative aux règlements d'administration publique à intervenir pour l'application de la loi de 1874."

Série F[17]. Instruction publique.
    9327   "Inspection des écoles primaires," Isère à Loire Inférieure, 1855–1856.
    9338   Hérault à Manche, 1857–1858.
    9344   Landes à Orne, 1859.
    9347   Creuse à Loire, 1860.

Série F[1c]. Supplément à la série F.
    III   Rapports: Loire 4, 7, 8, 9.
    V   Conseils généraux, séries départementales: Loire 1–3.
    VII   Conseil d'arrondissement: Loire.

Archives de la Préfecture de la Police de Paris (APP)
Série B/A. 171.

Archives du Ministère de la Guerre, Vincennes
Série MR. Reconnaissances militaires.
1266   "Rapport sur les environs de Saint-Chamond," 1843.
        "Rapport sur la reconnaissance de la route de Saint-Etienne à Saint-Chamond," 1837.

Archives Départementales de la Loire (ADL)
Sous-série 3E. Etat civil.
208   Naissances, mariages, et décès, Saint-Chamond, 1816–1865 (cartons 15–30).
Série M. Administration générale.
3M   Elections: 11, 13, 21, 22, 23.
6M   Elections: 13, 20.
10M   Evénements et affaires politiques: 15, 21, 28, 30, 31, 32, 53, 62, 67, 72, 102, 103, 113, 115, 147.
21M   Commissaire de police, rapports: 48.
27M   Cercles: 1, 2.
28M   Sociétés: 1, 4.
35M   Service d'hygiène—agents sanitaires, commissions cantonales de salubrité, commissions sanitaires . . . rapports, 1813–1889: 1–5.
40M   "Etablissements dangereuses et insalubres": 93, 118.
47M   Population—instructions, statistiques, états récapitulatives: 147.
48M   "Mouvement de la population": 5, 68.
49M   "Dénombrements de la population": 226, 285.
56M   Statistique industrielle: 4.
76M   Ecoles d'arts et métiers: 125.
81M   "Questions industrielles et commerciales": 22.
88M   "Surveillance du travail des enfants et des femmes": 8, 16, 18.
90M   "Enquêtes et renseignements divers sur la situation des ouvriers": 1.
92M   Grèves: 12, 13, 14, 15, 21, 39, 42, 49, 190.
93M   Syndicats: 11, 67.
M244   Sociétés de l'arrondissement de Saint Etienne, dossiers: tr. 427/6.
Série S. Archives de la Chambre de Commerce de Saint-Etienne: Cartons 25, 25A, 59, 131, 139, 141, 142.
Série T. Instruction publique.
505   Laicisation.
594   Saint Chamond, 1833–1882.
718, 720, 721
        Instruction primaire, "Rapports des délégués cantonaux."
883   Cours d'adults, 1864–1867.
2058   "Pétition pour les écoles libres de Saint-Chamond, 1870–1871."
Séries B, E, F, G, H, X, 24j. Hôpital de Saint Chamond.
24j (H) Cartons 102, 118, registre 30bis.
24j (E) Carton 59, registres 30bis, 30ter.

24j (F)   Cartons 5, 106, 134.
G107   Hospice de la Charité, 1792–1868.
X   Hospices de Saint-Chamond, 1873–1883.

Archives municipales de Saint-Chamond (Hôtel de Ville)
Etat civil de Saint-Chamond: naissances, mariages, et décès, 1866–1882.
Cadastres, 1884.

Palais de Justice, Saint-Etienne
Greffe du Tribunal de Grande Instance (GTGI): Etat Civil de Saint-Chamond; naissances, mariages, et décès, 1816–1914.

Bibliothèque de la Chambre de Commerce de Saint-Etienne
7.433 (V.R.)   Association des Fabricants de Lacets. *Question du travail de nuit dans les fabriques de lacets de Saint-Chamond.* Saint Etienne, 1890.
Chambre de Commerce de Saint Etienne. *Enquête commerciale sur les traités de 1860.* Saint Etienne: Thiollier, 1871.
Compagnie des Aciéries de la Marine. *Usines de Saint Chamond.* 3 vols. Paris: E. Mesière, 1900–1914.

Archives Paroissiales du Rhône, Diocèse de Lyon
Rapports des visites paroissiales du canton de Saint Chamond [uncatalogued]

Newspapers
La Croix de Saint-Chamond, 7 July 1891; 6 Jan. 1901; 26 Jan. 1901; 27 Jan. 1901; 3 Feb. 1901; 17 March 1901; 7 April 1901; 26 May 1901; 28 July 1901; 25 Aug. 1901; 5 May 1902; 10 Aug. 1902; 20 Aug. 1902; 23 Nov. 1902; 30 Jan. 1903; 24 Feb. 1910.
L'Eclaireur, 7 July 1891; 17 Nov. 1895.
L'Eclaireur de Saint-Chamond, 30 Aug. 1902.
Le Moniteur de la Loire et la Haute-Loire, 16 Aug. 1877.
Le Tribunal, 10 March 1901.

Worker Congresses
Congrès ouvrier de France session de 1876 tenu à Paris du 2 au 10 octobre. Paris: Librairie Sandoz et Fischbacher, 1877. (Musée Sociale.)
Séances du congrès ouvrier de France, Lyon, 28 janvier à 8 fevrier, 1878. Lyon: Jules Trichot, 1878. (Musée Sociale.)
Seilhac, Léon de. *Les congrès ouvriers en France de 1876 à 1897.* Paris: A. Colin, 1899.
Tonim, pseudonym of Albert Minot. *La question sociale et le congrès ouvrier de Paris: conditions rationnelles de l'ordre économique, social et politique: état de la capacité morale et politique du prolétariat.* Paris: M. Blanc, 1877.

Government Publications

Bureau de la Statistique Générale. *Statistique de la France: résultats généraux de l'enquête effectuée dans les années 1861–1865.* Nancy: Berger-Levrault, 1873.

———. *Statistique générale de la France,* série 2, vol. 21. Paris: Imprimerie Nationale, 1901, 1902, 1906.

Books, Pamphlets

Académie de Médecine. *Rapport annuel de la commission permanente de l'hygiène de l'enfance.* Paris: G. Masson, 1878.

Association Internationale pour la Protection Légale des Travailleurs. *Le travail de nuit des femmes dans l'industrie: rapports sur son importance et sa réglementation légale.* Paris: n.p., 1903.

Audiganne, A. *Les ouvriers en famille.* 5th edition. Paris: n.p., 1858.

———. *Les populations ouvrières et les industries de la France dans le mouvement social du XIXᵉ siècle.* Paris: Capelle, 1854.

———. *Les populations ouvrières et les industries de la France: études comparatives sur le régime et les ressources des différentes industries, sur l'état moral et matériel des ouvriers dans chaque branche du travail et les institutions qui les concernent.* 2 vols. 2d ed. Paris: Capelle, 1860.

Babu, L. *L'Industrie métallurgique dans la région de Saint-Etienne.* Paris: Dunot, 1899.

Balas Frères. *L'Industrie française des tresses et lacets.* Lyon: Association Typographique, 1890.

Baret, H. *Manuel de rubanerie, passementerie et lacets.* Paris: Ballière, 1924.

Bertholon, Stéphane. *Histoires de Saint-Chamond: notes et souvenirs d'un vieux couramiaud.* Saint Etienne: n.p., 1927.

Bouvier, Jeanne. *Mes mémoires ou 59 années d'activité industrielle, sociale et intellectuelle d'une ouvrière.* Paris: L'Action Intellectuelle, 1936.

Cetty, Henri. *La famille ouvrière en Alsace.* Rixheim: A. Sutter, 1883.

Condamin, James. *Histoire de Saint-Chamond et de la seigneurie de Jarez, depuis les temps les plus reculés jusqu'à nos jours.* Paris: A. Picard, 1890.

Du Chevalard, Jules. *Notice biographique sur M. J.-M. Gaudet, ancien maître des forges de Rive-de-Gier.* Saint Etienne: n.p., 1887.

Duplessy, J. *Essai statistique sur le département de la Loire.* Montbrison: n.p., 1818.

Fournier, M. *L'Essor d'une ville ouvrière: l'oeuvre sociale de la municipalité de Saint-Chamond.* Saint Etienne: Imprimerie de la Loire Républicaine, 1934.

———. *Les forgerons.* Saint Chamond: Bordron, 1939.

———. *Tableaux de la vie saint-chamonaise.* Saint Chamond: Bordron, 1949.

———. *La vallée ardente: scènes de la vie populaire.* Saint Etienne: Librairie Dubouchet, 1938.

Gonon, J. F. *Histoire de la chanson stéphanoise et forézienne depuis son origine jusqu'à notre époque.* Saint Etienne: Imprimerie Cooperative, Union Typographique, 1906.

Halbwachs, Maurice. *La classe ouvrière et les niveaux de vie.* Reims: Action

Populaire, 1908.

"Histoire des forges et aciéries de la marine et d'Homecourt." Unpublished manuscript, circa 1920. Archives of the Forges et Aciéries de la Marine.

Jury, L. "L'Industrie des lacets." 2:1–20 in *L'Association pour l'Avancement des Sciences, XXVIᵉ session tenue à Saint-Etienne, août 1897.* 2 vols. Saint Chamond: A. Poméon, 1898.

Le Play, F. *Fréderic Le Play: On Family, Work and Social Change.* Edited, translated, and with an introduction by Catherine Bodard Silver. Chicago: University of Chicago Press, 1982.

———. *Les ouvriers européens, étude sur les travaux, la vie domestique et la condition morale des populations ouvriers de l'Europe, précédé d'un exposé de la méthode d'observation.* Paris: Imprimerie Impériale, 1855.

———. *La réforme sociale en France, déduite de l'observation comparée des peuples européens.* 2 vols. 6th ed. Tours: Mame, 1878.

Leroy-Beaulieu, Paul. *De l'état moral et intellectuel des populations ouvrières et de son influence sur le taux des salaires.* Paris: Librairie Guillaumin, 1868.

———. *Le travail des femmes au XIXᵉ siècle.* Paris: Charpentier, 1888.

Nansouty, Max. *Compagnie des hauts fourneaux, forges et aciéries de la marine.* Paris: Le Génie Civil, 1894.

Raymond, F. *Les hospices de Saint-Chamond: histoire, administration, origines, agrandissements, biens et revenus d'après les documents conservés dans leurs archives.* Saint Chamond: A. Poméon, 1888.

Reybaud, Louis. *Etudes sur le régime des manufactures: Conditions des ouvriers en soie.* Paris: Michel Levy, 1859.

———. *Le fer et la houille.* Paris: Michel Levy, 1874.

———. *Rapport sur la condition morale, intellectuelle et matérielle des ouvriers qui vivent de l'industrie de coton.* Paris, 1863.

———. "Rapport sur la condition morale, intellectuelle et matérielle des ouvriers qui vivent de l'industrie du fer, 1866–1871." (Musée Sociale, no. 9920, vol. 4.)

Rondot, Natalis. *Les soies.* Paris: Imprimerie Nationale, 1887.

Roule, Antoine. *Petits poèmes et chansons.* Saint Etienne: n.p., 1921.

Simon, Jules. *L'Ouvrière.* Paris: Hachette, 1891.

Turgan, L. *Les grandes usines de la France.* 16 vols. Paris: Michel Levy, 1865–1884; vols. 4, 15.

Valserres, J. *Les industries de la Loire.* Saint Etienne: n.p., 1862.

Villermé, Louis René. *Tableau de l'état physique et moral des ouvriers employés dans les manufactures de coton, de laine et de soie.* 2 vols. Paris: Renouard, 1840.

SECONDARY SOURCES

Accampo, Elinor. "Entre la classe sociale et la cité: identité et intégration chez les ouvriers de Saint Chamond, 1815–1880." *Mouvement Social* 118 (January-March 1982): 39–59.

————. "Industrialization and the Working Class Family: Saint Chamond, 1815–1880." Ph.D. diss., University of California, Berkeley, 1984.

Ackerman, Bernette. *Village on the Seine: Tradition and Change in Bonnières, 1815–1914.* Ithaca: Cornell University Press, 1978.

Agulhon, Maurice. *La République au village.* Paris: Plon, 1970.

Anderson, Michael. *Approaches to the History of the Western Family, 1500– 1914.* London: Macmillan, 1980.

————. *Family Structure in Nineteenth Century Lancashire.* Cambridge, Eng.: Cambridge University Press, 1971.

————. "Sociological History and the Working Class: Smelser Revisted." *Social History* 3 (1973): 317–54.

Ariès, Philippe. *Centuries of Childhood: A Social History of Family Life.* New York: Vintage Books, 1962.

————. *Histoire des populations françaises.* Paris: Editions du Seuil, 1971.

Armengaud, André. *La famille et l'enfant en France et en Angleterre du XVIᵉ au XVIIIᵉ siècle.* Paris: Société d'Edition d'Enseignement Supérieur, 1975.

————. *La population française au XIXᵉ siècle.* Que sais-je? no. 1420. Paris: Presses Universitaires de France, 1971.

————. "Mouvement ouvrier et néo-malthusianisme au début de XXᵉ siècle." *Annales de démographie historique.* Paris: Sirey, 1966.

————. *La population française au XIXᵉ siècle.* Que sais-je? no. 1420. Paris: Presses Universitaires de France, 1971.

Bardet, Jean-Pierre. *Rouen aux XVIIᵉ et XVIIIᵉ siècles: les mutations d'un espace social.* 2 vols. Paris: Société d'Edition d'Enseignement Supérieur, 1983.

Berg, Maxine. *The Age of Manufactures: Industry, Innovation and Work in Britain, 1700–1820.* New York: Oxford University Press, 1986.

Berkner, Lutz. "The Use and Misuse of Census Data for the Historical Analysis of Family Structure." *Journal of Interdisciplinary History* 4 (1975): 721–38.

Bezucha, Robert J. *The Lyon Uprising of 1834: Social and Political Conflict in the Early July Monarchy.* Cambridge, Mass.: Harvard University Press, 1974.

Blacker, John G. C. "Social Ambitions of the Bourgeoisie in Eighteenth Century France and Their Relation to Family Limitation." *Population Studies* 11 (1957): 46–63.

Boissier, Albert. "Essai sur l'histoire et sur les origines de l'industrie du clou forgé dans la région de Firminy." *Revue de folklore français* 19 (April– June 1941): 65–101.

Bourdieu, P. "Marriage Strategies as Strategies of Social Reproduction." Pp. 117–44 in *Family and Society: Selections from the Annales.* Edited by R. Forster and O. Ranum. Baltimore: Johns Hopkins University Press, 1972.

Boxer, Marilyn. "Women in Industrial Homework: The Flowermakers of Paris in the Belle Epoque." *French Historical Studies* 12 (Spring 1982): 401–23.

Boyer, Laurent. *Les élections politiques dans le département de la Loire au temps de l'assemblée nationale et du Maréchal MacMahon.* Paris: Sirey, 1963.

Bravard, Jean-Paul. "La clouterie dans la région de Firminy." *Notes d'histoire: au pays de cloutiers.* Firminy: Maison de la Culture de Firminy, February 1977: 1–18.

Brooke, Michael Z. *Le Play, Engineer and Social Scientist: The Life and Work of Frederick Le Play.* London: Longman, 1970.

Cameron, Rondo. "Economic Growth and Stagnation in France, 1815–1914." Pp. 328–53 in *The Experience of Economic Growth*, edited by B. E. Supple. New York: Random House, 1963.

Chatelard, Claude. *Crime et criminalité dans l'arrondissement de Saint-Etienne au XIXᵉ siècle.* Saint Etienne: Centre d'Etudes Foréziennes, 1981.

Chevalier, Louis. *Laboring Classes and Dangerous Classes in Paris during the First Half of the Nineteenth Century.* Translated by Frank Jellinek. Princeton: Princeton University Press, 1973.

Coale, Ansley J. "The Decline of Fertility in Europe from the French Revolution to World War II." Pp. 3–24 in *Fertility and Family Planning: A World View*, edited by S. J. Behrman, Leslie Corsa, and Ronald Freedman. Ann Arbor: University of Michigan Press, 1969.

Coale, Ansley J., and T. James Trussell. "Technical Note: Finding the Two Parameters That Specify a Model Schedule of Marital Fertility." *Population Index* 44 (1978): 203–11.

Coleman, William. *Death Is a Social Disease: Public Health and Political Economy in Early Industrial France.* Madison: University of Wisconsin Press, 1982.

Courtheoux, Jean Paul. "Privilèges et misères d'un métier sidérurgique au XIXᵉ siècle: le puddleur." *Revue d'Histoire Economique et Sociale* 2 (1952): 161–84.

Crew, David. *Town in the Ruhr: A Social History of Bochum, 1860–1914.* New York: Columbia University Press, 1979.

Dawley, Alan. *Class and Community: The Industrial Revolution in Lynn.* Cambridge, Mass.: Harvard University Press, 1979.

Demos, John, and S. S. Boocock, eds. *Turning Points: Historical Sociological Essays on the Family.* Chicago: University of Chicago Press, 1978.

Donzelot, J. *The Policing of Families.* Translated by Robert Hurley. New York: Pantheon, 1979.

Dublin, Thomas. *Women at Work: The Transformation of Work and Community in Lowell, Massachusetts, 1826–1860.* New York: Columbia University Press, 1979.

Dubos, R., and J. Dubos. *The White Plague.* London: Little, Brown, 1952.

Dunham, Arthur L. *The Industrial Revolution in France, 1815–1848.* New York: Exposition Press, 1955.

Duveau, Georges. *La vie ouvrière sous le Second Empire.* Paris: Gallimard, 1946.

Elwitt, Sanford. *The Making of the Third Republic: Class and Politics in France, 1868–1884.* Baton Rouge: Louisiana State University Press, 1975.

Engels, Friedrich. *The Condition of the Working Class in England in 1844.* Stanford: Stanford University Press, 1958.

Farber, Bernard. *Guardians of Virtue: Salem Families in 1800*. New York: Basic Books, 1972.

Faure, Petrus. *Histoire de la métallurgie au Chambon Feugerolles*. Le Chambon-Feugerolles: Jué, 1931.

————. *Histoire du mouvement ouvrier dans le département de la Loire*. Saint Etienne: Dumas, 1956.

Flandarin, Jean-Louis. *Families in Former Times: Kinship, Household and Sexuality*. Translated by Richard Southern. Cambridge, Eng.: Cambridge University Press, 1976.

Fleury, M., and L. Henry. *Nouveau manuel de dépouillement et d'exploitation de l'état civil ancien*. Paris: Editions de l'Institut National d'Etudes Démographiques, 1965.

Flinn, Michael W. *The European Demographic System, 1500–1820*. Baltimore: Johns Hopkins University Press, 1981.

Foucault, Michel. *Discipline and Punish: The Birth of the Prison*. Translated by Alan Sheridan. New York: Pantheon, 1977.

Franzoi, Barbara. "Domestic Industry: Work Options and Women's Choices." Pp. 256–69 in *German Women in the Nineteenth Century: A Social History*. Edited by John C. Fout. New York: Holmes & Meier, 1984.

Fuchs, Rachel. *Abandoned Children: Foundlings and Child Welfare in Nineteenth-Century France*. Albany: State University of New York Press, 1984.

Furet, François, and Jacques Ozouf. *Reading and Writing: Literacy in France from Calvin to Jules Ferry*. Cambridge, Eng.: Cambridge University Press, 1982.

Furet, F., and W. Sachs. "La croissance de l'alphabétisation en France, XVIIIe–XIXe siècles." *Annales ESC* 3 (May-June 1974): 714–37.

Garden, Maurice. *Lyon et les lyonnais au XVIIIe siècle*. Paris: Flammarion, 1975.

————. "Ouvriers et artisans au XVIIIe siècle." *Revue d'Histoire Economique et Sociale* 48 (1970): 28–45.

Gautier, Etienne, and Louis Henry. *La population Crulai, paroisse normande*. Paris: Institut National d'Etudes Démographiques, 1958.

Gildea, Robert. *Education in Provincial France, 1800–1914: A Study of Three Departments*. Oxford: Clarendon Press, 1983.

Gille, Bertrand. "Analyse de l'industrie sidérurgique française à la veille de 1830." *Revue d'Histoire de la Sidérurgie* 3 (April-June 1962): 83–111.

————. "La formation du prolétariat ouvrier dans l'industrie sidérurgique française." *Revue d'Histoire de la Sidérurgie* 4 (October-December 1963): 244–51.

————. *La sidérurgie française au XIXe siècle: Recherches historiques*. Geneva: Droz, 1968.

Gillis, John. *For Better, for Worse: British Marriages, 1600 to the Present*. New York: Oxford University Press, 1985.

Glass, D. V., and D. E. C. Eversley, eds. *Population in History*. London: E. Arnold, 1965.

Goody, Jack, Joan Thirsk, and E. P. Thompson. *Family and Inheritance: Ru-*

ral Society in Western Europe, 1200–1800. Cambridge, Eng.: Cambridge University Press, 1976.

Gordon, David. *Merchants and Capitalists: Industrialization and Provincial Politics in Mid-Nineteenth-Century France*. University: University of Alabama Press, 1985.

Gordon, Michael, ed. *The American Family in Social-Historical Perspective*. New York: St. Martin's Press, 1978.

Gras, L.-J. *Le conseil de commerce de Saint-Etienne et les industries locales au commencement du XIXᵉ siècle*. Saint Etienne: Théolier, 1899.

———. *Essai sur l'histoire de la quincaillerie de petite métallurgie à Saint-Etienne et dans la région stéphanoise*. Saint Etienne: Théolier, 1904.

———. *Histoire de la rubanerie et des industries de la soie à Saint-Etienne et dans la région stéphanoise suivie d'un historique de la fabrique de lacets de Saint-Chamond*. Saint Etienne: Théolier, 1906.

———. *Histoire du commerce locale et des industries qui s'y rattachent dans la région stéphanoise et forézienne*. Saint Etienne: Théolier, 1910.

———. *Histoire économique de la métallurgie de la Loire, suivie d'une notice de la construction mécanique et l'industrie des cycles et des automobiles dans la région stéphanoise*. Saint Etienne: Théolier, 1908.

Guilbert, Madeleine. *Les femmes et l'organisation syndicale avant 1914: Présentation et commentaire de documents pour une étude du syndicalisme féminin*. Paris: Centre National de la Recherche Scientifique, 1966.

———. *Les fonctions des femmes dans l'industrie*. Paris: Mouton, 1966.

Guilbert, Madeleine, and V. Isambert-Jamati. *Travail féminin et travail à domicile*. Paris: Centre National de la Recherche Scientifique, 1956.

Guitton, Henri. *L'Industrie des rubans de soie en France*. Paris: Sirey, 1928.

Haines, Michael. *Fertility and Occupation: Population Patterns in Industrialization*. New York: Academic Press, 1979.

Hanagan, Michael. *The Logic of Solidarity: Artisans and Industrial Workers in Three French Towns, 1871–1914*. Urbana: University of Illinois Press, 1980.

———. "Urbanization, Worker Settlement Patterns and Social Protest in Nineteenth-Century France." Pp. 208–29 in *French Cities in the Nineteenth Century*, edited by John M. Merriman. New York: Holmes & Meier, 1981.

Hareven, Tamara. *Family and Kin in Urban Communities, 1700–1930*. New York: New Viewpoints, 1977.

———. *Family Time and Industrial Time*. New York: Cambridge University Press, 1982.

Hareven, Tamara, ed. *Transitions: The Family and the Life Course in Historical Perspective*. New York: Academic Press, 1978.

Hareven, Tamara, and Randolph Langenbach. *Amoskeag: Life and Work in an American Factory-City*. New York: Pantheon, 1978.

Hélias, Pierre-Jakez. *The Horse of Pride: Life in a Breton Village*. Translated by June Guicharnaud. New Haven: Yale University Press, 1978.

Henry, Louis. *Anciennes familles genevoises: étude démographique, XVIᵉ–XXᵉ siècles*. Paris: P.U.F., 1956.

———. *Techniques d'analyse en démographie historique*. Paris: INED, 1980.

Henry, Louis, and Jacques Houdaille. "Célibat et âge au mariage aux 18ᵉ et 19ᵉ siècles en France. II: Age au premier mariage." *Population* 34 (March 1979): 403–41.

———. "The Verification of Data in Historical Demography." *Population Studies* 22 (1968): 61–81.

Hewitt, Margaret. *Wives and Mothers in Victorian Industry*. London: Rockliff, 1948.

Humphries, Jane. "Class Struggle and the Persistence of the Working Class Family." *Cambridge Journal of Economics* 1 (September 1977): 241–58.

———. "The Working Class Family, Women's Liberation, and Class Struggle: The Case of Nineteenth-Century British History." *Review of Radical Political Economics* 8–9 (1976–1977): 25–41.

Imbert, Jean. *Histoire des hôpitaux en France*. Toulouse: Editions Privat, 1982.

Jardin, André, and André-Jean Tudesq. *Restoration and Reaction, 1815–1848*. Translated by Elborg Forster. Cambridge, Eng.: Cambridge University Press, 1983.

Jones, Gareth Stedman. "Working Class Cultures and Working Class Politics in London, 1870–1900: Notes on the Remaking of a Working Class." *Journal of Social History* 7 (Summer 1974): 460–508.

Joyce, Patrick. *Work, Society and Politics: The Culture of the Factory in Later Victorian England*. New Brunswick: Rutgers University Press, 1980.

Kaplan, Steven L., and Cynthia J. Koepp, eds. *Work in France: Representations, Meaning, Organization, and Practice*. Ithaca: Cornell University Press, 1986.

Knodel, John E. *The Decline of Fertility in Germany, 1871–1939*. Princeton: Princeton University Press, 1974.

———. "European Populations in the Past: Family Level Relations." Pp. 21–45 in *The Effects of Infant and Child Mortality on Fertility*, edited by Samuel H. Preston. New York: Academic Press, 1978.

———. "Family Limitation and the Fertility Transition: Evidence from the Age Patterns of Fertility in Europe and Asia." *Population Studies* 31 (1977): 219–49.

———. "Two and a Half Centuries of Demographic History in a Bavarian Village." *Population Studies* 3 (1970): 353–76.

Knodel, John E., and Etienne van de Walle. "Breast-Feeding, Fertility and Infant Mortality: An Analysis of Some Early German Data." *Population Studies* 21 (1967): 109–31.

Laslett, Peter. *Family Life and Illicit Love in Earlier Generations*. Cambridge, Eng.: Cambridge University Press, 1977.

Laslett, Peter, and R. Wall. *Household and Family in Past Time*. Cambridge, Eng.: Cambridge University Press, 1972.

Lehning, James R. "Family Life and Wetnursing in a French Village." *Journal of Interdisciplinary History* 12 (Spring 1982): 645–56.

———. *The Peasants of Marlhes: Economic Development and Family Organiza-*

tion in Nineteenth-Century France. Chapel Hill: University of North Carolina Press, 1980.

Lequin, Yves. "Classe ouvrière et idéologie dans la région lyonnaise à la fin du XIXe siècle." *Mouvement Social* 6 (October-December 1969): 3–20.

———. "La formation du prolétariat industriel dans la région lyonnaise au XIXe siècle: approches méthodologiques et premiers résultats." *Mouvement Social* 97 (October-December 1976): 121–37.

———. *Les ouvriers de la région lyonnaise (1848–1914)*. Vol. 1: *La formation de la classe ouvrière régionale*. Vol. 2: *Les intérêts de classe et de la république*. Lyon: Presses Universitaires de Lyon, 1977.

Levine, David. *Family Formation in an Age of Nascent Captialism*. New York: Academic Press, 1977.

Levine, David, ed. *Proletarianization and Family History*. New York: Academic Press, 1984.

Lévy-Leboyer, M. *Les banques européennes et l'industrialisation internationale dans la première moitié du XIXe siècle*. Paris: Presses Universitaires de France, 1964.

Lucas, Colin. *The Structure of the Terror: The Example of Javogues and the Loire*. London: Oxford University Press, 1973.

McLaren, Angus. *Reproductive Rituals: The Perception of Fertility in England from the Sixteenth Century to the Nineteenth Century*. New York: Methuen, 1984.

———. *Sexuality and Social Order: The Debate over the Fertility of Women and Workers in France, 1780–1920*. New York: Holmes & Meier, 1983.

Markovitch, T. J. "The Dominant Sectors of French Industry." Pp. 226–40 in *Essays in French Economic History*, edited by Rondo Cameron. Homewood, Ill.: Richard Irwin, 1970.

———. *L'Industrie française de 1789 à 1946: analyse des faits*. Paris: Cahiers de l'ISEA, May 1966.

Medick, Hans. "The Proto-Industrial Family Economy: The Structural Function of Household and Family during the Transition from Peasant Society to Industrial Capitalism." *Social History* 3 (1976): 291–315.

Mendels, Franklin F. "Proto-Industrialization: The First Phase of the Industrialization Process." *Journal of Economic History* 32 (1972): 241–61.

Merley, Jean. *L'Industrie en Haute-Loire de la fin de la monarchie de juillet au début de la IIIe République*. Lyon: Centre d'Histoire Economique et Sociale de la Région Lyonnaise, 1972.

Merriman, John M. *The Agony of the Republic: The Repression of the Left in Revolutionary France, 1848–1851*. New Haven: Yale University Press, 1978.

———. "The *Demoiselles* of the Ariège." Pp. 87–118 in *1830 in France*, edited by John M. Merriman. New York: New Viewpoints, 1975.

———. *The Red City: Limoges and the French Nineteenth Century*. New York: Oxford University Press, 1985.

Mitterauer, Michael, and Reinhard Sieder. *The European Family: Patriarchy to Partnership from the Middle Ages to the Present*. Translated by Karla Oosterveen and Manfred Horzinger. Chicago: University of Chicago Press, 1983.

Moch, Leslie Page. *Paths to the City: Regional Migration in Nineteenth-Century France.* Beverly Hills: Sage, 1983.

Moch, Leslie Page, and Gary D. Stark, eds. *Essays on the Family and Historical Change.* Arlington: Texas A&M University Press, 1983.

Nadot, Robert. "Evolution de la mortalité infantile endogène en France dans la deuxième moitié du XIXe siècle." *Population* 25 (January-February 1970): 49–58.

Perrin, Maxime. *La population de la région de Saint-Etienne: étude de géographie humaine.* Tours: Arrault, 1937.

———. *Saint-Etienne et sa région économique: un type de vie industrielle en France.* Tours: Arrault, 1937.

Perrot, Michelle. *Les ouvriers en grève: France, 1871–1890.* 2 vols. Paris: Mouton, 1974.

———. "The Three Ages of Industrial Discipline in Nineteenth-Century France." Pp. 149–68 in *Consciousness and Class Experience in Nineteenth-Century Europe,* edited by John M. Merriman. New York: Holmes & Meier, 1979.

Pierrard, Pierre. *L'Eglise et les ouvriers en France (1840–1940).* Paris: Hachette, 1984.

———. *La vie ouvrière à Lille sous le Second Empire.* Paris: Bloud and Gay, 1965.

Plessy, Bernard. *La vie quotidienne en Forez avant 1914.* Paris: Hachette, 1981.

Prost, Antoine. *L'Enseignement en France, 1800–1967.* Paris: A. Colin, 1968.

Rabb, Theodore K., and Robert Rotberg, eds. *The Family in History: Interdisciplinary Essays.* New York: Harper Torchbooks, 1973.

Rainwater, Lee. *And the Poor Get Children: Sex, Contraception and Family Planning in the Working Class.* Chicago: Quadrangle Books, 1960.

Ranum, Orest, and Patricia Ranum. *Popular Attitudes toward Birth Control in Pre-Industrial France and England.* New York: Harper Torchbooks, 1972.

Reddy, William M. "Family and Factory: French Linen Weavers in the Belle Epoque." *Journal of Social History* 8 (Winter 1975): 102–12.

———. *The Rise of Market Culture: The Textile Trade and French Society, 1750–1900.* Cambridge, Eng.: Cambridge University Press, 1984.

Reid, Donald. "Industrial Paternalism: Discourse and Practice in Nineteenth-Century French Mining and Metallurgy." *Comparative Studies in Society and History* 27 (October 1985): 579–607.

———. *The Miners of Decazeville: A Genealogy of Deindustrialization.* Cambridge, Mass.: Harvard University Press, 1985.

Rollet, C. "Allaitement, mise en nourrice et mortalité infantile en France à la fin du XIXe siècle." *Population* 6 (1978): 1189–1203.

Rollet, H. *L'Action sociale des catholiques en France, 1871–1901.* Paris: Bovin, 1947.

Ronsin, Francis. *La grève des ventres: propagande néo-malthusienne et baisse de la natalité en France, 19ᵉ–20ᵉ siècles*. Paris: Aubier Montaigne, 1980.

Ross, Ellen. "'Fierce Questions and Taunts': Married Life in Working-Class London, 1870–1914." *Feminist Studies* 8 (1982): 575–602.

Ross, Steven J. *Workers on the Edge: Work, Leisure, and Politics in Industrializing Cincinnati, 1788–1890*. New York: Columbia University Press, 1985.

Ryan, Mary P. *The Cradle of the Middle Class: The Family in Oneida County, New York, 1790–1865*. Cambridge, Eng.: Cambridge University Press, 1981.

———. "The Explosion of Family History." *Reviews in American History* 10 (December 1982): 181–95.

Salber, Eva J., Manning Feileib, and Brian MacMahon. "The Duration of Post-Partum Amenorrhea." *American Journal of Epidemiology* 82 (1966): 347–58.

Sanderson, Michael. "Literacy and Social Mobility in the Industrial Revolution in England." *Past and Present* 56 (August 1972): 75–104.

Schnetzler, Jacques. *Les industries et les hommes dans la région de Saint-Etienne*. Lille: Service de Reproduction des Thèses, Université de Lille III, 1976.

Scott, Joan W. *The Glassworkers of Carmaux: French Craftsmen and Political Action in a Nineteenth-Century City*. Cambridge, Mass.: Harvard University Press, 1974.

Scott, Joan W., and Louise A. Tilly. "Women's Work and the Family in Nineteenth Century Europe." *Comparative Studies in Society and History* 17 (1975): 36–64.

Seccombe, Wally. "Patriarchy Stabilized: The Construction of the Male Breadwinner Wage Norm in Nineteenth-Century Britain." *Social History* 11 (January 1986): 53–76.

Segalen, Martine. *Nuptialité et alliance: mémoires d'anthropologie française*. Paris: G. P. Maisonneuve et Larose, 1972.

Sewell, William H. "La classe ouvrière de Marseille sous la IIᵉ République: structure sociale et comportement politique." *Mouvement Social* 76 (July-September 1971): 27–66.

———. *Structure and Mobility: The Men and Women of Marseille, 1820–1870*. Cambridge, Eng.: Cambridge University Press, 1985.

———. *Work and Revolution in France: The Language of Labor from the Old Regime to 1848*. Cambridge, Eng.: Cambridge University Press, 1980.

Shorter, Edward. *The Making of the Modern Family*. New York: Basic Books, 1975.

Shorter, Edward, and Charles Tilly. *Strikes in France, 1830–1968*. London: Cambridge University Press, 1974.

Smelser, Neil. *Social Change and the Industrial Revolution*. Chicago: University of Chicago Press, 1959.

Smith, Bonnie. *Ladies of the Leisure Class: The Bourgeoises of Northern France in the Nineteenth Century*. Princeton: Princeton University Press, 1981.

Stearns, Peter. *Paths to Authority: The Middle Class and the Industrial Labor Force in France, 1820–1848*. Urbana: University of Illinois Press, 1978.

Stone, Judith. *The Search for Social Peace: Reform Legislation in France, 1890–1914.* Albany: State University of New York Press, 1985.

Stone, Lawrence. *The Family, Sex and Marriage in England, 1500 to 1800.* New York: Harper and Row, 1977.

Sussman, George. "The End of the Wet-Nursing Business in France, 1874–1914." *Journal of Family History* 2 (Fall 1977): 237–58.

———. "The Wet-Nursing Business in Nineteeth-Century France." *French Historical Studies* 9 (1975): 304–28.

Thompson, E. P. *The Making of the English Working Class.* New York: Vintage Books, 1963.

Tilly, Charles. "Did the Cake of Custom Break?" Pp. 17–44 in *Consciousness and Class Experience in Nineteenth-Century Europe,* edited by John M. Merriman. New York: Holmes & Meier, 1979.

———. "Flows of Capital and Forms of Industry in Europe, 1500–1900." *Theory and Society* 12 (1983): 123–42.

Tilly, Charles, ed. *Historical Studies of Changing Fertility.* Princeton: Princeton University Press, 1978.

Tilly, Charles, and E. A. Wrigley. *Population Growth and Early Industrialization.* Princeton: Princeton University Press, 1975.

Tilly, Louise. "Individual Lives and Family Strategies in the French Proletariat." *Journal of Family History* 4 (Summer 1979): 137–52.

———. "Paths of Proletarianization: Organization of Production, Sexual Division of Labor, and Women's Collective Action." *Signs* 7 (Winter 1981): 400–417.

Tilly, Louise, and Miriam Cohen. "Does the Family Have a History?" *Social Science History* 2 (Spring 1982): 131–79.

Tilly, Louise A., and Joan W. Scott. *Women, Work and Family.* New York: Holt, Rinehart and Winston, 1978.

Trempé, Roland. *Les mineurs de Carmaux, 1858–1914.* 2 vols. Paris: Les Editions Ouvrières, 1971.

Truant, Cynthia M. "Solidarity and Symbolism among Journeymen Artisans: The Case of *Compagnonnage.*" *Comparative Studies in Society and History* 21 (April 1979): 214–26.

Van de Walle, Etienne. *The Female Population of France in the Nineteenth Century: A Reconstruction of Eighty-Two Departments.* Princeton: Princeton University Press, 1974.

Van de Walle, Etienne, and Francine van de Walle. "Allaitement, stérilité et contraception: les opinions jusqu'au XIXᵉ siècle." *Population* 27 (1972): 686–701.

Vial, Jean. *Industrialisation de la sidérurgie française, 1814–1864.* 2 vols. Paris: Mouton, 1967.

Vincent, David. "Love and Death in the Nineteenth Century Working Class." *Social History* 2 (May 1980): 223–47.

Weber, Eugen. *Peasants into Frenchmen: The Modernization of Rural France, 1870–1914.* Stanford: Stanford University Press, 1976.

Weir, David. "Fertility Transition in Rural France, 1740–1829." Ph.D. diss., Stanford University, 1982.

Wheaton, Robert, and Tamara K. Hareven, eds. *Family and Sexuality in French History*. Philadelphia: University of Pennsylvania Press, 1980.

Wrigley, E. A., and R. Schofield. *The Population History of England, 1541–1871*. Cambridge, Mass.: Harvard University Press, 1981.

Zeldin, Theodore. *Emile Ollivier and the Liberal Empire of Napoleon III*. Oxford: Clarendon Press, 1963.

———. *France, 1848–1945: Politics and Anger*. Oxford: Oxford University Press, 1979.

Index

Abortion, 134, 135
Aciéries de la Marine. *See* Compagnie des Hauts Fourneaux, Forges et Aciéries de la Marine et des Chemins de Fer
Alamagny, Emile, 78, 155, 158, 182
Alamagny family, 160–61
Alsace-Lorraine, 135, 258n.21
Anarchism, 201
Anarchists, 194, 195
Anderson, Michael, 10, 11
Anticlericalism: and Catholics, 168, 202, 215; and challenges to paternalism, 167, 170; negative reaction to, 181, 203, 204; and politics, 191–92, 215
Apprenticeship, 27, 31, 42
Ardèche, department of, 98
Association of Catholic Employers, 79, 172, 183–84
Associations, of workers: and problems of uprootedness, 106, 214; recreational, 207; and worker independence, 20, 150, 193, 207. *See also* Clubs
Associations Law of 1901, 202, 204
Audiganne, Armand, 9, 83, 149

Bergé, Paul, 179, 189
Birth control. *See* Contraception; Family limitation; Fertility, decline in
Birth intervals: and breast-feeding, 59–60; following infant death, 61, 67, 126–27; as measure of fertility control, 58–59, 120–22
Birthrates, crude, 119. *See also* Fertility
Birth records, 25, 52
Blanc, Louis, 51, 152, 265–66n.46
Boissieu. *See* De Boissieu
Bourgeoisie, 15, 114, 149, 179–80; and perceptions of working class, 211–12, 213; and response to infant mortality, 128; values of, 74, 123. *See also* Elite; Employers; Merchant manufacturers

Braid industry: and economic crisis, 199; female labor in, 79–86; length of work day in, 82, 84–85, 129–30, 196–97; male labor in, 86, 91; night work in, 129–30; origins and growth of, 19, 77–80; wages in, 91, 96, 196–97. *See also* Oriol and Alamagny factories
Braid manufacturers, 156, 157, 160, 172, 180
Braid workers: age of, 84; and marriage, 96; and migration, 103; portrayal of, 79–86, 198, 257n.5; strikes of, 188, 196–97
Breast-feeding: and fertility, 59–60, 67, 72, 121–22; practice of, 133, 247n.29; and women's work, 64, 210
Briand, Aristide, 203, 207
Brothers of the Christian Doctrine, 148–49, 183
Brun, Irenée, 78, 158, 172, 183
Budgets, of workers, 89–90

Capitalism, 73, 141
Carnot, Sadi, 196
Catholic Committee, 184, 186, 200, 201, 202–4
Catholicism: appeal of, to workers, 167–68, 173, 200–201; and employers, 142, 167–73, 183–85; and high fertility, 50; norms of, 54; strength of, 261n.4
Census data, 119–20
Cetty, Henri, Abbé, 7–8, 135, 214
Chambon-Feugerolles, Le, 175, 205
Charity: administration of, 167; and industrialization, 155; and moralization of recipients, 150, 173, 263–64n.32; in Mulhouse, 8; and religious orders, 203; in response to socialism, 193, 200–201; and social harmony, 145, 152–54; worker dependency on, 146, 161–63. *See also* Hospice; Material assistance; Paternalism

Compositor:	G&S Typesetters, Inc.
Text:	10/13 Palatino
Display:	Palatino
Printer:	Braun-Brumfield, Inc.
Binder:	Braun-Brumfield, Inc.